The Writer's Response

A Reading-Based Approach to College Writing

FOURTH EDITION

Stephen McDonald
Palomar College

William Salomone
Palomar College

THOMSON

WADSWORTH

Australia   Brazil   Canada   Mexico   Singapore   Spain
United Kingdom   United States

DEDICATION

With love to George and Joan McDonald
and to Kathryn and Michelle Salomone

THOMSON

WADSWORTH

The Writer's Response
A Reading-Based Approach to College Writing
Fourth Edition
Stephen McDonald/William Salomone

Publisher: *Lyn Uhl*
Acquisitions Editor: *Annie Todd*
Development Editor: *Cathy Richard Dodson*
Editorial Assistant: *Daniel DeBonis*
Technology Project Manager: *Joe Gallagher*
Marketing Manager: *Kate Edwards*
Marketing Assistant: *Kathleen Remsberg*
Marketing Communications Manager:
Darlene Amidon-Brent
Content Project Manager: *Karen Stocz*

Senior Art Director: *Cate Rickard Barr*
Print Buyer: *Elizabeth Donaghey*
Production Service: *Hearthside Publishing Services*
Text Designer: *Hearthside Publishing Services*
Photo Manager: *Sheri Blaney*
Cover Designer: *Laurie Anderson*
Compositor: *International Typesetting and Composition*
Printer: *Edwards Brothers*

Cover Image: © age fotostock/Superstock

Thomson Higher Education
25 Thomson Place
Boston, MA 02210-1202
USA

For more information about our products, contact us at: **Thomson Learning Academic Resource Center 1-800-423-0563**
For permission to use material from this text or product, submit a request online **at http://www.thomsonrights.com** Any additional questions about permissions can be submitted by e-mail to **thomsonright@thomson.com**

Library of Congress Control Number: 2006940143

13-Digit ISBN: 978-1-4130-2930-7
10-Digit ISBN: 1-4130-2930-2

Credits appear on pages 478–479, which constitute a continuation of the copyright page.

Contents

Readings Listed by Rhetorical Mode

Articles that illustrate several modes may appear more than once.

Argument and Persuasion

The premise of *The Writer's Response* is that it is nearly impossible to write well without also reading well, that college courses today demand not only that students write clearly and read accurately but also that they write effectively *about* what they have read. *The Writer's Response* is designed as an introductory text to academic writing, the type of writing based on the careful, deliberate reading and the clear, critical thinking demanded of students throughout their college careers.

THE REASON FOR THIS TEXT

WRITING IN RESPONSE TO READING

College courses outside of our English departments rarely ask students to write personal experience essays, nor do they ask students to write papers on topics *similar* to those they have read in some textbook. Rather, such classes more often ask that students write papers and essays in direct response to ideas they have encountered in assigned reading. Such writing assignments demand careful reading and clear summary. They demand that students be able to recognize and respond to specific points in the material they have read, to synthesize ideas from several reading selections, and to evaluate and to argue about the ideas they have found in their reading material. *The Writer's Response* introduces students to these and other skills they will need to write successful college-level papers.

USING PERSONAL EXPERIENCE

Although *The Writer's Response* introduces students to academic writing, it does not at all ignore the importance of their personal experiences, nor does it fail to recognize that writing about themselves is often the best way for writers to find their own voices and to discover that they do indeed have something to say. For this reason, the assignments throughout *The Writer's Response* ask students to use personal experience to respond to the material they have read in the text when it is appropriate to do so. Chapters 1–4 in particular emphasize personal responses. Then, when the students are writing more directly *about* what they have read in Chapters 5–8, optional assignments allow instructors to assign personal experience responses when they want to do so.

ABOUT THE TEXT

The Writer's Response integrates reading, writing, sentence combining, and editing. Its writing instruction is kept simple and clear, and its reading selections consist of over sixty short articles, most of which are both recent and timely in their subject matter.

ORGANIZATION

Part One: The Reading-Writing Conversation

Part One, consisting of the first four chapters, introduces students to the reading and writing processes and to the concepts of unity, coherence, and development. Each of these chapters contains a variety of reading selections to illustrate the points being made and to provide material that students can respond to using their own personal experience. In these first four chapters we want students to become comfortable with the writing process and familiar with the elements of well-written paragraphs and essays. At the same time, we want students to become careful readers and to recognize that accurate reading is an integral part of clear thinking and good writing.

Part Two: Writing about Reading

Part Two consists of four chapters that introduce students to ways of writing about what they have read. We start Part Two with a chapter on how to write brief summaries, extended summaries, and summary-response essays because so often students have trouble doing much more than identifying the central idea of what they have read. Writing the summary gives them practice in recognizing and expressing both the central idea and the supporting points of a reading selection. We then move to a chapter on evaluating the effectiveness of material they read. In this chapter students must read accurately as well as explain why they have or have not found a selection convincing, persuasive, or effective. In the next chapter, students synthesize the issues involved in several reading selections. Here, students must not only summarize what they have read but also recognize connections among reading selections and explain those connections in their papers. The final chapter of Part Two asks students to argue from several reading selections, using material from a number of brief articles to support their positions.

Part Three: Editing Skills

Part Three of *The Writer's Response* is meant to act as a supplement to the primary instruction provided in Parts One and Two. It serves as a brief handbook for those students who need help with grammar, punctuation, or usage problems, and it allows the instructor to cover such material as needed. We have arranged it as a separate part of the text rather than spreading its material throughout each chapter so that the student can quickly and conveniently use it as an aid in the editing process.

Part Four: Additional Readings for Writing

Part Four includes twenty reading selections for the instructor to use in addition to those in the body of the text. The first eight selections cover a variety of topics appropriate for the writing assignments in the first six chapters. The remaining twelve selections are then grouped into three specific topic areas so that they can be used as synthesis and argument topics in Chapters 7 and 8. All of the reading selections reflect the criteria discussed below.

Appendix: Writing the Research Paper

The Appendix covers the writing of a research paper for those instructors who prefer to assign a full research paper at this level. We discuss choosing a topic, developing a thesis, doing the research using library services (including the Internet and library online subscription services), integrating research into the paper, and using MLA documentation methods. The Appendix also includes a sample student research paper.

FEATURES

The Reading Selections

In choosing the reading selections for *The Writer's Response*, we have kept several criteria in mind. First, we wanted most of the selections to be relatively brief since this text is, after all, an introduction to academic writing. For that reason, the majority of the selections are only a few pages in length. However, we also wanted our students to have to "stretch" their mental muscles at times, so we have included some longer, more complex articles for instructors to use as they see fit. Second, we wanted the reading selections to be both timely and interesting, appealing to as wide a range of students as possible. To achieve this end, we have chosen articles that challenge the students to think about who they are as well as about how they fit into our increasingly multicultural world. Titles ranging from "Are You Living Mindlessly?" to "A Generation of Bigots Comes of Age" to "The Changing Face of America" reflect the variety of topics to be found in this text. Finally, to allow for the kind of synthesis and argument that *The Writer's Response* is meant to encourage, we have included several articles grouped around common topics, such as "Should Drugs Be Legalized?" "Flag Burning and Free Speech," "The Minimum Legal Drinking Age," "Animal Experimentation," and "Physician-assisted Suicide."

Evaluating Sample Student Papers

In addition to writing instruction and brief reading selections, each of the chapters in Parts One and Two includes a section on evaluating sample student papers. This section has two purposes. First, it is designed to provide students with "models" of successful papers that can be used to discuss what is expected of well-written paragraphs or essays. Second, it is meant to teach students to distinguish between successful and less successful papers so that they can better evaluate the effectiveness of their own writing.

Sentence Combining

Each chapter in Parts One and Two includes a section on sentence combining. Since so many student writers rely primarily upon compound and relatively brief complex sentences, the sentence combining sections are designed to give students practice in writing sentences that move beyond the patterns they are most comfortable with. Beginning with simple exercises in recognizing when modifiers in one sentence can easily be "embedded" within another sentence, these sections gradually introduce more difficult sentence structures involving the use of coordination, parallelism, subordination, participial phrases, appositives, and sentence variety.

Online Activities

Every chapter includes links to supplemental instruction and exercises available on the Internet. Designed to assist the student who desires more information or further practice, the *Exploring Online* links provide valuable resources for more study.

Group Work

Throughout the text, exercises and writing assignments encourage students to work together, discussing the reading selections, comparing their responses to those selections, and helping each other develop their papers. While individual instructors will, of course, use such group work as they see fit, we have found it to be an invaluable teaching device, helping students clarify their own thinking as they work with those around them.

NEW TO THIS EDITION

In this fourth edition of *The Writer's Response*, we have made the following improvements:

- We have added an appendix entitled *Writing the Research Paper* for those instructors who prefer to introduce a research paper assignment. It covers how to choose topics; how to do the research, including making full use of the Internet; how to evaluate researched material; how to integrate researched paraphrases and quotations; and how to use MLA documentation within the text as well as on a Works Cited page. This new appendix also includes a sample student research paper.

- We have added a chapter entitled *ESL Issues* in Part Three: Editing Skills.
- Throughout the text we have added *Exploring Online* links, which direct the student to valuable online resources for supplemental instruction and exercises.
- Every chapter in Part Three: Editing Skills has a new exercise presented in paragraph form, testing the appropriate skills for that chapter.
- Eleven new reading selections have been added, covering topics ranging from how one decides who does or does not deserve charity ("Charity Means You Don't Pick and Choose," Chapter Two) to a discussion of the benefits of video games ("Video Games Can Be Helpful to College Students," Chapter Four) to arguments in favor of and opposed to same-sex marriages ("Desecration? Dedication!" and "Societal Suicide," Part Four).
- As in all previous editions, cultural diversity and reactions to it are emphasized in articles throughout the text.

INSTRUCTOR'S MANUAL

The Instructor's Manual for *The Writer's Response* provides suggestions for teaching the course on a chapter-by-chapter basis and offers comments about the reading selections. It also includes answers to all exe cises in the text.

ACKNOWLEDGMENTS

We want to thank our friends and colleagues at Palomar College for their unflagging encouragement and suggestions as we have revised this text. We particularly wish to acknowledge Jack Quintero, whose encouragement and suggestions have improved this text from the very beginning. A special thanks also goes to Brent Gowen, who consistently sends new reading selections our way. We are also grateful for the many English instructors at Palomar College who have taken the time to suggest ideas or respond to our questions about the text.

We also wish to extend our gratitude to the many professionals at Wadsworth who have worked with us on this text, especially Stephen Dalphin, our former Senior Acquisitions Editor; Karen Judd; and Ron Montgomery. We particularly thank Cathlynn Richard Dodson, who kept us focused and on task during this revision and who has always been ready with help when we needed it.

We are especially grateful to the following students, who graciously allowed us to use their work as models for evaluation: Nancy Kwan, Elizabeth Santos, Rosemarie Tejidor, Gabriel Borges, Sherrie Kolb, Jason Pauley, Brian

Schmitz, Rosendo Orozco, Alicia Sanchez, Saori Kurosawa, Tami Jacobs, Desiree Gharakanian, Scott Tyler, Jung Yun Park, Katrina Zanini, Rosa Contreras, Jeannine Welch, Elizabeth Harding, Danielle Colon, Tracy Thornton, Jayne Nash, Alison Martin, Lisa Brand, Louise Homola, Justin John, Junior Monta, and Ryan Roleson.

Finally, we are grateful to the following professors who took their time to provide valuable input for this text.

Fourth Edition Reviewers:
Chris Partida, *North Harris College*
Annmarie Chiarini, *Community College of Baltimore–Essex Campus*
Bev Neidefman, *Kent State University*
Victoria Sansome, *Los Medanos College*
Bernie Rihn, *Spokane Falls Community College*
Geoff Kirsch, *University of Alaska at Anchorage*
Jody Sterling, *Dutchess Community College*

Third Edition Reviewers:
Susan Hermann, *Mira Costa College*
Steve Mohr, *Terra State Community College*
Cheryl Scott, *Community College of Baltimore–Essex Campus*

Second Edition Reviewers:
Nancy Anter, *Wayne State University*
Debra Bailin, *Lyndon State University*
Kathleen Beauchene, *Community College of Rhode Island*
Joyce Malek, *Anoka Ramsey Community College*
Linda Ranucci, *Kent State University*

First Edition Reviewers:
William Bernhardt, *College of Staten Island;*
Linda J. Daigle, *Houston Community College*
Dianne Gregory, *Cape Cod Community College*
Kathleen M. Krager, *Walsh University*
Milla McConnell-Tuite, *College of San Mateo*

Stephen McDonald
William Salomone

PART ONE

The Reading-Writing Conversation

Have you ever talked to someone who wouldn't listen or listened to someone who just rambled on and on without making a clear point? Probably you tried not to have many more conversations with that person.

After all, in a conversation, both listening well and speaking clearly are important, and a poor listener or a confusing speaker is not a very enjoyable person to talk to.

Writing and reading are very much like speaking and listening. When you read, you listen to what someone else has to say; when you write, you speak your own ideas. Together, reading and writing make a conversation between the reader and the writer, and a poor reader or a poor writer can pretty much spoil that conversation.

As students in college classes, you will be asked to participate in this reading-writing conversation by writing in response to what you read. Depending on the instructor or the class, you might be asked to summarize the ideas you have found in textbooks, to analyze topics after reading about them, to evaluate opinions expressed by a writer, to define concepts discussed in several articles, or to respond in any number of other ways to what you have read.

Obviously, to write clearly and accurately in response to what you have read, you need to read clearly and accurately too. Part One of this text will help you work on both activities at the same time—clear and accurate reading and writing.

© ZITS Partnership, King Feature Syndicate

Writing with a Central Idea

THE WRITING PROCESS

Writing is a messy business. It is full of stops and starts and sudden turns and reversals. In fact, writing an essay can sometimes be one of the most confusing, frustrating experiences a college student will encounter. Fortunately, writing does not have to be a horrible experience. Like almost anything in life, writing becomes much easier as you become familiar with the "process" that makes up the act of writing.

Writing is often called a *recursive process*. This means that the many steps to writing an effective paper do not necessarily follow neatly one after the other. In fact, often you will find yourself repeating the same step a number of different times, in a number of different places, as you write a paper. For example, you might jot down notes on scratch paper before you start writing your first draft, but at any time while you write, you might stop to jot down more notes or to rethink what you are writing. To help yourself understand this writing process, think of it as being divided roughly into three stages: **prewriting, writing,** and **rewriting.**

PREWRITING

Prewriting involves anything you do to help yourself decide what your central idea is or what details, examples, reasons, or content you will include. Freewriting, brainstorming, and clustering (discussed below) are types of prewriting. Thinking, talking to other people, reading related material, outlining or organizing ideas—all are forms of prewriting. Obviously, you can prewrite at *any* time in the writing process. Whenever you want to think up new material, simply stop what you are doing and start using one of the techniques you will study in this chapter.

WRITING

The writing stage of the process involves the actual writing out of a draft. Unfortunately, many people try to start their writing here, without sufficient prewriting. As you may know from firsthand experience, trying to start out this way usually leads directly to a good case of writer's block. During this stage of the writing process, you should be ready to do more prewriting whenever you hit a snag or cannot think of what to write next.

REWRITING

Rewriting consists of revising and editing. You should plan to revise every paper you write. When you *revise,* you examine the entire draft to change what needs to be changed and to add what needs to be added. Perhaps parts of your paper will need to be reorganized, reworded, or thoroughly rewritten to express your ideas clearly. Perhaps your paper will need more examples or clearer explanations. Unfortunately, people pressed for time often skip this stage, and the result is a very poorly written paper. Finally, after you have revised your work, you must edit it. When you *edit,* you correct spelling, grammar, and punctuation errors. A word of warning: Do not confuse editing with revising. Merely correcting the spelling, grammar, and punctuation of a poorly written paper will not make much difference in the overall quality of the paper.

PREWRITING: FROM WRITER'S BLOCK TO WRITING

Have you ever had a writing assignment that absolutely stumped you? Have you ever found yourself *stuck,* staring at a blank sheet of paper for fifteen minutes (or thirty? or sixty?), wondering what in the world you could write to meet the assignment?

If you have not had this experience, you are a lucky person. Certainly almost everyone knows the frustrated, sinking feeling that comes as minute after minute passes and nothing seems to get written. In fact, for many writers, *getting started* is the most agonizing part of the entire writing process.

What we're talking about here is **writer's block,** a problem as common to professional writers as it is to student writers. Because it is so common, you need to learn how to get past it quickly and painlessly so that you can get on with your assignment. Here are a few prewriting techniques to help you.

FREEWRITING

Because writer's block means that you aren't writing, one of the quickest ways to get around it is to write anything at all, a technique called *freewriting*. You can write whatever you are thinking, feeling, wondering about, or trying to get out of your mind—just start writing.

Look at the *Zits* cartoon that opens this chapter. Jeremy, like many online writers, uses a form of freewriting as he writes his blog. (A *blog*, short for *weblog*, is a form of online journal.) He does not sit down wondering what to write. Instead, he writes about whatever is on his mind—in this case, his conversation with his mother.

When freewriting, don't stop to correct spelling, grammar, punctuation, or other elements of the writing. Set a time limit for yourself—five or ten minutes—and just keep writing. Here is how some freewriting might look from a person who was asked to write a paper explaining how a significant event affected his or her life:

> An event that affected my life. What event could I choose? There haven't been a lot of things that have really affected me. The death of Heidi did, I guess. My marriage, of course. Having a child. What else? How about when I was a child? I don't remember much that really affected me from then. No big traumatic events or anything. Nothing particularly wonderful either. How about in elementary or high school? Well—Heidi's death, like I said. My mom's alcoholism. That's a big event. I wonder how it affected me. I wasn't really home all that much then. I wonder if it counts as an "event." Something major. I'm trying to think of something major. How about moving to Boulder? That was big event for me. I'd never been away from home for so long. Yes. I like that one.

As you can see, freewriting is very informal. Notice that the above freewriting moves from questions ("What event could I choose?") to answers that the writer might be able to use in a paper ("The death of Heidi," "My marriage," "My mom's alcoholism," "moving to Boulder.") This movement—from searching for ideas that you might use to focusing on possible topics—is very common in freewriting.

BRAINSTORMING

Brainstorming is similar to freewriting in that you write down whatever ideas come to mind. Don't censor or correct them. However, in this case, write the ideas in **list** form. Don't be surprised if you find one technique—brainstorming or freewriting—working better than the other. Use the one you find most productive. Here's an example, again responding to an assignment to explain how a significant event affected your life:

Heidi's death
- depressed me
- made me feel guilty
- made me love my life more
- helped me realize how short life can be
- made me re-evaluate how I was living my life

Mom's alcoholism
- I was angry at her
- I avoided her
- I wouldn't talk to her when she was drinking
- I avoided going home
- I was embarrassed to be out with her

Moving to Boulder
- extreme loneliness
- didn't talk to anyone for days
- had to learn how to meet people
- had to learn to organize my time
- learned to balance play time with class time
- rethought my religious beliefs
- learned to value my friends more
- became stronger and more independent
- discovered what I wanted to major in
- saw the effects of drug and alcohol abuse
- helped me define myself
- learned to love nature even more

As you can see, brainstorming might help you discover which topic will provide the most ideas and details. The writer of the above lists can see that he has quite a few thoughts about his experiences in Boulder, so he chose that topic for his paper.

CLUSTERING

A third technique to help you generate ideas is called *clustering*. It differs from brainstorming and freewriting in that what you write is almost like an informal map. To cluster your ideas, start with a topic or question and draw a circle around it. Then connect related ideas to that circle and continue in that way. Look at the following example of clustering using the topic "How Moving to Boulder Affected Me." As you can see, clustering provides a mental picture of the ideas you generate. As a result, it can help you organize your material as you think of it.

Freewriting, brainstorming, and clustering are only three of many techniques to help you get past writer's block. When you use them, you should feel free to move from one to the other at any time. And, of course, your instructor may suggest other ways to help you get started. Whatever technique you use, the point is to start writing. Do your thinking on paper (or at a computer), not while you are staring out the window. Here's something to remember whenever you have a writing assignment due: **Think in ink.**

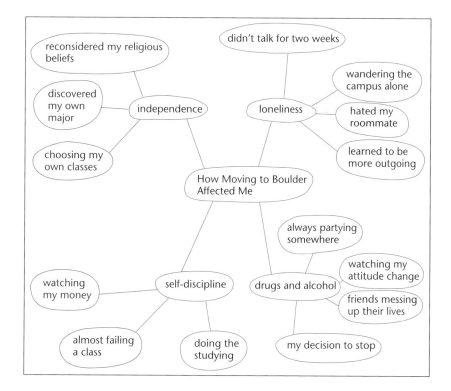

The Writer's Response website includes links for further discussion of prewriting. Go to www.thomsonedu.com/devenglish/mcdonald. Under "Chapter Resources" for Chapter 1, click on "Exploring Online."

Exploring **ONLINE**

READINGS

Read the following articles. Then practice your prewriting techniques by responding to the questions at the end of each article.

Live Each Moment for What It's Worth

ERMA BOMBECK

Until her death, Erma Bombeck was one of the most popular newspaper columnists in the United States. Her humorous stories about the everyday events of her life were often full of wisdom and insight. In this brief essay, she reminds us all of an important life lesson.

BEFORE YOU READ

1. Look up the words *carpe diem* in a dictionary. What do they mean? What do you think about them as an approach to life?

2. Where would you like to go, what would you like to do, or who would you like to see if you had the time or were not as busy as you are? What prevents you from going to those places, doing those things, or seeing those people?

I have a friend who lives by a three-word philosophy, "Seize the   1
moment." Just possibly, she might be the wisest woman on this
planet. Too many people put off something that brings them joy
just because they haven't thought about it, don't have it on their
schedule, didn't know it was coming, or are too rigid to depart
from the routine.

I got to thinking one day about all those women on the *Titanic*   2
who passed up dessert at dinner that fateful night in an effort to
"cut back." From then on, I've tried to be a little more flexible.

How many women out there will eat at home because their   3
husband suggested they go out to dinner AFTER something had
been thawed? Does the word *refrigerator* have no meaning for you?

How often have your kids dropped in to talk and sat there   4
in silence while you watched *Jeopardy?*

I cannot count the times I called my sister and said, "How   5
about going to lunch in half an hour?" She would gasp and stam-
mer, "I can't." Check one: "I have clothes on the line." "My hair is
dirty." "I wish I had known yesterday." "I had a late breakfast." "It looks
like rain." And my personal favorite, "It's Monday." She died a few
years ago. We never did have lunch.

Because Americans cram so much into our lives, we tend to   6
schedule our headaches. We live on a sparse diet of promises we
make to ourselves when all the conditions are perfect. We'll go
back and visit the grandparents . . . when we get Stevie toilet-
trained. We'll entertain . . . when we replace the carpet in the living room. We'll go on a second honeymoon . . . when we get two
more kids out of college.

Life has a way of accelerating as we get older. The days get   7
shorter and the list of promises to ourselves gets longer. One
morning we awaken and all we have to show for our lives is a
litany of "I'm going to," "I plan on," and "Someday when things are
settled down a bit."

When anyone calls my "seize the moment" friend, she is   8
open to adventure, available for trips and keeps an open mind on
new ideas. Her enthusiasm for life is contagious. You can talk to
her for five minutes and you're ready to trade your bad feet for a
pair of roller blades and skip an elevator for a bungi cord.

My lips have not touched ice cream in 10 years. I love ice   9
cream. It's just that I might as well apply it directly to my hips with
a spatula and eliminate the digestive process.

The other day I stopped the car and bought a triple-decker.   10
If my car hit an iceberg on the way home, I'd have died happy.

PREWRITING PRACTICE

1. Freewrite for five minutes (or for a time specified by your instructor)
   to react to Bombeck's article in any way that you want. Write whatever
   comes to your mind.

2. Discuss your freewriting with other members of your class. Did they
   have similar responses?

3. Respond to one of the following questions by using the prewriting
   techniques of freewriting, brainstorming, and/or clustering:

   a. What does Erma Bombeck mean by "seize the moment"? Do you live
      by that philosophy, or do you avoid doing things that are sponta-
      neous or unscheduled? Give some examples to illustrate your
      response.

   b. Think about your friends, relatives, and acquaintances. Do any of
      them "seize the moment"? Do any carefully avoid living in a spon-
      taneous way? Describe any people you know who do or do not
      "seize the moment."

4. Discuss your responses to the above questions with other members of
   your class. Explain to them why you or people you know do or do not
   "seize the moment."

Without Emotion   G. GORDON LIDDY

*The following selection, drawn from G. Gordon Liddy's autobiography, narrates an
experience from his childhood. As you read it, consider your reactions to the events
he describes. Do they offend you? Do you find them understandable given the circumstances of the times?*

BEFORE YOU READ

1. What do you make of the title "Without Emotion"? What does it make you expect to find in the reading selection?

2. Who is G. Gordon Liddy? If you don't know, ask other members of your class or your instructor. Does his background affect how you read this selection?

Squirrel hunting was a popular sport in West Caldwell in the 1940s. I loaded my homemade rifle, cocked the spring, and waited on the steps of the porch. A squirrel was in the top of the pear tree. I raised the rifle. The movement startled the squirrel and he jumped to the oak tree and froze as I stepped off the porch. I sighted along the side of the barrel, aimed for the squirrel's head, and fired.   1

I missed the squirrel's head and gut-shot him. Bravely, he clung to the tree as long as he could, then started to come down, clutching piteously at branches as he fell, wounded mortally.   2

I didn't know it, but the shot alerted my mother. She watched the furry creature's descent until it fell to the ground and I shot it again, this time through the head at point-blank range, to put it out of its suffering, then cut off its tail to tie to the handlebars of my bicycle as an ornament.   3

When I came into the house my mother told me reproachfully that she had seen from the kitchen window the suffering I had caused. I went off and wept. The dying squirrel haunted me. I kept seeing it fall, clutching and clawing from what must have been a terribly painful wound. I was furious with myself—not because I'd caused the pain, though I regretted that, but because I hadn't been able to kill without emotion. How could I expect to be a soldier in the war? I had to do something to free myself from this disabling emotionalism.   4

I cast about for an idea and found it across the street. Bill Jacobus's father, to help combat the wartime food shortage and to supplement rationing, had built a chicken coop in his backyard. He and his son used to butcher the chickens, then drain, scald, pluck, and clean them for sale.   5

I asked young Bill if I could help kill the chickens. He was glad to have the help. He showed me how to grasp the bird in such a way as to have control of both wings and feet, lay its neck on an upended stump, and then decapitate it with one chop of an ax held in the other hand. Bill explained that the shock made the corpse convulse and, if I let go, the body would run about, wings flapping, and bruise the meat. I'd need to control the corpse until   6 the shock wore off and the limp body could be hung up by the feet to drain the remaining blood. I should wear my old clothes.

Using the ax tentatively rather than making a bold stroke, I made a mess of my first chicken kill; it took me a number of chops to get the head off. The bird slipped out of my grasp and half flew, half jumped about, blood spurting from its neck all over me and everything else in range. Bill was good about it and gave me another chance.   7

I got better at it, and over a period of time I killed and killed and killed, getting less and less bloody, swifter and swifter, surer with my ax stroke until, finally, I could kill efficiently and without emotion or thought. I was satisfied: when it came my turn to go to war, I would be ready. I could kill as I could run—like a machine.   8

PREWRITING PRACTICE

1. Freewrite for five minutes (or for a time specified by your instructor) to react to Liddy's article in any way that you want. Write whatever comes to your mind.

2. Discuss your freewriting with other members of your class. Did they have similar responses?

3. Respond to one of the following questions by using the prewriting techniques of freewriting, brainstorming, and/or clustering:
   a. Did your feelings or thoughts change as you moved from the start of this article to the end of it? If so, what parts of the article caused them to change?
   b. Have you ever had to act "without emotion"? Describe any times you can remember when you had to repress or ignore your emotions.

4. Discuss your responses to the above questions with other members of your class. Did they develop ideas that had not occurred to you?

A View from Mount Ritter
                                                    JOSEPH T. O'CONNOR

Joseph T. O'Connor was an eighteen-year-old senior at Lee High School in Stanton, Virginia, when this article was first published in Newsweek. *In it, he discusses an event that changed the way he thinks about life. Notice the way O'Connor moves from the event itself to his reflections on the significance of it.*

BEFORE YOU READ

1. As you read this selection, watch for the "view" to which the writer refers. What does he see from Mount Ritter?

2. Has any experience with nature ever changed your attitude toward life? In what way?

"I hate this," I thought. We were on our way to the top of Mount   1
Ritter in northeastern California. You would think everyone, near
one of the tallest ridges in the Sierra Nevadas, would be in high
spirits. But on this particular day the rain fell in torrents. Quarter-
size hailstones pelted our protective helmets as thunder echoed
through the canyons.

It was the second week of my mountain expedition in   2
California. The first week there had not been a cloud in the sky,
but on Tuesday of week two, a dark cover crept in from the west,
painting the sunlit, blue sky black. The storm came in so fast we
didn't even notice it until our shadows suddenly disappeared.

"Here it comes," our guide warned. As if God himself had   3
given the order, the heavens opened, just a crack. Huge drops began falling but abruptly stopped, as if to say, "You know what's
coming; here's a taste." As we began searching for shelter, a bolt of
lightning ripped open the blackish clouds overhead and in unison
thunder cracked, leaving everyone's ears ringing. We were in the
midst of a huge July thunderstorm. Ethan, our guide, had said that
during the summer in the high Sierras it might rain twice, but
when it does, it's best not to be there. Suddenly lightning struck a
tree not 20 feet from where I was standing.

"Lightning positions!" Ethan yelled frantically. A little too   4
frantically for my taste. I thought he was used to this kind of thing.
As scared as I was, squatting in a giant puddle of water and hailstones, with forks of lightning bouncing off the canyon walls
around me, I couldn't help chuckling to myself at the sight of
Ethan's dinner-plate–size eyeballs as he panicked like an amateur.
Soon after the lightning died down some, we hiked to the shelter
of nearby redwoods to put on rain gear. While we prayed for the
rain to subside, I watched the stream we stood beside grow into
a raging, whitewater river. Another expeditioner, Mike, and I were
under a full redwood donning our not-so-waterproof equipment
when I realized we were standing on a small island.

"Mike! Let's go!" I yelled, my exclamation nearly drowned   5
out by the roar of water surrounding us and another roll of
thunder.

"I'm way ahead o' ya!" he screamed in his thick New York   6
accent, and his goofy smile broke through the torrents. "Ya ready?"

"Yeah!" I yelled back, and jumped from our island into the   7
knee-deep water. He followed as we slopped through the storm,
losing our footing every few feet.

The unforgiving downpour lasted all day and into the night   8
as we stumbled down the rocky cliffs seeking the driest place to set
up camp. It was dusk before we found a small clearing in a pine for-
est and began what was to be the worst night of my life. We constructed our tents in the dark, fumbling with the ropes with our
frozen hands and finishing just as a stiffness like rigor mortis set in.
We lay awake all night, shivering in our wet sleeping bags while rain
poured down and a small stream made its way through our tent.

It's funny how these memories keep coming back to me as   9
if it were just yesterday. All this happened last summer, after my junior year in high school. I had decided to attend a mountaineering
program in the Sierras. Two weeks in the back country with no sign
of civilization. It sounded exciting and slightly dangerous, and I've always been up for a good adventure. I found out on that trip that
nature is underestimated. The experience was the most invigorating,
fulfilling, stimulating two weeks of my life. For the first time since I
could remember, my head was crystal clear. I felt born again, only
two weeks old. On top of Mount Ritter, 13,000 feet above sea level,
I was entranced at the sight of the orange-red sun as it peeked
over the glistening peaks far off in the east. Cumulous clouds appeared transparent as they glowed bright red in the morning glory.

The wonder of all I'd experienced made me think seriously   10
about what comes next. "Life after high school," I said to myself.
"Uh-oh." What had I been doing for the last three years? I was so
caught up in defying the advice of my parents and teachers to
study and play by the rules that I hadn't considered the effects my
actions would have on me.

"Youth is wholly experimental," Robert Louis Stevenson   11
wrote. Sure, there will be mistakes, but there will also be successes.
I was a confused kid. Everyone—my parents, teachers and
coaches—offered suggestions, but I chose to ignore them. I had
"potential," they told me. As a typical teen, I thought I could make
it on my own. I didn't want any help, and the more people tried to
give it the more distant I grew. I was the kid who thought he could
be perfect at anything without any preparation. I was lost in the
daydream that I didn't need to study; I was going to play professional soccer. My game was good and I thought that practice, or
getting good grades, for that matter, was unnecessary. Stubbornness and rebellion can be terrible things if they get out of control.

"To get back one's youth one has merely to repeat one's   12
follies." A day before my awakening on that fateful July sunrise,

I would have disagreed with this quotation from Oscar Wilde. But after recognizing the results of my own follies for the first time, I thoroughly agree.

This year, my final year in high school, I've at last cleared   13
my head and buckled down. Judging by the past semester, I'm on the right track. My D average has U-turned into this report card's three B's and one A, landing me on my first Honor Roll. I intend to be on the Principal's List after this semester: then I hope to graduate and attend a community college in northern California, near the mountains, before transferring to a four-year school.

Thanks to that morning's conversion, I am a new person.   14
Now, I know I'll have to work hard. The sun streaming over the eastern Sierras wiped out the dark clouds that blurred my vision. Jonathan Harker in Bram Stoker's "Dracula" must have felt exactly the same way when he wrote in his journal: "No man knows 'till he has suffered from the night how sweet and how dear to his heart and eye the morning can be."

PREWRITING PRACTICE

1. Freewrite for five minutes (or for a time specified by your instructor) to react to O'Connor's article in any way that you want. Write whatever comes to your mind.

2. Discuss your freewriting with other members of your class. Did they have similar responses?

3. Respond to one of the following questions by using the prewriting techniques of freewriting, brainstorming, and/or clustering:

   a. Halfway through his article, Joseph O'Connor writes, "I found out on that trip that nature is underestimated." Have you ever had an encounter with nature that affected you deeply? Briefly describe any such encounters that you can remember.

   b. O'Connor goes on to write, "The experience was the most invigorating, fulfilling, stimulating two weeks of my life." Have you ever experienced something that affected you in such a way? Briefly describe any such experiences.

   c. Consider the final quotation from the article: "No man knows 'till he has suffered from the night how sweet and how dear to his heart and eye the morning can be." What do you make of this statement? Do you think it expresses a truth about life? Describe any instances from your own life or from the lives of people you know that might illustrate its truth.

4. Discuss your responses to the above questions with other members of your class. Explain to them why you reacted to any specific experiences the way that you did.

PREWRITING: CHOOSING A PRELIMINARY TOPIC SENTENCE OR THESIS STATEMENT

Once you have developed some ideas by using the prewriting techniques discussed so far, you are ready to decide on the topic and central idea of your paper and to focus those two elements into a *topic sentence* (for a single paragraph) or a *thesis statement* (for an entire essay). Your ability to write clear topic sentences or thesis statements can determine whether or not your readers will understand and be able to follow the points you want to make in the papers you write. In college classes, that ability can make the difference between a successful paper and one that is barely passing (or not passing at all).

FINDING THE TOPIC

In academic writing, deciding upon the topic of your paper is often not very difficult because it is assigned by your instructor. You may be asked to write about child abuse or a piece of literature or a particular political issue—but rarely (if ever) will your assignment simply be to "write about something." Of course, many times you may be asked to choose your own topic, but even then you will know which topics are appropriate and which are not. (For example, in a class studying the history of the Arab-Jewish tension in the Middle East, you probably would not choose state lotteries as the topic of your paper, right?)

FINDING THE CENTRAL IDEA

This is where many student writers get stuck. The problem is not "What is my topic?" but "What should I be *saying* about my topic?" For example, if you were asked to write a paragraph or essay explaining how an event in your life affected you, you might decide on an event easily enough, but you might not have any idea *how* it affected you. To put it another way, you wouldn't know what your *central idea* is, so how could you possibly write a topic sentence or a thesis statement? How do you decide what your central idea is? Here are two suggestions:

1. **Read your prewriting to find a central idea.**   As you examine your prewriting, watch for recurring ideas or for any idea that sparks your interest. For example, in the prewriting on pages 5, 6 and 7, you might notice that the writer listed a variety of ways his move to Boulder affected him. A preliminary central idea might be expressed this way:

central idea

My move to Boulder, Colorado, to go to school <u>affected me many ways</u>.

2. **Start writing your first draft to find a central idea.**   You may have been taught in the past that you should not even *start* writing until you have focused your central idea into a topic sentence or thesis statement—and you might have found that such advice led you right back to a good case of writer's block. Certainly, it would be convenient if you could simply sit down, think up a

perfect topic sentence or thesis statement, and start writing, but the process of writing is just not that neat and orderly. So if you are not sure what your central idea is but do have details or ideas you know you want to write about, just start writing about them. Many times your precise central idea will develop while you write.

FORMING THE PRELIMINARY TOPIC SENTENCE OR THESIS STATEMENT

Once you are somewhat sure what your topic and central idea will be, write them as a single sentence. If your assignment is to write one paragraph, this sentence will serve as its topic sentence. If you are writing an essay, this sentence will serve as its thesis statement. In either case, it will state the topic and central idea of the assignment. As you prepare this sentence, keep these points in mind:

1. *Make a statement that demands explanation. Do not merely state a fact.* Because a central idea demands some explanation, argument, or development, a simple statement of fact will not work as a topic sentence or thesis statement. Note the difference between the following two statements:

FACT   Several years ago I moved to Boulder, Colorado, to go to school.

DEMANDS EXPLANATION   My move to Boulder, Colorado, to go to school changed the way I think about my parents.

2. *Make a limited statement that can be reasonably supported with facts or examples. Do not be too general, vague, or broad.* Very general topic sentences and thesis statements result in very general papers. When you choose a topic and a central idea, *limit* your choice to something that can be covered in detail.

           broad topic   **vague central idea**

INEFFECTIVE   Many events have affected my life.

The sentence above commits the writer to discussing *many* events from his or her life (a very broad topic), and its central idea could refer to any changes at all—from insignificant to life-changing.

                limited topic   **vague central idea**

INEFFECTIVE   My move to Boulder, Colorado, to go to school was very interesting.

In the above sentence the topic "My move to Boulder, Colorado, to go to school" is limited well enough, but the central idea—that the move was "interesting"—is much too vague.

                limited topic

EFFECTIVE   My move to Boulder, Colorado, to go to school caused me to

                limited central idea

change in ways that would affect the rest of my life.

The statement above would work as a topic sentence for an extended paragraph or a thesis statement for an essay because it is focused on a limited topic (*My move to Boulder, Colorado, to go to school*) and because its central idea (*caused me to change in ways that would affect the rest of my life*) could be fully explained in one assignment.

EXERCISE 1.1

Examine each of the following sentences. If the sentence would be an effective topic sentence or thesis statement, underline its topic once and its central idea twice. If the sentence would not be an effective topic sentence or thesis statement, explain why not.

EXAMPLES

Two weeks ago, the Beach Boys gave a concert at the stadium.
Not effective because it merely states a fact.

Current movies are very enjoyable to watch.
Not effective because its topic and central idea are too general.

<u>Attending Marine Corps boot camp</u> was the most <u>challenging experience of my life</u>.
Effective because the topic is quite limited and the central idea demands explanation and support.

1. I have played on our college basketball team for two years.
2. My first job taught me how rude some customers can really be.
3. My family consists of some of the most obnoxious people you will ever meet.
4. Last January, a friend and I skipped work and went to the mountains.
5. This paper will be about affirmative action.
6. If people listened to all the warnings about eating sugar, fat, caffeine, or cholesterol, they would never have any fun at all.
7. Many food labels today are both confusing and misleading.
8. I love watching the seagulls and listening to the waves at the beach.
9. Although I don't approve of lying, sometimes a lie is both necessary and ethical.
10. If we are going to advance as a democracy, we need to improve our society.

EXERCISE 1.2

Look at the writing assignments on pages 25–26. With them in mind, reread the prewriting you did in response to the prewriting questions at the end of "Live Each Moment for What It's Worth," "Without Emotion," or "A View from Mount Ritter." Write a sentence that you could use either as a preliminary topic sentence for a paragraph or as a preliminary thesis statement for an essay. Compare your results with those of other members of your class to determine which sentences contain specific topics and clear central ideas.

PLACING THE TOPIC SENTENCE OR THESIS STATEMENT

As we mentioned above, the primary difference between a topic sentence and a thesis statement is that the topic sentence identifies the central idea of a paragraph and the thesis statement does the same for an essay. As you will see in Chapter 2, topic sentences and thesis statements can appear many places, depending on the purpose of a particular piece of writing. However, in college classes you will be writing academic papers, and in almost all academic writing the topic sentences and thesis statements must be placed very carefully.

1. ***Place the topic sentence at the start of the paragraph.***   Although there are exceptions, the first sentence of most academic paragraphs should be the topic sentence. The body of the paragraph should explain and support that topic sentence. (See Chapter 3 for a discussion of support within a paragraph.)

topic sentence

> **One serious problem for many newly arrived immigrants is that they do not speak English well, if they speak it at all.** For example, when my parents left Hong Kong in 1972 and came to America, they couldn't understand what people were saying, so they didn't know how to respond to them. Not knowing how to speak English was a horrible experience for them. Because everything was in English, they couldn't even watch TV, go to the store, or read the newspaper. The only thing they could do at that time was to stay home. One of the most terrible experiences that my mom had happened when she got lost while trying to pick me up at school. Because she didn't speak English, she couldn't even ask for directions, so she just drove around in circles for hours. Although people in the neighborhood tried to help her, my mom just couldn't understand what they were saying. One group of people just pointed and laughed as my mom drove by. After that experience she said, "If I don't learn to speak English soon, people will take advantage of me all the time."
>
> *Nancy Kwan, student writer*

2. ***Place the thesis statement at the end of the introductory paragraph.***   Again, there are many exceptions, as you will see in Chapter 2, but the thesis statement in most academic essays appears as the last sentence of the introductory paragraph. (See Chapter 3 for a discussion of writing introductory paragraphs.)

> Doesn't almost everyone want a good education? That is why most people, after graduating from high school, go on to college. Whether it is at a community college or a four-year university, people young and old spend their mornings, afternoons, or evenings in class studying and getting closer to a college diploma. Currently, I am completing my second year at Palomar College, and my attitude today about my education has drastically changed from when I started my first semester. **I believe that**

thesis statement   **if I had known how important education is when I first enrolled in college, I probably would have done things quite differently during my freshman year.**

> *Elizabeth Santos, student writer*

PREWRITING: PREPARING A ROUGH OUTLINE

If you have ever been required to turn in a complete outline of a paper before the final paper was due, you know how difficult—even impossible,
sometimes—it is to predict exactly what you will include in a paper, much
less what *order* it will follow. So rest easy—although preparing a *rough outline*
is part of the prewriting process, it is not at all the same as writing a complete, perfect, formal outline. Instead, it involves looking at what you have
written so far in your prewriting, deciding what ideas you *may* use, and list-
ing those ideas in the order in which you will *probably* use them. Essentially,
you are trying to give yourself some direction before you start writing the
first draft.

GROUPING RELATED POINTS

Let's continue to use the topic of "How My Move to Boulder, Colorado, Affected Me" as an example of how to write the rough outline. The first step is
to look at the prewriting on pages 5–7 and group any details that seem related. (You might notice, by the way, that the clustering example has already
grouped some of them.) They could be organized this way:

Group A	Group B	Group C	Group D
chose my own classes	didn't talk for two weeks	alcohol and drug use	learning to study
discovered my own major	wandered the campus alone	watched my attitude change	watching my own money
reconsidered my religious beliefs	hated my roommate	went to lots of parties	almost failing a class
	learned to be more outgoing	friends messed up their lives	
		decided to stop	

IDENTIFYING GROUP TOPICS

Once you have grouped the details you want to include, you need to identify
the topic that each group seems to focus on. This step is particularly important if you are writing an essay rather than a paragraph. Because each group
will most likely be developed into a separate paragraph, the topic of each
group will help to form its topic sentence.

Group Topics	
Group A:	Learning to think for myself
Group B:	Learning how to deal with loneliness
Group C:	Learning how to deal with drugs and alcohol
Group D:	Learning self-discipline

Choosing a Tentative Organization

After grouping the details and identifying their topics, you need to decide in what order you will discuss them. Here are three common ways to organize your material.

Emphatic Order

If you think some of your details should receive more emphasis than others because they are more important, complex, colorful, or memorable, arrange them so that they move from the least important to the most important. This type of organization will leave your readers with a strong impression of your most effective details.

For example, when organizing the above material about moving to Colorado, the writer might decide to save Group A for last because the idea of learning to think for himself is most important to him. On the other hand, another writer might choose to save Group C for last because learning not to abuse alcohol or drugs was a powerful, life-changing lesson.

Chronological Order

Chronological order presents details in the order they actually occurred. Whatever occurred first is discussed first, whatever occurred second is discussed second, and so on. This type of organization is very effective when you want to describe an event or explain how something happened. If the first major change that affected the writer who moved to Boulder, Colorado, was the sense of loneliness he experienced, then he would present Group B first.

Spatial Order

Spatial order consists of describing a place or an object in such a way that a reader can clearly picture the various details and their relationship to one another. One way to do so is to describe the larger elements of a scene first, identifying where they are in relation to other elements, and then moving to a description of the smaller details. The writer of the paper about moving to Boulder, Colorado, would not use spatial order because he is not describing a place or an object.

EXERCISE 1.3

Using the prewriting you did for "Live Each Moment for What It's Worth," "Without Emotion," or "A View from Mount Ritter," group the ideas or examples that you have developed so far into a rough outline, identify the topic of each group, and decide on a tentative organization. If you need to, do more prewriting to develop more details.

WRITING: THE FIRST DRAFT

If you have a preliminary topic sentence or thesis statement and have prepared a rough outline, you have everything you need to write your paper. So now is the time to sit and write. However, now is still *not* the time to worry about whether everything is spelled exactly right or worded perfectly. If you try to write your first draft and avoid all errors at the same time, you will end up right back where you probably started—stuck. Of course, you can correct some errors as they occur, but don't make revising or editing your primary concern at this point. What you want to do *now* is to write out your ideas. You can "fix" them later.

THE SINGLE PARAGRAPH: A FIRST DRAFT

If your assignment is to write one paragraph, open the paragraph with your *preliminary topic sentence*. Then use the details from your rough outline to explain and support the central idea of your topic sentence. Here is the first draft of a paragraph about the effects of moving to Boulder, Colorado, to go to school.

preliminary topic sentence

My move to Boulder, Colorado, to go to school affected me several ways. First, when I arrived, I was very lonely, so I had to learn to deal with that. I wandered around the campus for weeks without speaking to anyone. After a while I learned to be more outgoing by talking to people in the lobby of my dorm. I also had to learn to be more disciplined about my study habits as well as my spending habits. Because there was no one to tell me to do my homework, I almost failed my physics class, and I spent the money that was supposed to last for a month in the first two weeks I was there. My parents were not very happy when I had to phone home for more money so soon. As the year away from home went by, I began to feel more and more independent. I realized that I had chosen engineering as a major to please my dad, not because I was interested in it. My new independent attitude helped me find the major I really loved, which was journalism. I even found myself rethinking the religious beliefs I was raised with. Some of them I kept, but others I left behind. As I look back over my year in Colorado, I think what it really taught me was to take responsibility for my own life.

EXERCISE 1.4

Respond to the following questions.

1. What is the central idea of the paragraph? Where is it stated?
2. Which of the organizational patterns from page 20 is the writer using?
3. What details that appear in the rough outline on page 19 has the writer left out?
4. What idea in the final sentence could be used to improve the central idea of the preliminary topic sentence?
5. What advice would you give this writer to improve his paragraph?

THE BRIEF ESSAY: A FIRST DRAFT

If you are writing an essay, open your draft with an introductory paragraph that ends with a *preliminary thesis statement*. Then start each body paragraph with a *preliminary topic sentence* that supports or explains the central idea of the thesis statement.

preliminary thesis statement

preliminary topic sentence

preliminary topic sentence

preliminary topic sentence

A few years ago I had the opportunity to go to school in Boulder, Colorado. I had always lived in San Diego, California, so this move was a big change for me. **As I look back on it today, I realize that moving to Boulder to go to school affected me several ways.**

First, when I arrived, I was very lonely, so I had to learn to deal with that. I wandered around the campus for weeks without speaking to anyone. After a while I learned to be more outgoing by talking to people in the lobby of my dorm.

I also had to learn to be more disciplined about my study habits as well as my spending habits. Because there was no one to tell me to do my homework, I almost failed my physics class, and I spent the money that was supposed to last for a month the first two weeks I was there. My parents were not very happy when I had to phone home for more money so soon.

As the year away from home went by, I began to feel more and more independent. I realized that I had chosen engineering as a major to please my dad, not because I was interested in it. My new independent attitude helped me find the major I really loved, which was journalism. I even found myself rethinking the religious beliefs I was raised with. Some of them I kept, but others I left behind.

As I look back over my time in Colorado, I think what it really taught me was to take responsibility for my own life.

EXERCISE 1.5

Respond to the following questions:

1. What is the central idea of the essay? Where is it stated?
2. What is the central idea of each preliminary topic sentence?
3. What would you add to each body paragraph to expand and develop it?

REWRITING: REVISING AND EDITING

REVISING

As we mentioned at the start of the chapter, rewriting consists of two stages: revising and editing. Unfortunately, many people—especially if they are pressed for time—omit the revising stage and move directly to editing, often with disastrous results.

The problem is that editing will correct grammar, spelling, and punctuation errors *without* improving either the content or the organization of your paper, and these larger areas do need to be addressed before you submit your work. Now is the time to *read* what you have written, *think* about it, and *decide* what changes you should make. Here are some suggestions.

1. **Refine your topic sentence or thesis statement.**   Usually, writing the first draft of a paper will help you become more specific about what your central idea really is. In fact, if you look at the concluding sentences of your first draft, you will often find a statement that sums up your central idea better than your preliminary topic sentence or thesis statement did.

   When the writer of the first draft about the move to Colorado read the last sentence of the draft, he realized that *taking responsibility for my own life* was the central idea that tied all three points together. When you read the revised draft below, note how he refined the central idea.

2. **Reorganize your material.**   The writer of the above first draft reorganized the groups of details (A, B, C, D) listed on page 19 so that they appear in the order B, D, A (leaving out Group C). This reorganization allowed the writer to follow a chronological pattern.

3. **Add details.**   One of the most effective ways to improve a paper is to add more specific and descriptive details to illustrate the points you are making. Note how the writer has added details to the draft below.

4. **Reword sentences.**   Many times you will find that your original wording of sentences can be improved. Note the changes made in the middle of the revised draft below.

THE SINGLE PARAGRAPH: REVISED DRAFT

Here is a revised version of the paragraph on page 21. Changes are shown in boldface.

refined topic sentence

reworded sentences and added details

added details

reworded sentences

> **My move to Boulder, Colorado, to go to school taught me to take responsibility for my own life.** My first lesson occurred soon after I arrived. I didn't know a soul, so I wandered from my classrooms to the cafeteria to the library for weeks without speaking to anyone. When I realized that no one was going to introduce himself to me, I took responsibility for my own life and introduced myself to a guy reading a magazine in the lobby of my dorm. I also had to take responsibility for my own study and spending habits. Because there was no one to tell me to do my homework, I kept putting it off to go to parties. As a result, I almost failed my physics class. To make things worse, I spent the money that was supposed to last for a month the first two weeks I was there. My parents were not very happy when I had to phone home for more money so soon. Finally, as the first year away from home went by, I learned to take responsibility for my own interests and values. I realized that I had chosen engineering as a major to please my dad, not because I was interested in it. My new attitude helped me find the major I really loved, which was journalism. I even found myself rethinking the religious beliefs I was raised with. Some of them I kept, but others I left behind. As I look back over my time in Colorado, I can say for sure that is where I learned to take responsibility for myself.

EXERCISE 1.6

Identify the central idea in the topic sentence. Then point out words throughout the paragraph that emphasize that central idea.

THE BRIEF ESSAY: REVISED DRAFT

Here is a revised version of the brief essay on page 22. Changes are shown in boldface.

expanded
introduction

refined thesis
statement
refined topic
sentence

added details

refined topic
sentence

added details

refined topic
sentence

expanded
conclusion

A few years ago I had the opportunity to go to school in Boulder, Colorado. None of my friends from my home in San Diego were going with me. I would be living in a dorm with people I had never met before, so I knew I was in for some big adjustments. **As I look back on it today, I realize that moving to Boulder to go to school was my first step in learning to take responsibility for my own life.**

My first lesson occurred soon after I arrived. I didn't know a soul except for my roommate, and I really disliked him. So I wandered from my classrooms to the cafeteria to the library for weeks without speaking to anyone. When I realized that no one was going to introduce himself to me, I took responsibility for my own life and introduced myself to Marty, a guy reading a magazine in the lobby of my dorm. He ended up becoming one of my closest friends.

I also had to take responsibility for my own study and spending habits. Because there was no one to tell me to do my homework, I kept putting it off to go to parties with Marty. (He was from Denver, so he knew a lot of people at our school in Boulder.) As a result, I almost failed my physics class. To make things worse, I spent the money that was supposed to last for a month in the first two weeks I was there. My parents were not very happy when I had to phone home for more money so soon.

Finally, as the first year away from home went by, I learned to take responsibility for my own interests and values. I realized that I had chosen engineering as a major to please my dad, not because I was interested in it. My new attitude helped me find the major I really loved, which was journalism. I even found myself rethinking the religious beliefs I was raised with. Some of them I kept, but others I left behind.

As I look back over my time in Colorado, I can say for sure that is where I learned to take responsibility for myself. Some of my learning experiences were painful, but they all helped me to grow and become the person I am today.

EXERCISE 1.7

Identify the central idea in the thesis statement. Then point out words in the topic sentences of the body paragraphs and in the details of each paragraph that emphasize the central idea.

Editing

Now for the final step. You need to edit your draft before submitting your final copy. Read over your draft carefully, looking for spelling, grammar, and punctuation errors. Use your spell checker, but don't rely on it to catch every error. Many words used incorrectly (such as *there* instead of *their*) will not be highlighted by a spell checker. When you are satisfied with your draft, print it—and then do what every professional writer does: *Read the hard copy with a pen in hand, looking closely for errors you might have missed.*

Once you have corrected any errors and are satisfied with the final product, prepare a clean copy (double-spaced) and submit it to your instructor.

Exploring
ONLINE

For more information on the writing process, including instruction on writing topic sentences and thesis statements, go the website for *The Writer's Response*: www.thomsonedu.com/ devenglish/mcdonald. Under "Chapter Resources" for Chapter 1 click on "Exploring Online."

WRITING ASSIGNMENTS

WRITING WITH A CENTRAL IDEA

Write a paragraph or a short essay, whichever your instructor assigns, in response to one of the following assignments. If you write a paragraph, be sure to include a topic sentence. If you write an essay, include a thesis statement.

1. After reading "Live Each Moment for What It's Worth," write a paper in response to one of the following suggestions:
    a. Explain whether you do or do not live by the "seize the moment" philosophy. As you give examples to illustrate the type of person you are, be sure to make clear what you think about your approach to life.
    b. What do you think about Bombeck's idea that we should "seize the moment" more often? Give examples from your own life or from the lives of friends, relatives, and acquaintances to illustrate and explain your reaction.
    c. Discuss this article with your classmates or with people you know outside of class. Have any of them "seized the moment" in ways that you particularly admire? Describe one or more of those people, making it clear how they have lived by Bombeck's philosophy.

2. After reading "Without Emotion," write a paper in response to one of the following suggestions:
    a. If your reactions to G. Gordon Liddy or to the events in the article changed as you read it, explain which parts of the article caused your reactions to change.
    b. If you have found that at times you have had to repress or ignore your emotions, write a paper in which you describe specific situations that have caused you to do so.
    c. Interview other members of your class about this article. How did they react to it? Write a paper in which you explain the different types of reactions you discovered.

3. After reading "A View from Mount Ritter," write a paper in response to one of the following suggestions:

   a. Has nature been an important part of your life? Do you camp in the mountains, walk in the woods, listen to the waves at the beach? If you do, choose one particular event that you remember vividly. Briefly describe it, and then explain how or why the event affected you. Give examples to illustrate your points.

   b. Choose any event that affected you deeply, that somehow changed how you think or feel, that helped you to become a different person. Briefly describe the event and then explain in what ways you were changed by it. Give examples to illustrate your points.

   c. Choose a quotation from the article that seems to express a truth about life. Explain what the quotation means to you, and then illustrate its truth with examples from your own life or the lives of people you know.

4. Write a paper in response to one of the articles in Part Four, as assigned by your instructor.

EVALUATING SAMPLE PAPERS

At one time or another, most students have had the experience of turning in a paper they were *sure* they had done a good job on, only to have it returned a few class meetings later with a grade much lower than they expected. Even professional writers have the disappointing experience of having their manuscripts returned by editors with less-than-favorable responses. Perhaps you can *never* be 100% sure that your writing is perfect, but you can *greatly* improve the odds of submitting a successful paper if you learn how to judge the quality of what you have written.

One way to become a good judge of your own writing is to practice judging what others have written. You can get such practice by evaluating sample papers. In this text, each chapter will provide you with several student paragraphs and essays. Practice your judging skills by using the following checklist (or a format provided by your instructor) to determine which paper is the most effective. If your instructor asks you to, use the same checklist to evaluate the papers of some of your fellow students.

STUDENT MODEL CHECKLIST

1. Thesis statement or topic sentence:

   a. If you are reading an essay, underline the thesis statement and circle its central idea. If you are reading a single paragraph, underline the topic sentence and circle its central idea.

   b. Can the thesis statement or topic sentence be more exact or specific? Is it too broad? Should the thesis statement or topic sentence be revised to incorporate a term used in the last few sentences of the paper?

c. Rank the overall effectiveness of the thesis statement or topic sentence:

   1   2   3   4   5   6

ineffective   *excellent*

2. Support:

Look at the examples used. Do they refer to specific personal experiences and exact details, or are they general and vague? Rank the overall effectiveness of the examples:

   1   2   3   4   5   6

general and vague   *specific and detailed*

3. Organization:

Can you tell where one idea or example ends and another begins? Rank the clarity of the organization:

   1   2   3   4   5   6

unclear, confusing   *clear*

4. Spelling, punctuation, grammar:

Underline or circle any spelling, punctuation, or grammar errors that you find. Rank the effectiveness of the spelling, punctuation, and grammar:

   1   2   3   4   5   6

ineffective   *excellent*

5. Rank the overall effectiveness of the paper:

   1   2   3   4   5   6

ineffective   *excellent*

SAMPLE STUDENT PAPERS

The following paragraphs and essays were submitted as first drafts that would later be revised. To evaluate these papers, follow these steps:

1. Read the *entire* paper through before making any judgments about it.
2. Reread the paper to identify its topic sentence or thesis statement.
3. Identify the major sections of the paper.
4. Respond to the items on the student model checklist or to questions provided by your instructor.

PARAGRAPHS

The students who wrote the following papers were asked to write a 250- to 300-word paragraph responding to one of the writing assignments on pages 25–26.

Student Paragraph 1

My interpretation of Erma Bombeck's "seize the moment" is that one should live his or her life to the fullest. If some opportunity crosses your pathway you need to jump on it. A "just go for it" type of attitude is necessary. In my own life, I see this being needed in three areas. The first area is being able to have the "just go for it" attitude no matter what the cost. Who knows if I will have the chance to ever go to that place or do that something ever again. I tend to have too much to do to be able to drop every thing and seize the moment. Also, now everything tends to cost so much money and I don't have the resources to pay the expenses. The second problem I have is the lack of ability to stand up for and tell people what I believe in. That is the perfect time to seize the moment, express your feelings and tell people your personal views. You might help other people to understand, learn, and grow. So, it's important to stand up strong and speak out. When ever you are given the opportunity. For me, I struggle when I tell people about how God has changed my life. The last problem I have deals with grabbing job opportunities to move up in the working world. My employer demands a lot from me, and I should be able to stand up for my rights and demand things as well. I also need to jump on any opportunity to move up or to take on different responsibilities. So, these are the three problems I have with the quote "seize the moment." However, I do believe people need to seize the moment whenever given the opportunity. Never let it slip by, because once its gone who knows if you will ever have the opportunity again.

Student Paragraph 2

The article "Without Emotion" stirred up a few unpleasant feelings inside of me that I certainly was not expecting. When I first started this article and read about how the author went outside, lifted his rifle, and shot a small defenseless squirrel, I felt very horrified and sad. Still, I was able to make it okay in my head because he was only a boy and all kids do mean things. Then he went on and wrote, that after his mother had told him it was wrong to kill things it made him cry. This made me feel very relieved to know that he didn't really enjoy causing pain to another creature. It was certainly a shock to me when I read that he wasn't crying because of the pain he had inflicted, but because he couldn't shoot the squirrel without feelings. I felt sick to my stomach at this point and I actually did not want to continue reading. My curiousity lead me to the next surprise which was him wanting to kill chickens so that he wouldn't feel anything. By this time the author could have said just about anything and it still wouldn't have shocked me. However, I did become a little scared and I was even more frightened when I read that he was able to kill and not feel bad. I wasn't only afraid of him doing the killing, but mainly of him wanting to do the killing. At the end of this horrible article I felt shivers inside of me and kept thinking of this person being out in the world with me. This article certainly did arouse quite a few negative feelings inside of me. It amazes me that such a short article could bother me so much.

Student Paragraph 3

After reading "A View from Mount Ritter," I was reminded of a humbling experience that I also had with nature. The summer after my freshman year in high school, my family and I decided to raft down the Grand Canyon on a six-day, seven-night adventure. The first day was uneventful as we floated through several class one rapids, but day two was exciting as soon as we got back on the raft in the morning. Immediately our raft was bombarded by a class three rapid, followed by a class four rapid named Triple Threat. The sheer force of the water was unbelievable, we were completely at the mercy of the river. I knew that if I fell overboard, I would have to fight for my life. For the first time in my life I was faced with my own mortality. By day four we had already floated through about one hundred seventyfive miles of the Grand Canyon. By this time the walls of the canyon beside us were so tall that I could only see a tiny strip of blue sky when I looked up. In the middle of day five we hit the bottom of the canyon. We were told that the jagged rock walls beside us were over ten million years old. As we floated past canyon walls which had been here since before prehistoric times, I suddenly realized how small I really was and just how wrapped up in my little life I had become. The force of nature is truly awe inspiring. I realized how insignificant my life and contributions are and will be in comparison to the mighty canyon walls and the incredible force of the river that caused them. Before my trip river rafting down the Grand Canyon, I took the wonders of nature for granted. I always thought of man, myself included, as superior. This trip changed my thinking and made me realize that the force of nature is far superior to anything man could ever invent.

BRIEF ESSAYS

The students who wrote the following papers were asked to write a brief essay responding to one of the writing assignments on pages 25–26.

Student Essay 1

I have always been the kind of person who likes to take all opportunities. Erma Bombeck's "Live Each Moment for What It's Worth" could have been written about me. From an adventurous trip to a tropical country to hang gliding, mountain climbing, and bungee jumping. I've done them all.

I try to do everything possible to enjoy my life, and seize all moments, making the best out of them. My friend Alan is also like me. Last summer we went to Rio de Janeiro, and all we did was meet women and play volleyball. I'm happy for being a spontaneous person, it makes life less boring.

However, nothing beats the fear and adrenalin rush of a high altitude sport. I remember as if it was yesterday when my cousin asked me if I wanted to go hang gliding. I didn't think twice and I said yes. Hang gliding was alot of fun and I'll never regret that day.

My cousin also took me mountain climbing. Although I didn't quite like being two thousand feet up on a mountain with a little rope tied around my waist and a heavy bag on my back. It was an experience I'll never forget.

The last of my crazy high altitude adventures was bungee jumping. Until last year I was eager to feel the wind going against my face and the adrenaline rush on a hundred mile per hour vertical dive. However, on November 25, about 3:30 p.m., I bungee jumped and turned into a human yo-yo.

As I finished reading the article "Live Each Moment for What It's Worth," I realized how important it is to take chances and seize the moment. There are opportunities that only come up once in a lifetime. People should take their chances because they might not get another one.

Student Essay 2

When I first read Liddy's "Without Emotion," I was horrified by his desire to kill without feeling anything. However, the more I thought about it, the more I realized that there have been times in my own life when I needed to act without feeling too. In fact, many times I have had to repress my personal feelings just to make it through an unpleasant experience.

For instance, in 1984 I had to face the realization that a divorce was in order. I had no emotional or financial support, and I had an eleven-month-old son to take care of. It was a time when emotions had to be shelved, temporarily, and all of my attention directed toward how I would handle the more pressing issues. Those issues being: food, shelter, clothing, and a job. I struggled through the transition from marriage to solo living by remaining unemotional and methodical. There would be time enough to process feelings once the necessary tasks were taken care of.

A few years later, after the divorce was final and I was well settled into the daily living as a single parent, I was laid off from a typesetting position with a local newspaper. This time, also, I did not allow myself the luxury of feeling frightened, not even for a minute. I immediately busied myself with the task of finding a job. I didn't take time to feel sad or to feel sorry for myself; I just proceeded with what needed to be done, never once allowing myself to give in to everyone's barrage of "What if's?"

I think Liddy was trying to get to a point where he could kill without feeling emotion if he had to. He was aware of the "kill or be killed" probability that faced him as a soldier. For me, it was either conquer the challenges that had befallen me or be conquered by them.

Student Essay 3

When my parents separated, it was a very difficult and tough time for not only myself but my whole family. It changed my life forever. Everything was going great, and then my parents began to fight. It seemed to be no big deal, but after weeks and weeks of fighting, I started to get scared. One morning my mom told my brother and me that she was going to move into our other house so my dad and her could have some time apart. Since that time about two years ago, my parents are still not the best of friends, and I still cry at night when I think about the situation. This whole event caused me a lot of pain, but I have learned to bring a lot of positive things out of the whole situation.

I've learned to not take things for granted and to cherish every single day and everyone I love. This event has made me realize that one day I may have everything I need but the next day it all could be lost. That was how I felt when my parents separated. The whole time I was growing up I thought I had the perfect family and I was the luckiest kid. The family trips together to Utah and Canada were the greatest, and I thought it would always be that way. This event made me change the way

I felt. I felt I had lost everything I had loved. Now everyday I live that day as if the next may take some bad turn. I don't want to look back and wonder, "What if?"

Now if I have a problem or I see that someone else needs some help, I'm always the first to ask for help and the first to give. Two weeks ago one of my good friends was having some girl trouble, so I decided to ask him what was wrong. He told me that they had got into a fight, so I sat down and had a nice talk with him. I helped them solve their differences. Before this event happened, I felt afraid to talk about my problems or others' problems. Today, I am more open as a person. I really enjoy helping others during their troubled times.

This event made me feel like I can do more things on my own and not be dependent on everyone else all the time. I used to go places with others and have them help me with stuff I could have done on my own. Last week I went to a movie by myself where before this event I would have been afraid to go by myself. This event made me realize that everyone else won't always be there for me but that I should always be there for myself as well as for others.

At the beginning this was a very tough time for me, and it is still very hard to handle. It is a tough subject, but it has taught me a lot of great lessons that would have been hard for me to figure out. Don't get me wrong, I would give anything to have my family back the way it used to be, but I know that's never going to happen. So I'm really glad I was able to learn such a valuable lesson at an early age and take something out of my parents separation other than anger and pain. Some people never have a chance to learn these valuable lessons. They can change the way you look at life.

SENTENCE COMBINING: EMBEDDING ADJECTIVES, ADVERBS, AND PREPOSITIONAL PHRASES

As you have worked through the writing process presented in this chapter, we hope you have discovered that good writing develops as you write. Many times, for instance, you will not know exactly what your central idea is until you have done a substantial amount of prewriting, and sometimes you may not know exactly how your ideas or paragraphs should be organized until you have tried one or two different organizations to see which works best. This willingness to make changes and to rethink material as you discover new ideas is at the heart of all good writing—and it works at the level of individual sentences as well as at the larger levels related to the central idea or the organization of a paper.

As you write the initial drafts of your papers, you will express your ideas in sentence structures that are comfortable to you because they reflect your personal style of writing. (You *do* have a personal style, even if you write very rarely.) However, as you become more and more proficient in using the writing process, you will find that you can improve your personal style. At the level of sentence structure, this improvement can include, among other things, recognizing when separate sentences contain related ideas that should be expressed in one sentence and learning how to use different types of sentence structures to express different types of ideas.

EXERCISE **1.8**

To illustrate what we mean, let's compare the following versions of a passage drawn from an article by Lois Sweet entitled "What's in a Name? Quite a Lot." One passage is just as Lois Sweet wrote it. The other is written as a beginning writer might have written it. Which is which? How can you tell?

1 Over the years, a lot of my friends have changed their names. 2 A number of them began to take an interest in their cultural backgrounds. 3 Their parents had wanted to deny cultural differences. 4 As a result, their parents had anglicized their names. 5 My friends were horrified. 6 They had been pushed into the great bland melting pot. 7 They felt more like they were being drowned than saved. 8 For them, their culture was a source of pride. 9 They demanded recognition for their "ethnic" names.

1 Over the years, a lot of my friends have changed their names. 2 A number of them began to take an interest in their cultural backgrounds and became horrified that their parents had anglicized their names in an effort to deny cultural differences. 3 To my friends, being pushed into the great bland melting pot felt more like being drowned than saved. 4 Their culture was a source of pride and they demanded recognition for their "ethnic" names.

As you can see, these two versions are quite different from each other, although they both express the same ideas. The first version uses nine sentences and eighty-two words. The second version uses nearly the same number of words (seventy-five) but only four sentences.

The second version is Lois Sweet's original. In it, you can see a professional writer's ability to combine related ideas into sentences that are longer and more varied than those written by an inexperienced writer. In her version, Sweet has written in a single sentence (sentence 2) what it took three sentences (sentences 2, 3, and 4) for the first writer to express. And Sweet has written in two sentences (sentences 3 and 4) what the first writer expressed in four sentences (sentences 6, 7, 8, and 9). Of course, combining related ideas is a skill all writers have to some degree, no matter how experienced or inexperienced they may be. For example, when you see that two or more ideas are related, you probably combine them without thinking much about it. Would you write this?

My brother is an auto mechanic. I asked my brother to fix my car. My car had not run properly for weeks.

Probably not. But you might express yourself any one of these ways:

My brother is an auto mechanic, so I asked him to fix my car because it had not run properly for weeks.

I asked my brother, who is an auto mechanic, to fix my car because it had not run properly for weeks.

Because my car had not run properly for weeks, I asked my brother, an auto mechanic, to fix it.

I asked my brother to fix my car, which had not run properly for weeks, because he is an auto mechanic.

My car had not run properly for weeks, so I asked my brother to fix it because he is an auto mechanic.

Which sounds better to you? Each of the above sentences might work in your speech or in your writing, depending on the situation. The point is that you already can and do combine related ideas in many different ways. And with practice, you will become even better at what you already do.

EXERCISE 1.9

To see what we mean when we say you already know how to combine related ideas, rewrite the sentences below. Join those ideas that seem obviously related into sentences that make sense to you. Don't worry about getting the "right" answer—just combine the ideas that seem as if they should go together.

The woman held a book. It was in her left hand. She was tired. The book was thick. She waited for her ride. She was in the parking lot. Finally a car stopped. It was small and blue. It stopped next to her. She opened the door to the car. A poodle jumped out. It was white. It ran into the parking lot. It ran quickly. It disappeared between the parked cars.

THE EMBEDDING PROCESS

One of the most common ways to combine ideas is to use adjectives and adverbs to modify other words. For instance, in the exercise above, if you described the book the woman was holding as a "thick" book, you used *thick* as an adjective. If you wrote that the poodle ran "quickly" into the parking lot, you used *quickly* as an adverb.

What's the difference? It is that adjectives modify nouns and pronouns while adverbs modify verbs, adjectives, and other adverbs. However, knowing these definitions is not as important here as recognizing when a word in one sentence is related to a word in another sentence.

In sentence combining, the act of placing words or phrases from one sentence into another is called *embedding*. Look at the following examples. Note how the underlined adjective or adverb in the second sentence can be embedded within the first sentence.

EXAMPLES

The movie was about a tomato.
The tomato was <u>enormous</u>. (adjective)
   The movie was about an <u>enormous</u> tomato.

The lamp fell to the floor.
It fell <u>suddenly</u>. (adverb)
   The lamp <u>suddenly</u> fell to the floor.

Prepositional phrases also modify words, so in a sense they are adjectives and adverbs too. You use them all of the time in your speech and in your writing. You use prepositional phrases when you write that you are <u>in the house</u> or <u>on the step</u> or <u>at the store</u> or <u>from Indiana</u>.

Each prepositional phrase starts with a preposition and ends with a noun (or a pronoun), called the *object* of the preposition. Between the preposition and its object you may find modifiers. For example, in the prepositional phrase "from the tired old man," *from* is the preposition, *man* is the object, and the words between the two are modifiers.

preposition	modifiers	object of the preposition
from	the tired old	man

Here is a list of common prepositions:

above	before	for	on	under
across	behind	from	onto	until
after	below	in	over	up
among	beside	into	past	upon
around	between	in spite of	through	with
as	by	like	till	without
at	during	near	to	
because of	except	of	toward	

Prepositional phrases should be embedded in sentences they are related to, just as adjectives and adverbs should be. Look at the following examples:

EXAMPLES

The lawnmower was old and rusty.
The lawnmower was <u>in the garage</u>. (prep. phrase)
 The lawnmower <u>in the garage</u> was old and rusty.

Wild Bill Hickok was killed when he was shot.
He was killed <u>during a poker game</u>. (prep. phrase)
He was shot <u>in the back</u>. (prep. phrase)
 Wild Bill Hickok was killed <u>during a poker game</u> when he was shot <u>in the back</u>.

EXERCISE 1.10

Rewrite each of the following groups of sentences into one sentence by embedding the underlined adjective, adverb, or prepositional phrase in to the first sentence of the group:

EXAMPLE

We washed the dishes.
We washed them <u>after dinner</u>.
We washed them <u>carefully</u>.
The dishes were <u>expensive</u>.
 <u>After dinner</u>, we <u>carefully</u> washed the <u>expensive</u> dishes.

1. The dolphins leaped.
The dolphins were <u>sleek</u>.
They leaped <u>out of the water</u>.
They leaped <u>in arcs</u>.

The arcs were <u>long</u>.

The arcs were <u>graceful</u>.

2. The monster walked out.

It was <u>green</u>.

It was <u>ugly</u>.

It walked out <u>of the lagoon</u>.

The lagoon was <u>black</u>.

It walked <u>slowly</u>.

3. A goose waddled

It was <u>fat</u> and <u>white</u>.

It was a goose <u>with a mean look in its eye</u>.

It waddled <u>toward the tourist</u>.

The tourist was <u>unsuspecting</u>.

4. A dog guarded the entrance.

The dog was <u>ferocious</u>.

It was a dog <u>with three heads</u>.

It had <u>the tail of a serpent</u>.

The entrance was <u>to the underworld</u>.

5. The singer named himself.

The singer is <u>crude</u>.

The singer is <u>vulgar</u>.

He is named <u>after a brand of candy</u>.

The brand of candy is <u>popular</u>.

EXERCISE 1.11

Combine each of the sets of sentences into one sentence by embedding adjectives, adverbs, and prepositional phrases:

1. The skier gazed at the mountain.

The skier was disappointed.

The mountain was bare.

The mountain was rocky.

The mountain was above her.

2. The hikers shouted.

The hikers were starving.

They shouted loudly.

They shouted at the helicopter.

The helicopter was circling.

3. The violinist and his daughter played.

The violinist was blind.

They played in the square.

The square was crowded.

They played beautifully.

4. One swing sent the baseball flying.
   It was a strong swing.
   It was a swing of the bat.
   The baseball was flying out of the ballpark.
   The ballpark was his favorite.
5. The ranger explained the plan.
   The plan was dangerous.
   The ranger was patient.
   She explained the plan to the campers.
   The campers were eager.

EXERCISE 1.12

Combine each of the following sets of sentences into one sentence by embedding adjectives, adverbs, and prepositional phrases.

1. The novel was about a murder.
   It was a mystery novel.
   It was new.
   The murder was violent.
   The murder was in St. Patrick's Cathedral.
   St. Patrick's Cathedral is in New York City.
2. The newspapers carried the story.
   The story was on the front pages.
   These newspapers were in almost every city.
   They carried the story prominently.
   The story was of the murder.
3. The basketball game was held in the gym.
   It was for the state championship.
   It was in a small town.
   The town was on the banks of a river.
   The river was wide and muddy.
4. The game was held in the afternoon.
   The game was sold out.
   It was on a Saturday.
   It was held between one team and another team.
   One team was from a small town.
   The other team was from a large city.
5. When the team won, the town held a parade.
   The team from the small town won.
   The town was surprised.
   The parade was big.
   It was held in celebration of the players.

EXERCISE 1.13

Combine each group of sentences into one sentence. Use the first sentence as the base sentence. Adjectives, adverbs, and prepositional phrases that can be embedded into the base sentence are underlined in the first five groups. In each group, the original version of the sentence can be found in one of the reading selections in this chapter.

EXAMPLE

Hunting was a sport. <u>Squirrel</u> hunting was a <u>popular</u> one in <u>West Caldwell</u>. This was in the <u>1940s</u>.
　　Squirrel hunting was a <u>popular</u> sport in <u>West Caldwell in the 1940s</u>.

1. I loaded my rifle, cocked the spring, and waited. I was waiting <u>on the steps of the porch</u>, and it was my <u>homemade</u> rifle.

2. When I came in, my mother told me that she had seen the suffering I had caused. She told me this <u>reproachfully</u>. I came <u>into the house</u>. She said that she had seen me <u>from the kitchen window</u>.

3. Bill Jacobus's father, to help combat the shortage and to supplement rationing, had built a coop. It was the <u>wartime food</u> shortage he was combatting. He built a <u>chicken</u> coop. It was <u>in his backyard</u>.

4. Just possibly, she might be the woman. She might be the <u>wisest</u> of all the women <u>on this planet</u>.

5. I got to thinking one day. I was thinking <u>about all those women who passed up dessert</u>. They were <u>on the Titanic</u>. The dessert was <u>at dinner that fateful night</u>. The women had passed it up <u>in an effort to "cut back."</u>

6. We live on a diet. It is a sparse diet. It is a diet of promises we make when all conditions are perfect. They are promises we make to ourselves.

7. It's just that I might as well apply it and eliminate the process. I would apply it directly. I would apply it to my hips. I would apply it with a spatula. The process is digestive.

8. We constructed our tents, fumbling and finishing just as a stiffness set in. We constructed them in the dark. We were fumbling with the ropes. We were fumbling with our frozen hands. The stiffness was like rigor mortis.

9. I was on top of Mount Ritter. I was 13,000 feet above sea level. I was entranced by the sight. The sight was of the sun. It was orange-red. It peeked over the peaks. The peaks were glistening. They were far off in the east.

10. Clouds appeared transparent as they glowed. They were cumulous clouds. They glowed red. The red was bright. They were in the morning glory.

Exploring
ONLINE

For more practice combining sentences, go to www.thomsonedu.com/devenglish/mcdonald. Under "Chapter Resources" for Chapter 1, click on "Exploring Online."

Hagar the Horrible, by Chris Browne. © *King Features Syndicate.*

Reading for the Central Idea

In Chapter 1, you read that part of the writing process consists of developing a clearly worded statement of your central idea. Such a statement—whether it is a topic sentence or a thesis statement—serves as a guide for your readers, identifying for them the point you are trying to make.

In the "writing-reading conversation," you are a reader as often as you are a writer, and your ability to identify a central idea as a reader is certainly as important as your ability to express a central idea as a writer. In fact, in many college situations you will find that your ability to write a clear central idea depends first upon your ability to identify central ideas in what you read.

In the cartoon on the facing page, Hagar the Horrible and his companion have apparently not identified the central idea of the signs they have just read. (And the writer of the signs has not yet learned how to use *lay* and *lie*.) Of course, the message that Hagar and his friend have overlooked is a fairly clear one. Unfortunately, however, the central ideas of many paragraphs and essays are not always as clear—not necessarily because the paragraph or essay is written poorly, but because it is complex and demands close attention.

In this chapter, you will practice reading to identify and to summarize central ideas, and you will practice writing in response to those ideas.

PARAGRAPHS AND TOPIC SENTENCES

In a paragraph, the sentence that states the central idea is called the topic sentence. It is often the first sentence (or two) of the paragraph, although a paragraph often has its topic sentence in the middle or at the end. Look at the following paragraphs. Their topic sentences are in italics. Following each paragraph is an example of how you could state its central idea in your own words.

> *Football has replaced baseball as the favorite American spectator sport largely because of television.* A comparison between a telecast of a football game on one channel and a baseball game on another could reveal baseball as a game with people standing around seemingly with little to do but watch two men play catch. Football would appear as twenty-two men engaged in almost constant, frenzied action. To watch baseball requires identification with the home team; to watch football requires only a need for action or a week of few thrills and the need for a touch of vicarious excitement.
>
> —*Jeffery Schrank, "Sport and the American Dream"*

SUMMARY OF CENTRAL IDEA

Television has helped football to replace baseball as the favorite American spectator sport.

In the next paragraph, the "topic sentence" actually consists of more than one sentence.

> *Some people say the business about the jolly fat person is a myth, that all of us chubbies are neurotic, sick, sad people. I disagree. Fat people may not be chortling all day long, but they're a hell of a lot* nicer *than the wizened and shriveled.* Thin people turn surly, mean, and hard at a young age because they never learn the value of a hot-fudge sundae for easing tension. Thin people don't like gooey soft things because they themselves are neither gooey nor soft. They are crunchy and dull, like carrots. They go straight to the heart of the matter while fat people let things stay all blurry and hazy and vague, the way things actually are. Thin people want to face the truth. Fat people know there is no truth. One of my thin friends is always staring at complex, unsolvable problems and saying, "The key thing is. . . ." Fat people never say that. They know there isn't any such thing as the key thing.
>
> —*Suzanne Britt, "That Lean and Hungry Look"*

SUMMARY OF CENTRAL IDEA

The writer of this paragraph thinks that fat people are more pleasant to be around than thin people.

PARAGRAPHS WITHOUT TOPIC SENTENCES

Some paragraphs that you read will not have topic sentences. In these paragraphs, the topic sentence is *implied* (that is, it is not stated), but you can tell what the central idea is without it. Here is an example:

> The loose bones of Lincoln were hard to fit with neat clothes; and, once on, they were hard to keep neat; trousers go baggy at the knees of a storyteller who has the habit, at the end of a story, where the main laugh comes in, of putting his arms around his knees, raising his knees to his chin, and rocking to and fro. Those who spoke of his looks often mentioned his trousers creeping to the ankles and higher; his rumpled hair, his wrinkled vest. When he wasn't away making speeches, electioneering or practicing law on the circuit, he cut kindling wood, tended to cordwood for the stoves in the house, milked the cow, gave her a few forks of hay, and changed her straw bedding every day.
>
> —*Carl Sandburg*, Abraham Lincoln: The Prairie Years

SUMMARY OF CENTRAL IDEA

Abraham Lincoln was an ordinary man who was not concerned about his appearance and who was willing to do ordinary work.

Many paragraphs in newspapers also do not have topic sentences. The columns in newspapers are so narrow that every third or fourth sentence is indented—not because a new topic idea has started, but because an article is easier to read that way. Look at the following three paragraphs from a newspaper, and notice how they all support the same topic sentence in the first paragraph:

> *First, economists are virtually unanimous on the fact that jobs will be lost if the minimum wage is increased.* The Minimum Wage Study Commission concluded in 1981 that every 10 percent increase in the minimum wage could eliminate 70,000 to 200,000 jobs for teenagers alone. Total job loss could be substantially higher.
>
> Given a 40 percent increase, the legislation proposed by Kennedy and Hawkins would jeopardize an additional 400,000 to 800,000 jobs, denying opportunities to thousands more.
>
> Simply put, the minimum wage won't mean a thing—whatever the rate is—if people are forced out of their jobs. A higher wage is little consolation for someone who doesn't have a job.
>
> —*Senator Orrin G. Hatch,*
> *"Raising the Minimum Wage Will Put People Out of Work"*

SUMMARY OF CENTRAL IDEA

If the minimum wage is increased, fewer jobs will be available.

EXERCISE 2.1

Read each of the following paragraphs. Underline the topic sentence of each one. Then summarize its central idea in your own words. Remember that the topic sentence might be the first sentence, or it might occur later in the paragraph. It might consist of more than one sentence, or it might be implied.

1. Don't meddle with old unloaded firearms, they are the most deadly and unerring things that have ever been created by man. You don't have to take any pains at all with them; you don't have to have a rest, you don't have to have any sights on the gun, you don't have to take aim, even. No, you just pick out a relative and bang away, and you are sure to get him. A youth who can't hit a cathedral at thirty yards with a Gatling gun in three-quarters of an hour, can take up an old empty musket and bag his grandmother every time at a hundred.

    —*Mark Twain, "Advice to Youth"*

2. In the warmth of the inner Solar System a comet releases clouds of vapor and dust that form the glowing head and then leak into the tail, which is the cosmic equivalent of an oil slick. Pieces of the dust later hit the Earth, as meteors. A few survivors among the comets evolve into menacing lumps of dirt in tight orbits around the Sun. For these reasons comets are, in my opinion, best regarded as a conspicuous form of sky pollution.

    —*Nigel Calder,* The Comet Is Coming

3. A TV set stood close to a wall in the small living room crowded with an assortment of chairs and tables. An aquarium crowded the mantelpiece of a fake fireplace. A lighted bulb inside the tank showed many colored fish swimming about in a haze of fish food. Some of it lay scattered on the edge of the shelf. The carpet underneath was sodden black. Old magazines and tabloids lay just about everywhere.

    —*Bienvenidos Santos, "Immigration Blues"*

ESSAYS AND THESIS STATEMENTS

The central idea of a complete essay is called its *thesis statement.* Usually, it appears toward the start of the essay (in the introduction), although, like a topic sentence in a paragraph, it can appear in the middle or at the end of an essay, or it might not appear at all because it is implied.

Sometimes a thesis statement is quite straightforward and easy to see. For example, in the following brief essay, the thesis (shown in italics) is clearly stated in the first paragraph:

Three Passions I Have Lived For   BERTRAND RUSSELL

Bertrand Russell was a British philosopher, mathematician, Nobel Prize–winner, and political activist. He is recognized as one of the most productive writers and thinkers of the twentieth century. In the following selection, he identifies three passions that have influenced his life.

Three passions, simple but overwhelmingly strong, have governed my life: the longing for love, the search for knowledge, and unbearable pity for the suffering of mankind. These passions, like great winds, have blown me hither and thither, in a wayward course over a deep ocean of anguish, reaching to the very verge of despair.   1

I have sought love, first, because it brings ecstasy— ecstasy so great that I would often have sacrificed all the rest of my life for a few hours of this joy. I have sought it, next, because it relieves loneliness—that terrible loneliness in which one shivering consciousness looks over the rim of the world into the cold unfathomable lifeless abyss. I have sought it, finally, because in the union of love I have seen, in a mystic miniature, the prefiguring vision of the heaven that saints and poets have imagined. This is what I sought, and though it might seem too good for human life, this is what—at last—I have found.   2

With equal passion I have sought knowledge. I have wished to understand the hearts of men. I have wished to know why the stars shine. . . . A little of this, but not much, I have achieved.   3

Love and knowledge, so far as they were possible, led upward toward the heavens. But always pity brought me back to earth. Echoes of cries of pain reverberate in my heart. Children in famine, victims tortured by oppressors, helpless old people a hated burden to their sons, and the whole world of loneliness, poverty, and pain make a mockery of what human life should be. I long to alleviate the evil, but I cannot, and I too suffer.   4

This has been my life. I have found it worth living, and would gladly live it again if the chance were offered me.   5

SUMMARY OF CENTRAL IDEA

Bertrand Russell states that his life has been governed by the search for love and for knowledge and by a sense of pity for those who suffer.

Unfortunately, not everything you read will have a thesis statement as clear as the one above. Sometimes essays, articles, or chapters in texts will have their thesis statements in the second or third paragraph—or even later in the work. Sometimes the thesis statement will be most clearly worded in the conclusion. And sometimes it will not be stated directly at all. The point is that you need to read college material carefully and closely. Certainly one of the most important reading skills you will need to develop in college classes is the ability to recognize the central idea of what you read, even when it is not directly stated.

READINGS

Read the two articles below. After you have read each one, write a sentence that briefly summarizes its central idea. Underline any sentences that seem to state the thesis of the article.

Jailbreak Marriage   GAIL SHEEHY

> *Gail Sheehy's text* Passages, *from which the following selection is taken, and her many subsequent texts examine the stages of life that men and women pass through as they grow. Sheehy is a six-time recipient of the New York Newswomen's Club Front Page Award for distinguished journalism.*

BEFORE YOU READ

1. Consider the title. In what sense might a marriage be called a "jailbreak"?
2. As you read this selection, watch for sentences that will express the author's central idea about "jailbreak" marriages.

Thesis is

Although the most commonplace reason women marry young   1
is to "complete" themselves, a good many spirited young women gave another reason: "I did it to get away from my parents." Particularly for girls whose educations and privileges are limited, a *jailbreak marriage* is the usual thing. <u>What might appear to be an act of rebellion usually turns out to be a transfer of dependence</u>.

A lifer: that is how it felt to be Simone at 17, how it often   2
feels for girls in authoritarian homes. The last of six children, she was caught in the nest vacated by the others and expected to "keep the family together." Simone was the last domain where her mother could play out the maternal role and where her father could exercise full control. That meant goodbye to the university scholarship.

Although the family was not altogether poor, Simone had   3
tried to make a point of her independence by earning her own money since the age of 14. Now she thrust out her bankbook. Would two thousand dollars in savings buy her freedom?

"We want you home until you're 21." 4

Work, her father insisted. But the job she got was another 5 closed gate. It was in the knitting machine firm where her father worked, an extension of his control. Simone knuckled under for a year until she met Franz. A zero. An egocentric Hungarian of pointless aristocracy, a man for whom she had total disregard. Except for one attraction. He asked her to marry him. Franz would be the getaway vehicle in her jailbreak marriage scheme: "I decided the best way to get out was to get married and divorce him a year later. That was my whole program."

Anatomy, uncontrolled, sabotaged her program. Nine 6 months after the honeymoon, Simone was a mother. Resigning herself, she was pregnant with her second child at 20.

One day, her husband called with the news, the marker 7 event to blast her out of the drift. His firm had offered him a job in New York City.

"Then and there, I decided that before the month was out I 8 would have the baby, find a lawyer, and start divorce proceedings." The next five years were like twenty. It took every particle of her will and patience to defeat Franz, who wouldn't hear of a separation, and to ignore the ostracism of her family.

At the age of 25, on the seventh anniversary of her jailbreak 9 marriage (revealed too late as just another form of entrapment), Simone finally escaped her parents. Describing the day of her decree, the divorce sounds like so many women whose identity was foreclosed by marriage: "It was like having ten tons of chains removed from my mind, my body—the most exhilarating day of my life."

How to Stay Alive   ART HOPPE

Art Hoppe, a graduate of Harvard University, wrote for the San Francisco Chronicle *for over fifty years. His work as a political satirist and humorist is recognized as some of the best of its kind. In the following selection, he tells the story of Snadley Klabberhorn.*

BEFORE YOU READ

1. Read the title. What does it suggest will be the topic of this reading selection? What might be the central idea?
2. Read the first four words of this selection. What do they suggest to you?

Once upon a time there was a man named Snadley Klabberhorn   1
who was the healthiest man in the whole wide world.

Snadley wasn't always the healthiest man in the whole wide   2
world.

When he was young, Snadley smoked what he wanted,   3
drank what he wanted, ate what he wanted, and exercised only with
young ladies in bed.

He thought he was happy. "Life is absolutely peachy," he   4
was fond of saying. "Nothing beats being alive."

Then along came the Surgeon General's Report linking   5
smoking to lung cancer, heart disease, emphysema and tertiary
coreopsis.

Snadley read about The Great Tobacco Scare with a frown.   6
"Life is so peachy," he said, "that there's no sense taking any risks." So
he gave up smoking.

Like most people who went through the hell of giving up   7
smoking, Snadley became more interested in his own health. In
fact, he became fascinated. And when he read a WCTU tract which
pointed out that alcohol caused liver damage, brain damage, and acute
weltanschauung, he gave up alcohol and drank dietary colas instead.

At least he did until The Great Cyclamate Scare.   8

"There's no sense in taking any risks," he said. And he switched   9
to sugar-sweetened colas, which made him fat and caused dental
caries. On realizing this he renounced colas in favor of milk and
took up jogging, which was an awful bore.

That was about the time of The Great Cholesterol Scare.   10

Snadley gave up milk. To avoid cholesterol, which caused   11
atherosclerosis, coronary infarcts and chronic chryselephantinism,
he also gave up meat, fats and dairy products, subsisting on a diet
of raw fish.

Then came The Great DDT Scare.   12

"The presence of large amounts of DDT in fish . . ." Snadley   13
read with anguish. But fortunately that's when he met Ernestine.
They were made for each other. Ernestine introduced him to home-
ground wheat germ, macrobiotic yogurt and organic succotash.

They were very happy eating this dish twice daily, watching   14
six hours of color television together and spending the rest of their
time in bed.

They were, that is, until The Great Color Television Scare.   15

"If color tee-vee does give off radiations," said Snadley,   16
"there's no sense taking risks. After all, we still have each other."

And that's about all they had. Until The Great Pill Scare.   17

On hearing that The Pill might cause carcinoma, thromboses   18
and lingering stichometry, Ernestine promptly gave up The Pill—and
Snadley. "There's no sense taking any risks," she said.

Snadley was left with jogging. He was, that is, until he read   19
somewhere that 1.3 percent of joggers are eventually run over
by a truck or bitten by rabid dogs.

He then retired to a bomb shelter in his back yard (to avoid   20
being hit by a meteor), installed an air purifier (after The Great
Smog Scare) and spent the next 63 years doing Royal Canadian Air
Force exercises and poring over back issues of *The Reader's Digest.*

"Nothing's more important than being alive," he said   21
proudly on reaching 102. But he never did say anymore that life
was absolutely peachy.

Exploring
ONLINE

The website for *The Writer's Response* contains more exercises to assist you with clear and accurate reading. Go to www.thomsonedu.com/devenglish/mcdonald. Under "Course Resources," click on "Reading Quizzes."

PARTICIPATING ACTIVELY IN THE WRITER-READER DIALOGUE

What would you do if a friend showed up at your door with something important to tell you? Would you tell her to go ahead and talk while you finished watching a television show? Probably not. If you believed what she had to say was important, you'd invite her in, turn off the TV, and sit down to talk to her. If her message was complicated, you might find yourself asking her to repeat parts of it, or you might repeat to her what you thought she had said. Perhaps you would nod your head as she spoke to show that you were listening to her and understood her.

The point is, when you think something is important, you listen to it *actively.* You ask questions; you look for clarification; you offer your own opinions. Above all, you *participate* in the conversation. As we said earlier, reading and listening are very similar. Sometimes we read very casually, just as sometimes we listen very casually. After all, not everything needs (or deserves) our rapt attention. But some reading, like some listening, *does* demand our attention. The reading that you will do in college classes will, of course, demand active participation from you. So will reading related to your job or to major decisions that you must make in your life. In each of these cases, you must read in a way that is quite different from the casual way you might read a newspaper in the morning.

So what is active reading? How does one go about it? Here are some steps that you should learn to apply to all the reading you do in your college classes.

STEPS FOR ACTIVE READING

1. *Establish your expectations.*   Before you read an article or chapter or book, look at its title. Does it give you an idea of what to expect? Does it sound as if it is announcing its central idea? Read any background information that comes with the reading material. Does it tell you what to expect?

2. *First reading: underline or mark main points.*   With a pen, pencil, or high-lighter in hand, read the material from start to finish, slowly and carefully. During the first reading, you're trying to get an overall sense of the central idea of the selection. Don't try to take notes during this first reading. Instead, just underline or highlight sentences or ideas that seem significant to you as you read. Often these sentences will express the thesis of the reading selection or the topic ideas of individual paragraphs. In addition, mark any details or explanations that seem more important than others.

3. *Second reading: annotate.*   This step is of major importance if you intend to understand fully what you have read. *Reread* what you underlined. As you do, briefly summarize those points in the margin. If you think a point is especially important, make a note of it in the margin. If you have questions or disagree with something, note that in the margin.

4. *Summarize the reading.*   Briefly write out the central idea of the reading. In your own words, state the thesis of the entire essay and the supporting topic ideas of the paragraphs.

5. *Respond to the reading.*   Write out your own response to what you have read. Do you agree with the writer's idea? Did it remind you of anything that you have experienced? Did it give you a new insight into its topic? You might write this response in a journal or as an assignment to be used for class discussion. Your instructor will guide you here.

Should you go through these five steps every time you read? Absolutely not. Who would want to underline, annotate, and summarize when relaxing with a good novel on a Saturday afternoon? However, you should take these steps when what you are reading demands close attention—when you read material you must analyze for a report or a paper, for example.

Here is an example of an article that has been read by an active reader:

Printed Noise   GEORGE WILL

Most of us are used to the strange names that businesses use to draw attention to their products. In the following essay, George Will takes a second look at these names and suggests that they are a form of language pollution. Will is a former philosophy professor and a Pulitzer Prize–winning columnist for the Washington Post *and* Newsweek.

The flavor list at the local Baskin-Robbins ice cream shop is an anarchy of names like "Peanut Butter 'N Chocolate" and "Strawberry Rhubarb Sherbet." These are not the names of things that reasonable people consider consuming, but the names are admirably businesslike, briskly descriptive.

cuteness in commerce

Unfortunately, my favorite delight (chocolate-coated vanilla flecked with nuts) bears the unutterable name "Hot Fudge Nutty Buddy," an example of the plague of cuteness in commerce. There are some things a gentleman simply will not do, and one is announce in public a desire for a "Nutty Buddy." So I usually settle for a plain vanilla cone.

a gentleman won't say "Nutty Buddy"!

Example of man who wouldn't say "Yumbo"

I am not the only person suffering for immutable standards of propriety. The May issue of *Atlantic* contains an absorbing tale of lonely heroism at a Burger King. A gentleman requested a ham and cheese sandwich that the Burger King calls a Yumbo. The girl taking orders was bewildered.

"Oh," she eventually exclaimed, "you mean a Yumbo."

Gentleman: "The ham and cheese. Yes."

Girl, nettled: "It's called a Yumbo. Now, do you want a Yumbo or not?"

Gentleman, teeth clenched: "Yes, thank you, the ham and cheese."

Girl: "Look, I've got to have an order here. You're holding up the line. You want a Yumbo, don't you? You want a Yumbo!"

Whereupon the gentleman chose the straight and narrow path of virtue. He walked out rather than call a ham and cheese a Yumbo. His principles are anachronisms but his prejudices are impeccable and he is on my short list of civilization's friends.

=outdated, but the author likes him

That list includes the Cambridge don who would not appear outdoors without a top hat, not even when routed by fire at 3 A.M., and who refused to read another line of Tennyson after he saw the poet put water in fine port. The list includes another don who, although devoutly Tory, voted Liberal during Gladstone's day because the duties of prime minister kept Gladstone too busy to declaim on Holy Scripture. And high on the list is the grammarian whose last words were: "I am about to—or I am going to—die: either expression is correct."

more examples

Gentle reader, can you imagine any of these magnificent persons asking a teenage girl for a "Yumbo"? Or uttering

Hah! This is funny!

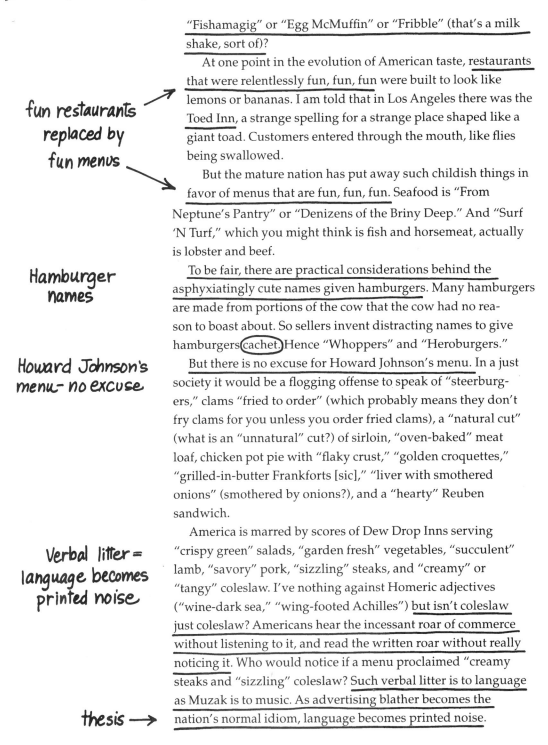

"Fishamagig" or "Egg McMuffin" or "Fribble" (that's a milk shake, sort of)?

At one point in the evolution of American taste, restaurants that were relentlessly fun, fun, fun were built to look like lemons or bananas. I am told that in Los Angeles there was the Toed Inn, a strange spelling for a strange place shaped like a giant toad. Customers entered through the mouth, like flies being swallowed.

But the mature nation has put away such childish things in favor of menus that are fun, fun, fun. Seafood is "From Neptune's Pantry" or "Denizens of the Briny Deep." And "Surf 'N Turf," which you might think is fish and horsemeat, actually is lobster and beef.

To be fair, there are practical considerations behind the asphyxiatingly cute names given hamburgers. Many hamburgers are made from portions of the cow that the cow had no reason to boast about. So sellers invent distracting names to give hamburgers cachet. Hence "Whoppers" and "Heroburgers."

But there is no excuse for Howard Johnson's menu. In a just society it would be a flogging offense to speak of "steerburgers," clams "fried to order" (which probably means they don't fry clams for you unless you order fried clams), a "natural cut" (what is an "unnatural" cut?) of sirloin, "oven-baked" meat loaf, chicken pot pie with "flaky crust," "golden croquettes," "grilled-in-butter Frankforts [sic]," "liver with smothered onions" (smothered by onions?), and a "hearty" Reuben sandwich.

America is marred by scores of Dew Drop Inns serving "crispy green" salads, "garden fresh" vegetables, "succulent" lamb, "savory" pork, "sizzling" steaks, and "creamy" or "tangy" coleslaw. I've nothing against Homeric adjectives ("wine-dark sea," "wing-footed Achilles") but isn't coleslaw just coleslaw? Americans hear the incessant roar of commerce without listening to it, and read the written roar without really noticing it. Who would notice if a menu proclaimed "creamy" steaks and "sizzling" coleslaw? Such verbal litter is to language as Muzak is to music. As advertising blather becomes the nation's normal idiom, language becomes printed noise.

Handwritten margin notes:

fun restaurants replaced by fun menus

Hamburger names

Howard Johnson's menu— no excuse

Verbal litter = language becomes printed noise

thesis →

SUMMARY OF THE READING

George F. Will calls advertising language, especially the kind we see on menus, "printed noise." He gives examples of many silly or unnecessary names given to food (like the "Yumbo"), and he admires people who resist what he calls "verbal litter."

PERSONAL RESPONSE TO THE READING

I thought this article was really funny. I remember feeling stupid the first time I had to ask for an "Egg McMuffin." The name sounds like something on a kindergarten menu. But I don't really think about those names anymore. I guess I've just gotten used to them. The article reminded me how much they are all around us, even though I don't notice them. How about "Wienerdude"? That's the stupidest name I've ever heard. When I first heard it, I thought I'd never order one of those, just because the name is so insulting to any intelligent person. But maybe it's really a good hot dog—so I guess I really would order one. I suppose I agree with the article's point that after a while you don't even notice these things anymore. They are like "verbal litter."

READINGS

Read each of the following essays *actively*. That is, as you read each essay, *underline* or *highlight* its thesis statement, topic sentences, and any examples or ideas that seem important to you. Then reread the parts you have marked and *annotate the* essay. Finally, write a brief *summary* of the article and a brief *personal response paragraph*.

Ordinary People Produce Extraordinary Results   PAUL ROGAT LOEB

Paul Rogat Loeb is the author of Soul of a Citizen: Living with Conviction in a Cynical Time, *from which the following selection is adapted. He is an associated scholar at Seattle's Center for Ethical Leadership, and he comments on social issues for the* New York Times, The Washington Post, CNN, NPR, *and elsewhere.*

BEFORE YOU READ

1. What do you know about Rosa Parks? Where did you first hear about her?

2. Would you consider Rosa Parks to be an "ordinary" woman? Why, or why not?

We learn much from how we present our heroes. A few years 1
ago, on Martin Luther King Day, I was interviewed on CNN. So
was Rosa Parks, by phone from Los Angeles. "We're very honored
to have her," the host said. "Rosa Parks was the woman who
wouldn't go to the back of the bus. She wouldn't get up and give
her seat in the white section to a white person. That set in motion the yearlong bus boycott in Montgomery. It earned Rosa
Parks the title of 'mother of the civil rights movement.'"

I was excited to be part of the same show. Then it occurred 2
to me that the host's familiar rendition of her story had stripped
the Montgomery, Ala., boycott of its most important context. Before refusing to give up her bus seat, Parks had spent 12 years helping lead the local NAACP chapter. The summer before, Parks had
attended a 10-day training session at Tennessee's labor and civil
rights organizing school, the Highlander Center, where she'd met an
older generation of civil rights activists and discussed the recent U.S.
Supreme Court decision banning "separate but equal" schools.

In other words, Parks didn't come out of nowhere. She 3
didn't single-handedly give birth to the civil rights efforts. Instead,
she was part of an existing movement for change at a time when
success was far from certain.

This in no way diminishes the power and historical 4
importance of her refusal to give up her seat. Yet it does
remind us that this tremendously consequential act might never
have taken place without the humble and frustrating work that
she and others did earlier on. It reminds us that her initial step of
getting involved was just as courageous and critical as the fabled
moment when she refused to move to the back of the bus.

People like Parks shape our models of social commitment. 5
Yet the conventional retelling of her story creates a standard so
impossible to meet that it may actually make it harder for the rest
of us to get involved. This portrayal suggests that social activists
come out of nowhere to suddenly materialize to take dramatic
stands. It implies that we act with the greatest impact when we
act alone or when we act alone initially. It reinforces a notion that
anyone who takes a committed public stand—or at least an effective one—has to be a larger-than-life figure, someone with more
time, energy, courage, vision or knowledge than any normal person could ever possess.

This belief pervades our society, in part because the media 6
rarely represent historical change as the work of ordinary human

beings who learn to take extraordinary actions. And once we en-
shrine our heroes on pedestals, it becomes hard for mere mortals
to measure up in our eyes. We go even further, dismissing most
people's motives, knowledge and tactics as insufficiently grand or
heroic, faulting them for not being in command of every fact and
figure or not being able to answer every question put to them.
We fault ourselves as well for not knowing every detail or for
harboring uncertainties and doubts.

We find it hard to imagine that ordinary human beings with   7
ordinary hesitations and flaws might make a critical difference in
worthy social causes. Yet those *who* act have their own imperfec-
tions and ample reasons to hold back.

"I think it does us all a disservice," a young African American   8
activist from Atlanta said, "when people who work for social
change are presented as saints, so much more noble than the rest
of us. We get a false sense that from the moment they were born
they were called to act, never had doubts, were bathed in a circle
of light."

She added that she was much more inspired to learn how   9
people "succeeded despite their failings and uncertainties." That
would mean that she, too, had a "shot at changing things."

Our culture's misreading of the Rosa Parks story speaks to a   10
more general collective amnesia by which we forget the examples
that might most inspire our courage and conscience. Most of us
know next to nothing of the grass-roots movements in which ordinary men and women fought to preserve freedom, expand the
sphere of democracy and create a more just society: the abolition-
ists, the populists, the women's suffragists, the union activists who
spurred the end of 80-hour work weeks at near-starvation wages.

These activists teach us how to shift public sentiment,   11
challenge entrenched institutional power and find the strength to
persevere despite all odds. Yet their stories, like the real story of
Parks, are erased in an Orwellian memory hole.

Parks' actual story conveys an empowering moral that is   12
lost in her public myth. She began modestly, by attending one
meeting and then another. Hesitant at first, she gained confidence
as she spoke out. She kept on despite a profoundly uncertain
context as she and others acted as best they could to challenge
deeply entrenched injustices with little certainty of results. Had
she and others given up after their 10th or 11th year of commitment, we might never have heard of the Montgomery boycott.

Parks' journey suggests that social change is the product of   13
deliberate, incremental action whereby we join together to try to
shape a better world. Sometimes our struggles will fail, as did
many earlier efforts of Parks, her peers and her predecessors.
Other times, they may bear modest fruit.

And at times, they will trigger a miraculous outpouring of   14
courage and heart, as happened in the wake of Parks' arrest. For
only when we act, despite all our uncertainties and doubts, do we
have the chance to shape history.

SUGGESTIONS FOR SUMMARIZING

1. What does this article suggest is true about many of the people we usually consider to be "extraordinary"?
2. Write three or four more sentences to summarize the major supporting
   ideas that are presented in the article.

SUGGESTIONS FOR PERSONAL RESPONSES

1. Have you ever known someone whom others might call extraordinary? If you have, describe that person's ordinary qualities that somehow led him or her to be an extraordinary person.
2. Describe situations from your experiences or observations that illustrate Loeb's statement that "ordinary human beings with ordinary hesitations and flaws can make a critical difference . . ."
3. Talk to other members of the class about the idea that all great actions
   start out with small steps, full of "uncertainty and doubt." For what areas of life might this statement hold true?

A Required Course in Beating the Freshman Blues   RENE SANCHEZ

*For some students, the first year of college can be a frustrating and lonely experience.
In the following article, Rene Sanchez reports on the efforts of colleges and universities around the country to improve that experience for college freshmen.*

BEFORE YOU READ

1. What are the "freshman blues"? Define what they might mean to you.
2. Have you taken any courses designed to help you through your first
   year of college? What were they? How did they affect you?

It's early morning in Gerri Strumpf's class at the University of   1
Maryland, and a batch of bleary-eyed freshmen is busy taking
notes. Today's lesson: surviving college.

Strumpf begins by collecting her students' latest diary   2
entries about campus life. An assistant dean stops by with tips on
how to study and pleads, "We really want to get to know you."
Then Strumpf details the tasks ahead: a seminar on date rape, assignments on cultural diversity, outlines of every student's academic goals for the next two years.

This is "The Student and the University," a semester-long   3
course in which Maryland freshmen earn college credit simply by
examining issues in their academic and personal lives. The idea is
not unique. At universities across the nation, it has become a
prime tactic in ever more elaborate campaigns to keep students
happy, improve their social skills and prevent them from quitting
or transferring.

By some estimates, about one-third of college freshmen   4
nationally don't return for their sophomore years. Many universities have long looked upon the loss of students as either a fact of
life or a testament to their academic rigor, but from the Ivy
League to large state universities that attitude is being discarded.

An age of sensitivity has begun on American campuses, and   5
it is changing how many of them are run. Stung by persistent criticism that they are indifferent to undergraduates—and competing
like never before to attract and keep students, particularly minorities—hundreds of universities are creating courses, revamping orientation programs, redesigning dormitories, and hiring counselors
and tutors in an attempt to ease students' transition to college life.

"What you're seeing is a profound rethinking of a habit and   6
an attitude that has guided how undergraduates have been treated
for generations," says John Gardner, director of freshman programs
at the University of South Carolina. "Colleges are admitting that
they have not done enough to help students. Now they're taking
the initiative. They're being much more intrusive in student lives."

At Maryland, there are 60 sections of the freshman seminar   7
course, including one taught by the university president. At the
University of Michigan, hundreds of freshmen are in a program
that requires them to live in the same dormitory, take the same
seminar course on personal and campus issues and have regular
evening talks about it led by staff members. At the University of
Pennsylvania, students attend "life sketches," skits that promote
racial diversity and sexual health and discourage drinking. Students
also are taught how to report a crime and use the campus peer
crisis hot line.

For the first time this fall, new students at Florida A&M   8
University could take workshops about dating relationships. There
also are men-only and women-only sessions with topics that range
from academics to the problems in African American communities.

At the University of South Carolina, there's a course called   9
"University 101." To forge a common academic experience, all
freshmen are assigned the same novel, which they later discuss in
small groups led by faculty members. At the University of Colorado, which has a "First Year Experience" office, faculty and administrators are even telephoning new students a few weeks into
the semester to see how they're doing.

An important part of many initiatives is to get senior   10
faculty to devote more time to undergraduates and less to research and writing projects. That focus reflects the growing concern among university leaders that students need more academic
and personal guidance from experienced faculty members and
get bored with large lecture classes taught by graduate students.

One of the freshmen in Strumpf's class illustrated that   11
problem the other day when she explained why she had not
completed an assignment to interview a professor on Maryland's
campus. "I don't have one, and it's hard to find one," she says.

In a recent survey of more than 2,500 colleges, American   12
College Testing, a group that administers a widely used
college entrance exam, reported that one-third of freshmen
did not return for their sophomore years, the highest rate
since the survey began in 1983. In a report this summer, the
American Association of State Colleges and Universities said its
members graduate only 40 percent of their freshman after six
years. The report also noted that for years colleges have used the
freshman year as a "gatekeeping experience" and judged their academic quality in part by how many students "washed out."

"Now it's considered irresponsible to think that way," says   13
Joyce Jones, an assistant dean of students at Northwestern
University.

It's also costly. The drive to make students more comfortable   14
on campus is not merely a matter of conscience. Many universities
simply can no longer afford to lose them.

The nation's pool of college-aged students has declined this   15
decade, forcing universities to compete more vigorously against
each other. In many states, lawmakers struggling to cut budgets
also are taking a hard look at why colleges lose so many students

and questioning whether state higher education aid is being used wisely.

"We've been a revolving door," says Strumpf, who directs Maryland's student orientation programs. "For a long time here at Maryland and other places, people did not care much about how many freshmen stayed or left. But they're worried about it now." 16

"The bottom line is retention," says Richard Mullendore, vice chancellor for student affairs at the University of North Carolina-Wilmington. "Colleges need the tuition." 17

Others suggest that the new courses and coping programs are simply a sign of the times. With campuses more racially diverse than ever before, there are concerns that minority students in particular are at risk of being ignored, feeling isolated and leaving. Students are also facing difficult questions on other issues—such as AIDS or date rape—that were not cause for alarm a generation ago. For all of those reasons, universities are trying to do more parenting than ever before. 18

Still, there are worries that the new approaches could coddle students too much. "There's definitely that risk," Gardner says. Others contend that an important role of college has long been to allow young adults to fend for themselves for the first time, not to have faculty members hold their hands whenever they confront a new problem. 19

Strumpf insists that's not the intent. "These students still have tremendous freedoms," she said. "We're only trying to help with some of it. When they first come to campus, they're totally optimistic. But as the semester goes on, and reality sets in, it can be much different than what they expected." 20

Strumpf's class meets once a week for nearly two hours. She has about two dozen students, all freshmen. The course lasts for three months. Students are graded and earn one college credit. That's standard practice at other universities with similar seminars; most other academic courses are worth three credits. Once a week, either in writing or through electronic mail, students turn in journal entries in which they are supposed to reflect on their campus experiences. 21

Already this fall, the freshmen in Strumpf's course have taken personality tests to help them decide what kind of career to choose. There also have been class sessions on time management and studying skills. One session included tips on how using a highlighting pen while reading or working past 8 p.m. might be bad habits. 22

Soon, as part of a lesson in racial diversity and prejudice, the class will be required to read "The Diary of Anne Frank" and will visit the Holocaust Museum to learn how intense hatred can be.   23

Many other universities have designed similar courses. The University of South Carolina's "University 101," for example, includes sessions on public speaking, study skills, campus diversity, and "sex and the college student."   24

The students in Strumpf's class say they welcome the help. Midway through their first semester, many are facing problems they never anticipated a few months ago—such as struggling in courses that seemed easy in high school, second-guessing the major they selected, getting little sleep, or sitting in classes for the first time with many students of other races or from other countries.   25

"There's so much going on in your head all of a sudden—it's draining," says Kevin Davidson, 18, a freshman from southern Maryland. "Managing your time is hard. You have so many new things to worry about."   26

"It can be intimidating," says Anna Paule, 18, a freshman from Olney, Maryland. "It's nothing like high school. Everything was basically done for you there. Being on your own like this can be tough. But this class gives good directions."   27

Chanda Littlefield, a freshman from Hyattsville, Maryland, says that at first the size of the campus community and its racial diversity can be daunting. "It's good to have a class like this where you can ask questions and try to figure things out," she says.   28

Some universities are going beyond course work to help undergraduates by hiring more counselors and tutors. Others, like Michigan, are trying to create "learning communities" of freshmen by placing them in the same seminar class and the same dormitory wing staffed with veteran students trained to lead discussion groups.   29

Several hundred randomly chosen students are taking part in Michigan's housing program, which began several years ago and is rapidly being expanded. More than 1,000 students are also taking freshman seminar courses there.   30

To keep class sizes small and have senior professors to teach them, the university is spending several hundred thousand dollars to hire more faculty and staff members.   31

"This has become a priority," says Mary Hummel, who directs the program. "Large colleges are always accused of not paying enough attention to their students, especially the new ones.   32

That's what we're trying to break down. We've finally realized that helping students succeed takes much more than what we've been doing."

SUGGESTIONS FOR SUMMARIZING

1. Does this article seem to be *explaining* what colleges are now doing or *arguing* a point about what they should be doing? As you summarize the article's central idea, write a sentence that reflects which approach the article is taking.

2. After you state the central idea of the article, write one sentence of summary for each major supporting section of the article.

SUGGESTIONS FOR PERSONAL RESPONSES

1. In what ways do your own experiences during your first semester in college correspond to those described in this article?

2. Have you taken any courses similar to the University of Maryland's "The Student and the University," courses designed to help you adjust to college life? If you have, what was your reaction to them?

3. Did you feel isolated and ignored during your first few months in college? Why, or why not? What might have helped to change that experience?

4. Talk to other members of the class or to people you know about their early experiences in college. Were their experiences difficult ones? Would programs such as those described in Sanchez's article have helped them?

Charity Means You Don't Pick and Choose   PATRICIA O'HARA

In the following selection from Newsweek, *Patricia O'Hara discusses a common occurrence on the streets of many cities across the United States. As you read the article, consider how you would respond to the situations she describes.*

BEFORE YOU READ

1. Consider the word "charity." What does it mean? What associations or feelings do you associate with the word?

2. The title of this selection makes an assertion. What is that assertion, and what is your initial response to it?

"If you're not going to eat that, little boy, I will," said the man   1
sitting on the sidewalk to my son, who was holding a doggie bag
of restaurant leftovers. It was the first time my son had ever seen a

homeless person. He was 5 years old, and we were spending the weekend visiting museums in Washington, D.C. It was a March night of unusually raw weather—not a night to be sitting on a cold, hard sidewalk. I tightened my grasp on my son's hand as I made eye contact with the man.

"Spare anything, ma'am?"

My son looked up at me uneasily, so I left him with my husband   2 and went over to the man, dollar extended. He thanked me and asked my son again for his doggie bag. I motioned him over, nodding my assurances. "I didn't finish my steak sandwich," my son told him proudly, as he handed the man his bag. The man thanked him and said, "Be good to your mommy."

At just that moment a father and his two teenage sons walked   3 past and, without breaking his stride, barked out: "It'd be better if they got a job!"

I was startled by the intensity of the man's disapproval, but I,   4 too, have had doubts about offering handouts to the homeless. Under the watchful eyes of my child, I chose the action that I hoped would speak to my son about the principles of charity I hold dear, but the truth is, my decision to give has seldom been so clear-cut.

Like most people, I'm more comfortable giving when the   5 people on the receiving end are anonymous. I happily participate in the clothing drives sponsored by my son's school, and I drop my spare change in the big metal kettle at the mall, where a man dressed like Santa Claus rings his bell and smiles at shoppers.

Giving directly to the street person shambling across my   6 pathway—well, that's another matter. Hollywood tends to portray the homeless as lovable rogues (think Eddie Murphy in *Trading Places*), but in real life, the person asking for money is often suffering the effects of mental illness or addiction. I'm not proud to admit it, but even the few seconds it takes to look the other person in the eye, extend my hand and offer some change can feel like more of a connection than I want to make.

I've heard the intellectual arguments against giving handouts: 7 the money will be used to buy drugs or alcohol, handouts breed dependency, giving money discourages the homeless from going to shelters. I don't want to undermine the efforts of the mental-health professionals who work to get the homeless off the streets. But what I know in my head doesn't square with what I feel in my heart.

Pretending that people don't exist and withholding a couple of quarters or a dollar bill feels like the wrong thing to do.

Several years after our encounter with the homeless man   8
in Washington, my son and I visited New York City. As we walked down the street, a thin, drugged-out young man approached us and asked us for change. It was midtown at midday, so there was nothing particularly threatening about the circumstances. Nevertheless, the man was, by anyone's standards, unsavory-looking with his dirty clothes and unhealthy skin. I passed him by. Half a block later, my son stopped walking and asked: "Why didn't you give him anything?" I fumbled through a rationale about how we hadn't had time to stop and why we couldn't possibly give to everyone. My son interrupted and said, "Yeah, I don't think you should give money to people like that."

"People like that."

In his words and his tone of voice were echoes of the man   9
who told the panhandler to get a job. I had shown my son that it was acceptable to classify people as the deserving and the undeserving poor.

Last spring I traveled to London to do some work-related   10
research. Each day on the way to the library, I passed a group of homeless men lying on the steps of St. Pancras Old Church. Perhaps spending time in one of Charles Dickens's old neighborhoods set me thinking about his righteous anger at society's neglect of its poor. Or maybe I finally accepted that I'm in no position—and who is?— to judge another person's worthiness of a small act of kindness. Whatever the reason, I decided that I would always give when asked, even when it means weathering the sidelong glances of those who think I'm a fool or worse.

My son is now a teenager and will have to decide for himself   11
if and how he'll give to the poor. For all of my inconsistencies, I hope that I've taught him that it's better to set the needle of his compass to the magnetic pull of kindness than to contempt. But time alone will tell.

SUGGESTIONS FOR SUMMARIZING

1. What is this writer's central idea regarding giving money or handouts to people who ask? Write a sentence that states that central idea.

2. Write three or four more sentences to summarize the supporting ideas that are presented in the article.

SUGGESTIONS FOR PERSONAL RESPONSES

1. Has an apparently homeless person ever asked you for money or a handout? Have you been with friends or relatives when they were approached? Describe some specific instances from your own experiences or observations of others. How did you or others respond?

2. Have you noticed that people respond in a variety of ways to being approached for money or a handout by a homeless person? What different responses have you observed (in yourself or in others)? What might be the motivations behind these differing responses?

3. Talk to other members of the class or to people you know about how they respond to requests for money or handouts. What reasons do they give for their reactions? What do you think of those reasons?

WRITING ASSIGNMENTS

WRITING WITH A PERSONAL RESPONSE

1. Write a paper that responds to one of the following questions about "Ordinary People Produce Extraordinary Results."

   a. Paul Rogat Loeb says of Rosa Parks that "her initial step of getting involved was just as courageous and critical as the fabled moment when she refused to move to the back of the bus." Consider your own life. Have you found that the first step toward some event or accomplishment was sometimes the most difficult one? Write a paper in which you describe several different "first steps" that have led to significant changes or events in your life.

   b. Consider people in your life whom you do or do not love, respect, or admire. What specific actions caused them to gain or lose your love, respect, or admiration? Write a paper in which you explain the everyday, ordinary actions that eventually helped you to form your opinion about that person.

   c. According to Loeb, "We find it hard to imagine that ordinary human beings with ordinary hesitations and flaws might make a critical difference in worthy social causes." Have you ever participated in a social cause? Write a paper describing the cause you were part of, your role in it, and how you were affected by your participation in it.

2. Write a paper that responds to one of the following questions about "A Required Course in Beating the Freshman Blues."

   a. Analyze your first semester at college. Was it a pleasant and successful experience, a difficult and disconcerting one, or a little of both? As you develop examples to illustrate your points, explain your thoughts and reactions in an effort to help your reader understand why you reacted the way you did.

b. What do you see as the most serious problems a student entering college faces? Write a paper in which you use your own experiences or those of people you know to illustrate and explain your points.

c. Have you taken any courses similar to those described in the article? If you have, explain why they were or were not helpful and illustrate your points with examples. If you have not taken such courses, do you think they might have helped you? Explain why or why not, using examples to support your points.

3. Write a paper that responds to one of the following questions about "Charity Means You Don't Pick and Choose."

a. Patricia O'Hara writes that she is aware of "the intellectual arguments against giving handouts" but that "what I know in my head doesn't square with what I feel in my heart." Have you ever felt a similar conflict regarding giving money or handouts to the homeless? Write a paper in which you examine that conflict. Use examples of your own experiences to illustrate what you thought and felt in different situations. Which won—your heart or your head—and why?

b. People react in a variety of ways to requests from the homeless—or even to the presence of homeless people. Write a paper in which you use examples of your own experiences or the experiences of people you know to illustrate different ways people react to the homeless and to speculate about the reasons for those different reactions.

c. O'Hara writes that "in real life, the person asking for money is often suffering from the effects of mental illness or addiction." Have you ever known any homeless people? If you have, write a paper describing how they ended up homeless and the problems they encountered living without a home. As you describe the person (or persons), include your own thoughts and feelings regarding the situation. Do you feel compassion for them? Critical of them? What were your reactions?

4. Write a paper that responds to one of the following questions about "Printed Noise."

a. George Will describes some of the ridiculous ways restaurants will name or advertise their food. If you think his observations have merit, write a paper that gives examples of your own. If you would like to, use a different type of product, such as cigarettes, liquor, cars, or grocery items. If you think Will is overreacting or has missed the purpose of such advertising, write a paper that explains why, and illustrate your points with examples of actual products.

b. George Will has focused on one specific change in our culture—the trend toward silly names of food items in restaurants. Are there other specific cultural changes that you object to? Think of the places you visit, the people you see, the situations you encounter. Choose one particular change that you object to and illustrate it with examples from your own experiences and observations. Explain what you find objectionable as you present each example.

EVALUATING SAMPLE PAPERS

Using the Student Model Checklist on pages 26–27, evaluate the effectiveness of the following student essays.

Student Essay 1

Reading George Will's article made me realize that I am bothered by many changes in our culture. I don't like the way that people have changed the way they drive around ambulances. As a driver on the road I have seen ambulance drivers experience rudeness in the worst ways.

For example one day I heard sirens and immediately looked for the direction the ambulance was coming in so to be prepared. A car coming to the left of me seemed to do nothing to prepare, so the driver either did not hear the sirens or did not care. He continued to drive but at the last minute he panicked, for now the ambulance was directly behind him, and he didn't know where to go. The driver is entirely rude because it slows down the ambulance from getting to its destination.

Another time I witnessed a car that had to have seen the ambulance coming in the drivers' direction, but still kept on driving as he watched the ambulance speed by. What I had just witnessed left me in awe wondering if these kinds of drivers think they are excluded from the pull over and wait law! I see many drivers do this but have never seen anyone be cited. The law needs to be enforced to act as a reminder to those who are not just rude but endangering lives.

Finally the worst rudeness I have seen on the road is the drivers who think they can make it through an intersection before the ambulance, so they do not have to wait. I actually have witnessed this near miss myself. I saw a black pick-up in front of me and the driver looking to see where the sirens were coming from. The ambulance was speeding towards us from the right hand side of the road. I pulled over, but to my dismay the pick-up hit the gas and flew through the intersection just seconds before the ambulance. How the driver made it without causing an accident I still do not know.

These kinds of people also have no idea to the lives they are putting endanger. The endangerment is more than the life in question or the ambulance drivers but also the idiots who impose this potential hazard. This type of driving should not be tolerated and the drivers need to be reminded of the dangers involved when not following the rules of the road.

Student Essay 2

After I graduated from Vista High School, I really looked forward to the future that lay ahead. I was looking forward to my first semester in college because all my friends were going to the same school I was planning to attend. I had heard great things about Palomar College from friends and people I knew that had attended school there for at least a year, and had me anxious to start my first semester. When the time finally came and I attended my first semester, I was stunned by all the troubles and difficulties that I had to go through during my fist semester of school.

Having heard that Palomar had a phone registration system, I thought it would be all too easy to enroll in my classes with the comfort of being at home. I soon found out that this was all but true. The phone system Palomar College was using was experiencing technical difficulties and was down on a daily basis, making it really hard to add the classes I desired. Sometimes I would be in the process of registering when the whole system would shut down and leave me waiting to see when the system would be up again. Other times, the system was busy because there was an overload of calls from students that were also desperately trying to enroll in the classes they needed. Finally, when I had enrolled and thought that everything was ready to go, I received a letter from school that confirmed the classes I had chosen, and found out that the system had made a mistake in my schedule. At this point, I had no alternative but to go to the administration office and personally register because I knew that it was going to be an impossible task to register through the phone. When I was finally enrolled in my classes, I looked back at all the troubles and difficulties I had to go through, and could not believe how hard it was to register. I had commenced my first college semester on a bad note.

To make my first semester even worse, Palomar College was under construction. The campus was full of trenches that had been excavated with tractors, and there were dozens of dirt mountains all across the school. There were work trucks, tractors, lumber, bricks, and other equipment on the passageways students would use to walk to class. Many times I was forced to walk around one or two buildings to find a different path to class. I also had to find myself a way to get through the maze of fences that were temporarily put up while the construction workers worked. I found this to be a real hassle for myself and the rest of the students. I also had to put up with all the loud noises that the workers created while they worked the tractors and the trucks right next to the class. It was hard for the instructors to give a class and not be disrupted by all the noises. I remember times when the instructor had to pause and wait until the noises dimmed to continue with his lesson; other times he had to repeat himself so we could listen to what he had said. Because of the construction that was taking place, it was difficult for me to concentrate on the lectures and to keep focus on what was being taught; therefore, the construction added to the difficulties and troubles I faced my first semester in college.

I thought that Palomar College, a well-known school that has many students, would have sufficient parking and facilities for all of them. On my first day of school, it took me thirty minutes to find a parking lot that was a ten-minute walk to my first class. I could not believe that there was not enough parking for the students and that the parking lots were so far away from the classes. This fact caused me to be late many times, and had me waking up forty minutes earlier so I could find a parking space and not be late to class. I struggled constantly throughout my first semester of school to wake up earlier, which made it difficult for me to have enough time to properly prepare myself to go to school. Because I had to leave forty minutes earlier to get a parking space, I would miss breakfast and found myself going to school on an empty stomach, which affected me physically. I think that students have too many things to worry about as it is to have to worry about parking. Furthermore, I was also late to class on a few occasions because I could not find a place to park, and I personally think that it was rude and distracting to my instructors for me to walk in late. Even though the school was a little better with its facilities, I found that a few more restrooms could be added to the campus as well as more desks in the classrooms. I remember having to sit on the floor for a week in one of my classes until I brought in a desk from a different class. This also contributed to one of the many difficulties that I went through during my first semester in college.

Throughout the last ten years of school I have attended, I have never experienced what I did that first semester of college. The difficulties and troubles that I endured my first semester in college caused me to have some the worst memories of my first semester of school. For those who are going to college for the first time and are expecting great things in their first semester in school, don't get your hopes too high on how great it's going to be because you might find yourself in a world of troubles and difficulties.

The reading selection on which Student Essay 3 is based can be found in Part Four of the text.

Student Essay 3

In the article "Are You Living Mindlessly?," Michael Ryan explains that "mindlessness" is lacking control of our responses in particular situations that we believe are familiar to us. A simple example of mindless behavior is putting milk in the cupboard and cereal in the refrigerator without thinking about it. Michael Ryan cites several examples from a psychology professor, Ellen Langer, to indicate different mindless behaviors. Ryan and Langer believe mindlessness can cause problems in our lives because it limits our minds from seeing different possibilities. Langer suggests that we should always think creatively and flexibly to prevent mindless behavior. I agree with Langer that acting mindlessly is a dangerous human behavior which confines our creativity and makes us narrow-minded; however, we may defeat narrow-mindedness by thinking creatively and flexibly.

Mindlessness makes us narrow-minded by limiting our behavior and creativity, but these limiting behaviors and creations may be overcome by using our imaginations. Ellen Langer's example of one woman who habitually would cut one end of her holiday turkey before putting it in the oven just because her mother had done it that way demonstrated narrow-mindedness. This example reminded me of the time when I could not accept how my roommate, Natalie, made miso soup. The way she was making it did not seem right to me since it was not the way that I had learned to make it from my mother. Miso soup is a Japanese tradition that is a simple side dish with one or two vegetables in it; however, Natalie cooked it with garlic, tomatoes, bell peppers, carrots and cabbage and called it "miso soup." I instantly said "It is not miso soup." Because of my cultural tradition, I could not see any other way to make it. Even though Natalie's soup did not look like miso soup to me, it ended up tasting better than mine; as a result, now I have started making miso soup in my own creative way. I have become more open minded and creative after this experience, and it has helped me to improve my cooking skills. The way I reacted made Natalie feel uncomfortable. I agree with Langer, and I think that I can try to improve my behavior by being more flexible.

In addition to narrow-minded behavior regarding recipes and eating traditions, mindlessness can cause misunderstandings in relationships, but these misunderstandings may be overcome by thinking flexibly and seeing everyone as unique. Langer says that mindlessness assumption can cause prejudice; for example, people see either "black or white, Jew or non-Jew." This example led me to think about the times when I could not think any other possible situations except "black or white." One of my situations was when I noticed my food was disappearing almost every time I came home. I was mad and just assumed that my roommate was eating my food to take advantage of me. I could not accept another cause for the food's disappearance. I found out later that she'd had a head injury from a car accident; consequently, it became a struggle for her not to eat the food around her whenever she felt lonely. I realized how inflexible I was in judging my friend. My false judgment caused me to misunderstand my roommate. This experience proved to me that mindless behavior can hurt relationships. I agree with Langer, and I think that I want to be more flexible to see individuals' unique personalities.

Thinking creatively and flexibly helped me to improve my cooking skills and to have better friendships. These experiences opened up my eyes to see different possibilities in similar situations. I agree with Langer that acting mindlessly limits our views to familiar things and damages our lives because it prevents us from living creatively and flexibly.

SENTENCE COMBINING: COORDINATION

In Chapter 1, you practiced *embedding* simple modifiers (adjectives, adverbs, and prepositional phrases) next to the words they modify in a sentence. Such embedding may have seemed rather easy to you, for it is something we all learned to do quite automatically at an early age. (Almost everyone would automatically change "I wrote a letter. It was long." to "I wrote a long letter.") However, not all combining of related ideas is as easily performed. As writers become more and more proficient, they develop the ability to create quite sophisticated sentence structures as well as very simple ones—but they develop that ability gradually, after much practice.

In this section, you will practice *coordinating* ideas. Like embedding simple modifiers, the process of coordination can be natural and easy. However, effective coordination also has its complexities, which we will take up in this section.

USING COORDINATING CONJUNCTIONS

Coordination consists of joining ideas that are grammatically alike, usually by using one of the seven **coordinating conjunctions:** *and, but, or, nor, for, so,* and *yet.* You can easily memorize these seven conjunctions by learning the acronym BOYSFAN. (An acronym is a word made up from the first letters of other words.)

But Or Yet So For And Nor

Of course, when we talk, we use each of these seven words all of the time. They are so common to our language, in fact, that we rarely think about them. When we want to join two ideas, it takes practically no thought at all to stick an *and* or a *but* or some other coordinating conjunction into our speech and to go on.

Writing, however, is more precise than speech. When someone else reads what we have written, we are usually not there to clarify things that might be confusing, so a careful choice of words the first time through is much more important in writing than in speech. For instance, is there a difference between these two sentences?

> Huck Finn was very superstitious, and he knew he was in trouble when he spilled the salt.
>
> Huck Finn was very superstitious, so he knew he was in trouble when he spilled the salt.

Both sentences suggest a relationship between the ideas of Huck's being superstitious and of his spilling the salt, but only the second sentence is *precise* in stating the relationship clearly. By using the word *so,* the second sentence makes it clear that Huck's belief about spilling salt was a *result* of his being superstitious.

When you use the coordinating conjunctions, keep their *precise* meanings in mind:

> **And** suggests *addition.* It is used to "add" one idea to a similar one.
> My grass needs to be mowed, <u>and</u> my garden needs to be weeded.
>
> **Nor** also suggests *addition,* but it adds two negative ideas.
> I have not mowed my lawn in the past two weeks, <u>nor</u> have I weeded the garden.
>
> **But** suggests a *contrast* or *opposition.*
> I should mow the lawn today, <u>but</u> I think I'll watch a movie instead.
>
> **Yet** also suggests a *contrast* or *opposition.*
> I feel guilty about not mowing the lawn, <u>yet</u> I really don't want to work today.
>
> **Or** suggests *alternatives.*
> I will mow the lawn tomorrow, <u>or</u> perhaps I'll wait until next weekend.
>
> **For** suggests a *cause.*
>
>   cause
> My yard is becoming the neighborhood eyesore, <u>for</u> I hate to do yardwork.
>
> **So** suggests a *result* relationship.
>
>   result
> My neighbors have stopped talking to me, <u>so</u> maybe I should clean up my yard today.

EXERCISE 2.2

Combine the following sentences using the coordinating conjunctions that most accurately express the relationship between them.

EXAMPLE

The forecast was for rain with strong winds. I decided to cancel our picnic.

The forecast was for rain with strong winds, so I decided to cancel our picnic.

1. There were no Roman emperors before the time of Julius Caesar. Julius Caesar himself was not a Roman emperor.
2. Julius Caesar was a renowned Roman general who became dictator of Rome. He was never called an emperor.
3. Augustus, the adopted son of Julius Caesar, was the first Roman emperor. The despotic Nero was the last emperor who could trace his lineage directly back to Julius Caesar.
4. The title of *Caesar* became synonymous with authority and leadership. Many subsequent emperors also called themselves *Caesars.*
5. On a military campaign in Asia, Julius Caesar sent the famous message "I came, I saw, I conquered" back to the Roman Senate. It had asked him to report on his progress.
6. In Shakespeare's famous play, Julius Caesar is warned to "Beware the Ides of March." That is the day he is assassinated by, among others, his friend Brutus.
7. The title *Caesar* has come to refer to a leader with great power and authority. Many world leaders have adopted the term.
8. The Russian czars take their title from *Caesar.* The German emperors did the same, calling themselves "kaisers."
9. In a world history class, one might read about the first Russian czar in 1547, Ivan the Terrible. He might study instead the defeat of Kaiser Wilhelm II in World War I.
10. In the United States, the Commissioner of Major League Baseball is sometimes called the "Baseball Czar." The Director of National Drug Control Policy is commonly referred to as the "Drug Czar."

EXERCISE 2.3

Each of the following sentences uses *and* as a coordinating conjunction. Where needed, change the *and* to a more precise and accurate coordinating conjunction. Some of the sentences may not need to be changed.

EXAMPLE

Last year I spent $300 on a membership to a local gym, <u>and</u> I used the gym only two times all year long.

Last year I spent $300 on a membership to a local gym, but I used the gym only two times all year long.

1. The horn of a rhinoceros is one of its unique features, <u>and</u> the commercial value of that feature threatens the survival of the rhinoceros.
2. Rhino horns are sought by many poachers, <u>and</u> they are currently worth more than their weight in gold.
3. In some cultures rhino-horn walking sticks are symbols of prestige, <u>and</u> in other cultures rhino-horn products are used for everything from headaches to labor pains.
4. In North Yemen, daggers carved from rhino horns were so expensive, costing as much as $12,000, that very few people could buy them, <u>and</u> today oil wealth has put that price within reach of many Yemeni.
5. Today, an East African farmer can double his annual income by killing a single rhino, <u>and</u> the temptation to hunt rhinos illegally is hard to resist.
6. Game wardens may try to stop poachers, <u>and</u> they may themselves be lured into this very lucrative activity.
7. Rhinos are not difficult to approach, <u>and</u> they are not hard to kill with today's advanced weapons.
8. Professional poachers today use many sophisticated hunting techniques, <u>and</u> they are able to decimate entire populations of rhinos with very little effort.
9. One can tell that the mature rhino is disappearing, <u>and</u> the average size of the illegal rhino horn has dropped 60% since 1973.
10. The poachers cut off the horns of the dead rhinos, <u>and</u> then they ship the horns out of the country.

In each of the above exercises and examples, a comma has been placed before the coordinating conjunction because the statements being combined could stand alone as separate sentences. However, when a coordinating conjunction joins two sentence parts that can *not* stand alone as separate sentences, do not use a comma before the conjunction. (For a further discussion of this comma rule, see Chapter 17.)

EXAMPLE

COMMA	Mario worked all night on the new computer program, and his brother worked with him.
NO COMMA	Mario worked all night on the new computer program and all the next day on his accounting work.

USING SEMICOLONS

So far, we have seen that using a comma and a coordinating conjunction is one way to combine related sentences. Another way to combine sentences is to use a *semicolon,* usually (but not always) with a conjunctive adverb. On the next page are some common **conjunctive adverbs:**

accordingly	however	otherwise	as a result
also	instead	similarly	for example
besides	meanwhile	still	for instance
consequently	moreover	then	in addition
finally	namely	therefore	in fact
further	nevertheless	thus	on the other hand
furthermore	next	undoubtedly	
hence	nonetheless		

EXAMPLES

Henry ate all of the potato chips; however, he was still hungry.

Tuan knew that he should buy a new car; on the other hand, he really wanted a motorcycle.

The movie was too violent for Sabrina; the concert was too dull for Rocky.

If you use a semicolon to combine related sentences, remember these points:

1. Most writers—professional and nonprofessional—use semicolons *much less frequently* than the other methods of combining sentences that are discussed in this and other sections.
2. Conjunctive adverbs *are not* coordinating conjunctions and should *not be used to combine sentences with commas.*

EXAMPLES

INCORRECT   Sylvia had always wanted to visit the Far East, however she never had enough money to do so.

CORRECT   Sylvia had always wanted to visit the Far East; however, she never had enough money to do so.

3. It is the *semicolons* that join sentences, not the conjunctive adverbs. As a result, conjunctive adverbs may appear *anywhere that makes sense* in the sentence.

EXAMPLES

It rained for fifteen straight days. <u>Nevertheless</u>, my father jogged every day.

It rained for fifteen straight days; my father, <u>nevertheless</u>, jogged every day.

It rained for fifteen straight days; my father jogged every day, <u>nevertheless</u>.

EXERCISE 2.4

Combine the following sentences, either by using a comma with a coordinating conjunction or by using a semicolon with or without a conjunctive adverb.

EXAMPLE

Hillary wanted to attend college full-time. She needed to work forty hours a week to support her family.

> Hillary wanted to attend college full-time, but she needed to work forty hours a week to support her family.

or

> Hillary wanted to attend college full-time; however, she needed to work forty hours a week to support her family.

1. For hundreds of years, people have considered the number thirteen to be unlucky. Surveys have shown that the fear of the number thirteen is the most widespread of all bad-luck superstitions.

2. The French, for instance, never issue the house address thirteen. The Italian national lottery omits the number thirteen.

3. Americans also fear the number thirteen. Some modern skyscrapers, condominiums, and apartment buildings label the floor that follows twelve as fourteen.

4. When a new luxury apartment building labeled a floor thirteen, it rented units on all other floors. It could rent only a few units on the thirteenth floor.

5. The owners recognized the problem. They changed the floor number to twelve-B and were soon able to rent out the rest of the apartments.

6. Fear of the number thirteen has been attributed to the Last Supper, when Christ with his apostles numbered thirteen. It has an older source in Norse mythology.

7. According to Norse mythology, the evil god Loki grew angry when he was not invited to a banquet with twelve other gods. He decided to attend anyway, bringing the total to thirteen.

8. The other gods battled Loki. Balder, the favorite of the gods, was killed.

9. In the United States, thirteen should be considered a lucky number. The nation started with thirteen colonies.

10. On the Great Seal of the United States, the bald eagle holds in one claw an olive branch with thirteen leaves and thirteen berries. It holds in the other claw thirteen arrows.

Exploring ONLINE

For more practice combining sentences using commas and semicolons, go to www.thomsonedu.com/devenglish/mcdonald. Under "Course Resources" click on "Online Grammar Quizzes." On the page that appears, choose the "Self-Tests" under "Combining sentences using the three methods of coordination."

COMBINING PARTS OF SENTENCES

So far, we have focused on using coordination to combine *separate sentences.* Another way to improve your writing is to use a coordinating conjunction to join *part* of one sentence to *part* of another sentence. This type of sentence combining is more difficult than the simple joining of entire sentences, but it usually results in more concise and direct writing. For instance, here are two sentences as they might have been written by Gail Sheehy in "Jailbreak Marriage." The parts of each sentence that could be combined are underlined.

> Simone was the last domain <u>where her mother could play out the maternal role</u>. She was also the last place <u>where her father could exercise complete control</u>.

Of course, Sheehy recognized that these two ideas could really be expressed as one sentence, so she wrote this:

> Simone was the last domain <u>where her mother could play out the maternal role</u> and <u>where her father could exercise complete control.</u>

Here is another example, taken from "A Required Course in Beating the Freshman Blues," by Rene Sanchez. When discussing the program at the University of Michigan, Sanchez could have written three sentences. The parts of each sentence that could be combined are underlined.

> At the University of Michigan, hundreds of freshmen are in a program that requires them to <u>live in the same dormitory.</u> These freshmen must also <u>take the same seminar course on personal and campus issues</u>. Finally, to help them make good use of each seminar, they <u>have regular evening talks about it led by staff members.</u>

Here is how Sanchez actually wrote the sentence:

> At the University of Michigan, hundreds of freshmen are in a program that requires them to <u>live in the same dormitory,</u> <u>take the same seminar course on personal and campus issues</u> and <u>have regular evening talks about it led by staff members.</u>

Note When joining three or more items, as has been done here, you need to use the coordinating conjunction only before the last item.

PARALLEL SENTENCE STRUCTURE

When you use coordination to join ideas, you should do your best to word those ideas similarly so they are clear and easy to read. Coordinate ideas that are worded similarly are said to be *parallel* in structure. Notice the difference between the following two examples:

NONPARALLEL STRUCTURE

My favorite sports are <u>swimming</u> and <u>to jog</u>.

PARALLEL STRUCTURE

My favorite sports are <u>swimming</u> and <u>jogging</u>.

Do you see how much clearer the parallel sentence is? Now let's look once more at the examples from the articles by Gail Sheehy and Rene Sanchez. Notice how the coordinate ideas have been written so that they are parallel in structure.

Simone was the last domain

       <u>where her mother could play out the maternal role</u>
and <u>where her father could exercise complete control</u>.

At the University of Michigan, hundreds of freshmen are in a program that requires them to

       <u>live in the same dormitory</u>,
       <u>take the same seminar course on personal and campus issues</u>
and <u>have regular evening talks about it led by staff members.</u>

As you can see, recognizing related ideas and combining them in parallel structure can result in sentences that are more direct and less repetitious than the original sentences.

$\mathcal{N}ote$ For a more thorough discussion of parallel sentence structure, see Chapter 6.

EXERCISE 2.5

Combine each group of sentences into one sentence by using coordinating conjunctions to join related ideas. Wherever possible, use parallel sentence structure. Parallel ideas that can be combined are underlined in the first three groups.

EXAMPLE

People <u>who stereotype others</u> are often insensitive to the pain they cause. The same is true for people <u>who tell ethnic jokes</u>.
    People <u>who stereotype others</u> or <u>who tell ethnic jokes</u> are often insensitive to the pain they cause.

1. According to legend, Calamity Jane was a <u>fierce Indian fighter</u>. She also was a <u>brave scout</u>. In addition, legend describes her as <u>a beautiful, vivacious tamer of the Old West.</u>

2. In reality, however, she often brought misfortune <u>into her own life</u>. She brought misfortune <u>into the lives of others</u>, too.

3. Although born in Princeton, Missouri, she spent most of her life in Deadwood, South Dakota, a town notorious for its collection of <u>miners</u> and <u>Civil War veterans</u>. It was also full of <u>gamblers</u> and <u>outlaws</u>, and it was the home of many <u>prostitutes</u>.

4. It is said that she drank as heavily as any mule skinner. In addition, she cursed as coarsely as the roughest of men.

5. Calamity's life was characterized by drunkenness. It was also full of lawlessness. It even included prostitution.

6. Dime-store novels helped to spread her legend by describing her as a natural beauty. She was referred to as the sweetheart of Wild Bill Hickok.

7. Calamity Jane did know Wild Bill Hickok. She was part of his gang for a while, but there is no evidence that he romanced her. There is also no evidence that he even paid much attention to her.

8. Easterners viewed the westward movement as adventurous. To them, it was romantic. It was exciting, so they preferred stories that idealized the West. They also liked stories that made their heroes seem larger than life.

9. Calamity Jane may have received her nickname from her many hard-luck experiences. It may also have come from the problems she caused others. It may even have resulted from her willingness to help victims of smallpox during an epidemic in Deadwood.

10. In her last years, Calamity drifted from place to place, selling a poorly written leaflet about her life. She also could be found performing as a sharpshooter in Wild West shows. In addition, she performed as a wild driver of six-horse teams in these same shows.

Supporting the Central Idea

Poor Irving! He wants a nice, fuzzy, somewhat vague relationship, but Cathy wants specifics. She wants Irving to explain *why* he had a great time, to elaborate upon *what* was great about it. We're often the same way, aren't we? If we ask a friend how he or she liked a movie, we're not usually satisfied with answers like "Great!" or "Yuck!" We want to know specifically *why* the person liked or disliked it. Was it the plot or the acting or the special effects or the quality of the popcorn that caused our friend to react in a certain way? The more specific our friend can be, the more he or she will help us to decide whether we want to see the film too.

The same is true of responses to other media, such as novels and television, or to public issues, such as elections or gun control or capital punishment. The more specific information we have on these issues, the better informed our decisions will be.

In the same way, the more you can support your topic sentence or your thesis statement with specific information, the more convincing your writing will be. The most common types of support are brief or extended examples, statistics, and expert opinion or testimony.

BRIEF EXAMPLES

From Personal Experience or Direct Observation

One of the most interesting and convincing ways to support your ideas is by relating brief examples drawn from your own personal experiences or observations. When we are discussing issues casually with acquaintances, we just naturally share our own experiences. Note how several brief examples are used in the following paragraph to support its central idea:

> People, at least the ones in my town, seem to have become ruder as the population has increased. Twice yesterday drivers came up behind me and gestured rudely even though I was driving ten miles per hour over the speed limit. The other day, as my friend and I were sitting on the seawall watching the sunset and listening to the ocean waves, a rollerblader with a boom box going full blast sat down next to us. When we politely asked him to turn off his radio, he cursed at us and skated off. Every day I see perfectly healthy people parking in spaces reserved for the handicapped, smokers lighting up in no-smoking areas and refusing to leave when asked, and people shoving their way into lines at movie theaters and grocery stores.

Personal examples are usually not enough to prove a point, but they do help to illustrate your ideas and make your writing more specific and interesting. In fact, good writing is always moving from the general to the specific, with the emphasis on the specific, and the use of brief examples is one of the most effective ways of keeping your writing interesting, convincing, and informative. Notice how the lack of examples in the following paragraph results in uninteresting, lackluster writing:

> There are a lot of animals to be found in Carlsbad. They come in all sizes and shapes. There are all kinds of birds and other animals besides dogs and cats.

Now let's see if it can be improved with the addition of brief examples:

> The typical yard in Carlsbad is visited by a wide variety of animals. Birds, especially, are present in abundance. House finches and sparrows flit through the trees and search the ground for seeds. Mockingbirds sing day and night, claiming their territory. The feisty and mischievous scrub jays, with their blue plumage, raid the food set out for cats. The homely California towhee, whose call sounds like a squeaky wheel, rustles among the fallen leaves looking for insects. And the exotic and mysterious ruby-throated hummingbirds go from flower to flower, searching for nectar, or visit feeders hung out for them. At night the slow-witted possum rambles about, getting into garbage cans and dog dishes. The elegant and clever raccoons compete with the possums. Occasionally one can sense that a skunk has visited someone's yard. In some places, bands of escaped domestic rabbits can be seen frolicking and raiding gardens. Lizards and snakes ply the underbrush, searching for insects and small rodents. If one is observant and lucky, one can experience a multitude of critters right in the backyard.

As you can see, the many brief, specific examples in this paragraph improve it immensely, giving it texture, color, and interest. They also make the writing believable. Any reader would easily be convinced that this writer knows what he is talking about and has taken the time to observe the animals in Carlsbad carefully and to report them accurately.

From Other Sources

Brief examples from other sources are quite similar to brief personal examples or anecdotes. They may come from places such as books, magazines, television, films, or lectures, or they may come from the experiences of people you know. Like personal examples, they make your abstract ideas and arguments concrete and therefore convincing.

Here are some brief examples from recent news broadcasts that were offered in support of a gun control bill:

> Larry and Sharon Ellingsen were driving home from their 29th wedding anniversary party in Oakland, California, when a passing driver on the freeway sent a bullet through their window, killing Mr. Ellingsen instantly.
>
> Mildred Stanfield, a 78-year-old church organist from quiet Broad Ripple, Indiana, was shot twice in the chest at a bus stop when she tried to stop a 15-year-old boy from stealing her purse.
>
> Cesar Sandoval, a 6-year-old kindergartener, was shot in the head while riding home on a county school bus in New Haven, Connecticut. He and six classmates were caught in drug-related crossfire among three teenagers.

EXTENDED EXAMPLES

From Personal Experience or Direct Observation

Extended examples from personal experiences or observations are longer, more detailed narratives of events that have involved you or people you know. Sometimes several brief examples just won't have the emotional impact that an extended example will. Sometimes people need to hear the full story of something that happened to a real person to understand fully the point you are trying to make. Suppose, for instance, that you are writing about the senseless violence that seems to be occurring more and more frequently in today's society. You could illustrate that violence with several brief examples, or you could emphasize its heartlessness and brutality with an extended example such as the following:

> The senseless, brutal violence that we read about in the newspapers every day seems very distant from the average person, but it is really not far away at all. In fact, it can strike any of us without any warning—just as it struck my uncle Silas last week. After having dinner with his wife and two children, Silas had driven to the Texaco gas station at the corner of Vista Way and San Marcos Drive, where he was working part-time to earn extra money for a down payment on a house. Some time around 11:00 p.m., two young

men carrying Smith and Wesson 38's approached him and demanded money. Uncle Silas was a good, brave man, but he was also a realistic person. He knew when to cooperate, and that's just what he did. He opened the cash register and the safe, then handed the intruders the keys to his new truck. They shot him in the head anyway.

Wouldn't you agree that the above extended example carries an emotional impact that brief examples might not carry? This anecdote might be used in a pro–gun control essay or even in an anti–gun control essay (Uncle Silas should have had his own gun). Or it could be part of an essay on capital punishment. In any case, it would add dramatic interest to a piece of writing. As you can see, examples of personal experience can be brief, perhaps only one sentence long, or extended, taking up several paragraphs.

From Other Sources

Extended examples taken from magazines, newspapers, books, or newscasts can also provide dramatic and persuasive support for your papers. Professional writers know the effect that extended examples can have on the reader, so they use such examples frequently. Notice how Ellen Goodman, a nationally known writer, uses the following extended example in an article debating the right of people to commit suicide:

> It is certain that Peter Rosier wouldn't be on trial today if he hadn't been on television two years ago. If he hadn't told all of Fort Myers, Florida, that "I administered something to terminate her life." 1
>
> His wife Patricia, after all, a woman whose lung cancer had spread to her other organs, had told everyone that she intended to commit suicide. Indeed she planned her death as a final elaborate production. 2
>
> Perhaps it was a dramatic attempt to control, or shape, or choose the terms of her death. Perhaps it was an attempt to win some perverse victory over her cancer. Either way, Patricia Rosier, forty-three, picked the date, the time, even the wine for her last meal. She picked out the pills and she swallowed them. 3
>
> Death, however, didn't play the accommodating role that had been scripted for it. While the Rosier children slept in the next room, the deep coma induced by twenty Seconal pills began to lighten. Her husband, Peter, a pathologist, went desperately searching for morphine. And then, as he said a year later, he "administered something." 4
>
> —*Ellen Goodman,* Making Sense © *1989 by the Boston Globe Newspaper Co./Washington Post Writers Group. Reprinted by permission.*

The details of Patricia Rosier's death, particularly the descriptions of the cancer that had spread throughout her body and of her careful plans to take her own life, help the reader to understand the complexity of the decision that Peter Rosier had to make. Is he guilty of murder? Should he have ignored his wife's desire to avoid a painful death by cancer? In the face of detailed, real experience, answering such questions is not easy.

EXERCISE 3.1

Examine "Jailbreak Marriage" on pages 44–45 and "Printed Noise" on pages 48–50 (or examine other articles assigned by your instructor) to determine whether the authors are using brief or extended examples. Discuss the effectiveness (or ineffectiveness) of the types of examples used in each article.

EXERCISE 3.2

Choose one of the following sentences, and support it with at least three brief examples. Then choose another of the sentences, and support it with one extended example.

1. People who think they can fix anything often end up making things worse.
2. My brother (or other relative or friend) has one particular characteristic that consistently causes problems.
3. Many high school students today lead remarkably busy lives outside of school.
4. Racial intolerance (or religious, gender, or sexual intolerance) is alive and well in our community.
5. Ignorance of other cultures and traditions can cause people to act in offensive ways even though they don't mean to be offensive.

STATISTICS

Examples are very effective ways to support your ideas, but sometimes examples just aren't enough. Sometimes you need support that is more objective and measurable than an example. Sometimes you need support that covers more situations than one or even several examples could possibly cover. At times like these, statistics are the perfect support. In fact, if statistics are used fairly and correctly and are drawn from reliable sources, they are just about the most credible and effective type of support. We are impressed, perhaps overly impressed, when a writer can cite clear numbers to support an argument. Notice how the editorial writer Joseph Perkins uses statistics in his article about the effect of TV violence on young people:

> In fact, according to a study by the American Psychological   1
> Association, the average American child will view 8,000 murders

and 100,000 other acts of violence before finishing elementary school. The average 27 hours a week kids spend watching TV— much of it violent—makes them more prone to aggressive and violent behavior as adolescents and adults.

Of course, TV executives have known this for a long time. One of the most comprehensive studies of the impact of violent TV was commissioned by CBS back in 1978. It found that teenage boys who watched more hours of violent TV than average before adolescence were committing such violent crimes as rape and assault at a rate 49 percent higher than boys who watched fewer than average hours of violent TV.

2

—*Joseph Perkins, "It's a Prime-Time Crime"*

As the above paragraphs illustrate, statistics can be quite impressive. It is startling to read that the average child will view over 100,000 acts of violence before he or she leaves elementary school or that children spend an average of 27 hours per week watching television. Be aware, however, that statistics can also be misleading. How many of these acts of violence consist of Wile E. Coyote chasing the Road Runner in Saturday morning cartoons? Is there any difference between that kind of violence and the violence found in police shows or murder mysteries?

EXPERT OPINION OR TESTIMONY

Another kind of support that can be quite convincing is information from or statements by authorities on the subject about which you are writing. Let's suppose that you are trying to decide whether to have your child vaccinated against the measles. You have heard other parents say that a measles vaccination can harm a child, but you have never really known any parents who said their own children were harmed. So what do you do? Probably you call your pediatrician and ask for her expert opinion. After all, she is the one who has studied the field and who has vaccinated hundreds, perhaps thousands, of children.

In the same way, if you are writing a paper about a constitutional issue— such as the relationship of the Second Amendment to the need for gun control—you might decide to consult the experts for their opinions. And who are they? Probably legal scholars, political scientists, and even Supreme Court justices. Of course, you won't call these people on the phone; instead, you'll use quotations that you have found in articles and books from your college library. Here is an example of one such use of expert testimony:

Parents must strive to find alternatives to the physical punishment of children. Almost every effect of corporal punishment is negative. Dr. Bruno Bettelheim, famous psychologist and professor at the University of Chicago, and 70's," he said. "But the area of academic integrity is the only one where authority is still moving toward the students . . . ."

In 1976, 152 cadets were kicked out of the U.S. Military   5
Academy for cheating on an exam. After a long investigation, 98 were reinstated the following year. In 1984, 19 Air Force Academy seniors were suspended for cheating on a physics exam, and cadet honor boards' handling of academic cheating was temporarily halted.

The most excruciating cheating affair in the history of the   6
military service schools is still being played out on the stately campus of the U.S. Naval Academy at Annapolis. There, a panel of senior officers appointed by the Secretary of the Navy is hearing the last cases of as many as 133 midshipmen involved in cheating on an electrical engineering examination in December, 1992.

> —*From the* Los Angeles Times, *April 3, 1994, E1. Reprinted by permission of Rudy Abramson.*

EXERCISE 3.4

Examine "A Required Course in Beating the Freshman Blues" on pages 54–59 (or another article assigned by your instructor). Identify the types of support that have been discussed in this chapter.

EXPLAINING THE SIGNIFICANCE OF THE SUPPORT

Remember that better paragraphs and essays almost always move from the more general topic or thesis to the more specific example, statistic, or expert opinion. Specific, detailed support will give color and life to your papers, and it will help make your points clear and convincing.

However, once you have provided specific support, you are still not finished if you want your ideas to be as convincing as possible. Now is the time to *explain the significance* of your support. You might explain how your supporting details relate to the central idea of your paper, or you might emphasize the parts of your support that you consider the most significant. The point is that *your ideas* will become clearest when you elaborate upon your support, using your own words to explain the significance of the details you have given.

In the following example, note how the student writer elaborates upon her support.

topic sentence

    Sometimes it is very difficult not to respond to rude people with more rudeness of my own. For instance, one day last summer while I was working as a

supporting
example

cashier at Rice King, a Chinese restaurant, an old lady came in and said "Give me the damn noodles." I could not believe what she said. I was very angry. When I gave her the food, she opened the box in front of me and started picking through writes, "Punishment is a traumatic experience not only in itself but also because it disappoints the child's wish to believe in the benevolence of the parent, on which his sense of security rests."

If you do use expert opinion or testimony, don't believe too easily every thing you read. When choosing authorities, you should consider not onl their expertise but also their reputations for such qualities as integrity, hon esty, and credibility. Also, you should determine whether other experts in th same field disagree with the expert whose opinion you have cited. After al if the experts don't agree, testimony from just one of them won't be very con vincing. In fact, because experts often *do* disagree, it is a good idea to use e: pert testimony only *in combination with* the other types of support discussed this chapter.

COMBINING TYPES OF SUPPORT

Combining the different types of support is a very effective way to devel your ideas. Rarely will you find professional writers relying only on examp or statistics or expert testimony to support what they have to say. Instead, t more convincing writers provide many different types of support to ma their point. Usually, the better and wider the support you use, the better yc chance of persuading your reader.

EXERCISE 3.3

The following excerpt from an article on cheating appeared in the *Los Ang* *Times*. Examine it for each type of support discussed in this chapter.

> Cheating, studies show, is pervasive. It involves students struggling for A's and admission to prestigious graduate schools as well as those flirting with academic failure.
>
> A landmark survey of 6,000 students in 31 of the country's prestigious colleges and universities two years ago found that nearly 70% had cheated—if all manner of minor infractions were taken into account. The figure approached 80% for non–honor code schools and 60% for those with codes . . . .
>
> The move back to honor codes is symptomatic of a larger change on college campuses, said Gary Pavela, president of the National Center for Academic Integrity, a consortium of 60 colleges and universities collaborating on issues involving honor codes, student ethics and academic integrity.
>
> "All across the country, college administrators are beginning to take back authority that they gave up to students in the 60's

explaining the
significance

the noodles with her fingers. Then she said, "There is not enough meat." I knew there was more than enough meat in the box, but I ended up giving her more anyway. I suppose what I really wanted to do was to tell her what a disgusting person she was, but I'm glad that I didn't. After all, I didn't know her or what kind of problems she might be having in her life. Was she rude and obnoxious? Yes. Did that give me the right to be mean or hurtful in return? I didn't think so.

—*Jung Yun Park, student writer*

Exploring
ONLINE

The Writer's Response website includes links for further discussion of types of support. Go to www.thomsonedu.com/devenglish/mcdonald. Under "Chapter Resources" for Chapter 3, click on "Exploring Online."

WRITING INTRODUCTIONS AND CONCLUSIONS

So far in this chapter, we have been discussing how to *support* your ideas. In many ways, however, how you *introduce* and *conclude* your paper is as important as how you support it. In the next few pages, we will discuss some strategies you can use to write effective introductions and conclusions.

THE INTRODUCTORY PARAGRAPH

As we all know, first impressions can be deceptive, but they can also be of great importance. The opening paragraph of a paper provides the first impressions of the essay and of the writer. Thus, it is one of the most important paragraphs of your essay. Your introductory paragraph serves a number of important purposes:

- It gains the attention of your reader in the lead-in.
- It informs your reader about such details as the background of your subject and the purpose of your essay.
- It gives the reader some idea of you, the writer, particularly through its tone.
- It presents the thesis statement and often the plan or organization of your essay.

THE LEAD-IN

The lead-in generally consists of the first several sentences of the introduction. It may take any number of forms.

A General Statement

One of the most common ways of developing the introduction is to begin with a general statement and then follow it with ever more particular or specific statements leading to your thesis statement. This introductory strategy is sometimes referred to as a *funnel introduction* because, like a funnel, it is broad at the opening and narrow at the bottom. The following brief introduction from a student essay follows the general-to-particular pattern:

general
statement

specific thesis

> When disaster strikes, American people respond with their good hearts and numerous organized systems to help families cope with the disaster and its effects. There is beauty in a neighbor's heartfelt response to a disaster. My children and I discovered just how much caring and assistance Americans will help families with when a disaster strikes.

Here is another general-to-particular introduction. Note that the thesis in this introduction presents two particular points on which the paper will focus:

general
statement

specific thesis

> Some time around the middle of November, about half the population seems to begin griping about the "secularization" of Christmas. They become nostalgic for some old, ideal, traditional Christmas that may never have existed. They fume about artificial trees and plastic creches. However, P. H. Terzian, in an article entitled "A Commercial Christmas Is Not So Crass," states that these grouches are wrongheaded, and I agree. Terzian and I feel that the Christmas spirit is alive and well for several reasons: Christmas has always been a healthy mixture of the sacred and profane, and it has always been about joyfully getting, giving, and receiving.

A Question

Many writers open their essays with a question that is meant to attract the interest of the reader. Sometimes writers use a *rhetorical question*—that is, a question for which no answer is expected because the intended answer is obvious. Here is a rhetorical question: "Should we allow child abuse to continue?" Obviously, the answer to this question is no. Even so, a writer might open an essay with such a question to make the reader wonder why she or he is asking it and to draw the reader into the essay. Other times a writer might open an essay with a question that requires an answer—and the need to hear the answer keeps the reader reading. Here is a student's introductory paragraph that begins with a question:

question

specific thesis

> Is Tipper Gore overreacting? In her article "Curbing the Sexploitation Industry," Gore emphasizes the dangers posed for our children by what she calls the sexploitation industry. She claims that entertainment producers do not take our children into consideration when they present violent material. She says we should be concerned about the mental health of our children and the dignity of women. I do not think she is overreacting at all. Our society is facing a serious threat from the sexploitation industry: TV networks show excessive sex scenes, movie producers make films with excessive graphic violence, and rock recordings contain explicit sexual lyrics.

An Anecdote or Brief Story

We all enjoy stories. For most of us, reading about real people in real situations is far more convincing and interesting than reading about general ideas. For that reason, opening an essay with a short description of a person, place, or event can be an effective way of grabbing your reader's attention. The following introduction opens with a short anecdote:

anecdote

> I found a *Penthouse* magazine in my twelve-year-old's room last week, and I panicked. I recalled that Ted Bundy, who roamed the country mutilating, murdering, and raping, had said right before his execution that he had been influenced by pornography. Was my son on his way to a life of violent crime? Probably not. But a recent article, "Ted Bundy Shows Us the Crystallizing Effect of Pornography," raises some serious concerns. We need to be more vigilant about what our children (and our fellow citizens of all ages) are experiencing in all of the media, and we need to make our lawmakers

specific thesis

> aware of our concern. However, we need to accomplish these missions without weakening the First Amendment to the Constitution and without harming the world of art.

A Quotation

A quotation from someone connected with your topic, from an article you're writing about, or from an expert on your subject can be a good way of opening your introduction. Or you might look up a famous quotation on your subject in a book such as *Bartlett's Familiar Quotations.* Notice how the following student paragraph moves from a quotation to a specific thesis statement:

question

> Martin Luther King, Jr., once said, "I have a dream that my four little children will one day live in a nation where they will not be judged by the color of their skin, but by the content of their character." Dr. King would certainly be disappointed if he could read a recent article by Richard Cohen in the *Washington Post,* entitled "A Generation of Bigots Comes of Age." The author claims that we are seeing an increase in bigotry, especially from the generation just coming of age (those in their twenties). He cites a great deal of information and statistics from the Anti-Defamation League and from a Boston polling

specific thesis

> firm. I believe Mr. Cohen because lately I have experienced an increase in prejudice at work, at school, at shopping malls, and at many other places.

A Striking Statement or Fact

"Coming soon to your local cable system: VTV, violent television, 24 hours a day of carnage and mayhem." This quotation was the lead-in for a recent article on the amount of violence children see on television and the effects it may be having on them. Later in the article, the writer pointed out that one hundred acts of violence occur on television each hour. This fact could also be used as a striking lead-in to your essay. Once you have captured the attention of your reader through a strategy like this, he or she will tend to keep reading. Here is an introduction based on the above quotation:

striking
statement

specific thesis

"Coming soon to your local cable system: VTV, violent television, 24 hours a day of carnage and mayhem." So writes Joseph Perkins in his article "It's a Prime-Time Crime." Perkins cites the American Psychological Association and the quarterly journal *The Public Interest* to support his idea that the enormous amount of violence viewed by American children may be doing them irreparable harm. I find the overwhelming evidence that violence on TV is making children overly aggressive and is having a negative effect on their mental health quite convincing, especially because so many of my own observations confirm that evidence.

EXERCISE 3.5

Examine the introductions to "Live Each Moment for What It's Worth" (pages 7–8), "A View from Mount Ritter" (pages 11–14), "Jailbreak Marriage" (pages 44–45), "A Required Course in Beating the Freshman Blues" (pages 54–59), and "Charity Means You Don't Pick and Choose" (pages 59–61). Pay particular attention to the type of lead-in used by each article. Be prepared to discuss which introductions you find to be most effective.

THE CONCLUDING PARAGRAPH

Final impressions are as important as initial ones, especially if you want to leave your reader with a sense of completeness and confidence in you. Although the content of your conclusion will depend on what you have argued or presented in your essay, here are some suggestions as to what you might include:

- A restatement of your thesis, presented in words and phrases different from those used in your introduction
- A restatement of your supporting points, presented in words and phrases different from those used in your body paragraphs
- Predictions or recommendations about your proposals or arguments
- Solutions to the problems you have raised
- A quotation or quotations that support your ideas
- A reference to an anecdote or story that appeared in your introduction

Following are some concluding paragraphs that use some of these strategies.

A Restatement of the Main Points, and a Prediction or Recommendation

The following is a concluding paragraph from an article on the effects of TV violence on children. The author summarizes his main points and also offers a recommendation.

Given the overwhelming evidence that violent TV has deleterious effects on children, that it increases the level of violence throughout American society, it hardly seems unreasonable that the government ask that [the] TV industry tone down its violent programming. Those who find that request objectionable should forfeit their privileged use of public airwaves.

—*Joseph Perkins, "It's a Prime-Time Crime"*

A Solution to a Problem That Has Been Raised

Here is a conclusion from a rather unusual essay. Its thesis is that laws allowing men but not women to go topless at the beach are discriminatory and reflect our male-dominated culture. It offers two possible solutions to the problem.

It was not too long ago that the law also attempted to shield children from pregnant teachers. But the Supreme Court held pregnancy no grounds for a forced leave of absence. Another court has ruled that unmarried pregnant students cannot be excluded from public schools—not unless unmarried expectant fathers are also excluded. It is time for the same equality to be applied to bathing attire. Whether that is accomplished by allowing all people to go topless or by requiring men to wear tops, the end result will be the same: discarding one more premise of a male-defined society.

A Restatement of the Main Points, and a Quotation That Supports the Ideas

The following conclusion to a student essay sums up the writer's ideas on her subject and then presents an effective quotation from the author of the article to which she is responding.

Diversity, in America, is supposed to be good. This country was formed for freedoms like religion, speech, and sexual preference. America was formed for all ethnic groups and all traditions. When a certain group thinks that they are above all, that is when the problems begin. It is important to educate others on your background and to celebrate your heritage, to a certain extent. It is also important to learn about other cultures so that we feel comfortable and not threatened by others. As Schoenberger says, "I would much prefer them to hate or distrust me because of something I've done, instead of hating me on the basis of prejudice."

A Restatement of the Main Points, a Reference to an Anecdote or Story from the Introduction, and a Solution to a Problem That Has Been Raised

This conclusion is drawn from the article "Getting to Know about You and Me," which appears later in this chapter. Its introduction tells the story of the author's being invited to join the Diversity Committee at her high school, an invitation she declined. The conclusion refers again to that invitation.

I'm now back at school, and I plan to apply for the Diversity Committee. I'm going to get up and tell the whole school about my religion and the tradition I'm proud of. I see now how important it is to celebrate your heritage and to educate others about it. I can no longer take for granted that everyone knows about my religion, or that I know about theirs. People who are suspicious when they find out I'm Jewish usually don't know much about Judaism. I would much prefer them to hate or distrust me because of something I've done, instead of them hating me on the basis of prejudice.

EXERCISE 3.6

Examine the conclusions to "Live Each Moment for What It's Worth" (pages 7–8), "A View from Mount Ritter" (pages 11–14), "Jailbreak Marriage" (pages 44–45), "A Required Course in Beating the Freshman Blues" (pages 54–59), and "Charity Means You Don't Pick and Choose" (pages 59–61). Be prepared to discuss which conclusions you find to be most effective.

READINGS

As you read each of the following selections, pay particular attention to the type of support each writer uses and to the introduction and conclusion of each article.

Male Fixations   DAVE BARRY

Dave Barry, one of the most popular humor columnists in the United States, writes for the Miami Herald *and is published in more than five hundred newspapers. According to his official website (www.davebarry.com), he also "plays lead guitar in a literary rock band called the Rock Bottom Remainders, whose other members include Stephen King, Amy Tan, Ridley Pearson, and Mitch Albom."*

BEFORE YOU READ

1. What could the title "Male Fixations" possibly refer to? What is a fixation?
2. What assumptions do you or people you know have about what a man should or should not know how to do?

Most guys believe that they're supposed to know how to fix   1
things. This is a responsibility that guys have historically taken upon themselves to compensate for the fact that they never clean the bathroom. A guy can walk into a bathroom containing a colony of commode fungus so advanced that it is registered to vote, but the

guy would never dream of cleaning it, because he has to keep himself rested in case a Mechanical Emergency breaks out.

For example, let's say that one day his wife informs him that the commode has started making a loud groaning noise, like it's about to have a baby commode. This is when the guy swings into action. He strides in, removes the tank cover, peers down into the area that contains the mystery commode parts, and then, drawing on tens of thousands of years of guy mechanical understanding, announces that *there is nothing wrong with the commode*.   2

At least that's how I handle these things. I never actually fix anything. I blame this on tonsillitis. I had tonsillitis in the ninth grade, and I missed some school, and apparently on one of the days I missed, they herded the guys into the auditorium and explained to them about things like carburetors, valves, splines, gaskets, ratchets, grommets, "dado joints," etc. Because some guys actually seem to understand this stuff. One time in college my roommate, Rob, went into his room all alone with a Volvo transmission, opened his toolbox, disassembled the transmission to the point where he appeared to be working on *individual transmission molecules,* then put it all back together, and it *worked*. Whereas I would still be fumbling with the latch on the toolbox.   3

So I'm intimidated by mechanical guys. When we got our boat trailer, the salesman told me, one guy to another, that I should "re-pack" the "bearings" every so many miles. He said this as though all guys come out of the womb with this instinctive ability to re-pack a bearing. So I nodded my head knowingly, as if to suggest that, sure, I generally re-pack a couple dozen bearings every morning before breakfast just to keep my testosterone level from raging completely out of control. The truth is that I've never been 100 percent sure what a bearing is. But I wasn't about to admit this, for fear that the salesman would laugh at me and give me a noogie.   4

The main technique I use for disguising my mechanical tonsillitis is to deny that there's ever anything wrong with anything. We'll be driving somewhere, and my wife, Beth, who does not feel that mechanical problems represent a threat to her manhood, will say, "Do you hear that grinding sound in the engine?" I'll cock my head for a second and make a sincere-looking frowny face, then say no, I don't hear any grinding sound. I'll say this even if I have to shout so Beth can hear me over the grinding sound; even if a hole has appeared in the hood and a large, important-looking engine part is sticking out and waving a sign that says HELP.   5

"That's the grommet bearing," I'll say. "It's supposed to do   6
that."

Or, at home, Beth will say, "I think there's something wrong   7
with the hall light switch." So I'll stride manfully into the hall, where
volley-ball sized sparks are caroming off the bodies of recently electrocuted houseguests, and I'll say, "It seems to be working fine now!"

Actually, I think this goes beyond mechanics. I think guys   8
have a natural tendency to act as though they're in control of the
situation even when they're not. I bet that, seconds before the Titanic slipped beneath the waves, there was some guy still in his
cabin, patiently explaining to his wife that it was *perfectly normal* for
all the furniture to be sliding up the walls. And I bet there was a guy
on the *Hindenburg* telling his wife that, oh, sure, you're going to get
a certain amount of flames in a dirigible. Our federal leadership is
basically a group of guys telling us, hey, *no problem* with this budget
deficit thing, because what's happening is the fixed-based long-term
sliding-scale differential appropriation forecast has this projected
revenue growth equalization sprocket, see, which is connected via
this Gramm-Rudman grommet oscillation module to . . . .

AFTER YOU READ

Work with other students to develop responses to these questions or to compare responses that you have already prepared.

1. Now that you've read the article, explain the male fixation referred to
   in the title.
2. What is Barry's point about this male fixation?
3. What does Barry mean when he says that he has "mechanical
   tonsillitis"?
4. What is Dave Barry's thesis idea? Identify any sentences that seem to
   express it.
5. What types of support does Dave Barry use? Identify any brief or extended examples. Does he use any statistics or expert opinions?
6. Examine the introduction and conclusion to this article. How does each
   accomplish its purpose?

Fear of Heights: Teachers, Parents, and Students Are Wary of Achievement   BOB CHASE

The following selection was originally published as a paid advertisement in the
Washington Post. *In it, the President of the National Education Association claims
that the educational values of the average American need an overhaul. Do you agree?*

BEFORE YOU READ

1. Bob Chase is President of the National Education Association. In light of his position and the title of this article, what point do you expect him to be making about a "fear of heights"?

2. Which person do you worry about more, the C student involved in many extracurricular activities or the A student who spends most of his time studying? Why?

Imagine you're a high school chemistry teacher. One of your students is a shy, brilliant girl who routinely does "A" work. Another constantly chats on her cell phone during lab time. She plays varsity soccer, chairs the homecoming committee, and earns unspectacular grades.   1

Which student troubles you more?   2

Shockingly, a majority of teachers say they're more worried about the star pupil than the "C" student. And their sentiments mirror those of most parents. A recent survey by the research group Public Agenda found that 70 percent of parents said they'd be upset if their child received excellent grades but had a limited extracurricular life. Only 16 percent wanted their children to get "mostly A's."   3

Similarly, 53 percent of America's public school teachers worried about "A" students with two or three friends, while only 29 percent worried about "C" students who were popular.   4

Why? According to the survey, a majority of the population agrees that "People who are highly educated often turn out to be book smart but lack the common sense and understanding of regular folks." Unsurprisingly, this perception filters down to students. Research by Public Agenda also reveals that "most teens view the academic side of school as little more than 'going through the motions.'" Explained one Alabama boy, "My parents don't care if I make a C."   5

In many communities, after-school activities are more sacrosanct than academics. High school football victories garner more newspaper ink than math decathlons. School plays confer greater status on their participants than spelling bees. In perhaps the most bizarre example, in 1991 a mother in Channelview, Texas, hired a man to murder the mother of her daughter's rival for a spot on the cheerleading squad. The National Honor Society has never generated such feverish (albeit insane) competition!   6

Historically, Americans have embraced a degree of anti-intellectualism as a badge of our populist spirit. But as our economy   7 becomes increasingly reliant on technology, scientific research, and a highly skilled work force, this attitude undermines our best interests.

Proof came earlier this year, in the form of the Third International Mathematics and Science Study (TIMSS). A comparison of academic performance in 21 countries, TIMSS showed that U.S. 12th graders ranked at or near the bottom in math and science.   8

TIMSS underscores the need for more rigorous curricula, higher academic standards, and better teacher training. But policy changes alone will not improve students' performance. Our basic values need an overhaul. As long as teachers, parents, and students remain suspicious of intellectual excellence, we will function as a tripod for mediocrity—supporting a system that celebrates "averageness" over achievement.   9

What changes are in order?   10

TIMSS offers some important clues. The test revealed that American students spend less time doing homework and more time at after-school jobs than do their international peers. Indeed, says researcher Gerald Bracey, "The American vision of teenager-dom includes dating, malls, cars, jobs, and extracurricular activities." In the name of being "well rounded," many students are being spread too thin. We need to set new priorities, with academics enshrined as the centerpiece.   11

It's ironic that many teenagers are unenthusiastic about learning at a time in their lives when they're generally passionate about everything else. If we're going to cultivate world-class students, we adults may need some remedial lessons ourselves. Says Kay Armstrong, a public school librarian, "If children go into video arcades, it means they can operate a computer. If they can recite rap songs, they can quote Shakespeare. The problem is that we as educators have not learned what motivates this generation."   12

Poet William Butler Yeats once wrote, "Education is not filling up a pail but lighting a fire." Together, we must kindle the sparks fearlessly—and encourage the flames to burn as high and as bright as they can.   13

AFTER YOU READ

Work with other students to develop responses to these questions or to compare responses that you have already prepared.

1. Which person does Bob Chase think we should worry about more, the C student with extracurricular activities or the A student with a limited extracurricular life? Explain his reasoning.

2. "In many communities, after-school activities are more sacrosanct than academics." Do your own experiences or observations confirm this statement? Explain why or why not.

3. How would you express the thesis of this article? Use your own words. Then find any sentences in the article that express that idea.

4. What types of support does Bob Chase use?

5. Examine the introduction and conclusion to this article. Explain how each accomplishes its purpose.

Getting to Know about You and Me   CHANA SCHOENBERGER

"Ignorance [. . .] leads to misunderstandings, prejudice and hatred." So writes Chana Schoenberger in the following selection, which was published when she was only sixteen years old. Her stories revealing the ignorance of her professor as well as her classmates may remind you of situations you have encountered in your own life.

BEFORE YOU READ

1. What do you know about religions or denominations other than your own?

2. Do you feel uncomfortable around people who are different from you? Have you ever felt uncomfortable around any particular group of people?

3. What does the title suggest will be the focus of this article?

As a religious holiday approaches, students at my high school who will be celebrating the holiday prepare a presentation on it for an assembly. The Diversity Committee, which sponsors the assemblies to increase religious awareness, asked me last spring if I would help with the presentation on Passover, the Jewish holiday that commemorates the Exodus from Egypt. I was too busy with other things, and I never got around to helping. I didn't realize then how important those presentations really are, or I definitely would have done something.

This summer I was one of 20 teens who spent five weeks at the University of Wisconsin at Superior studying acid rain with a National Science Foundation Young Scholars program. With such a small group in such a small town, we soon became close friends and had a good deal of fun together. We learned about the science of acid rain, went on field trips, found the best and cheapest restaurants in Superior and ate in them frequently to escape the lousy cafeteria food. We were a happy, bonded group.

Represented among us were eight religions: Jewish, Roman   3
Catholic, Muslim, Hindu, Methodist, Mormon, Jehovah's Witness
and Lutheran. It was amazing, given the variety of backgrounds, to
see the ignorance of some of the smartest young scholars on the
subject of other religions.

On the first day, one girl mentioned that she had nine   4
brothers and sisters. "Oh, are you Mormon?" asked another girl,
who I knew was a Mormon herself. The first girl, shocked, replied,
"No, I dress normal!" She thought Mormon was the same as Men-
nonite, and the only thing she knew about either religion was the
Mennonites don't, in her opinion, "dress normal."

My friends, ever curious about Judaism, asked me about   5
everything from our basic theology to food preferences. "How
come, if Jesus was a Jew, Jews aren't Christian?" my Catholic roommate asked me in all seriousness. Brought up in a small Wisconsin
town, she had never met a Jew before, nor had she met people
from most of the other "strange" religions (anything but Catholic or
mainstream Protestant). Many of the other kids were the same way.

"Do you all still practice animal sacrifices?" a girl from a   6
small town in Minnesota asked me once. I said no, laughed, and
pointed out that this was the 20th century, but she had been absolutely serious. The only Jews she knew were the ones from
the Bible.

Nobody was deliberately rude or anti-Semitic, but I got the   7
feeling that I was representing the entire Jewish people through
my actions. I realized that many of my friends would go back to
their small towns thinking that all Jews liked Dairy Queen Bliz-
zards and grilled cheese sandwiches. After all, that was true of all
the Jews they knew (in most cases, me and the only other Jewish
young scholar, period).

The most awful thing for me, however, was not the benign   8
ignorance of my friends. Our biology professor had taken us on a
field trip to the EPA field site where he worked, and he was telling
us about the project he was working on. He said that they had to
make sure the EPA got its money's worth from the study—he
"wouldn't want them to get Jewed."

I was astounded. The professor had a doctorate, various   9
other degrees and seemed to be a very intelligent man. He apparently had no idea that he had just made an anti-Semitic remark. The other Jewish girl in the group and I debated whether or
not to say something to him about it, and although we agreed we

would, neither of us ever did. Personally, it made me feel uncomfortable. For a high-school student to tell a professor who taught her class that he was a bigot seemed out of place to me, even if he was one.

What scares me about that experience, in fact about my whole visit to Wisconsin, was that I never met a really vicious anti-Semite or a malignantly prejudiced person. Many of the people I met had been brought up to think that Jews (or Mormons or any other religion that's not mainstream Christian) were different and that difference was not good.   10

Difference, in America, is supposed to be good. We are expected—at least, I always thought we were expected—to respect each other's traditions. Respect requires some knowledge about people's backgrounds. Singing Christmas carols as a kid in school did not make me Christian, but it taught me to appreciate beautiful music and someone else's holiday. It's not necessary or desirable for all ethnic groups in America to assimilate into one traditionless mass. Rather, we all need to learn about other cultures so that we can understand one another and not feel threatened by others.   11

In the little multicultural universe that I live in, it's safe not to worry about explaining the story of Passover because if people don't hear it from me, they'll hear it some other way. Now I realize that's not true everywhere.   12

Ignorance was the problem I faced this summer. By itself, ignorance is not always a problem, but it leads to misunderstandings, prejudice and hatred. Many of today's problems involve hatred. If there weren't so much ignorance about other people's backgrounds, would people still hate each other as badly as they do now? Maybe so, but at least that hatred would be based on facts and not flawed beliefs.   13

I'm now back at school, and I plan to apply for the Diversity Committee. I'm going to get up and tell the whole school about my religion and the tradition I'm proud of. I see now how important it is to celebrate your heritage and to educate others about it. I can no longer take for granted that everyone knows about my religion, or that I know about theirs. People who are suspicious when they find out I'm Jewish usually don't know much about Judaism. I would much prefer them to hate or distrust me because of something I've done, instead of them hating me on the basis of prejudice.   14

AFTER YOU READ

Work with other students to develop responses to these questions or to compare responses that you have already prepared.

1. What point is Schoenberger making in her references to the girl who responded that she "dressed normal" when she was asked if she was a Mormon?

2. What is her point about the professor who said he "wouldn't want [the EPA] to get Jewed"?

3. How would you express the thesis of this article? Use your own words. Then find any sentences in the article that express that idea.

4. What kind of support does Schoenberger use? Identify the different types of support that you see.

5. Where does the introduction end? In what way does it introduce the article? Which paragraphs make up the conclusion? Why is it an effective conclusion?

Attention Shoppers: Your Dreams in Aisle 3   Sharon Zukin

Sharon Zukin is a professor of sociology at Brooklyn College and the City University of New York Graduate Center. Her latest book, Point of Purchase: How Shopping Has Changed American Culture, *was recently published by Routledge.*

BEFORE YOU READ

1. What kind of shopper are you? Do you buy items impulsively? Do you search from store to store to find the best buy?

2. Do you find shopping a frustrating or an enjoyable experience? Why?

3. Do you enjoy shopping with someone of the opposite sex? Explain why or why not.

For a long time, I didn't realize that I was born to shop. I am not amused when I enter my local Kmart during the holiday season and come face to face with a pair of life-size, gyrating mannequins in red velvet suits—Mr. and Mrs. Santa Claus—just past the security sensors. Neither am I cheered by the slogan on the window of a nearby Virgin Mega-store: "Merry Savings to You!" But since I have published a book about the culture of shopping in America, I take those spurs to buy things more seriously than does the average shopper.

Ten years ago, it hit me that shopping had become a highly visible part of the landscape and an important part of my life. At first I thought that just reflected personal changes. After my daughter was born, in 1990, I bought enough disposable diapers and plastic playthings to support the expansion of Toys "R" Us around the world. Then I began to notice that more newspapers and magazines were publishing articles about what to buy, and that more, and bigger, stores were springing up around me. When Kmart opened a discount superstore in my neighborhood—a unique event in lower Manhattan—my neighbors and I shopped there for six-packs of Bounty paper towels.

This wasn't happening just in store-rich New York City. All around the country, Americans were shopping more than ever before—and talking more about it.   3

By 1987, the United States had more shopping malls than high schools. Financial companies issued more than one billion credit cards. Mail-order merchants sent out five billion catalogs a year. Then, in the mid-'90s, the Internet brought Amazon.com, eBay, and pop-up advertisements into our homes and offices. Now we can shop anywhere, anytime, even if we don't have much money.   4

Most social critics blame us for buying stuff we don't need. "Affluenza": We have more money, so we spend it. "Luxury fever": We want the good things that others have. "Greed": We have an urge to splurge. As baby boomers, we were never taught self-control.   5

But the supply side should come in for blame as well. Since the 1970s, the amount of retail space per person has quadrupled, and America has had too many stores chasing too few sales. Wal-Mart—the discount store whose policies toward its work force recall Scrooge McDuck's—has grown to be the largest private employer on the planet. Nor is it that Americans have an irrational desire to buy things. These days, few of us bake our own bread, sew our own clothes, or know how to build a car. We depend on shopping to buy what we need for survival.   6

Each time we shop, however, we are surrounded by visions of abundance. We think not only of what we need, but also of what we could have. The more we see, the more we want to see, because whether entering a store or accessing a retail Web site, we invest time, money, and emotion in the means of our seduction.   7

Even if we don't make a purchase, the social space of stores is a material image of our dreams. Low prices? Wal-Mart, where men and women of all income levels shop together, offers us a vision of democracy. Brand names? Sony and Band-Aids represent our means to a better life. Designer labels? The Armani suit or Miss Sixty jeans will win us the job or a social partner.   8

The seduction of shopping is not about buying goods.   9
It's about dreaming of a perfect society and a perfect self. As Walter
Benjamin knew when he wrote about the Paris Arcades, shopping
encourages us to get lost in daydreams while giving us a way to pursue our dreams rationally. We're looking for truth with a capital T,
beauty *and* economic value. In a society where we no longer have
contact with nature or beauty in our daily lives, shopping is one of
the few ways we have left to create a sense of ultimate value.

Yet shopping also often plunges us into conflict. We can't   10
find what we want. What we find is too expensive. And it doesn't fit.

Take Cindy, who shopped for a year to find "the perfect   11
pair of leather pants." When she begins to tell me her story, I can't
help thinking she's a narcissist. Cindy sees herself as a practical
shopper. She firmly believes that she will find what she wants: "a
classic pair of leather pants." Cindy has a good job, but she doesn't
want to spend too much money. She wants good quality, but her
search is complicated because, like many women, she has a size
problem. Most women tell me they can't find the size they need
because their hips, or thighs, or arms are out of proportion to the
rest of their body. In Cindy's case, her size is too small for most
stores to carry—she's a size 2 petite.

Cindy is not out of sync with the zeitgeist. But she is   12
persuaded by the whole infrastructure of consumer society—
stores, advertisements, magazines—that she will find what she
wants. So she keeps on shopping.

Meanwhile, armies of market researchers and merchandise   13
managers try to discover what Cindy wants, so they can sell it to
her. For the past 30 years, market researchers have prided themselves on their ability to identify our values. Abandoning demo-
graphics for psychographics, they have stopped emphasizing our
SES, or socioeconomic status (income, education, and social class),
and turned to our VALS (values and lifestyles). They ask us not
only about what we buy, but also about our dogs and cats,
spouses, parents, religious attendance, and what we keep in our
bathroom cabinets. On the basis of our replies, they place us in
composite categories initially derived from Abraham Maslow's
psychology of needs and David Riesman's studies of social conformity: We're inner-directed, outer-directed, traditionalists, or
mavens of the avant-grade.

Whether they are pushing soft drinks, political candidates,   14
or leather pants, however, market researchers think in terms of

only a small number of options. Cindy's daydreams (or those of my mother, who can't find housedresses like the ones she bought in the '50s) may not fit into them.

The failure to find what we want is not the only reason   15
shopping isn't satisfying. Most of us feel a conflict between shopping the way our mothers taught us and shopping the way stores, Web sites, and magazines urge. Nearly all of us still learn to shop with our moms: the trips to the supermarket in car seats and strollers, the tantrum in the cereal aisle over frosted or plain, the begging for a treat when we get to the cashier. When we are 9 or 10 (or sometimes even younger, if TV viewing has made us precocious consumers): arguing with our mothers over buying clothes with cool brand names. When we're 15 or 16: shopping with our friends. Those are rites of passage.

Teenagers whom I interview in East New York, a low-income   16
neighborhood in Brooklyn, tell rueful stories about friends who bought Air Jordans or Tommy Hilfiger shirts cheap, on the street, only to find that the logos were spelled wrong. These young men claim to be savvier shoppers now. Chris makes a list of the clothing he needs before going to a store. Kwame heads for the outlet malls beyond the city.

All of the young men agree on one point: Going shopping   17
with a girl is like "committing suicide," because girls insist on going back and forth between stores to find the "cutest" style at the lowest price. Even among teenagers, shopping becomes a source of tension in gender relations.

The mothers of the teenagers, with whom I also speak,   18
are sadder and wiser shoppers. Like all parents of modest means, they stopped indulging their desire to shop for themselves when they began to have children. Leading small kids around a store is not conducive to daydreams about leather pants, or even jeans. Balancing a budget requires passing by the hair ornaments and teaching your children that Payless sneakers are just as good as Nikes. Revealing their own tensions over gender, the mothers claim that the children's fathers are more likely to buy the kids brand-name shirts or sneakers.

But when someone mentions the designer jeans that were   19
popular when they were growing up, everyone chuckles fondly. "Gloria Vanderbilt!" they exclaim in unison. "Sergio Valente!!!"

America has always been a nation of shoppers. The dawn   20
of mass production brought new ways to sell goods at affordable

prices, and the department store, mail-order catalog, and five-and-dime expanded our cultural horizons. When the German economist Werner Sombart asked, in 1906, "Why is there no socialism in the United States?" he found the answer in the fact that American workers wore better clothes, and lived in bigger, more comfortable homes, than their European counterparts did.

In the 20th century, supermarkets and discount stores made shopping universal. Today, mass consumption has become an entitlement, like Social Security and veterans' benefits. Whether we study consumer guides or push our wire carts from warehouse club to outlet mall, we are searching for our dreams.   21

We can't be blamed if we see our dreams in stores.   22

After you Read

Work with other students to develop responses to these questions or to compare responses you have already prepared.

1. In paragraph 9, Zukin writes, "The seduction of shopping is not about buying goods. It's about dreaming of a perfect society and a perfect self." Read the rest of paragraph 9, and then explain what her point seems to be.

2. Zukin moves into the second half of her essay when she writes, "Yet shopping also often plunges us into conflict." What conflicts does she discuss?

3. How would you express the thesis of this article? Use your own words. Then find any sentences in the article that express that idea.

4. What kind of support does Zukin use? Identify the different types of support that you see.

5. Examine the introduction and conclusion to this article. Explain how each accomplishes its purpose.

WRITING ASSIGNMENTS

As you write a paper in response to one of the following assignments, pay particular attention to the support that you use as well as to the paper's introduction and conclusion.

1. Dave Barry's article "Male Fixations" takes a humorous look at the behavior of some males who act as if they can fix everything. Have you ever known such a person? Have you known more than one? Write a paper in which you use examples drawn from personal experiences or observations to illustrate and explain the consequences of one particular kind of behavior practiced by a person (or persons) you know.

2. In "Fear of Heights," Bob Chase suggests that we should worry less about the A student with two or three friends and more about the C student with an active extracurricular life. What do you think? Write a paper in which you use examples drawn from personal experiences or observations to illustrate and explain your response.

3. Chase writes that "teachers, parents, and students [are] suspicious of intellectual excellence . . . supporting a system that celebrates 'averageness' over achievement." Write a paper in which you use examples drawn from personal experiences or observations to support or contradict this statement.

4. What do you think of Chase's idea that the American teenager is "spread too thin" and that too much emphasis is placed on extracurricular activities over academics? Write a paper in which you use examples drawn from personal experiences or observations to illustrate and explain your response.

5. In "Getting to Know about You and Me," Chana Schoenberger argues that widespread, often unintentional, religious intolerance exists in the United States. On a broader scale, diversity in various forms—religion, race, gender, sexual preference and so forth—is often not very tolerated in America. Compose an essay in which you use examples drawn from personal experiences or observations to explain the ways you and/or other people have experienced intolerance, whether as victim or perpetrator.

6. Consider Schoenberger's idea that intolerance is often unintentional. Write a paper in which you explain how such unintentional intolerance occurs, and support your ideas with examples drawn from personal experiences or observations.

7. In "Attention Shoppers: Your Dreams in Aisle 3," Sharon Zukin writes, "Most social critics blame us for buying stuff we don't need. 'Affluenza': We have more money, so we spend it. 'Luxury fever': We want the good things that others have. 'Greed': We have an urge to splurge." Have you found such criticism to be true of you or people you know? Write a paper in which you use examples drawn from personal experiences or observations to support or contradict this criticism of our shopping habits.

8. Zukin writes, "Whether we study consumer guides or push our wire carts from warehouse club to outlet mall, we are searching for our dreams." What do you think of Zukin's idea that we are pursuing our dreams as we shop? Write a paper in which you use examples drawn from personal experience or observation to illustrate the dreams that shopping habits reveal about you or others.

9. In the second half of her essay, Zukin suggests that in some ways shopping can be deeply dissatisfying and often full of conflict. Do you agree? Write a paper in which you use examples drawn from personal experience or observation to illustrate a variety of ways that you or others find shopping to be a dissatisfying experience.

EVALUATING SAMPLE PAPERS

Use the following checklist to determine which of the student essays on the next few pages is most effective.

1. Thesis Statement

   Underline the thesis statement of the essay. Does it express a clear and specific central idea?

   1   2   3   4   5   6

2. Introduction

   Does the introduction clearly introduce the central idea of the writer's paper? Does it end with a thesis statement?

   1   2   3   4   5   6

3. Topic Sentences

   Underline the topic sentence of each paragraph. Does each one clearly state the central idea of its paragraph?

   1   2   3   4   5   6

4. Support

   Examine the supporting details in each paragraph. Are they specific and clear? Should they be more detailed, or should more support be included?

   1   2   3   4   5   6

5. Conclusion

   Does the conclusion adequately bring the essay to a close?

   1   2   3   4   5   6

6. Sentence Structure

   Do the sentences combine ideas that are related, using coordination and subordination when appropriate? Are there too many brief, choppy main clauses? (See the *Sentence Combining* section later in this chapter for a discussion of subordination.)

   1   2   3   4   5   6

7. Mechanics, Grammar, and Spelling

   Does the paper contain a distracting number of these kinds of errors?

   1   2   3   4   5   6

8. Overall Ranking of the Essay

   1   2   3   4   5   6

Student Essay 1

"Getting to Know about You and Me" by Chana Schoenberger shows how unaware people are about the differences in religions. Schoenberger says that because of this unawareness/ignorance, people tend to hate or distrust someone because of their background or religion. Schoenberger, a teen, was amazed at the ignorance of even the most intelligent of her fellow students.

Too many people try to force their religion on others. Ever had strange men in suits come to your front door selling their religion? Those men and going to church on a regular basis has made me aware of other religions. According to Schoenberger, "If there weren't so much ignorance about other people's backgrounds, people wouldn't hate each other as badly as they do now." This ignorance leads to prejudice and hatred. Many of society's problems are based on prejudice and hatred. As for those men who go door to door, I believe it is intolerable for people to try to force their religion on you. I understand that they want you to learn about their religion, but I do not like to be pushed or harassed into something I do not agree with. "If people were educated in other backgrounds, then hatred would be based on facts and not flawed beliefs," says Schoenberger.

I became a victim of religious intolerance in my own church. Some members of the church went on a weekend trip up north to "spread the word." Although I willingly went, I felt I was pressured into going. I felt as if I was one of those men selling my religion, which I disagree with very much. This incident has made me hesitant to go to church. Do not get me wrong, I know what I believe in I just do not like being pressured into things I do not want to do. My friend took a religious studies course at school, and she said the teacher tried to force his religion on the class. It is good to be proud of your background, but thinking it is best for all is intolerable.

Diversity, in America, is supposed to be good. This country was formed for freedoms like religion, speech, and sexual preference. America was formed for all ethnic groups and all traditions. When a certain group thinks that they are above all, that is when the problems begin. It is important to educate others on your background and to celebrate your heritage, to a certain extent. It is also important to learn about other cultures so that we feel comfortable and not threatened by others. As Schoenberger says, "I would much prefer them to hate or distrust me because of something I've done, instead of hating me on the basis of prejudice."

Student Essay 2

According to the article "Fear of Heights," Public Agenda conducted a survey which found that 53% of America's school teachers worried about "A" students with a couple of friends, while only 29% worried about "C" students who were popular. Most of the current high school students I have spoken to fit in one of these two categories. For example, Shelly Beeby, a senior attending Oceanside High, has a 4.0 GPA and no real social life to speak about. Shelly would like to be a computer engineer in the future. On the other hand, Drew Gillespie, a junior attending La Costa Canyon High, has a 2.4 GPA, plays field hockey and works. In the future she would like to be a social worker. Natalie DelFrancia, a junior attending Carlsbad High, has a 4.3 GPA, works, attends dance classes and plays soccer. Natalie would like to make a career out of teaching math at the college level. What these three girls have in common is that they are all individuals with different capacities. I believe that we need not worry about the "A" student with a minute social life nor the average student with an abundant one, nor should we deny that there are students who can handle both a successful academic life and an active social one.

Most of the "A" students with minute social lives that I have spoken with seem to be geared toward careers that don't have a great amount of emphasis on social skills. Shelly Beeby, future computer engineer, explained to me that she has always felt most comfortable working on her own. In Shelly's case becoming a computer engineer fits her perfectly. She has the smarts to do it, and she enjoys one-sided situations. In high school a boy named Tom, who sat behind me in U.S. history, was a straight "A" student with about two or three friends. Our teacher would give us the option to work in groups; however, Tom always choose to do the projects on his own. He always talked about being some kind of scientist. Tom is another example of a straight "A" student who likes doing things alone. I feel that we do not need to worry about these students. It has been my observation that they often pick careers that fit their intelligence as well as their personality.

Contrary to the "A" students with minute social lives, most average students with abundant social lives that I have come in contact with seem to be interested in careers that focus on social skills. For instance, Drew Gillespie wants to become a social worker. Drew possesses average intelligence, has a passion for people, and loves to be involved; therefore, I believe that one day she will make a fine social worker. My friend Raymond, who was an average high school student, worked, played football, and was a part of the Orange Police Department's Explorer program. Raymond's dream of being a police officer finally came true last March when he was hired to work for the Santa Ana police department. Not only is Raymond good at what he does, but he also enjoys it. I believe we should not worry about these students because they see themselves in positions that require average intelligence with a major focus on people.

What the article failed to mention are those students who can maintain both an academic and social life. These students seem to be drawn to intellectual and prestigious careers. Natalie DelFrancia wants to be a math teacher at the college level. She has everything going for her, a high amount of intelligence and a wide array of people skills. My cousin Mike, who would like to be an international lawyer, graduated this summer with a 3.8 GPA. During his high school years, Mike played football, ran track and worked. He now attends the University of Michigan and is working towards his Master's degree in international law. Again, Mike has the high academic and social skills needed to achieve his dreams. These students should not be left out, for they too play a vital role in America's education system.

All the students I have mentioned in this paper are individual and highly important people. I don't believe that we need to worry that certain percentages of students are smart with no friends or average with many. What we need to focus on are students as individuals with certain capacities. We need to "encourage the flames to burn as high and as bright as they can." After all, if everyone in this world operated on the same level, how could life possibly go on?

Student Essay 3

While reading Dave Barry's article "Male Fixations," I couldn't help but to think of my neighbor's who have different types of fixations. The fixations that I see in some of my neighbors are similar to Barry's because they seem to be know-it-alls who refuse to admit that they really don't know as much as they claim, they will be embarrassed at their mistakes, and go into a state of denial when proven wrong.

Many of my neighbors seems to have a know-it-all attitude when it comes to certain things, only later to learn that they really don't know much about what they were talking about. For example, my neighbor Gabe seems to know everything about the O.J. Simpson trial because he is always telling me what the defense team is going to do everyday in court with the prosecution's witnesses, only later to find that he was only guessing and didn't really know that much about it to begin with. Another example of a know-it-all neighbor is Bob. I remember the time that I had bought my computer, and Bob came over to my house to help get it set up because he believed that he was a computer expert. He said that to set up a computer was a basic thing and that anyone with half a brain should be able to set it up without having to use the enclosed instructions. After an hour of watching him getting frustrated and calling the machine a few choice words, I told him that we could finish it the next day. When he left I referred to the instructions and got the job done in a timely manner, and the next day I just thanked him for his help and gave him lots of credit.

Some of my neighbors seem to get embarrassed when they are wrong about something simple. One morning I went outside to move my car off the street so I wouldn't get fined by the street sweeper. My neighbor Peg was outside, and she told me that the steet sweeper wasn't coming by that day and that it would be crazy for me to move my car. I believed her and later found a ticket on my windshield from the street sweeper for not moving my car. Even though I told her that it was a simple mistake, she was extremely embarrassed about it for weeks to follow.

Finally, the best example of a neighbor going into a state of denial is a situation with Bob in which he just wouldn't accept his wrong verdict of a problem and wouldn't let himself be proved wrong. Even though my washer broke down really late one night, Bob was quick to be on the scene to give his opinion on the mechanics of my washer that wasn't draining. He quickly came to the conclusion that something was in the pipe blocking the drain hose. I took his advice to try to unplug it, but it had then occurred to me that there is a filter on the washer to prevent such a thing from happening. I suggested to him that the problem could be an electrical failure, but he thought that I was kidding around with him. After we unsuccessfully tried looking for the blockage, I broke down and called a repairman the next day. Although it turned out that there was a problem with a switch, Bob just does not accept the fact that he was wrong and goes on by saying that whatever was blocking the pipe had been cleared.

My neighbors are good hearted persons that are eager to please. I believe that they do have practical ideas on how to fix things, but sometimes they are not always correct. It seems that whenever something goes wrong at my house with anything mechanical, a neighbor is there to assist because it is the neighborly thing to do. I guess I just have to accept the fact that they may have an opinion about everything, be embarrassed at their mistakes, and not accept their wrong solutions to certain problems.

SENTENCE COMBINING: USING SUBORDINATION

In Chapter 2, you practiced using appropriate coordinating conjunctions in your sentences. When you use coordination, you are suggesting that the ideas in your sentences are all of equal importance. On the other hand, when you employ subordination, you indicate to your reader which ideas are more important than others. The subordinate ideas in a sentence are usually the ones of lesser importance. Look at the following pairs of simple statements:

> I awoke from my nap.
> A burglar was smashing the window in my back door.

> The snow was falling lightly on the mountain road.
> A huge truck barrelled straight at us.

> The professor stomped toward me and began to yell.
> I would not stop talking.

> A very dear friend recently sent me a baby alligator.
> She lives in Pittsburgh.

As you can see, in each pair of sentences, one sentence contains much more important information than the other. In the first two pairs, the second sentences convey the more important ideas. In the last two pairs, the first sentences seem to be more important. (Admittedly, deciding which sentences are more "important" can be rather subjective, yet you must attempt to make such distinctions when you combine related ideas.)

SUBORDINATING CONJUNCTIONS AND RELATIVE PRONOUNS

One way to combine ideas is to write the less important information as a **subordinate clause.** Doing so will emphasize the relative importance of the ideas as well as clarify *how* the words are related. To write a subordinate clause, begin the clause with a **subordinator** (either a **subordinating conjunction** or a **relative pronoun**). Here is a list of subordinating conjunctions and relative pronouns that you can use to start subordinate clauses:

SUBORDINATING CONJUNCTIONS			RELATIVE PRONOUNS	
after	even though	until	that	whom(ever)
although	if	when	which	whose
as	since	whenever	who(ever)	
as if	so that	where		
as long as	than	wherever		
because	though	while		
before	unless			

You can combine the above four pairs of sentences by using subordinators. Here is how the sentences look when the less important sentences are written as subordinate clauses. Each subordinate clause is underlined.

> **When** I awoke from my nap, a burglar was smashing the window in my back door.

> **As** the snow was falling lightly on the mountain road, a huge truck barreled straight at us.

The professor stomped toward me and began to yell **because** <u>I would not stop talking</u>.

A very dear friend **who** <u>lives in Pittsburgh</u> recently sent me a baby alligator.

As you can see, each subordinate clause begins with a subordinator that expresses the relationship between the main clause and the subordinate clause. Notice also that the subordinate clause can appear at the start, at the end, or in the middle of the sentence.

EXERCISE 3.7

Each of the following sentences is drawn from one of the reading selections in this chapter. Underline each subordinate clause and circle its subordinator. Some sentences may contain more than one subordinate clause.

EXAMPLE

<u>If they can recite rap songs</u>, they can quote Shakespere.

1. One of your students is a shy, brilliant girl who routinely does "A" work.
2. As long as teachers, parents, and students remain suspicious of intellectual excellence, we will function as a tripod for mediocrity—supporting a system that celebrates "averageness" over achievement.
3. If we're going to cultivate world-class students, we adults may need some remedial lessons ourselves.
4. As a religious holiday approaches, students at my high school who will be celebrating the holiday prepare a presentation on it for an assembly.
5. This summer I was one of 20 teens who spent five weeks at the University of Wisconsin at Superior studying acid rain with a National Foundation Young Scholars program.
6. If there weren't so much ignorance about other people's backgrounds, would people still hate each other as badly as they do now?
7. Wal-Mart, where men and women of all income levels shop together, offers us a vision of democracy.
8. Take Cindy, who shopped for a year to find "the perfect pair of leather pants."
9. He said this as though all guys come out of the womb with this instinctive ability to re-pack a bearing.
10. So I'll stride manfully into the hall, where volley-ball sized sparks are caroming off the bodies of recently electrocuted houseguests, and I'll say, "It seems to be working fine now!"

PUNCTUATING SUBORDINATE CLAUSES

There are a few rules you need to know in order to punctuate sentences with subordinate clauses correctly.

1. Use a comma after a subordinate clause that precedes a main clause.

   <u>Because I have a meeting in the morning</u>, I will meet you in the afternoon.

2. In general, do not use a comma when the subordinate clause follows a main clause.

   I will meet you in the afternoon <u>because I have a meeting in the morning</u>.

3. Use commas to set off a subordinate clause beginning with *which, who, whom,* or *whose* if the information in the subordinate clause is not necessary to identify the word the clause modifies.

   Dave Barry, <u>who is a very funny man</u>, writes for the *Miami Herald*.

   (Because the information contained in the subordinate clause is not necessary to identify Dave Barry, it is set off with commas.)

4. On the other hand, do not use commas to set off a subordinate clause beginning with *which, who, whom,* or *whose* if the information in the subordinate clause is necessary to identify the word it modifies.

   The woman <u>who stepped on my toes in the theater</u> apologized profusely.

   (The clause "who stepped on my toes in the theater" is necessary to identify which "woman" you mean.)

5. No commas are used with subordinate clauses that begin with *that*.

   Subordinate clauses <u>that begin with *that*</u> are never enclosed in commas.

EXERCISE 3.8

Combine each of the following sets of sentences by changing at least one of the sentences in each set into a subordinate clause. Use commas where they are needed.

EXAMPLE

I was anxious. I prepared my tax return.

I was anxious after I prepared my tax return.

or

Because I was anxious, I prepared my tax return.

1. I always thought that my friends and I weren't prejudiced. I now know that we have our share of biases.

2. My cousin came over to my house. She didn't feel comfortable talking to her parents.

3. One night I was extremely happy and in good spirits. I felt I could not contain my energy.

4. I would describe myself as an energetic person. I don't like to sit around doing nothing.

5. *Neurotic* is another word I would use to describe myself. I am embarrassed to admit it.

6. My neighbor Gabe thinks he knows everything about the judicial system. He tells me what he thinks the verdict will be whenever there is a major trial.

7. Last week I bought a new computer. Bob came over to my house to help me set it up. He thinks he is a computer expert.

8. A friend of mine works as a mechanic at a local garage. He told me that my battery was weak and needed to be recharged.

9. One of my neighbors can no longer drive. She gave me a list and some money. I told her I would pick up some groceries for her.

10. He told me that he was going to do the dishes. I became upset with him. We were late for the party.

11. Josefina had always lived along the coast. She moved to Nevada. Her company offered her a better position there.

12. Snowboarding is my sister's favorite sport. She says it makes her feel as if she were surfing on snow. I don't really believe her.

13. I attended a trade school after high school. I met a student named Jack. He owned a black 1975 Corvette.

14. A couple of weeks ago a close friend and I were talking on the phone. He asked me a question. Would I consider dating someone of a different race?

15. Edna was driving home in the pouring rain. She decided to stop at Home Depot. She picked up fifteen pounds of lawn seed.

The Writer's Response website includes links for further practice using subordination. Go to www.thomsonedu.com/devenglish/mcdonald. Under "Chapter Resources" for Chapter 3, click on "Exploring Online."

EXERCISE 3.9

Combine each of the following groups of sentences into one sentence. Use subordination and coordination where appropriate. Embed adjectives, adverbs, and prepositional phrases. Use commas where they are needed.

1. The phoenix is a legendary bird.
   It supposedly lived for 500 years or longer.
   It has long been a symbol of resurrection.
   It also has been a symbol of immortality.

2. It was a beautiful scarlet-and-gold bird.
   Supposedly it would prepare for its own death.
   It would build a nest.
   The nest would be made of aromatic boughs and spices.

3. The phoenix would sing a melodious dirge.
   By flapping its wings, it would set the nest afire.
   It would be burned alive.
   It would emerge from the ashes newly born.

4. *Through the Looking Glass* was written by Lewis Carroll.
   In it, Humpty Dumpty told Alice that *slithy* was a portmanteau word.
   It was a combination of *slimy* and *lithe.*
   It was like a portmanteau (a traveling bag).
   A portmanteau packs two sides together.

5. *Chortle* is a portmanteau word,
   It combines *chuckle* and *snort.*
   Squawk is also one.
   It is a blend of *squall* and *squeak.*
   Blurt is probably also a combination.
   It blends *blow* and *spurt.*

6. A Pyrrhic victory refers to a battle fought against the Romans.
   King Pyrrhus fought the battle in 279 B.C.
   It is one in which both sides suffer losses.
   Both sides' losses are devastating.
   Even the victor seems to have lost.

7. *SOS* is not punctuated as *S.O.S.*
   It is not an abbreviation of "Save Our Ship" or "Save Our Souls."
   It was adopted as the international distress signal.
   It is a combination of three dots, three dashes, and three more dots.
   That combination is distinctive and easily transmitted.

8. The word *idiot* is derived from the Greek word *idiotes.*
   It refers to someone of remarkably low intelligence.
   In an insulting manner, it refers to someone whose judgments, ideas, or actions we strongly disapprove of.
   The Greek *idiotes* simply meant "private person."
   A "private person" was someone who did not hold public office.

9. In 1818, Dr. Thomas Bowdler decided to eliminate vulgar terms.
   The terms were in the plays of William Shakespeare.
   Dr. Bowdler was an English physician and editor.

He believed that the terms were not appropriate for virtuous women to read.

Shakespeare lovers around the world objected to his actions.

10. Many people know Pluto only as Mickey Mouse's dog.

He is actually the Greek god of the underworld.

He controls all that is under the ground.

As a result, he is also the giver of wealth in Greek mythology.

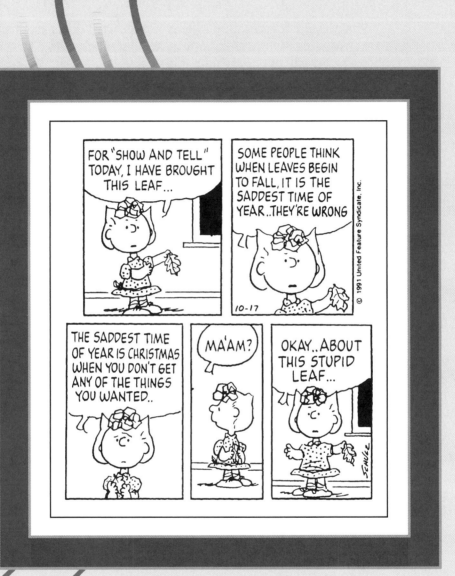

Peanuts: © United Feature Syndicate, Inc.

Unity and Coherence

UNITY

As you can see from the "Peanuts" cartoon on the facing page, Sally is having trouble staying focused on her topic. Her tendency to drift from the subject of her report ("this stupid leaf") to why Christmas is the saddest time of the year is called a break in **unity**.

Think about the word *unity* for a moment. It means *oneness* or *singleness of purpose.* A *unified* paragraph or essay is one that stays focused on its central idea. It does not wander into areas that are unrelated to that central idea. To put it another way, all the details, facts, examples, explanations, and references to authorities with which you develop a unified paper should clearly relate to and develop the central idea of that paper. If they do not do so, the paper lacks unity.

A good time to check the unity of your writing is after you have written the first draft. Until that time, you are still prewriting, and during the prewriting stage you really should not worry too much about unrelated material that creeps into your writing. Remember, when you prewrite, you concentrate on getting as many ideas on paper as you can. When you write, you produce your draft. And when you revise, you improve that draft. Checking your paper for unity will usually occur as you revise—before you submit your paper to your instructor but after you have produced a first draft.

EXERCISE 4.1

Read the following paragraphs, and identify the topic sentence of each one. Then identify any sentences that break the unity of the paragraph.

A. 1 The names of the seven days of the week have some rather interesting origins. 2 The names *Sunday* and *Monday,* for example, come from Old English words that refer to the sun *(sunne)* and moon *(mona),* respectively. 3 *Tuesday, Wednesday, Thursday,* and *Friday* all refer to gods in Germanic mythology. 4 Tiu (for Tuesday) was a god of war. 5 Most cultures have some kind of name for a war god. 6 The Roman name was Mars; the Greek name was Ares. 7 Woden (for Wednesday) was the chief Germanic god. 8 He is known to many people as Odin. 9 The corresponding chief god in Roman mythology is Jupiter, and in Greek mythology it is Zeus. 10 Thor (for Thursday) was the Germanic god of thunder; Freya (for Friday) was the goddess of love and beauty. 11 Interestingly, *Saturday* comes from the name of a Roman god, not a Germanic one. 12 Saturn was the Roman god of agriculture. 13 How agriculture is related to the huge planet we know as Saturn may be confusing to some people, but it obviously did not worry the Romans very much.

B. 1 Folk remedies, which are passed on from one generation to another, are sometimes quite effective and at other times absolutely worthless. 2 One example of effective folk wisdom is the advice to eat chicken soup when you have the flu. 3 Many people love the taste of chicken soup, especially during cold weather. 4 Several scientific studies have shown that chicken soup improves the functioning of the fibers in the upper respiratory tract that help people get rid of congestion. 5 Usually, people buy over-the-counter drugs to alleviate the symptoms of the flu, and today generic brands are much more popular than name brands. 6 Unfortunately, not all folk remedies are as effective as chicken soup. 7 Scientists say, for example, that slices of raw potato placed on the forehead will do nothing for a fever, although many people believe otherwise. 8 In fact, many people believe almost anything they are told. 9 A friend of mine once told some children that the world used to have only two colors—black and white—and that was why old movies looked that way. 10 And the children believed him! 11 Another bit of folk advice that scientists say is untrue is that taping a child's ears back at night will change the positions of ears that stick out too much. 12 Finally, scientists say that boiling skim milk for children with diarrhea is dangerous as well as ineffective.

C. 1 For many years, ice cream was a treat enjoyed only by the nobility. 2 When Marco Polo returned to Italy from China in 1271 with a recipe for a new dessert made of fruit mixed with ice and milk, the dish quickly became a favorite of the Italian nobility. 3 However, the nobility did not share the recipe with the common people. 4 Marco Polo went on to become one of the most famous travelers in history. 5 His book, *The Travels of Marco Polo*, describes China as a country far superior to his own in culture and technology. 6 Several hundred years later, in 1533, Catherine de Medici of Italy introduced the recipe to the French nobility when she married a son of the King of France. 7 A creative French chef experimented with the recipe, beating a mixture of fruit and cream in a bowl surrounded by ice. 8 Of course, French chefs are known for their creativity and imagination, which is why French restaurants are regarded as special, expensive places by most Americans. 9 The result was a dessert much like our ice cream of today, but the recipe was still kept a closely guarded secret. 10 When King Charles I of England brought the dessert to his country in 1625, he was so determined to keep the recipe secret that he even refused to tell his own nobility how to make it. 11 That is just like the English, though. 12 They are known for keeping things to themselves. 13 Finally, in 1670, ice cream appeared for the first time on the menu of a Paris restaurant, and soon people throughout the world were sharing this "new" taste treat.

COHERENCE

Another way to improve the clarity of your writing is to work on its **coherence,** which involves clarifying the *relationships* between ideas. When ideas (or sentences) are *coherent,* they are understandable. And when they are understandable, one sentence makes sense in relation to the sentence before it. When ideas (or sentences) are *incoherent,* they do not make much sense because they are not clearly related to each other or to the central idea of the paper.

For example, imagine someone passing you a note that read "Snow! Last winter! Trees! Gone!" What in the world could such a person possibly be trying to tell you? That the snow that fell on the trees last winter is gone? That the trees that were snowed on last winter are gone? That last winter's snow killed the trees? What is missing here is **coherence,** the connections between the ideas.

Of course, a person's writing is rarely as incoherent as the above example, but all writers—from students who are taking their first writing classes to professionals who make their living by writing—must consistently work on the clarity of what they have written. Here is an example of a paragraph that needs more work in coherence:

1 Some television viewers claim that Donald Duck cartoons are immoral. 2 For fifty years, Donald has kept company with Daisy. 3 Donald's nephews—Huey, Dewey, and Louie—are apparently the children of a "Miss Duck," who was last seen in a comic book in 1937. 4 Donald is drawn without pants. 5 The opinions of these persons have been largely ignored by the general public.

The above paragraph lacks coherence because each sentence seems to jump from one unrelated detail to the next. A careful reader will probably be able to figure out that each sentence is meant to be an example of the "immorality" of Donald Duck cartoons, but the relationship of each sentence to that central idea and to the idea in the sentence before it needs to be made much clearer. Clarifying such relationships involves working on the coherence of the paper.

A number of techniques will help you improve the coherence of your writing.

IMPROVING COHERENCE

1. *Refer to the central idea.*   One of the most effective ways to improve coherence is to use words that refer to the central idea of your paper as you write your support. In the above paragraph about Donald Duck cartoons, the central idea is that some people think they are "immoral," but none of the supporting sentences clearly refer to that idea. The relationship between the supporting sentences and the central idea will be clearer—and the coherence improved—if the writer uses words that connect her support to the central idea of immorality.

> 1 Some television viewers claim that Donald Duck cartoons are immoral. 2 For fifty years, Donald has kept company with Daisy, a relationship that to some seems **suspicious and dishonorable.** 3 Donald's nephews—Huey, Dewey, and Louie—are apparently the **illegitimate** children of a "Miss Duck," who was last seen in a comic book in 1937. 4 It seems **improper and indecent** to these critics that Donald is drawn without pants. 5 Donald's dressing habits **clearly upset** these particular television viewers. 6 The opinions of these persons have been largely ignored by the general public.

Now the relationship of each supporting idea to the central idea of the paragraph has become much clearer. Notice how the boldfaced words keep the emphasis of the paragraph on the "immorality" of Donald Duck cartoons.

2. *Use common transitional words and phrases.*   Transitions tell you what direction a sentence is about to take. When a sentence starts with *However,* you know that it is about to present a contrast; when it starts with *For example,* you know that it is about to move from a general statement to a specific illustration of that statement. Clear transitions will improve the coherence of your paper because they will signal to your readers how the sentence that they are about to read is related to the sentence that they have just finished reading.

Many transitions are so common that they are worded the same way no matter who is doing the writing. They are like road signs *(Stop, Yield, School Zone)* that all drivers are expected to recognize and respond to. These common transitions can improve your paper, but be careful not to overuse them. Too many of them will make your writing sound artificial and awkward.

- To show a movement in time: *first, second, next, finally, then, soon, later, in the beginning, at first, meanwhile*
- To move to an example: *for example, to illustrate, for instance, as a case in point*
- To add another idea, example, or point: *in addition, furthermore, and, also, second, third, next, moreover, finally, similarly*
- To show a contrast: *on the other hand, however, but, yet, instead, on the contrary, nevertheless*
- To show a result: *so, therefore, as a result, consequently, hence, thus*
- To conclude: *finally, in conclusion, as a result, hence, therefore, clearly, obviously*

Notice how the addition of these transitions helps to improve the paragraph about Donald Duck cartoons:

> 1 Some television viewers claim that Donald Duck cartoons are immoral. 2 **For example,** for fifty years, Donald has kept company with Daisy, a relationship that to some seems suspicious and dishonorable. 3 **In addition,** Donald's nephews—Huey, Dewey, and Louie—are apparently the illegitimate children of a "Miss Duck," who was last seen in a comic book in 1937. 4 **Finally,** it seems improper and indecent to these critics that Donald is drawn without pants. 5 Donald's dressing habits clearly upset these particular television viewers. 6 **However,** the opinions of these persons have been largely ignored by the general public.

3. *Write your own transitional phrases, clauses, or full sentences.*   The most effective transitions are those written in your own words as phrases, clauses, or complete sentences. Transitions such as these often **repeat a word or idea** from the previous sentence. They also often **refer to the central idea** of a paper to introduce a new element of support.

Note the transitional phrases, clauses, and full sentences in the following paragraph:

> 1 Some television viewers claim that Donald Duck cartoons are immoral. 2 **According to these viewers, Donald's relationship with Daisy is an example of his immorality.** 3 For fifty years, Donald has kept company with Daisy, a relationship that to some seems suspicious and dishonorable. 4 In addition, **some people question the morality of a cartoon that features three children of unknown parentage.** 5 Donald's nephews—Huey, Dewey, and Louie—are apparently the illegitimate children of a "Miss Duck," who was last seen in a comic book in 1937. 6 Finally, it seems improper and indecent to these critics that Donald is drawn without pants. 7 **Although few people ever expect to see any animal in pants,** Donald's dressing habits clearly upset these particular television viewers. 8 **Luckily for the famous duck,** the opinions of these persons have been largely ignored by the general public.

In the above paragraph, sentence 2 is a full *transitional sentence*. It replaces the phrase *for example,* and it emphasizes the central idea of the paragraph by using the word *immorality*. Sentence 3 is another *transitional sentence*. Again, this sentence improves the coherence of the paragraph by emphasizing the central idea of *morality*. Sentence 7 now includes a *transitional clause*. Notice that the clause refers to the idea of animals "in pants," which was mentioned at the very end of sentence 6. Sentence 8 contains a *transitional phrase* that allows the reader to move easily into the concluding idea of the paragraph.

EXERCISE 4.2

Work with several other students in a small group to identify the topic sentence and central idea in each of the following paragraphs. Write "C.I." above all references to the central idea. Circle all words or ideas that are repeated from one sentence to the next. Finally, underline all common transitional words and phrases.

EXAMPLE

TOPIC

1 Folk remedies, which are passed on from one generation to another, are sometimes quite effective and sometimes absolutely worthless. [CENTRAL IDEA] 2 One example of effective (folk wisdom) is the advice to eat chicken soup when you have the flu. 3 Several scientific studies have shown that (chicken soup) improves the functioning of the fibers in the upper respiratory tract that help people get rid of congestion caused by the flu. 4 Unfortunately, not all (folk remedies) are as effective as chicken soup. 5 Scientists say, for example, that slices of raw potato placed on the forehead will do nothing for a fever, although many people believe otherwise. 6 Another bit of (folk advice) that (scientists say) is untrue is that taping a child's ears back at night will change the position of ears that stick out too much. 7 Finally (scientists say) that boiling skim milk for children with diarrhea is dangerous as well as ineffective.

A.   1 If you think dainty butterflies are lily-livered weaklings, think again. 2 Most male butterflies are gutsy and aggressive within their own habitat and will pick a fight at the slightest provocation. 3 This trait is often seen when a male is on the prowl for a mate. 4 The European grayling butterfly, for example, will perch on a twig or leaf to wait for Ms. Right. 5 When he scents a female of his own species, he will begin an elaborate courtship dance and emit his own identifying scent. 6 But he will rough up almost anyone else who ventures into his territory, whether it's another butterfly twice his size, a dragonfly or a small bird. 7 He'll even lunge at his own shadow. 8 Black swallowtail butterflies, an especially aggressive species, have been known to chase after terrified birds for as long as half a minute. 9 When vying for the favors of the same female, two male butterflies will repeatedly ram each other in midair until one surrenders and flees.

—*Irving Wallace et al.,* Significa

B. 1 In competition, losing should not necessarily be seen as failing. 2 If a runner finishes behind Bill Rogers in the marathon but runs the race twenty minutes faster than he has ever before, one cannot say that he has failed. 3 If a person enters a city tennis tournament and is eliminated in the third round, he cannot be said to have failed if neither he nor anyone else expected him to survive the first round. 4 The point is simple: failure in competition is not to be identified with losing per se but rather with performing below reasonable expectations. 5 Only when one could reasonably have expected to win does losing mean failing. 6 In most competition, someone wins and someone or many lose, but this does not mean that many (or even *any*) have performed below reasonable expectations and have, therefore, failed.

—*Richard Eggerman, "Competition as a Mixed Good"*

C. 1 When a man and a woman walk together, convention says the man takes the curb side. 2 A common historical explanation of this custom is that in the days when garbage was hurled into the street from upper-story windows, it was the man's duty to bear the majority of the refuse. 3 More reasonable is the explanation that a man on the outside is in a better position to protect his female companion from the hazards of the street itself, which until fairly recently included runaway horses and street brawlers. 4 Though Emily Post dutifully approved the custom, she denied its usefulness in the days of automobiles. 5 Apparently she had never negotiated a New York City sidewalk just after a downpour.

—*Tad Tuleja,* Curious Customs

EXERCISE 4.3

Revise the following paragraphs to improve their coherence by referring more clearly to the central idea, by repeating words and ideas from one sentence to the next, and by adding appropriate transitional words and phrases. You may also need to add complete sentences to emphasize how the details are related to the central idea of the paragraph. Consider working with other students as you revise two of these paragraphs. Then revise one on your own.

A. 1 Driving on freeways today has become a frightening experience. 2 I glanced into my rear-view mirror to find a blue Ford pickup driving 65 miles per hour only two feet from my rear bumper. 3 When I changed lanes, he changed lanes too. 4 He pulled off the freeway at the next exit. 5 The local "freeway skiers" weave in and out of traffic as if they were in an Olympic slalom event. 6 Some small red sportscar will swing onto the freeway, race up the lane next to mine, change lanes, and then repeat the same maneuver as it weaves up the freeway. 7 There are the people who are much too busy to be driving. 8 They are reading reports, checking make-up, combing mustaches, drinking soft drinks, or talking on the telephone. 9 People have changed the nature of freeway driving.

B.   1 Most fathers that I know seem to be much more awkward and nervous than mothers when it comes to caring for their babies. 2 My brother's baby, Kaori, had a slight cold. 3 My brother insisted that she should be taken to the hospital. 4 His wife said that Kaori would be fine in a day or so. 5 The child recovered completely. 6 My brother became sick because he hadn't slept all night. 7 My father would always avoid holding my little brother when we were younger. 8 At Disneyland, my mother asked him to hold my brother while she used the restroom. 9 The entire time, my dad paced back and forth. 10 Whenever my mother held the child, she seemed completely at ease. 11 I suppose it is natural for mothers to feel comfortable with their young children. 12 I don't see any reason for fathers to be as awkward as they are.

C.   1 After reading G. Gordon Liddy's "Without Emotion," I was reminded of times in my own life when I felt that I had to act without emotion just to make it through an unpleasant experience. 2 I had to go through a divorce. 3 I had no financial support, and I had an eleven-month-old son to take care of. 4 I had to think about handling the pressing issues of finding food, clothing, shelter, and a job. 5 I was laid off from a typesetting position with a local newspaper. 6 I immediately busied myself with the task of finding another job. 7 Liddy was trying to get to the point where he could act without emotion if he ever really had to. 8 For me, it was either act without letting my emotions get to me or allow myself to be defeated by my circumstances.

Exploring **ONLINE**   Go to www.thomsonedu.com/devenglish/mcdonald for more practice with using transitions. Under "Chapter Resources" for Chapter 4, click on "Exploring Online."

IMPROVING UNITY AND COHERENCE WITH THESIS STATEMENTS AND TOPIC SENTENCES

So far we have discussed unity and coherence *within* paragraphs, but these elements of clear writing affect the entire essay, not just the single paragraph. Remember, *unity* refers to a writer's ability to stay focused on one central idea, and *coherence* involves clarifying relationships between ideas. When you move from one paragraph to another within an academic essay, you can stay focused on the central idea of the essay (unity) and clarify the relationships between paragraphs (coherence) by paying particular attention to the thesis statement of the essay and the topic sentence of each paragraph.

THESIS STATEMENTS AND TOPIC SENTENCES

1. *Write a thesis statement that clearly expresses the central idea of the essay.*   As we discussed in Chapters 1 and 2, academic essays need thesis statements that carefully and accurately state the central idea of the paper. Unless your instructor tells you otherwise, place the thesis statement at the end of your introductory paragraph.

2. *Write topic sentences that clearly express the central idea of each paragraph.* This point has been discussed in Chapters 1 and 2. Unless your instructor tells you otherwise, place your topic sentences at the start of each body paragraph.

3. *Write topic sentences that clearly develop the central idea of the thesis statement.*   This point relates to both the *unity* and the *coherence* of your essay. One way to emphasize the relationship between each topic sentence and the thesis statement is to repeat words and ideas from the central idea of the thesis statement within each topic sentence. To avoid repetitive wording, don't repeat exact phrases.

4. *Write topic sentences that use transitions to move away from the topic in the previous paragraph.*   This point relates the *coherence* of your essay. A transition within a topic sentence might be a brief reference to the central idea of the previous paragraph, a common transitional phrase, or a transitional phrase or sentence of your own.

SAMPLE STUDENT ESSAY

Examine the following essay, and note how the unity and coherence are emphasized as the writer moves from one paragraph to another. The central idea in the thesis and in each topic sentence is in boldface. The transition that opens each paragraph is underlined once. The words in each topic sentence that repeat the central idea of the thesis statement are in parentheses.

The Benefits of Competition

In the article "School Sports—Latest New Age Target," John Leo tells us that many gym teachers across America are opposed to competition in school sports because they think such competition harms the children who aren't outstanding players. He refers to an article from *The New York Times*, which he says "carries the implicit message that win-lose games are dangerous." Leo, however, disagrees with the *Times* article. He believes that one can "lose without humiliation and win without feeling superior." I agree with him. In fact, after the experiences I have had with school sports in my own life, **I believe that the competition in school sports benefits students in many ways.**

One of the (benefits of competition) in school sports is that it **motivates** students to do their best. For example, when I was taking a swim class last semester, I could not swim one hundred yards without stopping. When the teacher said that he was going to time every one of us to see who could finish one hundred yards in the least amount of time, I was worried because I was sure I could not swim that far. During the competition, the only thought that came into my mind was that I did not want to be the last one to finish, and that thought motivated me to continue swimming even though I was very tired. When I reached the finish line, I was astounded to find that I was in fourth place. From this experience and from many others like it, I can say the competition did indeed bring out the best in me.

In addition to motivating students, competition in school sports **(prepares** 3 **young people)** for the competition they will face in real life. My younger brother has (benefited) from school sports this way. Since he is the youngest member of our family, we always used to let him win when we played games with him because that was the only way we could keep him happy. Then one day he came home from school depressed. When I asked him what had happened, he said that he had lost to a friend in a school race. After I heard his story, I realized that my brothers and I had spoiled him and that school sports were giving him a dose of reality. I decided that the next time he wanted to beat me at checkers, he would have to really compete with me because that is the only way to teach him what life is really like.

Not only does competition benefit people by motivating them and teaching 4 them about life, but it also (benefits them) by **revealing their own inner strengths and weaknesses.** My friends Minh and Hoa are good illustrations of this point. Minh is a quiet person who never seems very secure about his tennis talent. On the other hand, Hoa, a talkative person, always brags about how well he plays tennis. Hoa was sure that he was a better tennis player than Minh, but one day he had to face Minh in a school tennis tournament. When Hoa lost the game, he realized that he really could not play tennis as well as he thought. This competition pointed out Hoa's weakness, but it also revealed to Minh his own hidden strength. If they had not competed, neither would have discovered the truth about himself.

Clearly, competition in school sports can (benefit) people in many ways. It 5 motivates students to do their very best, it teaches them about real life, and it reveals to them their own strengths and weaknesses. Like John Leo, I believe that school sports are a valuable part of school life.

EXERCISE 4.4

Examine the following sets of thesis statements and topic sentences. In each set, consider the following questions:

1. Does each thesis statement present one clear central idea? What is it?
2. Does each topic sentence introduce a central idea? What is it?
3. Does each topic sentence clearly develop the central idea in the thesis statement? What words or ideas from the thesis statement does it repeat?
4. Does each topic sentence open with some kind of transition to move it away from a previous paragragh?

A. *thesis statement*   Knowing many people myself who have attended college as freshmen, I agree that survival skill courses are extremely helpful in dealing with all the stress that comes along with college life.

	topic sentence	One of the main things that many freshmen stress about is the fact that they will no longer be living under the care of their parents.
	topic sentence	In addition to the stress of being away from home, college also introduces new financial stress.
B.	*thesis statement*	Will the "A" student or the "C" student get farther in life and have what it takes to survive everyday troubles?
	topic sentence	Surprisingly, most people would say that the "A" student would be better off because he puts academics first.
	topic sentence	I feel that the so-called smart kids get far too much praise for excellence in academics.
	topic sentence	Education is a great thing.
	topic sentence	I feel that education is incorrectly defined in other parts of the world, and that our international peers are becoming stupid by their schooling.
C.	*thesis statement*	Thanks to the counseling required by the college prior to registration, the helpful staff, and the job placement office, my first college semester was a success.
	topic sentence	As I analyzed my first college semester, I realized that the success I experienced was the result of the counseling I received before enrolling.
	topic sentence	During this first semester, I also found the staff to be informative and helpful.
	topic sentence	Most important, the job placement assistance I received from the college made it possible to succeed the first semester.
D.	*thesis statement*	Straight "A" students might end up making the most money, but most of them are creating a huge hole for themselves that will only get bigger until they can't get out.
	topic sentence	Many of the prestigious students might be book smart, but they lack social skills.
	topic sentence	One major factor in a happy life is health.
	topic sentence	America's job force has changed dramatically within the last couple of years, with the type of person they hire for positions.
E.	*thesis statement*	I agree that going through life "mindlessly" makes a person accept the norm and suppresses the creative side of human behavior.
	topic sentence	Being mindful involves forcing ourselves into looking at things from a different point of view.

topic sentence	Being mindful also means using your imagination and creativity to learn what works best for you as an individual.
topic sentence	One last definition of what being mindless means is best portrayed by elderly people at retirement homes.

READINGS

Are Families Dangerous?   BARBARA EHRENREICH

Barbara Ehrenreich is an award-winning political essayist and social critic whose scathing commentaries have appeared in dozens of magazines, including Time *magazine,* The Nation, Harper's, Z Magazine, *and* Mother Jones. *She is also the author or co-author of twelve books. In the following selection, she levels her critical gaze on one of the most cherished American institutions, the family.*

BEFORE YOU READ

1. Consider the title of this selection. What is your response to it?
2. Consider people you know. Would different people respond to the title of this selection in different ways?

A disturbing subtext runs through our recent media fixations. Parents abuse sons—allegedly at least, in the Menendez case—who in turn rise up and kill them. A husband torments a wife, who retaliates with a kitchen knife. Love turns into obsession, between the Simpsons anyway, and then perhaps into murderous rage: the family, in other words, becomes personal hell. 1

This accounts for at least part of our fascination with the Bobbitts and the Simpsons and the rest of them. We live in a culture that fetishes the family as the ideal unit of human community, the perfect container for our lusts and loves. Politicians of both parties are aggressively "pro-family," even abortion-rights bumper stickers proudly link "pro-family" and "pro-choice." Only with the occasional celebrity crime do we allow ourselves to think the nearly unthinkable: that the family may not be the ideal and perfect living arrangement after all—that it can be a nest of pathology and a cradle of gruesome violence. 2

It's a scary thought, because the family is at the same time our "haven in a heartless world." Theoretically, and sometimes actually, the family nurtures warm, loving feelings, uncontaminated by 3 greed or power hunger. Within the family, and often only within the family, individuals are loved "for themselves," whether or not they are infirm, incontinent, infantile or eccentric. The strong (adults and especially males) lie down peaceably with the small and weak.

But consider the matter of wife battery. We managed to dodge it in the Bobbitt case and downplay it as a force in Tonya Harding's life. Thanks to O.J., though, we're caught up now in a mass consciousness-raising session, grimly absorbing the fact that in some areas domestic violence sends as many women to emergency rooms as any other form of illness, injury or assault.   4

Still, we shrink from the obvious inference: for a woman, home is, statistically speaking, the most dangerous place to be. Her worst enemies and potential killers are not strangers but lovers, husbands and those who claimed to love her once. Similarly, for every child like Polly Klaas who is killed by a deranged criminal on parole, dozens are abused and murdered by their own relatives. Home is all too often where the small and weak fear to lie down and shut their eyes.   5

At some deep, queasy, Freudian level, we all know this. Even in the ostensibly "functional," nonviolent family, where no one is killed or maimed, feelings are routinely bruised and often twisted out of shape. There is the slap or put-down that violates a child's shaky sense of self, the cold, distracted stare that drives a spouse to tears, the little digs and rivalries. At best, the family teaches the finest things human beings can learn from one another—generosity and love. But it is also, all too often, where we learn nasty things like hate and rage and shame.   6

Americans act out their ambivalence about the family without ever owning up to it. Millions adhere to creeds that are militantly "pro-family." But at the same time millions flock to therapy groups that offer to heal the "inner child" from damage inflicted by family life. Legions of women band together to revive the self-esteem they lost in supposedly loving relationships and to learn to love a little less. We are all, it is often said, "in recovery." And from what? Our families, in most cases.   7

There is a long and honorable tradition of "anti-family" thought. The French philosopher Charles Fourier taught that the family was a barrier to human progress; early feminists saw a degrading parallel between marriage and prostitution. More recently, the renowned British anthropologist Edmund Leach stated that "far   8 from being the basis of the good society, the family, with its narrow privacy and tawdry secrets, is the source of all discontents."

Communes proved harder to sustain than plain old couples, and the conservatism of the 80s crushed the last vestiges of life-style experimentation. Today even gays and lesbians are eager to get married and take up family life. Feminists have learned to couch their concerns as "family issues," and public figures would sooner advocate free cocaine on demand than criticize the family. Hence our unseemly interest in O.J. and Erik, Lyle and Lorena: they allow us, however gingerly, to break the silence on the hellish side of family life.   9

But the discussion needs to become a lot more open and forthright. We may be stuck with the family—at least until some-one invents a sustainable alternative—but the family, with its deep, impacted tensions and longings, can hardly be expected to be the moral foundation of everything else. In fact, many families could use a lot more outside interference in the form of counseling and policing, and some are so dangerously dysfunctional that they ought to be encouraged to disband right away. Even healthy fami-lies need outside sources of moral guidance to keep the internal tensions from imploding—and this means, at the very least, a pub-lic philosophy of gender equality and concern for child welfare. When, instead, the larger culture aggrandizes wife beaters, de-grades women or nods approvingly at child slappers, the family gets a little more dangerous for everyone, and so, inevitably, does the larger world.   10

AFTER YOU READ

Work with other students to develop responses to these questions or to compare responses that you have already prepared.

1. Use your own words to state the thesis of the article. Then identify any sentence or sentences in the article that seem to express the idea.
2. Divide the article into sections according to each major point that Ehrenreich makes.
3. In three or four sentences, briefly summarize the thesis of the article and its major supporting points.
4. Identify the types of support that Ehrenreich uses. Does she use brief or extended examples, statistics, or expert testimony?
5. Look at paragraphs 4, 5, and 6 (or other paragraphs assigned by your instructor), and explain how the coherence is maintained from sen-tence to sentence.

A Generation of Bigots Comes of Age   RICHARD COHEN

Richard Cohen has been writing a twice-weekly column for The Washington Post *since 1976. Born in New York City, Cohen graduated from both New York University and the Columbia University Graduate School of Journalism. In the following column, he explores a disturbing trend in the attitudes of younger Americans.*

BEFORE YOU READ

1. Look at the title. What is a bigot? What does the title suggest will be the central idea of this article?
2. In what age group would you expect to find the most bigotry—older Americans, middle-aged Americans, or younger Americans? Why?

There's hardly a politician in the land who, when children are mentioned, does not say they are our future. That's true, of course—and nothing can be done about it—but the way things are going we should all be worried. A generation of bigots is coming of age.   1

The evidence for that awful prognostication can be found in a recent public opinion survey conducted for the Anti-Defamation League by the Boston polling firm of Marttila & Kiley—two outfits with considerable credentials in the field of public opinion research.   2

For the first time, a trend has been reversed. Up to now, opinion polls have always found that the more schooling a person has, the more likely he is to be tolerant. For that reason, older people—who by and large have the least education—are the most intolerant age group in the nation.   3

But no longer. The ADL found a disturbing symmetry: Older and younger white Americans share the same biases. For instance, when white people were asked if blacks prefer to remain on welfare rather than work, 42 percent of the respondents 50 years old and over said the statement was "probably true." Predictably, the figure plummeted to 29 percent for those 30 to 49. But then it jumped to 36 percent for respondents under 30.   4

Similarly, a majority of younger respondents thought blacks "complain too much about racism" (68 percent) and "stick together more than others" (63 percent). For both statements, the young had a higher percentage of agreement than any other age category.   5

The pattern persisted for the other questions as well—questions designed to ferret out biased attitudes. In the words of Abraham Foxman, the ADL's national director, the generation that's destined to run this country is either racist or disposed to   6 racism to a degree that he characterized as "a crisis." It's hard to disagree with him.

What's going on? The short answer is that no one knows for sure. But some guesses can be ventured and none of them are comforting. The first and most obvious explanation has to do with age itself: The under-30 generation is pathetically ignorant of recent American history.   7

Younger people apparently know little about—and did not see on television—the civil rights struggles of the 1950s and 1960s, everything from the police dogs of Birmingham to the murder of civil rights workers. They apparently do not understand that if blacks tend to see racism everywhere, that's because in the recent past, it was everywhere and remains the abiding American sickness.   8

But historical ignorance is not the only factor accounting for the ADL's findings. Another, apparently, is affirmative action. It has created a category of white victims, either real or perceived, who are more likely than other whites to hold prejudicial views.   9

For instance, when the ADL asked "Do you feel you have ever been a victim of reverse discrimination in hiring or promotion," only 21 percent said yes. But the percentage rose to 26 percent for college graduates and 23 percent for people with post-graduate degrees. Since the ADL found that "about one-third" of the self-described victims of reverse discrimination fell into the "most prejudiced" category, these numbers are clearly worth worrying about.   10

Too many of the American elite are racially aggrieved—although possibly some of them were bigoted in the first place.   11

One could argue that not all of the statements represent proof of bigoted attitudes. For instance, white college students who witness voluntary self-segregation on the part of black students—demands for their own dorms, for instance—have some reason to think that blacks "stick together more than others."   12

Nevertheless, the data strongly suggests that progress on racial attitudes is being reversed—with contributions from both races. Worse, this is happening at a time when the economic pie is shrinking and competition for jobs increasing. If the economic trend continues, racial intolerance is likely to grow.   13

It's nothing less than a calamity that a generation has come of age without a deep appreciation of the recent history of African-Americans. At the same time, black leaders who advocate or condone separatism had better appreciate the damage they are doing.   14

And finally, affirmative action programs, as well-intentioned   15
as they may be, need to be re-examined—and without critics automatically being labeled as racist. No doubt these programs have
done some good. But there's a growing body of evidence—of
which the ADL poll is only the latest—that they also do some bad.

AFTER YOU READ

Work with other students to develop responses to these questions or to
compare responses that you have already prepared.

1. Use your own words to state the thesis of the article. Then identify any
   sentence or sentences in the article that seem to express the idea.
2. Divide the article into sections according to each major point that Cohen makes.
3. In three or four sentences, briefly summarize the thesis of the article
   and its major supporting points.
4. Paragraphs 2 to 6 serve a purpose different from paragraphs 7 to 11.
   Explain that difference.
5. Identify the types of support that Cohen uses.
6. Look at paragraphs 12 and 13 (or other paragraphs assigned by your
   instructor), and explain how the coherence is maintained from sentence to sentence.

Colorblind   ALEX KOTLOWITZ

*Alex Kotlowitz is an award-winning writer whose articles on urban affairs, poverty,
social policy, and race appear in such national magazines as the* New Yorker *and
the* New York Times Sunday Magazine. *He is best known for his award-winning
nonfiction book* There Are No Children Here, *which examines life in a Chicago
housing project through the eyes of two young brothers.*

BEFORE YOU READ

1. "Colorblind" is a common term that some people use to refer to a racial
   attitude. What does it suggest to you? Do you consider yourself to be
   colorblind?
2. Kotlowitz suggests that black Americans and white Americans often
   see the same event from a different perspective. Consider why that
   might be so as you read the selection.

One Christmas day seven years ago, I'd gone over to the Henry   1
Horner Homes in Chicago to visit with Lafeyette and Pharoah, the
subjects of my book *There Are No Children Here.* I had brought
presents for the boys, as well as a gift for their friend Rickey, who

lived on the other side of the housing complex, an area controlled by a rival gang. Lafeyette and Pharoah insisted on walking over with me. It was eerily quiet, since most everyone was inside, and so, bundled from the cold, we strolled toward the other end in silence. As we neared Damen Avenue, a kind of demilitarized zone, a uniformed police officer, a white woman, approached us. She looked first at the two boys, neither of whom reached my shoulder, and then directly at me. "Are you O.K.?" she asked.

About a year later, I was with Pharoah on the city's North   2
Side, shopping for high-tops. We were walking down the busy street, my hand on Pharoah's shoulder, when a middle-aged black man approached. He looked at me, and then at Pharoah. "Son," he asked, "are you O.K.?"

Both this white police officer and middle-aged black man   3
seemed certain of what they witnessed. The white woman saw a white man possibly in trouble; the black man saw a black boy possibly in trouble. It's all about perspective—which has everything to do with our personal and collective experiences, which are consistently informed by race. From those experiences, from our histories, we build myths, legends that both guide us and constrain us, legends that include both fact and fiction. This is not to say the truth doesn't matter. It does, in a big way. It's just that getting there may not be easy, in part because everyone is so quick to choose sides, to refute the other's myths, and to pass on their own.

. . . While myths help us make sense of the incom-   4
prehensible, they can also confine us, confuse us, and leave us prey to historical laziness. Moreover, truth is not always easily discernible—and even when it is, the prism, depending on which side of the river you reside on, may create a wholly different illusion. Many whites were quick to believe Susan Smith, the South Carolina mother who claimed that a black man had killed her children. And with the reawakening of the Tawana Brawley case, we learn that, although a grand jury has determined otherwise, many blacks still believe she was brutally raped by a group of white men. We—blacks and whites—need to examine and question our own perspectives. Only then can we grasp each other's myths and grapple with the truths.

In 1992, I came across the story of a sixteen-year-old black   5
boy, Eric McGinnis, whose body had been found a year earlier floating in the St. Joseph River in southwestern Michigan. The river flows between Benton Harbor and St. Joseph, two small towns

whose only connections are two bridges and a powerful under-
tow of contrasts.

St. Joseph is a town of 9,000 and, with its quaint downtown   6
and brick-paved streets, resembles a New England tourist haunt.
But for those in Benton Harbor, St. Joseph's most defining characteristic is its racial makeup: It is 95 percent white. Benton Harbor,
a town of 12,000 on the other side of the river, is 92 percent
black and dirt poor. For years, the municipality so hurt for money
that it could not afford to raze abandoned buildings.

Eric, a high-school sophomore whose passion was dancing,   7
was last seen at the Club, a teen-age nightspot in St. Joseph,
where weeks earlier he had met and started dating a white girl.
The night Eric disappeared, a white man said he caught the boy
trying to break into his car and chased him—away from the river,
past an off-duty white deputy sheriff. That was the last known
moment he was seen alive, and it was then that the myths began.

I became obsessed with Eric's death, and so for five years   8
moved in and out of these two communities, searching for answers to both Eric's disappearance and to matters of race. People
would often ask which side of the river I was staying on, wanting
to gauge my allegiance. And they would often ask about the secrets of those across the way or, looking for affirmation, repeat
myths passed on from one generation to the next.

Once, during an unusually bitter effort by white school-   9
board members to fire Benton Harbor's black superintendent, one
black woman asked me: "How do you know how to do this? Do
you take lessons? How do you all stick together the way you do?"
Of course, we don't. Neither community is as unified or mono-
lithic as the other believes. Indeed, contrary to the impression of
those in St. Joseph, the black community itself was deeply divided
in its support for the superintendent, who was eventually fired.

On occasion, whites in St. Joseph would regale me with tales   10
of families migrating to Benton Harbor from nearby states for the
high welfare benefits. It is, they would tell me, the reason for the
town's economic decline. While some single mothers indeed moved
to Benton Harbor and other Michigan cities in the early 1980s to receive public assistance, the truth is that in the 1930s and 1940s, factories recruited blacks from the South, and when those factories
shut down, unemployment, particularly among blacks, skyrocketed.

But the question most often asked was: "Why us? Why write   11
about St. Joseph and Benton Harbor?" I would tell them that while

the contrasts between the towns seem unusually stark, they are, I believe, typical of how most of us live: physically and spiritually isolated from one another.

It's not that I didn't find individuals who crossed the river to spend time with their neighbors. One St. Joseph woman, Amy Johnson, devotes her waking hours to a Benton Harbor community center. And Eric McGinnis himself was among a handful of black teenagers who spent weekend nights at the Club in St. Joseph. Nor is it that I didn't find racial animosity. One St. Joseph resident informed me that Eric got what he deserved: "That nigger came on the wrong side of the bridge," he said. And Benton Harbor's former school superintendent, Sherwin Alien, made no effort to hide his contempt for the white power structure.   12

What I found in the main, though, were people who would like to do right but don't know where to begin. As was said of the South's politicians during Jim Crow, race diminishes us. It incites us to act as we wouldn't in other arenas: clumsily, cowardly, and sometimes cruelly. We circle the wagons, watching out for our own.   13

That's what happened in the response to Eric's death. Most everyone in St. Joseph came to believe that Eric, knowing the police were looking for him, tried to swim the river to get home and drowned. Most everyone in Benton Harbor, with equal certitude, believes that Eric was killed—most likely by whites, most likely because he dated a white girl. I was struck by the disparity in perspective, the competing realities, but I was equally taken aback by the distance between the two towns—which, of course, accounts for the myths. Jim Reeves, the police lieutenant who headed the investigation into Eric's death, once confided that this teenager he'd never met had more impact on him than any other black person.   14

I'm often asked by whites, with some wonderment, how it is that I'm able to spend so much time in black communities without feeling misunderstood or unwelcomed or threatened. I find it much easier to talk with blacks about race than with fellow whites. While blacks often brave slights silently for fear that if they complain they won't be believed, when asked, they welcome the chance to relate their experiences. Among whites, there's a reluctance—or a lack of opportunity—to engage. Race for them poses no urgency; it does not impose on their daily routines. I once asked Ben Butzbaugh, a St. Joseph commissioner, how he felt the two towns got along. "I think we're pretty fair in this community," he said. "I don't know that I can say I know of any out-and-out   15

racial-type things that occur. I just think people like their own better than others. I think that's pretty universal. Don't you? . . . We're
not a bunch of racists. We're not anything America isn't."
Butzbaugh proudly pointed to his friendship with Renee Williams,
Benton Harbor's new school superintendent. "Renee was in our
home three, four, five days a week," he noted. "Nice gal. Put herself
through school. We'd talk all the time." Williams used to clean for
Butzbaugh's family.

As I learned during the years in and out of these towns, the   16
room for day-to-day dialogue doesn't present itself. We become
buried in our myths, certain of our truths—and refuse to acknowledge what the historian Allan Nevins calls "the grains of stony
reality" embedded in most legends. A quarter-century ago, race
was part of everyday public discourse; today it haunts us quietly,
though on occasion—the Rodney King beating or the Simpson
trial or Eric McGinnis's death—it erupts with jarring urgency. At
these moments of crisis, during these squalls, we flail about—trying
to find moral ballast. By then it is usually too late. The lines are
drawn. Accusations are hurled across the river like cannon fire. And
the cease-fires, when they occur, are just that, cease-fires, tempo-
rary and fragile. Even the best of people have already chosen sides.

AFTER YOU READ

Work with other students to develop responses to these questions or to
compare responses that you have already prepared.

1. Use your own words to state the thesis of the article. Then identify any
   sentence or sentences in the article that seem to express the idea.
2. Divide the article into sections according to each major point that
   Kotlowitz makes.
3. In three or four sentences, briefly summarize the thesis of the article
   and its major supporting points.
4. Identify the types of support that Kotlowitz uses.
5. Choose one paragraph from the article, and explain how its coherence
   is maintained from sentence to sentence.

Video Games Can Be Helpful to College Students   SCOTT CARLSON

Scott Carlson is a staff reporter for The Chronicle of Higher Education. *In the
following selection, he discusses a report that suggests video games have little effect
on a college student's performance.*

BEFORE YOU READ

1. Consider your own experience with video games. Do you play them? If so, what kind do you play and how often?
2. In your experience, do video games interfere with your education? If you play video games, would you be a better student without them?

A report released last month suggests that video games are a vital and positive part of college students' social lives, even though games may be keeping them from their studies. 1

The study on which the report was based was conducted by the Pew Internet and American Life Project, which sponsors research to gauge the effect of the Internet on various aspects of everyday life. The researchers made distinctions among video games played online, those played through a personal computer, and those using a dedicated video-game console, such as a Sony PlayStation. 2

The study shows that for this generation of college students, gaming does not edge out other activities, says Steve Jones, a professor of communication at the University of Illinois at Chicago, who supervised the research. 3

"It's been with them forever, and they have never had to choose between gaming and other things," he says. "It's already been in the mix for them since the kindergarten days. . . . It's not that disruptive as a result." 4

The researchers distributed paper surveys to more than 1,100 students at colleges across the country. The findings are accurate to within 3.5 percentage points, the report says. 5

The study's least surprising finding is that most respondents— 65 percent—said they were regular video-game players. One in five college students said games had helped them develop, and even improve, friendships. Sixty percent said games provided a pastime when friends are not around. 6

The genders showed differences in the ways that they approached games: Women play computer and Internet games more than men, while the two sexes play console games at about the same rate. The researchers speculate that because console games are generally more violent and feature stereotyped gender roles, they are less attractive to women. 7

"The men were telling us that gaming was a standard part of the entertainment and media mix for them, and it was something they looked forward to doing," Mr. Jones says. "Women were telling us that they were doing it to kill time, so it wasn't as prominent an activity in their everyday lives." 8

The time spent on gaming and socializing does seem to cut into classwork. About half of the students said gaming distracts them from studying.   9

For one in 10, gaming is a procrastination tool. A third of the respondents said they played games during class.   10

However, in a somewhat contradictory finding, two-thirds of the students said video games had no effect on their college performance. The researchers noted that the amount of time the students spent studying closely matched the results of other surveys. Sixty-two percent of the students said they studied about 7 hours a week, and 15 percent said they studied 12 hours a week.   11

James Gee, a professor of education at the University of Wisconsin at Madison, is not heartened by the figures on students' reported study habits—merely an hour a day for a full load of college courses.   12

But the professor, whose book *What Video Games Have to Teach Us about Learning and Literacy* was published in May, says that in his research on high-school and middle-school students, he has had a hard time finding any whose schoolwork is, in fact, damaged by video games. "From the earliest ages, the game is one among multiple tasks that people do and switch between," he says.   13

Gaming is a much more integral part of students' social lives than the Pew study suggests, Mr. Gee believes. "The report is a good first swipe, but with any new technology, you want to know what the niches are," he says.   14

Mr. Jones says the study is only a beginning for research on video games—something that could be used to push the creation of educational games for students.   15

"Those of us working in higher education could do more to show some of the positive sides of gaming," he says. "In some ways, it's unfortunate that we call them games, because that makes it hard for us to take them seriously."   16

AFTER YOU READ

1. State the thesis of the article in your own words. Then identify any sentences in the article that express that idea.
2. Divide the article into sections according to each major point that Carlson makes.
3. In three or four sentences, briefly summarize the thesis of the article and its major supporting points.
4. Identify the types of support that Carlson uses.
5. Choose one or more paragraphs from the article, and explain how its coherence is maintained from sentence to sentence.

WRITING ASSIGNMENTS

1. In "Are Families Dangerous?" Barbara Ehrenreich writes, "At best, the family teaches the finest things human beings can learn from one another—generosity and love. But it is also, all too often, where we learn nasty things like hate and rage and shame." What do you think of this statement? Write a paper in which you illustrate your response with examples drawn from your own experiences and/or the experiences of people you know.

2. Ehrenreich suggests that we are all, in some sense, "in recovery" from our families. Do you suppose such a statement might be true even for loving, supportive families? Write a paper in which you illustrate your ideas with examples drawn from your own experiences and/or the experiences of people you know.

3. According to Richard Cohen, the national director of the Anti-Defamation League believes that "the generation that's destined to run this country is either racist or disposed to racism to a degree that he characterized as 'a crisis.'" Do your own experiences confirm or contradict this view? Write a paper in which you illustrate either in what ways attitudes of younger Americans are racist, intolerant, and bigoted or in what ways they are open, tolerant, and accepting of other races, religions, lifestyles, or cultures. Support your ideas with examples drawn from your own experiences and observations.

4. Toward the end of his essay, Richard Cohen offers three reasons for the apparent racism of young Americans. Write an essay in which you offer your own explanations for racism among the young. Use examples drawn from your own experiences and observations to support your reasons.

5. In "Colorblind," Alex Kotlowitz writes, "We—blacks and whites—need to examine and question our own perspectives. Only then can we grasp each other's myths and grapple with truths." Consider the perspectives with which you were raised concerning people of other races or colors. What were they? Write a paper in which you use examples to illustrate what Kotlowitz calls the "myths" about other groups you or members of your family might have held—or do hold.

6. Consider the community in which you live in light of Kotlowitz's "Colorblind." What groups might not be easily accepted by your community? Why not? Does your community's attitude suggest prejudice or intolerance? Write a paper that uses specific examples to illustrate your points. As you think about this topic, consider not only racial groups but also people of various religious persuasions, age ranges, income levels, or sexual orientations.

7. In "Video Games Can Be Helpful to College Students," Scott Carlson discusses a study that examined the effect of video games on college students. The report, he says, "suggests that video games are a vital and positive part of college students' social lives, even though games may be keeping them from their studies." What do you think of this

statement? Is it true for you or for people you know? Write a paper in which you offer your own analysis of the effects of video games on the people who play them. Use specific examples drawn from your personal experiences or observations.

8. According to Scott Carlson, the study of video games "made distinctions among video games played online, those played through a personal computer, and those using a dedicated video-game console, such as a Sony PlayStation." In your experience, what distinctions might one make among these three types? Do they offer different types of games? Do they attract different types of people? Does one type attract or repel one gender over another? Write a paper in which you use specific examples drawn from your personal experiences or observations.

EVALUATING SAMPLE PAPERS

As you read and evaluate the quality of the essays on the following pages, consider these areas:

1. Thesis Statement
   Underline the thesis statement of the essay. Does it express a clear and specific central idea?

   1   2   3   4   5   6

2. Topic Sentences
   Underline the topic sentence of each paragraph. Does it clearly state the central idea of the paragraph?

   1   2   3   4   5   6

3. Support
   Examine the supporting details in each paragraph. Are they specific and clear? Should they be more detailed, or should more support be included?

   1   2   3   4   5   6

4. Unity
   Does each paragraph clearly relate to and develop the central idea expressed in the thesis statement? Do the supporting details *within* each paragraph clearly relate to and develop the *central idea* expressed in the topic sentence of that paragraph?

   1   2   3   4   5   6

5. Coherence
   Does each paragraph open with a transition, a reference to the central idea of the thesis statement, and an identification of its own central idea? Are the sentences within each paragraph clearly related to each other by the use of transitions or by references to the central idea of the paragraph?

   1   2   3   4   5   6

6. Sentence Structure

   Do the sentences combine ideas that are related, using coordination and subordination when appropriate? Are there too many brief, choppy main clauses?

   1   2   3   4   5   6

7. Mechanics, Grammar, and Spelling

   Does the paper contain a distracting number of errors of these kinds?

   1   2   3   4   5   6

8. Overall Ranking of the Essay

   1   2   3   4   5   6

Student Essay 1

"At best, the family teaches the finest things human beings can learn from one another—generosity and love. But it is also, all too often, where we learn nasty things like hate and rage and shame." This quote couldn't be anymore true. Our family structure today is not one of the families portrayed on sitcoms like *The Brady Bunch* or *Leave It to Beaver*. On the contrary, when troubles rise up, families usually can't resolve their problems in a quick and civil manner. Sure, we learn about love and sharing in a family unit, but the sharing of living quarters seems to bring waves of awful situations that bring about hateful feelings. We learn about the worst attributes of human nature like jealousy, hate, revenge, and spite. Moreover, when families have issues of communication, these everyday quarrels can turn into a dangerous situation and teach harmful ways to solve them. I see in my friend's family and my own that these things have been developed at home because of the failure to communicate and resolve problems in a compromising and calm manner. Families can be the most dangerous place when problems are left to fester, stubbornness resides in the home, and communication ceases.

When a conflict is avoided and no one deals with it, the household can become a volcano ready to burst. My aunt Lily thought her newlywed would give up alcohol on his own as times passed because they were happy. Of course, Samuel was never confronted that his drinking was a problem for Lily, and the problem began to escalate. Samuel didn't get the help he needed right away, as my aunt got more and more upset about it, but said nothing. Time only made the problem grow enough for him to become an alcoholic. As a result, he became violent and mistreated Lily, blaming her for all his problems. Because they did not deal with the situation early on, the home they shared became a vault of drunken violence and anger. The household becomes a dangerous place when there is a lack of communication and problems are left to grow among the family.

As communication ceases, so does the chance of having healthy relationships in the family. Without communication, others under the same roof will become agitated, and everyone will go misunderstood and angry. My friend's mom is an example of this with her cousins. They had stopped communicating when a problem arose, and feelings of jealousy and spite festered within the family. When my friend wanted to learn Tongan, her mother's native language, she had only snapped at her. My friend Veronica was not encouraged to learn the language because her mom refused to let her know what their family said about them when they gathered, unpleasantly, for family occasions. When communication stops among a family, the household will become unpleasant and tense. The family begins to build up a wall of stubbornness and bitterness among each other, only making the household an even worse place to be.

If issues are dealt with in stubborn pride, then no one agrees to compromise, hostility is imminent, and people can become violent. In my own home, for the past few years, there has been a wall built up by my father and brother concerning the actions my brother chose to do, and the wrong path he has been following. Instead of finding an effective way to communicate with my brother in order to deal with the situation, my father shut Steve out, making him feel excluded and trying to bear shame for his actions on his shoulders. Instead, my brother was bitter and very stubborn (as is my father) making the family against each other when sides seemed to be picked. It split the family into pieces, causing pain and misery for everyone involved. Stubbornness gets us nowhere, yet it's only human to be defiant and protect your pride. So the home becomes violent, as my father did not know how to control my angry, bitter brother. Instead of talking it out, they both resorted in abuse, not of each other but the whole family because of their shared unhappiness. Emotional abuse, and in the case of my mother, Steve would use her and sometimes physically hurt her when she did not get him out of all the problems he put himself into. When Steve went to Juvenile Hall, our family seemed lost in a wave of disappointment in one another for letting this happen. Because of our pride, no one gave in to compromise and as a result my brother Steve did not change his ways. Letting things get out of control this way only makes the family a dangerous and scary place.

Problems are unavoidable, yet the way we handle them within the family can be either a learning experience for the better, or a nightmare to live with. The approach to the problem is how to judge the safety and security a home can have. When issues are left unfixed, family members stop speaking, and people let their pride get in the way of getting through it, the household is dangerous, and even unbearable. The home is supposed to be a place of escape from the dangers of the world, not a place you want to escape from.

Student Essay 2

Throughout my life I and people I know have experienced intolerance, racism, or bigotry. Richard Cohen explains in his article how people in America are still experiencing bigotry and intolerance for being the race they are. Cohen feels that we should be worried about the way things are going in America because a generation of bigots is coming of age. I feel that he is correct in this assumption.

This intolerance of other races comes from people who have never experienced intolerance in their lives. For example, when I was a little girl, my next door neighbors kids would come out and play with my sister and me, but they'd call us names and put us down by saying bad things about Mexicans, they obviously didn't like people of our race mixing with theirs. So, we tried to stay away from them as much as possible. These kids just didn't know to act any better because of the way they were raised. Some people are just raised to not like certain races and act differently toward them.

The reality of how people may be so intolerant toward other peoples races is being very closed minded. Like Cohen stated in his article ". . . if blacks tend to see racism everywhere . . . it was everywhere and remains the abiding American sickness." To live in America you have to get accustomed to their culture and race, but people want to stick to their own. For example, when we visit with the cousins on my moms side of the family, they want us to leave our Mexican customs and heritage behind because they want us to be like they are which is having a white tradition.

Cohen raises this bigotry issue that touches everyone who's been treated with intolerance in the past. But no one wants to have to change themselves to try to fit in more with other races than their own. Like me when I was little and played with my next door neighbors I just wished that we could all just play together without worrying about being a different race, so that meant we couldn't play together. Somehow almost everyone out there is guilty of being a racist or bigot because we don't all get along and we don't all like everyone else. Maybe this is just a part of living in America and it will never change.

Student Essay 3

In Richard Cohen's article "A Generation of Bigots Comes of Age," he suggests we should all be concerned that our children are growing up intolerant of other races. This reminds me of the billboard with a picture of an African-American child and a white child with their arms around each other's backs and a caption that read, "They are not born hating each other." The billboard reflects what I have experienced with children today. I believe children have a more open and accepting attitude toward other races. I think this can be credited to the education of children.

One example of how we are educating our children is through the television set. Television is often the sole exposure to images of minorities. The persuasiveness of the media can profoundly influence children's ideas of the world they live in. For example, Barney the dinosaur uses a variety of different races in his "backyard gang." There are Hispanic, African-American, and Asian, as well as Caucasian. Another example would be *Sesame Street,* where they promote friendship between children of many different races. Furthermore, they also use animals and friendly monsters to demonstrate that it is not important what you look like but how you treat others.

Through school, children are also being educated about racial tolerance. My oldest son started school in Valley Center, where he was enrolled in bilingual education. He was taught in both English and Spanish. One day all his lessons would be in English whether it be math or colors and shapes then the next day he would be taught in Spanish. Not only that but they encouraged friendship with all the children in class by making sure that they mixed the Spanish speaking students into study groups with the English speaking students, so that they could help each other understand the lessons. They have a large number of migrant workers and also Indians from a nearby reservation. They educated the children on the different cultures on national and religious holidays. For instance, St. Patrick's Day comes with a social studies lesson on Ireland. The students also celebrate the Chinese New Year, Cinco de Mayo, and they have a study of African-American history during which they celebrate Martin Luther King, Jr. Day.

Similarly, children are being taught tolerance through neighborhood friendships. When you come into our neighborhood, you will see all of the children playing together. We have children from all different races none of them are concerned with what color skin the other has. Some examples are Vanessa and David, who are American Indian; Aaron, Javier, and Claudia, who are Hispanic; Jovonne, Huesson, and Anjenneta, who are African-American; and Jennifer, Mark, and Kevin, who are Caucasian. This is a vastly different situation from when I was growing up, because we had no other races, the only differences were our hair or eye color. Of course, I had heard it said that friendship has a color all its own. I believe children today have proven that statement.

Consequently, as our children grow we will see many changes in this nation. One change is already taking effect at this time. This nation is moving toward a global economy, and with this move we need to understand that people, regardless of skin color, are a very important part of the picture. Furthermore, the friendships children are building now will last as they grow. As a result, the ignorance and bigotry of the past will continue to shrink. In fact, through education and knowledge bigotry cannot survive.

SENTENCE COMBINING: VERBAL PHRASES

The verbal phrase is an easy and effective way to add more information to your sentences without using a full clause to do so. In fact, you already use verbal phrases every day, both in your speech and in your writing. When you write "The man crossing the street waved at the irate motorists," you use a verbal phrase ("crossing the street"). The sentence "The plan to rob the bank was nearly flawless" also contains a verbal phrase ("to rob the bank").

Although people use verbal phrases unconsciously in their speech and writing, learning how to use them in a planned, conscious manner can improve your writing in two ways. First, using verbal phrases will allow you to add more action and description to your writing without using additional sentences. As a result, your writing will have a sense of depth and detail that will distinguish it from the prose of the average writer. Second, using these phrases will allow you to vary the structure of the sentences that you write, and a varied sentence structure makes for more interesting reading than sentence after sentence written exactly the same way.

A **verbal** is simply a verb form that is not used as a verb. For example, in the following sentences, the underlined verb forms are used as adjectives, not as verbs.

The <u>singing</u> cowboy made everybody angry.

The police officer assisted the <u>confused</u> motorist.

Each type of verbal has its own specific name. In the above examples, *singing* is a **present participle** and *confused* is a **past participle**.

PRESENT AND PAST PARTICIPLES

The **present participle** is the "-ing" form of a verb used as an adjective.

> A <u>traveling</u> sales representative decided that he needed a new pair of shoes.

> Mr. Ingham did not know what to do about the <u>barking</u> dogs.

The **past participle** is also used as an adjective. Some past participles end in "-d" or "-ed" *(picked, fired, tossed);* others end in "-n" or "-en" *(eaten, thrown, spoken);* still others have their own unique forms *(sung, brought, gone).* To determine the past participle form of any verb, ask yourself how you would spell the word if "have" preceded it.

> The <u>exhausted</u> jogger decided to rest for an hour.

> The patient with the <u>broken</u> leg was ready to leave the hospital.

PRESENT AND PAST PARTICIPIAL PHRASES

Present and past participial phrases consist of present and past participles with other words added to them to give more details. The following examples are drawn from "Attention Shoppers: Your Dreams in Aisle 3," "A Generation of Bigots Comes of Age," "Video Games Can Be Helpful to College Students," and "Colorblind."

> <u>Revealing their own tensions over gender,</u> the mothers claim that the children's fathers are more likely to buy the kids brand-name shirts or sneakers.

> The evidence for that awful prognostication can be found in a recent public opinion survey <u>conducted for the Anti-Defamation League by the Boston polling firm of Marttila & Kiley</u>. . . .

> A report <u>released last month</u> suggests that video games are a vital and positive part of college students' social lives. . . .

> We circle the wagons, <u>watching out for our own</u>.

INFINITIVE PHRASES

The **infinitive** is another type of verbal. It consists of the base form of a verb preceded by "to" *(to throw, to breathe, to eat).* The **infinitive phrase** consists of the infinitive with other words added to it to give more details. Here are some examples from "Are Families Dangerous?":

> Legions of women band together <u>to revive the self-esteem they lost in supposedly loving relationships</u> and <u>to learn to love a little less</u>.

> Even healthy families need outside sources of moral guidance <u>to keep the internal tensions from imploding</u>. . . .

USING VERBAL PHRASES

Participial and infinitive phrases can be used to improve your writing in several ways:

1. *Use Verbal Phrases to Develop Sentences by Adding Details and Ideas.* Participial phrases are particularly effective for adding details to your sentences. Since participles are verbals, they work especially well when you are describing actions. Notice how the writers of the articles in this text used verbal phrases to expand their sentences:

> Through sports, children learn how to handle defeat as well as victory.
>
> Through sports, children learn how to handle defeat as well as victory—<u>no sulking, gloating or rubbing it in.</u>
>
> Giving directly to the street person—well, that's another matter.
>
> Giving directly to the street person <u>shambling across my pathway</u>—well, that's another matter.

2. *Use Verbal Phrases to Combine Related Sentences.* Verbal phrases often can be used to create one sentence from two or more related sentences. Note how the following sentences can be combined using verbal phrases:

> **Two sentences:** Seymour stared at his lottery ticket in amazement. He could not believe that he had just won ten million dollars.
>
> **One sentence using a present participial phrase:** <u>Staring at his lottery ticket in amazement</u>, Seymour could not believe that he had just won ten million dollars.
>
> **Two sentences:** A body was found in the Alps last year. It had been frozen for over three thousand years.
>
> **One sentence using a past participial phrase:** A body <u>frozen for over three thousand years</u> was found in the Alps last year.
>
> **Two sentences:** Michelle wanted to pass the midterm on Monday. She knew that she should study all weekend.
>
> **One sentence using an infinitive phrase:** Michelle knew that she should study all weekend <u>to pass the midterm on Monday.</u>

3. *Use Verbal Phrases to Be Concise.* Many subordinate clauses can easily and more concisely be written as verbal phrases.

> The sycamore tree <u>that is growing next to our driveway</u> has started to drop its leaves.
>
> The sycamore tree <u>growing next to our driveway</u> has started to drop its leaves.
>
> <u>Because he thought that he had seen a ghost</u>, Herman began to scream.
>
> <u>Thinking that he had seen a ghost</u>, Herman began to scream.
>
> The person <u>who was accused of shoplifting</u> insisted that she had paid for all her items.
>
> The person <u>accused of shoplifting</u> insisted that she had paid for all her items.

EXERCISE 4.5

Develop the following sentences by adding verbal phrases to them where indicated. Use verbals derived from the verbs in parentheses.

EXAMPLE

∧Lyle stared at the paper in front of him. (confuse, determine)
> Confused by the unclear directions but determined to pass the test, Lyle stared at the paper in front of him.

1. ∧ Calvin jogged fifteen miles every day. (prepare)
2. ∧ The mangy alley cat slowly licked its lips. (stare)
3. The driver in the blue Isuzu was driving erratically ∧ . (honk, cut, weave)
4. ∧ George was not in the mood to shop for Christmas trees. (irritate, bother)
5. My six-year-old daughter ∧ walked out of the rain and into our living room. (wear, hold)
6. Narcissus stood before the mirror ∧ . (gaze, wonder)
7. Frankie looked at Annette and told her about his plans ∧ . (quit, buy, move)
8. The UFO ∧ flew into space and never returned. (observe, photograph)
9. ∧ The seven dwarfs headed for the mine. (whistle, sing)
10. Last summer we drove over three thousand miles. ∧ (visit, tour, relax)

EXERCISE 4.6

Combine each of the following groups of sentences* into one sentence. Change each underlined sentence into the type of verbal phrase suggested in parentheses.

EXAMPLE

The macaw emitted an earsplitting shriek.
It flew from the tree.
(present participial phrase)
> Emitting an earsplitting shriek, the macaw flew from the tree.

1. A rogue elephant separates itself from the herd and roams alone.
   It is often quite dangerous.
   (present participial phrase)
2. A solitary rogue elephant can be savage.
   It attacks and kills everyone it can.
   (present participial phrase)
3. A. A. Kinlock, a British authority, wrote that a rogue will often haunt a particular road.

It will stop traffic for as long as it remains.

(present participial phrase)

4. One particular rogue in India seemed determined.

It killed many people and even destroyed their homes.

(infinitive phrase)

5. Carl Ackley was seized and mutilated by a rogue elephant.

Carl Ackley, the father of modern taxidermy, became convinced that the elephant was the most dangerous of all animals.

(past participial phrase)

6. The Asian elephant is considered less temperamental than the African elephant.

It nevertheless more commonly turns rogue.

It accounts for the deaths of more than fifty persons per year.

(past participial phrase and present participial phrase)

7. A rogue elephant wants to destroy its victim.

It will catch him and dismember him.

It will smash him against the ground or a tree.

It will toss him into the air.

(infinitive phrase and two present participial phrases)

8. An elephant may turn rogue because it is suffering from a wound.

The wound may have been inflicted by another elephant or by hunters.

(past participial phrase)

9. In many instances, elephants were found to have been suffering from painful sores and old wounds.

These elephants had been identified as rogues and killed.

(past participial phrase)

10. One Indian rogue suffered from a huge sore at the end of its tail.

It caused great damage.

It chased travelers.

It killed several natives.

(present participial phrases)

*Adapted from Lawrence D. Gadd, The Second Book of the Strange (Amherst, NY: Prometheus Books). © 1981 by Newspaper Enterprise Association. Reprinted by permission of the publisher.

AVOIDING DANGLING MODIFIERS

Because verbal phrases are not verbs, they do not have subjects. However, they do express an action, and the "doer" of that action is usually the subject of the sentence. Whenever you open a sentence with a verbal phrase, be sure that the subject of the sentence is also the "doer." If the subject cannot logically perform the action in the verbal phrase, you have a dangling modifier that needs to be rewritten. (See Chapter 16 for a more thorough discussion of dangling modifiers.)

DANGLING MODIFIER

<u>Sighing with relief</u>, the golf ball rolled into the cup.
  A golf ball cannot sigh with relief.

POSSIBLE CORRECTION

<u>Sighing with relief</u>, the golfer watched as his golf ball rolled into the cup.
  A logical subject has now been supplied. A golfer can sigh with relief.

POSSIBLE CORRECTION

<u>As the golfer sighed with relief</u>, the golf ball rolled into the cup.
  The verbal phrase has been rewritten into a subordinate clause with its own subject and verb.

EXERCISE 4.7

Revise any dangling modifiers in the following sentences, either by supplying a logical subject or by rewriting the verbal phrase as a subordinate clause. Some sentences may be correct.

EXAMPLE

INCORRECT

<u>Surprised by the unexpected rainstorm</u>, our clothing was soon soaked.

CORRECT

<u>Surprised by the unexpected rainstorm</u>, we were all soon soaked.

CORRECT

<u>Because we were all surprised by the unexpected rainstorm</u>, our clothing was soon soaked.

1. Staring at the boiling noodles, the pasta was almost ready.
2. Damaged by the intense heat, Cheryl threw the videocassette into the trash.
3. Turning green with slime and algae, parts of Lake Elsinore soon became a local eyesore.
4. Breaking in through the kitchen window, the stereo equipment and television set were stolen.
5. Frightened by the low moaning sounds coming from the cellar, Herman's hand reached for the phone.

EXERCISE 4.8

Combine the following sentences using verbal phrases. In each case, the first sentence is the main sentence. Each following sentence should be revised as a verbal phrase and added to the beginning or to the end of the main sentence or, occasionally, within the main sentence. Be careful not to write a dangling modifier when you start a sentence with a verbal phrase.

1. According to many legends, a creature lives in the Himalayan mountains of Nepal.
   The creature is named the "abominable snowman" or "Yeti."
2. This creature is said to look half-human, half-ape.
   It stands eight feet tall.
   It is covered in long, white fur.
3. It has icy blue eyes and a second transparent eyelid.
   The second eyelid allows it to see in blowing snow.
   It also prevents its eyes from freezing in cold temperatures.
4. Some people refer to large, unidentifiable footprints.
   These people want to prove that the Yeti exists.
   The footprints have been discovered in the snows of Nepal.
5. The Sherpa, native people, keep the legend of the Yeti alive with stories.
   They live high in the Himalayan mountains.
   Their stories describe their encounters with the creature.
6. Another huge, ape-like creature has been reported.
   It is called Bigfoot in the United States.
   It is called Sasquatch by Canadian Indian tribes.
   It has been reported to exist in the northern United States and Canada.
7. Such a creature has reportedly been sighted in the Pacific Northwest, California, New Jersey, Pennsylvania, Ohio, Illinois, and British Columbia.
   It stands six to eight feet tall.
   It weighs eight hundred or more pounds.
8. Some researchers point to an ancient ape-like creature.
   It is named Gigantopithecus.
   They point to Gigantopithecus to support their theory that Bigfoot might be descended from it.
9. Brazilians tell stories about the Mapinguary.
   The Brazilians are frightened by attacks on their cattle and farms,
   They describe the Mapinguary as an immense, ape-like animal.
10. The Mapinguary fearlessly attacks wild cattle,
    It is also called the Bigfoot of Brazil.
    It leaves behind human-like footprints as long as eighteen inches.

Exploring **ONLINE** Go to www.thomsonedu.com/devenglish/mcdonald for more practice using verbal phrases to combine sentences. Under "Chapter Resources" for Chapter 4, click on "Exploring Online."

PART TWO

Writing about Reading

In the first four chapters of this text, you have written papers on topics similar to those in the reading selections. In a sense, you have used the topics in the reading selections as springboards for your own ideas, and then you have supported those ideas with examples drawn from real-life experiences.

In the next four chapters, you will move from writing on topics that are similar to those in the reading selections to writing about the reading selections themselves. Often called *academic papers* because they are required in many college-level courses, the writing assignments in the next four chapters will introduce you to summarizing accurately what you have read, to evaluating and responding to the ideas in a reading selection, to synthesizing ideas from several articles, and to arguing a point based on information drawn from a number of sources. In other words, you will be asked to write *about* what you have read.

Of course, academic writing does not mean that you will no longer use personal experiences to support your points. As a means of supporting your ideas, the real experiences of real people are just as important as ever. You will find, however, that much of your support will also be drawn from the articles you read. For that reason, the clear and accurate reading you have been practicing in Chapters 1 through 4 will be of critical importance. Obviously, you cannot write thoughtfully about an article if you have not first read it in a thoughtful manner.

Summarizing and Responding to Reading

5

Clear and accurate summarizing is one of the most important skills you can learn in college. Your ability to summarize effectively will help you study for and take tests, write reports and papers (particularly papers involving research), and give thorough, convincing oral presentations. Summarizing is also a skill in demand in the business world, especially when you must report information to other people. The person who can read and *accurately* report what he or she has read will always have an advantage over the person who cannot.

It seems as if summarizing should be such a simple task. After all, when you summarize, you merely explain what you have read to somebody else. And in many ways summarizing *is* simple. Yet it also can be quite a challenging assignment. A good summary demands that you read carefully, that you accurately identify the main points of what you have read, and that you then successfully communicate those ideas to another person. The following explanations should help you to write successful summaries.

Characteristics of a Successful Summary

- A summary accurately communicates the author's ideas.
- It includes all of the author's main points.
- It usually does *not* include supporting details.
- It does *not* include your opinions or reactions.
- It does *not* alter the author's meaning in any way.
- It uses your own words and writing style.

WRITING A BRIEF SUMMARY

Because most summaries present only the central idea and main points of a reading selection, they are usually quite brief, often no more than one or two paragraphs long. To write a summary, follow these steps:

1. As you read the material that you intend to summarize, underline or highlight whatever seems significant to you. Mark statements that seem to express the central idea and the main points of the reading selection. Even particularly vivid facts or other supporting details may be marked.

2. Reread the material, annotating it and dividing it into major sections so that each section reflects one main point.

3. Write the opening sentence of your summary. It should identify the name of the reading selection, the author, and the central idea, purpose, thesis, or topic of the reading.

4. After the opening sentence, briefly summarize each of the author's main ideas. Often you will need no more than one sentence to summarize each main idea.

5. Revise what you have written so that your summary is expressed in your own words and in your own style of writing. Where needed, add transitions that refer to the author between main points.

READING

Read the following article. As you do, identify its central idea and main points. Then reread the article, annotating it and dividing it into major sections. A sample brief summary follows the article. Note how the central idea and main points of the article are incorporated into the summary.

The Decline of Neatness   NORMAN COUSINS

Norman Cousins (1915–1990) was the editor of The Saturday Review *for the better part of forty years. He was also the author of a dozen books and hundreds of essays and editorials. Besides having been notably active in a variety of peace organizations, he was, in later years, on the faculty of the University of California at Los Angeles School of Medicine.*

Anyone with a passion for hanging labels on people or things   1
should have little difficulty in recognizing that an apt tag for our time is the Unkempt Generation. I am not referring solely to college kids. The sloppiness virus has spread to all sectors of society. People go to all sorts of trouble and expense to look uncombed, unshaved, unpressed.

The symbol of the times is blue jeans—not just blue jeans in   2
good condition but jeans that are frayed, torn, discolored. They don't get that way naturally. No one wants blue jeans that are crisply clean or spanking new. Manufacturers recognize a big market when they see it, and they compete with one another to offer jeans that are made to look as though they've just been discarded by clumsy house painters after ten years of wear. The more faded and seemingly ancient the garment, the higher the cost. Disheveled is in fashion; neatness is obsolete.

Nothing is wrong with comfortable clothing. It's just that   3
current usage is more reflective of a slavish conformity than a desire for ease. No generation has strained harder than ours to affect a casual, relaxed, cool look; none has succeeded more spectacularly in looking as though it had been stamped out by cookie cutters. The attempt to avoid any appearance of being well groomed or even neat has a quality of desperation about it and suggests a calculated and phony deprivation. We shun conventionality, but we put on a uniform to do it. An appearance of alienation is the triumphant goal, to be pursued in oversize sweaters and muddy sneakers.

Slovenly speech comes off the same spool. Vocabulary, like   4
blue jeans, is being drained of color and distinction. A complete sentence in everyday speech is as rare as a man's tie in the swank Polo Lounge of the Beverly Hills Hotel. People communicate in chopped-up phrases, relying on grunts and chants of "you know" or "I mean" to cover up a damnable incoherence. Neatness should be no less important in language than it is in dress. But spew and sprawl are taking over. The English language is one of the greatest sources of wealth in the world. In the midst of accessible riches, we are linguistic paupers.

Violence in language has become almost as casual as the   5
possession of handguns. The curious notion has taken hold that
emphasis in communicating is impossible without the incessant
use of four-letter words. Some screenwriters openly admit that
they are careful not to turn in scripts that are devoid of foul language lest the classification office impose the curse of a G (general) rating. Motion-picture exhibitors have a strong preference
for the R (restricted) rating, probably on the theory of forbidden
fruit. Hence writers and producers have every incentive to employ tasteless language and gory scenes.

The effect is to foster attitudes of casualness toward violence   6
and brutality not just in entertainment but in everyday life. People
are not as uncomfortable as they ought to be about the glamorization of human hurt. The ability to react instinctively to suffering
seems to be atrophying. Youngsters sit transfixed in front of television or motion-picture screens, munching popcorn while human
beings are battered or mutilated. Nothing is more essential in education than respect for the frailty of human beings; nothing is
more characteristic of the age than mindless violence.

Everything I have learned about the educational process   7
convinces me that the notion that children can outgrow casual attitudes toward brutality is wrong. Count on it: if you saturate
young minds with materials showing that human beings are fit
subjects for debasement or dismembering, the result will be de-
sensitization to everything that should produce revulsion or resistance. The first aim of education is to develop respect for life, just
as the highest expression of civilization is the supreme tenderness
that people are strong enough to feel and manifest toward one
another. If society is breaking down, as it too often appears to be,
it is not because we lack the brainpower to meet its demands but
because our feelings are so dulled that we don't recognize we
have a problem.

Untidiness in dress, speech and emotions is readily connected   8
to human relationships. The problem with the casual sex so fashionable in films is not that it arouses lust but that it deadens feelings and annihilates privacy. The danger is not that sexual
exploitation will create sex fiends but that it may spawn eunuchs.
People who have the habit of seeing everything and doing anything run the risk of feeling nothing.

My purpose here is not to make a case for a Victorian   9
decorum or for namby-pambyism. The argument is directed to

bad dress, bad manners, bad speech, bad human relationships. The hope has to be that calculated sloppiness will run its course. Who knows, perhaps some of the hip designers may discover they can make a fortune by creating fashions that are unfrayed and that grace the human form. Similarly, motion-picture and television producers and exhibitors may realize that a substantial audience exists for something more appealing to the human eye and spirit than the sight of a human being hurled through a store-front window or tossed off a penthouse terrace. There might even be a salutary response to films that dare to show people expressing genuine love and respect for one another in more convincing ways than anonymous clutching and thrashing about.

Finally, our schools might encourage the notion that few   10
things are more rewarding than genuine creativity, whether in the clothes we wear, the way we communicate, the nurturing of human relationships, or how we locate the best in ourselves and put it to work.

A SAMPLE BRIEF SUMMARY

In "The Decline of Neatness," Norman Cousins argues that a "sloppiness virus" is affecting all areas of our society. According to Cousins, the sloppy clothing that is so fashionable today reflects our desperate need to conform, making us look as if we had been "stamped out by cookie cutters." Our sloppy speech reflects the same need, but it goes beyond the slovenly to the violent. And this sloppily violent speech results in casual attitudes toward all violence and brutality. Cousins claims that we seem to be losing the ability to react to suffering. He says that the violence and brutality in movies and television are "desensitizing" our children and that such casual attitudes toward violence will not be outgrown. Finally, he suggests that our sloppy clothing, speech, and emotions affect human relationships, as is evident in the casual attitude toward sex in films, an attitude that is deadening our feelings and destroying our privacy. Cousins concludes by stating that he does not want to return to Victorian attitudes, although he does hope that our "calculated sloppiness" will soon disappear and that we will all begin to "locate the best in ourselves and put it to work."

EXERCISE 5.1

Identify the paragraph or paragraphs from "The Decline of Neatness" that are covered in each sentence of the above summary. Are all of the main points of "The Decline of Neatness" clearly and accurately summarized?

WRITING PARAPHRASES AND QUOTATIONS

Paraphrasing

As you can see from the above sample summary, most of what you write in a summary consists of the author's ideas put into your own words. Each time you reword what an author has written so that the *author's idea* is now expressed in *your writing style,* you have **paraphrased** the author. Here are some points to consider when you paraphrase:

1. Paraphrases must reflect your own writing style, not the author's.
2. Paraphrases must not change or distort the author's ideas in any way.
3. Paraphrases must be clearly identified as presenting the author's ideas, not your own.
4. Paraphrases use the present tense when referring to the author.

Here are some paraphrases that appeared in the sample summary of "The Decline of Neatness," along with the original passages:

ORIGINAL   The ability to react instinctively to suffering seems to be atrophying.

PARAPHRASE   Cousins claims that we seem to be losing the ability to react to suffering.

ORIGINAL   Untidiness in dress, speech, and emotions is readily connected to human relationships. The problem with the casual sex so fashionable in films is not that it arouses lust but that it deadens feelings and annihilates privacy.

PARAPHRASE   Finally, he suggests that our sloppy clothing, speech, and emotions affect human relationships, as is evident in the casual attitude toward sex in films, an attitude that is deadening our feelings and destroying our privacy.

Note that both of the above paraphrases accurately state the ideas in the original, yet they do so in a writing style quite different from that of the original. Both paraphrases clearly refer to the author of the article, and the words that refer to the author are written in the present tense.

Quoting

A quotation is an exact reproduction of an author's words. To let the reader know that the words are not your own, you must use quotation marks. However, you should be careful to use quotations sparingly in your writing. For the most part, *your* writing should be in *your* style, not in someone else's, so most references to what you have read should appear as paraphrases, not as quotations. In general, quote only those words, phrases, or sentences that you really want to emphasize or that would not be as emphatic if they were paraphrased. In fact, notice how *few* quotations appear in the brief summary of "The Decline of Neatness" above. With that said, let's discuss the points you should keep in mind when you use quotations in your writing:

1. Quotations must be accurate.

ORIGINAL   People go to all sorts of trouble and expense to look uncombed, unshaved, unpressed.

INACCURATE   As Cousins says, "People go to <u>a lot</u> of trouble and expense to look uncombed, unshaven, <u>and</u> unpressed."

2. *Every* quotation should be integrated into your text with a transition that refers to its source.

> Cousins says, "Slovenly speech comes off the same spool."
> Next, Cousins discusses sloppy speech, saying it "comes off the same spool" as sloppy dress.

3. Use correct punctuation to separate transitions from quotations.

   a. Use commas to set off transitional phrases that introduce a complete-sentence quotation.

   > According to Cousins, "The sloppiness virus has spread to all sectors of society."
   >
   > "The sloppiness virus," according to Cousins, "has spread to all sectors of society."
   >
   > "The sloppiness virus has spread to all sectors of society," according to Cousins.

   b. Use a colon to separate a complete-sentence quotation from a complete-sentence transition.

   > Cousins is emphatic in his assertion that sloppiness affects us all: "The sloppiness virus has spread to all sectors of society."

   c. Do not use any punctuation to set off partial quotations unless you would have used punctuation even if the quotation marks were not there.

   > Cousins insists that sloppiness affects "all sectors of society."

4. Use brackets if you need to add one or more of your own words for clarity and an ellipsis (three spaced dots) if you leave out material.

ORIGINAL   People go to all sorts of trouble and expense to look uncombed, unshaved, unpressed.

QUOTATION   Cousins claims that many people today go to great lengths to appear "uncombed, unshaved, [and] unpressed."

ORIGINAL   If society is breaking down, as it too often appears to be, it is not because we lack the brainpower to meet its demands but because our feelings are so dulled that we don't recognize we have a problem.

QUOTATION   According to Cousins, "If society is breaking down . . . it is not because we lack the brainpower to meet its demands. . . ."

Note   Words added in brackets must *not* alter the author's idea, and words omitted need *not* be replaced with an ellipsis if it is obvious that they have been omitted. Notice that none of the partial quotations in any of the above examples need ellipses. Also notice that the last example has *four* spaced dots. The fourth dot is a period.

5. Use single quotation marks to indicate a quotation that appears within another quotation.

> Cousins states that people today speak in "chopped-up phrases, relying on grunts and chants of 'you know' or 'I mean' to cover up a damnable incoherence."

6. Punctuate the end of a quotation correctly.

    a. Place periods and commas within quotation marks.

    > Cousins also states, "Nothing is wrong with comfortable clothing."
    > "Nothing is wrong with comfortable clothing," Cousins states.

    b. Place semicolons and colons outside quotation marks.

    > Cousin also states, "Nothing is wrong with comfortable clothing"; however, he does object to our "slavish conformity."

    c. Place question marks and exclamation points within quotation marks if the quotation is a question or exclamation. In all other situations, place them outside.

    > Do you agree when Cousins writes, "Violence in language has become almost as casual as the possession of handguns"?
    > In "Live Each Moment for What It's Worth," Erma Bombeck asks, "Does the word *refrigerator* have no meaning for you?"

 Note   For a further discussion of using and integrating paraphrases, summaries, and quotations within your paper, see pages 464–468.

EXERCISE 5.2

Write a brief summary of Michael Ryan's "Are You Living Mindlessly?" on pages 414–417 or an article assigned by your instructor. Your summary should identify the central point and main ideas of the article. Follow the above suggestions for writing paraphrases and quotations in your summary.

Exploring **ONLINE**   Go to www.thomsonedu.com/devenglish/mcdonald for more information about writing paraphrases, summaries, and quotations. Under "Chapter Resources" for Chapter 5, click on "Exploring Online."

WRITING AN EXTENDED SUMMARY

Although brief summaries are handy for expressing the main ideas of something you have read, many papers, reports, or presentations will require a more detailed summary of your source, one that explains the main ideas more thoroughly, pointing out which ideas the author has emphasized and how the author has supported those ideas. Writing an extended summary is excellent practice for such assignments. To write a successful extended summary, you need to read carefully and accurately and to communicate what you have read clearly and completely to someone else.

The steps in the writing of an extended summary are essentially the same as those in the writing of a brief summary. However, the extended summary is written as a brief essay, with individual paragraphs explaining the author's points in more detail than in a brief summary. Below is an extended summary of "The Decline of Neatness." Notice how each paragraph focuses on one of the article's main points.

A SAMPLE EXTENDED SUMMARY

In his article "The Decline of Neatness," Norman Cousins claims that a "sloppiness virus" has infected all areas of our society. His evidence focuses specifically on our style of dress, our casual speaking habits, our apathetic attitude toward violence and brutality, and our ineffective human relationships.

Cousins first examines the way we dress. He points out that the torn, sloppy jeans worn by so many people today can stand as a symbol of our times. According to Cousins, today it is fashionable to look disheveled, but such sloppiness is really not much more than a "slavish conformity." In fact, he says that today's sloppy dress makes people look as if they had been "stamped out by cookie cutters." It suggests, he says, a phoniness, as if the mere "appearance of alienation" were our goal.

In addition to the sloppiness in our dress, Cousins discusses the sloppy speech so common today. He says that people today speak in "chopped-up phrases," rarely use complete sentences, and lack the ability to use the English language effectively. Our speech, he says, is violent and foul, so foul in fact that screenwriters today resist turning in scripts that are too tame in order to avoid receiving any rating lower than an R (restricted).

Our foul and violent speech, according to Cousins, results in casual attitudes toward all violence and brutality. Cousins claims that we seem to be losing the ability to react to suffering, that "mindless violence" is the characteristic of our age. He says that the violence and brutality in movies and television are "desensitizing" our children and that such casual attitudes toward violence will not be outgrown.

Cousins's final point concerns human relationships. He suggests that our sloppy clothing, speech, and emotions affect human relationships, as is evident in the casual attitude toward sex in films. Our willingness to accept such casual sex, he says, deadens our feelings and destroys our privacy. It turns us not into lustful people, but into people who are incapable of feeling anything. Norman Cousins closes his article by stating that he does not want to return to Victorian attitudes, although he does hope that our "calculated sloppiness" will eventually disappear. He suggests that fashion designers and movie or television producers might someday discover that people would respond to clothes and movies that show respect for the human form and spirit, and he hopes that schools will find ways to encourage students to pursue "genuine creativity" in all areas of their lives.

EXERCISE 5.3

Work with other students to develop responses to these questions or to compare responses that you have already prepared.

1. Examine the introductory paragraph of the sample extended summary above. Where does it state the central idea of "The Decline of Neatness"? What other information does it include?
2. Identify the topic sentence of each body paragraph. Which paragraph or paragraphs from "The Decline of Neatness" does that topic sentence introduce?
3. Identify the transitions between paragraphs.
4. Examine the support within each paragraph. Have any points been left out of it that you think should have been included?

WRITING A SUMMARY-RESPONSE ESSAY

Many college writing assignments will ask that you both summarize what you have read and respond to it. After all, your ability to express your own reaction to a topic is certainly as important as your ability to summarize that topic. Although the structure of such an essay will vary, depending on the topic and the expectations of your instructor, one common format consists of a brief summary in your introductory paragraph, followed by a clear thesis statement of your own in the same introductory paragraph, followed by several body paragraphs that support and develop your thesis statement. When you write a summary-response essay, keep the following points in mind:

1. The introduction should include a brief summary of the article and its main points.
2. The introduction should include a thesis statement that expresses your response to the topic.
3. Each body paragraph should open with a topic sentence that clearly refers to and develops the thesis statement.
4. Each body paragraph should support its topic sentence with explanations, facts, examples, statistics, or references to authority.
5. Each sentence should reflect a sense of coherence by exhibiting a clear relationship to the sentence before it or to the topic sentence of the paragraph.

A SAMPLE SUMMARY-RESPONSE ESSAY

In "The Decline of Neatness," Norman Cousins argues that a "sloppiness virus" is affecting all areas of our society. According to Cousins, the sloppy clothing that is so in fashion today reflects our desperate need to conform, making us look as if we had been "stamped out by cookie cutters." Our sloppy speech reflects the same need, but it is more than just sloppy: it is foul and violent. He says that our sloppy language results in casual attitudes toward all violence and brutality and that, as a result, our children are losing the ability to react to suffering. Finally, he suggests that our sloppy clothing, speech, and attitudes affect human relationships, resulting in a sexual exploitation that "deadens feelings and annihilates privacy." I believe that Cousins's points are well worth considering. In fact, I have found that his "sloppiness virus" has affected my life and the lives of people I know in a number of significant areas.

A quick jaunt down the freeway will reveal the sloppiness virus at work in the way we drive our cars. Many drivers today either do not care about other people on the road or do not realize how dangerous their sloppy driving habits really are. Cars switch from one lane to the other and back again without signaling; they weave in and out of traffic; they race up to the rear bumper of the car in front of them—even if both cars are in the right lane—and tailgate for miles. Not too many months ago I was nearly killed by a sloppy driver in a white Celica. Traffic was heavy, moving at only about forty-five miles per hour, when he raced up behind me and began to flash his brights—as if there were anywhere I could go. As soon as he had the chance, he changed lanes to the left, raced past me, changed lanes again so that he was now in front of me, and then plowed into the rear of a bus. I had just enough time to brace myself before I smashed into him. I awoke in the hospital with a broken hip and a smashed ankle—all because of one person's sloppy driving habits.

As well as turning drivers into life-threatening idiots, the sloppiness virus affects our attitudes toward relationships. Many people today (myself included) act as if relationships should be easy, as if "love" should smooth out all the rough spots and keep us comfortable. I know of couple after couple who have separated or divorced or broken up after their relationship became more work than romance. But I also know a few couples who have managed to drop the sloppy expectation that relationships should be easy. One person in particular, a friend named Bob, nearly walked out of a sixteen-year marriage last year, but today he and his wife are closer than I have ever seen them. When I asked him what made the difference, he said that he decided to act *as if* he still loved his wife until he really did feel love for her again. He said, "I faked it until I made it." Don't misunderstand me. I'm not saying that we should never have the courage to end unhealthy relationships, but something is wrong when more than 50% of all marriages end in divorce.

Finally, I see the sloppiness virus at work every day in my own thinking and in the thinking of people I know. When a person is faced with a situation that is uncomfortable or that challenges his or her beliefs, it is easier *not* to think. It is easier to grab hold of the nearest, safest stereotype and believe in that. When the issue of gays in the military recently arose, for example, I had to laugh at how many people refused to consider the issues and took refuge in their stereotypical fears that gays are some sort of moral deformity that will invade the barracks and seduce all of our helpless young boys, destroying the "morale" of our troops. I see the same sort of thing happen when people from different races marry. When our new neighbors moved in—a recently married white woman and black man—many people around us were appalled (and yet these same people would never consider themselves racists). Unfortunately, it is just too easy for many of us to retreat into our sloppy thinking and hasty moral judgments.

Norman Cousins has raised an issue that touches us all, for all of us, in our sloppiness, want things to go *our* way. We do not want to have to change ourselves. The driver on the freeway wishes cars would part before him so he can be as reckless as he wants to be; the lover in a relationship wishes the other person would change so that he or she does not have to; and all people wish life itself would stop challenging them with situations that force them to think for themselves. We are, indeed, all victims of the sloppiness virus. Perhaps that virus is part of being a human being.

EXERCISE 5.4

Work with other students to develop responses to these questions or to compare responses that you have already prepared.

1. The introduction to the summary-response essay is much more developed than the introduction to the extended summary essay. Why? What is it doing that is different?

2. Identify the thesis statement of the essay.

3. Identify the topic sentence of each body paragraph. Does it clearly introduce the topic of the paragraph?

4. Identify the transitions between paragraphs. Also, explain how each topic sentence is clearly connected to the thesis statement.

5. Examine the support in each paragraph. Point out which sentences are generalized explanations and which are specific examples.

6. Examine the concluding paragraph, and explain what it does to bring the essay to a satisfactory close.

READINGS

The Bachelor: Silly, Sexist, and, to Many, Irresistible   MIMI AVINS

In the following selection, Mimi Avins, a staff writer for the Los Angeles Times, *considers the popularity of ABC's* The Bachelor, *and, by extension, the popularity of other similar "reality" shows. She finds the show "stupid, contrived, and . . . boring." And yet, she writes, "I was addicted too."*

BEFORE YOU READ

1. Have you watched *The Bachelor* or similar "reality" shows? If you have, what was your reaction to them?

2. Why do you think such shows have become so popular in the past few years?

Well, excuse me for coming late to the party, but it took "The Bachelor" to seduce me. Until Alex Michel, the highly eligible, soul mate–shopper of ABC's hit "reality" show came along, I was a confirmed hater of the unscripted programs that surfaced on television a few seasons ago.

Without ever having seen "Survivor," I decided it was stupid, contrived and boring. When "Who Wants to Be a Millionaire" was on at the gym, I'd leave the room. I feared that those relentlessly hyped phenomena and their sorry offspring would elbow out the unreal series I enjoy: well-crafted fare like "The West Wing" and "Six Feet Under."

I wish I could say I would have spent this spring's Monday evenings rereading the complete works of Virginia Woolf if I hadn't been flattened by a nasty bout of pneumonia. But, if truth be told, I didn't tune into "The Bachelor" just because I was weak and feverish. About halfway through its six-week run, in which 31-year-old Michel fishes for Mrs. Right in a pool of 25 carefully selected women, I began hearing murmurs from smart, sophisticated, highly evolved female friends. "I know it's sexist and ridiculous, but I'm addicted to 'The Bachelor,'" they confessed.

So I watched Episode 4. Ensconced in a Malibu mansion that is to the new millennium what the "Dynasty" homestead was to the '80s, Michel had winnowed the group down to a quartet of beauties. In a hometown-hopping hour, he met each of their families. Then, in the show's final minutes, one of the hopefuls was eliminated. Oh, my God, I thought. This is stupid, contrived and often slow enough to be boring. I was addicted too.

The scholarly component of my fascination stemmed from analyzing how cleverly a drama was constructed from the basic one-man, 25-women premise. "The Bachelor" (and for all I know, its unscripted predecessors) is a triumph of clever editing. The most romantic, amusing or titillating moments from hours of undoubtedly tedious encounters are shown. I write nonfiction for a living. Why wouldn't I be transfixed by the show's skill at spinning a compelling narrative from the dross of life? Part of the fun is busting the essential manipulativeness of the format.

For example, Michel has a wonderful time with Trista's   6
family in St. Louis. They're warm and welcoming. Talk flows, laughs come easily. When he meets Shannon's parents in Dallas, the atmosphere is so chilly it's a wonder he didn't put on a parka. Were the good times in Texas edited out? Were the conversational dead ends in Missouri trashed? Call me cynical, but I think so.

In a "reality" show, reality is plastic. The players' appeal,   7
their vulnerability and even wit can be adjusted as deliberately as a TV set's volume control. Michel would have been insufferable if he'd been too perfect. Thus the decision to show him losing his lunch, as he and Trista hover above Hawaii in a helicopter, only made him more endearing.

Enough intellectual rationalization. There's much more to a   8
"Bachelor" fixation than a desire to bust the show for being faux. Millions of women, and some men, have become obsessed with the program, whose audience and media presence steadily grew. As Diane Sawyer said on "Good Morning America" after admitting she'd fallen under "The Bachelor's" spell, "It's a strange thing we're all doing when we watch, but we are watching." Inquiring minds wonder why.

Everyone's a voyeur. With the exception of Monica   9
Lewinsky and her married boyfriend, we don't usually become privy to what goes on between men and women behind closed doors. But we are curious. "The Bachelor" is part of a genre that finds sport in the brutality of modern courtship. It's less cheesy than "Blind Date," "Shipmates," "Temptation Island" or "Change of Heart." Michel is a poised, personable management consultant with an MBA from Stanford. The show's bevy of bachelorettes is uncommonly telegenic, outgoing and seems to have triple-digit IQs. "The Bachelor" lets us see the sort of genetically blessed population you'd think would be immune to the more barbaric aspects of singlehood being humiliated. There's a certain wicked comfort in knowing no one is safe from the dating jungle's hazards.

Shallow is good. We come to know the characters we care 10
about in dramatic series over time. We know their back stories and idiosyncrasies. If "The Bachelor" moved at a more leisurely pace, it would have more depth. Yet its effectiveness is in direct proportion to its shallowness. Its cast is reduced to archetypes.

Michel is the catch, choosing among the good girl, the ditz, the hottie, the mystery woman and the neurotic handful. By skimming the surface, the show lets the audience fill in its many blanks, sparking the sort of debate that fueled its popularity.

Pass the popcorn. Let us not underestimate the howl   11
factor. It's so easy to mock Michel and the girls for their verbal tics, hairstyle goofs or awkward giggles. Nothing like sitting in front of the TV feeling superior to cap off a hard day.

Take this cringe-inducing exchange: As they ride home from   12
a date in one of the show's ubiquitous stretch limos, Michel asks Kim, a nanny from Arizona, what she likes to do in her free time. She tells him she finds turning the pages of magazines relaxing, but she doesn't really "read fiction/nonfiction." The very thought that a guy who majored in history and literature at Harvard might stroll into the sunset with a gal who confines her reading to Us magazine and self-help tomes makes you screech at the screen.

Women have organized "The Bachelor"–watching parties,   13
because the urge to nudge a friend while cackling is often irresistible. Most of the time, everyone involved seems in on the joke. On a pre-show broadcast just before Thursday's finale, it was evident that the producers and most of the participants have a sense of humor about themselves.

Champagne wishes and caviar dreams. Perhaps "The   14
Bachelor" hooked me when "Survivor" and "The Mole" didn't because romance is more entertaining than power struggles. The show has put Michel and his inamoratas into soft-focus fantasies sure to warm the heart of every woman who believed the glass slippers didn't give Cinderella blisters.

At every turn, Michel and the woman he's with are   15
pampered. The dazzling settings they find themselves in obscure the fact that nothing that might pass for interesting conversation ever occurs. In the snippets we see, the dates have all the charm of job interviews, as Michel grills the women about everything from the authenticity of their body parts to whether they expect relationships to follow a preordained sexual timetable. Michel may sound platitudinous when he tells each woman she's "awesome," but style trumps content. It can be hard to quibble with such a pretty fairy tale.

Repeat Steps 1 through 4. There's a notion currently   16
rampant in the culture that the right way to find a mate can be diagramed the way Popular Mechanics teaches you how to install

a carburetor. Some women are looking for tips, as if whatever wiles "The Bachelor" winner used could be practiced at home. For them, "The Bachelor" is the "Name That Tune" of relationship shows—"I can get that man to propose in six dates!"

If the mysteries of attraction could be reduced to a strategy, everyone would follow it. If there were a love potion, everyone would drink it. Just because Michel ultimately chose the bustiest, most blandly agreeable and sexually adventurous woman who, he said, "made him feel good," doesn't mean there aren't terrific single men looking for flat-chested, high-maintenance brunets who'll make them miserable. Just don't tell that to the faithful who think the show is a dating manual.   17

The big complaint about "The Bachelor" has been that it's demeaning to women. ABC, already casting for a sequel, may try to eviscerate that charge by letting one bachelorette choose from 25 men in a future edition. The really bold move would be to have a geriatric version, or even a middle-aged one. That would never fly, because the show is about people who look good in a mud bath looking for a partner. And it is very much about almost regular folks who want, more than anything, to be on TV. Women can't imagine why Michel would have to wife-hunt so publicly. Men don't understand why the women would risk getting their hearts broken in prime time.   18

In fact, the show is as much about the quest for fame as the search for love. As they've been doing the rounds on talk shows, the women who were dumped admitted that falling in love would have been nice. But being on TV was cool enough. "The Bachelor" isn't the story of the perfect union of Alex and Amanda Marsh. Between commercials for diamond rings and herpes medications, it celebrates the wedding of a voyeuristic audience and a group of exuberantly exhibitionist players—a match made in TV heaven.   19

AFTER YOU READ

Work with other students to develop responses to these questions or to compare responses that you have already prepared.

1. State the thesis of the article in your own words. What sentences in the article, if any, best express the idea?
2. Divide the article into sections according to each major point that Avins makes.
3. Briefly summarize the thesis of the article and its major supporting points.

Killing Women: A Pop-Music Tradition   JOHN HAMERLINCK

John Hamerlinck is a freelance writer in St. Cloud, Minnesota, who specializes in popular culture. He is currently working on a progressive history of women's sports and public policy in the 1920s and 1930s.

BEFORE YOU READ

1. Consider the title. Does it make sense to you? In what way is "killing women" a tradition in pop music?
2. Do you think lyrics in popular music affect the attitudes of the audience? Or do they merely reflect attitudes that are already there?

If there has been anything positive about the flood of media coverage of the O.J. Simpson trial, it has been an increased public awareness of the disturbing incidence of violence against women in our society. According to the Family Violence Prevention Fund, an act of domestic violence occurs every nine seconds in the United States. Even though the mainstream press seems to have only recently recognized this horrible reality, the signs of our tolerance toward domestic violence have long had a prominent profile in popular culture. This tragic phenomenon has often been reflected in novels and on film, but perhaps the most common occurrence of depictions of violence against women comes in popular music. Indeed, the often innocuous world of pop music has cultivated its own genre of woman-killing songs.

Violent misogyny in popular song did not begin with recent controversial offerings from acts like Guns 'N' Roses and 2 Live Crew. There's an old, largely southern, folk genre known as the "murder ballad." And as long as men have sung the blues, they have told stories of killing the women who have "done them wrong." In a common scenario, a man catches "his" woman with another man and kills them both in a jealous rage. In the 1920s, Lonnie Johnson sang a song called "Careless Love," in which he promises to shoot his lover numerous times and then stand over her until she is finished dying. In "Little Boy Blue," Robert Lockwood threatens to whip and stab his lover; while Robert Nighthawk's "Murderin' Blues" suggests a deliberate values judgment in the premeditation: the song says that prison chains are better than having a woman cheat and lie to you.

In many of the songs in this genre, the music belies the homicidal lyrics. A song like Little Walter's "Boom, Boom, Out Go the Lights'' (later turned into an arena-rock anthem by Pat Travers) features a smooth, catchy, danceable blues riff. Little Walter caresses the song's famous hook so softly that one gets the feeling that perhaps his bark is worse than his bite. There is, however, no doubt that retribution for emotional pain is going to come in the form of physical violence.

This theme is not limited to blues artists. The Beatles   4
provide harsh and frightening imagery in "Run for Your Life," a song which features premeditation along with traditional blues lines. It also incorporates stalking and threats sung directly to the target. The stalking transcends the mind-game variety we find in a song like the Police's "Every Breath You Take"; "Run for Your Life" is pure terror. Charles Manson aside, this Beatles offering is considerably more frightening than "Helter Skelter."

Another song in this vein is "Hey Joe," which was a minor   5
hit for a band called the Leaves in the 1960s and was later covered by numerous artists, including an electrifying version by Jimi Hendrix. Thanks to Hendrix, the song became a garage-band staple in the sixties and seventies: many a young vocalist cut his rock-and-roll teeth singing that musical question: "Hey, Joe/Where you goin' with that gun in your hand?" (The same bands probably also played Neil Young's contribution to the genre, "Down by the River.")

The woman-killing genre has also been embraced by the   6
MTV generation. One of the video age's most recent additions to the catalog of murder songs comes from the "man in black," Johnny Cash, who is only one of many country artists to record such songs. Cash recently released a single called "Delia's Gone" from his latest album, *American Recordings*. The stark and eerie video, which features Cash digging a grave for his victim, even made its way into an episode of MTV's "Beavis and Butt-Head."

Occasionally the genre attempts to even the odds by arming   7
the victim: for example, in Robert Johnson's "32-20 Blues," the heartbroken man gets his revenge despite the fact that the victim had a "38 Special." And sometimes the gender tables are turned: for example, Nancy Sinatra covered "Run for Your Life" shortly after the Beatles recorded it, changing the prey from "little girl" to "little boy." In real life, however, the victims are overwhelmingly women, and their primary form of defense usually consists of a mere piece of paper called a restraining order.

It should quickly be pointed out, however, that these songs   8
do not *cause* violence. Their singers are not wicked, evil people.

The perseverance of this genre, however, certainly reflects a disturbingly casual level of acceptance in society when it comes to so-called "crimes of passion." When we hear tales of real domestic abuse, we are appalled. Often, however, we rationalize the perpetrator's actions and say that we can understand how he was driven to commit such a crime. Shoulders shrug and someone ubiquitously adds, "Well, we live in a violent society." Just as metal detectors and X-rays have become an unquestioned, accepted part of the airport landscape, our culture comfortably places violence and terror in pop music's love-song universe.

"I-loved-her-so-much-I-had-to-kill-her" songs are not about   9
love; they are about power and control. But if the beat is good and the chorus has a catchy hook, we don't need to concern ourselves with things like meaning, right? We can simply dance on and ignore the violence around us.

AFTER YOU READ

Work with other students to develop responses to these questions or to compare responses that you have already prepared.

1. State the thesis of the article in your own words. What sentences in the article, if any, best express the idea?
2. Divide the article into sections according to each major point that Hamerlinck makes.
3. Briefly summarize the thesis of the article and its major supporting points.
4. Hamerlinck refers to "a disturbingly casual level of acceptance in society when it comes to so-called 'crimes of passion.'" What does he mean by this? In what way do we casually accept violence?
5. What other attitudes toward women does popular music reflect?

The Changing Face of America

OTTO FRIEDRICH

In the following article written for Time *magazine, Otto Friedrich considers questions raised by the latest waves of immigration to the United States. Although he acknowledges the concerns of many Americans over the changes they see all about them, he asserts that "These changes do not represent social decline or breakdown."*

BEFORE YOU READ

1. Consider the title. What do you assume the "changing face" of America refers to?
2. Friedrich discusses the concerns that many Americans have about the changing population. Do you have such concerns? Why, or why not?

Reina came from El Salvador because of "horrible things." She   1
says simply, "I got scared." When she finally reached Los Angeles
and found a job as a housekeeper at $125 a week, her new
employer pointed to the vacuum cleaner. Vacuum cleaner? Reina,
24, had never seen such a thing before. "She gave me a maid
book and a dictionary," says Reina, who now writes down and
looks up every new word she hears. "That's how I learn English. I
don't have time to go to school, but when I don't speak English, I
feel stupid, so I must learn...."

Lam Ton, from Viet Nam, is already a U.S. citizen, and he   2
did well with a restaurant, the Mekong, at the intersection of
Broadway and Argyle Street in Chicago. "When I first moved in
here, I swept the sidewalk after we closed," he recalls. "People
thought I was strange, but now everyone does the same." Lam
Ton's newest project is to build an arch over Argyle Street in
honor of the immigrants who live and work here. "I will call it
Freedom Gate," he says, "and it will have ocean waves with hands
holding a freedom torch on top. It will represent not just the
Vietnamese but all the minorities who have come here. Just look
down Broadway. That guy is Indian, next to him is a Greek, next to
him is a Thai, and next to him is a Mexican."

They seem to come from everywhere, for all kinds of   3
reasons, as indeed they always have. "What Alexis de Tocqueville
saw in America," John F. Kennedy once wrote, "was a society of
immigrants, each of whom had begun life anew, on an equal footing. This was the secret of America: a nation of people with the
fresh memory of old traditions who dared to explore new fron-
tiers." It was in memory of Kennedy's urging that the U.S. in 1965
abandoned the quota system that for nearly half a century had
preserved the overwhelmingly European character of the nation.
The new law invited the largest wave of immigration since the
turn of the century, only this time the newcomers have arrived not
from the Old World but from the Third World, especially Asia and
Latin America. Of the 544,000 legal immigrants who came in fiscal
1984, the largest numbers were from Mexico (57,000 or more
than 10%), followed by the Philippines (42,000) and Viet Nam
(37,000). Britain came in ninth, with only 14,000....

In addition to the half-million immigrants who are allowed   4
to come to the U.S. each year, a substantial number arrive illegally.
Estimates of the total vary widely. The Immigration and Naturaliza-
tion Service apprehended 1.3 million illegal immigrants last year

and guessed that several times that many had slipped through its net. . . .

The newest wave raises many questions: How many immigrants can the country absorb and at what rate? How much unskilled labor does a high-tech society need? Do illegals drain the economy or enrich it? Do newcomers gain their foothold at the expense of the poor and the black? Is it either possible or desirable to assimilate large numbers of immigrants from different races, languages and cultures? Will the advantages of diversity be outweighed by the dangers of separatism and conflict?   5

When asked about such issues, Americans sound troubled; their answers are ambiguous and sometimes contradictory. In a *Time* poll taken by Yankelovich, Skelly & White Inc., only 27% agreed with the idea that "America should keep its doors open to people who wish to immigrate to the U.S. because that is what our heritage is all about." Two-thirds agreed that "this philosophy is no longer reasonable, and we should strictly limit the number." Some 56% said the number of legal immigrants was too high, and 75% wanted illegal immigrants to be tracked down. On the other hand, 66% approved of taking in people being persecuted in their homelands.   6

"One of the conditions of being an American," says Arthur Mann, professor of history at the University of Chicago, "is to be aware of the fact that a whole lot of people around you are different, different in their origins, their religions, their life-styles." Yet most Americans do not know exactly what to make of those differences. . . . Much of the concern comes from people who favor continued immigration, but who fear the consequences if a slow-down in the economy were to heighten the sense that immigrants, especially illegal ones, take jobs away from Americans. . . .   7

The number of newcomers is large in itself . . . but their effect is heightened because they have converged on the main cities of half a dozen states. Nowhere is the change more evident than in California, which has become home to 64% of the country's Asians and 35% of its Hispanics. Next comes New York, followed by Texas, Florida, Illinois and New Jersey. Miami is 64% Hispanic, San Antonio 55%. Los Angeles has more Mexicans (2 million) than any other city except metropolitan Mexico City, and nearly half as many Salvadorans (300,000) as San Salvador.   8

These population shifts change all the bric-a-brac of life. A car in Los Angeles carries a custom license plate that says *Sie sie li,*   9 meaning, in Chinese, "Thank you." Graffiti sprayed in a nearby park send their obscure signals in Farsi. A suburban supermarket specializes in such Vietnamese delicacies as pork snouts and pickled banana buds. The Spanish-language soap opera *Tu o Nadie* gets the top ratings among independent stations every night at 8.

Such changes require adaptation not only in the schools and   10
the marketplace but throughout society. The Los Angeles County court system now provides interpreters for 80 different languages from Albanian and Amharic to Turkish and Tongan. One judge estimates that nearly half his cases require an interpreter.

These changes do not represent social decline or breakdown.   11
The newcomers bring valuable skills and personal qualities: hope, energy, fresh perspectives. But the success stories should not blot out the fact that many aliens face considerable hardships with little immediate chance of advancement. Avan Wong, 20, came from Hong Kong in 1983 and hoped to go to college. She lives in the Bronx with her aged father, commutes two hours by bus to a job of up to twelve hours a day in a suburban restaurant. "I don't even read the newspapers," she says. "You don't have time. Once you go home, you go to sleep. Once you get up, you have to go to work. The only thing I'm happy about is that I can earn money and send it back to my mother. Nothing else. You feel so lonely here." College is not in sight. . . .

Even with the best intentions on all sides, the question of   12
how to fit all these varieties of strangers into a relatively coherent American society remains difficult. Linda Wong, a Chinese-American official of the Mexican-American Legal Defense and Education Fund, sees trouble in the racial differences. "There is concern among whites that the new immigrants may be unassimilable," says Wong. "Hispanics and Asians cannot melt in as easily, and the U.S. has always had an ambivalent attitude toward newcomers. Ambivalent at best, racist at worst."

Many historians disagree. Hispanics, says Sheldon Maram,   13
a professor of history at California State University at Fullerton, "are moving at about the same level of acculturation as the Poles and Italians earlier in the century. Once they've made it, they tend to move out of the ghetto and melt into the rest of society." Asians often have it easier because they come from urban middle-class backgrounds. "They are the most highly skilled of any immigrant group our country has ever had," says Kevin McCarthy, a demographer at the Rand Corp. in Santa Monica, California. . . .

How long, how complete and how painful the process of   14
Americanization will be remains unclear. It is true that ethnic elit-
ists have bewailed each succeeding wave of Irish or Germans or
Greeks, but it is also true that the disparities among Korean merchants, Soviet Jews, Hmong tribesmen, French socialites and Hait-
ian boat people are greater than the U.S. or any other country
has ever confronted. On the other hand, Americans are probably
more tolerant of diversity than they once were. . . .

The question is not really whether the new Americans can   15
be assimilated—they must be—but rather how the U.S. will be
changed by that process.

AFTER YOU READ

1. State the thesis of the article in your own words. What sentences in the article, if any, best express the idea?
2. Divide the article into sections according to each major point that Friedrich makes.
3. Briefly summarize the thesis of the article and its major supporting points.
4. "Will the advantages of diversity be outweighed by the dangers of separatism and conflict?" What does Friedrich mean by this question? Explain the advantages and dangers that he seems to have in mind.
5. What changes in American life does Friedrich discuss in paragraphs 8 to 11? What sentences suggest his attitude toward these changes?

Serve or Jail

DAVE EGGERS

Dave Eggers is an author, editor, and publisher. He is best known for his memoir A Heartbreaking Work of Staggering Genius *(2000), which describes how he raised his brother, Christopher, after the death of his parents. Eggers founded Mc-Sweeney's, an independent publishing house, and has established writing centers for children in San Francisco and Brooklyn. In the following selection, Eggers suggests that public service should be required of college students.*

BEFORE YOU READ

1. What is your initial reaction to the idea of requiring public service as a requirement for graduation?
2. If you have ever performed community service, describe the service as well as your reaction to it.

About now, most recent college graduates, a mere week or   1
two beyond their last final, are giving themselves a nice respite.
Maybe they're on a beach, maybe they're on a road trip, maybe
they're in their rooms, painting their toenails black with a Q-tip
and shoe polish. Does it matter? What's important is that they
have some time off.

Do they deserve the time off? Well, yes and no. Yes, because   2
finals week is stressful and sleep-deprived and possibly involves
trucker-style stimulants. No, because a good deal of the four years
of college is spent playing football.

I went to a large state school—the University of Illinois—and   3
during my time there, I became one of the best two or three
football players in the Land of Lincoln. I learned to pass deftly between my rigid players, to play the corners, to strike the ball like a
cobra would strike something a cobra would want to strike. I also
mastered the dart game called Cricket, and the billiards contest
called Nine-ball. I became expert at whiffle ball, at backyard
archery, and at a sport we invented that involved one person
tossing roasted chickens from a balcony to a group of us waiting
below. We got to eat the parts that didn't land on the patio.

The point is that college is too long—it should be three   4
years—and that even with a full course load and part-time jobs
(I had my share) there are many hours in the days and weeks that
need killing. And because most of us, as students, saw our hours
as in need of killing—as opposed to thinking about giving a few of
these hours to our communities in one way or another—colleges
should consider instituting a service requirement for graduation.

I volunteered a few times in Urbana-Champaign—at a Y.M.C.A.   5
and at a home for senior citizens—and in both cases it was much
too easy to quit. I thought the senior home smelled odd, so I left,
and though the Y.M.C.A. was a perfect fit, I could have used nudging to continue—nudging the university might have provided. Just
as parents and schools need to foster in young people a "reading
habit"—a love of reading that becomes a need, almost an addiction—colleges are best-poised to create in their students a lifelong commitment to volunteering even a few hours a month.

Some colleges, and many high schools, have such a thing in   6
place, and last year Michael R. Veon, a Democratic member of
Pennsylvania's House of Representatives, introduced a bill that
would require the more than 90,000 students at 14 state-run universities to perform 25 hours of community service annually. That
comes out to more than two million volunteer hours a year.

College students are, for the most part, uniquely suited to have time for and to benefit from getting involved and addressing the needs of those around them. Unlike high school students, they're less programmed, less boxed-in by family and after-school obligations. They're also more mature, and better able to handle a wide range of tasks. Finally, they're at a stage where exposure to service—and to the people whose lives nonprofit service organizations touch—would have a profound effect on them. Meeting a World War II veteran who needs meals brought to him would be educational for the deliverer of that meal, I would think. A college history major might learn something by tutoring a local middle school class that's studying the Underground Railroad. A connection would be forged; a potential career might be discovered.   7

A service requirement won't work everywhere. It probably wouldn't be feasible, for example, for community college students, who tend to be transient and who generally have considerable family and work demands. But exempt community colleges and you would still have almost 10 million college students enrolled in four-year colleges in the United States. If you exempted a third of them for various reasons, that would leave more than 6 million able-bodied young people at the ready. Even with a modest 10-hour-a-year requirement (the equivalent of two mornings a year) America would gain 60 million volunteer hours to invigorate the nation's nonprofit organizations, churches, job corps, conservation groups and college outreach programs.   8

And with some flexibility, it wouldn't have to be too onerous. Colleges could give credit for service. That is, at the beginning of each year, a student could opt for service, and in return he or she might get credits equal to one class period. Perhaps every 25 hours of service could be traded for one class credit, with a maximum of three credits a year. What a student would learn from working in a shelter for the victims of domestic abuse would surely equal or surpass his or her time spent in racquetball class—at my college worth one full unit.   9

Alternatively, colleges could limit the service requirement to a student's junior year—a time when the students are settled and have more hours and stability in their schedules. Turning the junior year into a year when volunteering figures prominently could also help colleges bridge the chasm that usually stands between the academic world and the one that lies beyond it.   10

When Gov. Gray Davis of California proposed a service   11
requirement in 1999, an editorial in *The Daily Californian,* the student
newspaper at the University of California at Berkeley, opposed the
plan: "Forced philanthropy will be as much an oxymoron in action as
it is in terms. Who would want to receive community service from
someone who is forced to serve? Is forced community service in
California not generally reserved for criminals and delinquents?"

First of all, that's putting forth a pretty dim view of the soul   12
of the average student. What, is the unwilling college volunteer going to *throw food* at visitors to the soup kitchen? Volunteering is by
nature transformative—reluctant participants become quick converts every day, once they meet those who need their help.

Second, college is largely about fulfilling requirements, isn't   13
it? Students have to complete this much work in the sciences,
that much work in the arts. Incoming freshmen accept a tacit
contract, submitting to the wisdom of the college's founders
and shapers, who decide which experiences are necessary to
create a well-rounded scholar, one ready to make a contribution to the world. But while colleges give their students the
intellectual tools for life beyond campus, they largely ignore the
part about how they might contribute to the world. That is, until the commencement speech, at which time all the "go forth's"
and "be helpful's" happen.

But what if such a sentiment happened on the student's   14
first day? What if graduating seniors already knew full well how
to balance jobs, studies, family, and volunteer work in the surrounding community? What if campuses were full of underserved
high school students meeting with their college tutors? What if
the tired and clogged veins of thousands of towns and cities had
the energy of millions of college students coursing through them?
What if the student who might have become a football power—
and I say this knowing how much those skills have enhanced my
life and those who had the good fortune to have watched me—
became instead a lifelong volunteer? That might be pretty good
for everybody.

After You Read

Work with other students to develop responses to these questions or to
compare responses that you have already prepared.

1. State the thesis of the article in your own words. What sentences in the
article, if any, best express the idea?

2. Divide the article into sections according to each major point that Eggers makes.

3. Briefly summarize the thesis of the article and its major supporting points.

4. Describe any community service you have ever performed. In what context did you provide the service? What was your reaction to it?

5. What do you think the major objections would be to a community service requirement for college graduation? Compare your answers with those from other members of the class

WRITING ASSIGNMENTS

1. Write a brief summary of one of the reading assignments in this chapter or of a reading assignment from Part four of this text.

2. Write an extended summary of one of the reading assignments in this chapter or of a reading assignment from Part four of this text.

3. Write a summary-response essay in reaction to Mimi Avins's "*The Bachelor:* Silly, Sexist, and, to Many, Irresistible." After briefly summarizing her article, your introduction should include a thesis of your own that responds to one of the following topics or to a topic assigned by your instructor:

   a. Mimi Avins offers several reasons for the popularity of *The Bachelor.* Consider another popular television program, and write a paper in which you explain why that program is so popular. As you present each reason for the show's popularity, support that reason with specific examples drawn from actual episodes that you have seen.

   b. Toward the end of her article, Avins writes, "The big complaint about 'The Bachelor' is that it's demeaning to women." Consider in what way this show or other shows with which you are familiar may demean women or any other group of people. Support your points with specific examples drawn from shows that you have watched.

   c. Choose one of the reasons that Avins proposes for the popularity of *The Bachelor,* and consider in what way it makes a true statement about human nature. You might, for example, explain what she means by "Everyone's a voyeur" and then write a paper supporting that idea with examples of your own drawn from various areas of life. Or consider "Champagne wishes and caviar dreams." What does she mean by that? Consider writing a paper illustrating what her point reveals about human nature, illustrating your understanding with examples of your own.

4. Write a summary-response essay in reaction to John Hamerlinck's "Killing Women: A Pop-Music Tradition." After briefly summarizing his article, your introduction should include a thesis of your own that responds to one of the following topics or to a topic assigned by your instructor:

a. John Hamerlinck is careful not to claim that these "women killing" songs *cause* violence. Rather, he writes that they *reflect* "a disturbingly casual level of acceptance in society when it comes to so-called 'crimes of passion.'" Do the lyrics of popular music reflect other attitudes toward women as well? Write a paper in which you analyze any other attitudes that such music reflects, supporting your points with specific examples and clear explanations.

b. Although Hamerlinck suggests that violent lyrics do not cause violence, most people might agree that they are affected one way or another when they listen to music, whether the effect comes from the lyrics or the music. Consider many types of pop music. Write a paper in which you analyze ways that different types of pop music and/or its lyrics might affect the attitudes of its listeners, supporting your points with specific examples and clear explanations.

c. Hamerlinck focuses on depictions of violence against women, but on a more general level his article suggests that we have developed a casual attitude toward many instances of violence in our society. What do you think of that idea? Write a paper in which you analyze different types of violence toward which people have developed casual attitudes, supporting your points with specific examples and clear explanations.

5. Write a summary-response essay in reaction to Otto Friedrich's "The Changing Face of America." After briefly summarizing his article, your introduction should include a thesis of your own that responds to one of the following topics or to a topic assigned by your instructor:

a. Throughout his article, Friedrich says that Americans are "troubled" and "concerned" about the changes they see. Talk to other students about these concerns, and examine your own (if you have any). What concerns do people have? Write a paper in which you identify those concerns, explaining them as clearly and specifically as you can.

b. Choose one of the following statements from Friedrich's article (or a statement provided by your instructor), and respond to it with examples and explanations of your own.

- "These population shifts change all the bric-a-brac of life."
- "Such changes require adaptation not only in the schools and the marketplace but throughout society."
- "These changes do not represent social decline or breakdown. The newcomers bring valuable skills and personal qualities: hope, energy, fresh perspectives."

c. If you or your parents are immigrants to the United States, explain whether or not you have found the process of adapting to this society a difficult or painful one. Give specific examples to illustrate your points.

6. Write a summary-response essay in reaction to Dave Eggers's "Serve or Fail." After briefly summarizing the article, your introduction should

include a thesis of your own that responds to one of the following topics or to a topic assigned by your instructor:

   a. What is your position on requiring community service for a college degree? Write a paper in which you support or oppose such a requirement—using your own examples and explanations.

   b. Eggers provides several reasons to support his contention that public service should be required for a college degree. He also identifies and refutes possible objections. Write a paper in which you focus each of your body paragraphs on a separate point discussed by Eggers. Then use your own examples and explanations to support or refute what Eggers has to say.

  7. Write a summary-response essay in reaction to one of the reading assignments in Part four of this text. After briefly summarizing the article, your introduction should include a thesis of your own that responds to a topic assigned by your instructor.

EVALUATING SAMPLE PAPERS

EXTENDED SUMMARIES

As you read and evaluate the following extended summaries, consider these areas:

  1. Introduction

    Underline the sentences that state the central idea of the article. Is it accurate and clear? Does the introduction prepare the reader for an extended summary and not for a summary-response?

    1   2   3   4   5   6

  2. Unity

    Does each paragraph have a clear and specific topic sentence that accurately introduces one of the major sections of the article? Does the material in each paragraph clearly relate to its topic sentence?

    1   2   3   4   5   6

  3. Support

    Are all of the major points in the article summarized? Is each point accurately and fully explained?

    1   2   3   4   5   6

  4. Coherence

    Are transitions used between paragraphs? Where needed, are transitions used between sentences within each paragraph?

    1   2   3   4   5   6

  5. References to the Text

    Are direct quotations and paraphrases correctly introduced and smoothly incorporated into the text? Do they reflect the author's points accurately?

    1   2   3   4   5   6

6. Sentence Structure

   Do the sentences combine ideas that are related, using coordination, subordination, or verbal phrases when appropriate? Are there too many brief, choppy main clauses?

   1   2   3   4   5   6

7. Mechanics, Grammar, and Spelling

   Does the paper contain a distracting number of errors of these kinds?

   1   2   3   4   5   6

8. Overall Ranking of the Essay

   1   2   3   4   5   6

Student Summary 1

In his article, "The Decline of Neatness," Norman Cousins explains that a "sloppiness virus" has spread to all categories of life. His evidence of this virus is directed towards the way we dress, the way we speak, the way we treat one another, and the way we act in relationships.

In his first point, Norman Cousins speaks of our clothing. According to Cousins, "The symbol of the times is blue jeans." He describes our blue jeans as frayed, torn, and discolored, and he shows that the more worn and "ancient" the jeans look, the higher the price on the tag will be. Cousins writes, "Disheveled is in fashion; neatness is obsolete." He implies that this generation tries desperately to appear as individuals, but we come out looking like we stepped off an assembly line. He shows that in order to be different, we must be well groomed and even neat.

In the next section of his article, Cousins shows that our vocabulary has been "drained of color as well," and communication has progressed into grunts, chants, chopped up phrases, and "the incessant use of four letter words." He demonstrates this point by mentioning that screenwriters will not turn in a script without at least a handful of obscene words because they do not want to receive a "'G' rating." These screenwriters "employ tasteless language and gory scenes" so that they receive the strongly preferred "'R' rating."

Next, Cousins moves into the idea that our sloppiness in attitudes is directly related to our casualness toward violence. He states," People are not as uncomfortable as they ought to be about the glamorization of human hurt." He suggests that we take "debasement and dismembering" of human beings for granted and that if we continue to let this happen, the younger generation will be desensitized "to everything that should produce revulsion or resistance." He says our aim should be to educate the younger people to respect and cherish life.

Cousins' final point helps summarize the article by showing that our shortcomings in other aspects in life, such as clothing and vocabulary, have a direct impact on how we view our relationships. Cousins states, "Untidiness in dress, speech, and emotions is readily connected to human relationships." He implies that we have become apathetic because we have seen too much and have become immune to our feelings. He reminds us that because we are so casual with our feelings and our privacy, casual sex is as "fashionable" as our clothing.

In conclusion, Cousins points out that the outlook may be positive. Maybe a fashion designer will create a fashion that is not frayed and "grace[s] the human form." Maybe a screen writer will write a movie "to show people expressing genuine love and respect for one another." Maybe our schools could "encourage the notion that fewer things are more rewarding than genuine creativity." Cousins implies that the choice is ours: do we want to be "cookie cutters" or do we want to be unique?

Student Summary 2

According to Norman Cousins in his article, "The Decline of Neatness," the sloppiness virus has spread to all sectors of society. He thinks people go to great lengths and expense to look uncombed, unshaved, and unpressed. Anyone who is passionate about labels, he says, can tag us the Unkempt generation. He certainly makes us think about our appearance.

One factor he uses as a basis for that opinion is the fashion in blue jeans today. They are torn, discolored and look as though they have been discarded by a house painter. The fashion of today is disheveled. The author is not opposed to comfortable clothing. He thinks the desire for nonconformity has created people like cookie cutters. They are desperate not to be well groomed, their appearance takes on an uncaring quality.

Mr. Cousins attacks the modern day slovenly speech. He compares it to the blue jeans, and it is drained of color, with chopped up phrases, grunts, and chants. The violence in our language and the four letter words are a sign of decline. Some screen writers use four letter words so they don't get rated G. Violence is also affecting people. Battering and mutilations on TV and in movies leave us desensitized to the dismembering of humans. It also fosters attitudes of casualness, and children cannot outgrow the casualness.

Human relationships are connected to the lack of tidiness in dress, speech, and emotions. Sexual exploitation, which is fashionable in films today, does not create sex fiends, on the contrary, it deadens feelings. "People who have the habit of seeing everything and doing anything run the risk of feeling nothing."

He goes on to say that his purpose is not to make a case for the return to Victorian decorum, but rather to examine bad dress, manners, speech, and human relationships. He hopes fashion designers and motion picture producers will realize that there are people who want something better. Films that show genuine love and respect.

In conclusion, Norman Cousins says that schools may begin to encourage genuine creativity in clothes fashion, communication and human relationships. Perhaps, he says, we can locate the best in ourselves and put it to work.

SUMMARY-RESPONSE ESSAYS

As you read and evaluate the following summary-response essays, consider these areas:

1. Introduction

   Does the introduction contain a clear and accurate brief summary of the central idea and major supporting points of the article? Does it prepare the reader for a summary-response essay by moving to a thesis of the writer's own?

   1   2   3   4   5   6

2. **Thesis Statement**

   Underline the thesis statement of the essay. Does it express a clear and specific central idea?

   1   2   3   4   5   6

3. **Topic Sentences**

   Underline the topic sentence of each paragraph. Does it clearly state the central idea of the paragraph?

   1   2   3   4   5   6

4. **Support**

   Examine the supporting details in each paragraph. Are they specific and clear? Should they be more detailed, or should more support be included?

   1   2   3   4   5   6

5. **Unity**

   Does each paragraph clearly relate to and develop the *central idea* expressed in the thesis statement? Do the supporting details *within* each paragraph clearly relate to and develop the *central idea* expressed in the topic sentence of that paragraph?

   1   2   3   4   5   6

6. **Coherence**

   Does each paragraph open with a transition, a reference to the central idea of the thesis statement, and an identification of its own central idea? Are the sentences within each paragraph clearly related to each other by the use of transitions or by reference to the central idea of the paragraph?

   1   2   3   4   5   6

7. **Sentence Structure**

   Do the sentences combine ideas that are related, using coordination, subordination, and verbal phrases when appropriate? Are there too many brief, choppy main clauses?

   1   2   3   4   5   6

8. **Mechanics, Grammar, and Spelling**

   Does the paper contain a distracting number of errors of these kinds?

   1   2   3   4   5   6

9. **Overall Ranking of the Essay**

   1   2   3   4   5   6

Student Essay 1

In "Killing Women: A Pop-Music Tradition," John Hamerlinck writes that accepting violence toward women in pop music has somehow made society less sensitive to domestic abuse. Hamerlinck believes many artist have incorporate these kinds of lyrics into their songs. Even the MTV generation is not concerned with these disturbing images that can be produced by these kinds of woman-killing lyrics. He also points out that these songs do not cause violence but "reflect a disturbingly casual level of acceptance in society when it comes to so-called crimes of passion." We as a society have let ourselves understand and rationalize with why people commit these types of crimes. I believe Hamerlinck's view of woman in pop music is accurate. I feel music is extremely powerful and certain lyrics in songs can glamorize drug-induced lifestyles, while other lyrics in songs embrace drinking as a part of everyday life. Even a person's style of dressing and attitude can change.

Music lyrics have been known through the ages to glamorize drug-induced lifestyles. In Eric Clapton's "Cocaine" Clapton sings "If you wanna hang out, you've gotta take her out—cocaine," or "If you got that lose, you wanna kick them blues—cocaine." These lyrics could suggest that, if you want to have a good time or if you want to hang out and be cool you should take cocaine. I feel these lyrics send a false representation of drug use to people. These lyrics just mention the glamorous side of drugs use and not the deadly addiction it can have on a person. Another example are the musicians who lived drug-induced lifestyles. Janis Joplin and Jimi Hendrix are always being portrayed as wild drug-loving hippies that lived fast glamorous lives. On the cover of *Pearl*, Janis Joplin has a bottle of whiskey in one hand and a smoke in the other. This might send a negative message to people who want to be like their favorite musician. They could decide that they want to drink and use drugs like Janis Joplin did. I enjoy listening to these artists, but I do not feel we should glamorize their lifestyles.

In addition to lyrics that glamorize drug-induced lifestyles, there are also the lyrics in songs that seem to say, It's alright to have a drink or to get drunk whenever you feel like it. Country music is always portraying booze and bars as just a natural part of life. David Allan Coe writes "Mamma, train, truck, prison, and getting drunk, is the perfect country western song." I personally listen to country music and I realize that most of my country CD's I own have at least one song about getting drunk. People might get carried away with the lyrics and drink whenever they feel like it because the CD they are listening to promotes drinking. Country music can be good music, but I think some of these artists need to stop using alcohol as a way to fix problems. Next is another example of lyrics in pop music promoting drinking. In the famous song "Margaritaville" Jimmy Buffett tells the story of a man who is constantly drunk in order to forget about his lost love. I do not feel these lyrics will turn a person into an alcoholic, but these lyrics could urge someone to drink if they have had a fight with their boyfriend or girlfriend. The lyrics seem to say it's alright to drink when you are depressed and have problems in life.

Finally, some types of lyrics can influence people to dress a certain way and can change a person's attitude. Some people like to dress in clothes that reflect what kind of music they like. People who listen to country like to wear cowboy hats, Wrangler jeans, and ropers while rap music lovers like to dress in baggy, loose, hip-hop clothes. I think dressing this way is fine, but sometimes people attitudes reflect negatively on the music they listen to. When I worked in a music shop in high school young kids that listen to rap would come in and act rude. On some occasions they used vulgar language when they talked. Some of theses boys had no respect for women because many of the rap artists use insulting language about women in their music. This is not a message that we want to be sending our youth. Artist should be more careful when they write music because they have the power to mold young people in our society.

Clearly, music is powerful and wonderful today, but I feel artist need to be more observant when writing lyrics that could have negative effects on people that are looking for role models and are trying to deal with problems in their life.

Student Essay 2

In the article "The Changing Face of America" Otto Friedrich talks about American people's concern that new group of immigrants is changing American society in positive and negative ways. Friedrich discusses the new wave of immigrants from Asia and Latin America especially those immigrants who have come since 1965. According to Friedrich, immigration raises all sorts of questions that trouble and confuse American society because Americans do not know if the immigrants are positive or negative for our society. One expert states that America is a lot of different societies combined together. Friedrich explains that immigrants bring changes in "bric-a-brac of life" that require adaptation; however, changes might be good for American society to improve "valuable skills and personal qualities." Friedrich questions whether different people can fit in one society. He explains that one expert sees differences as a problem, but other experts don't see them as a problem. Friedrich concludes that new Americans are assimilated just as in the past. I believe that many American immigrants go through painful experiences to assimilate in American society as they adapt a new culture. I am an immigrant from Japan who came to live and study in America in 1995. As I have adapted to a new culture, I have had a number of painful experiences that caused confusion, frustration, and fear about myself.

One of my painful experiences while adapting to a new culture was speaking English with American people. I felt awkward speaking English in the beginning because I noticed that people avoided talking to me right after they found out I spoke different or funny. For example, one of the girls in my first semester of dance class asked me if she missed anything or not because she came in late. I tried to explain about the things that she needed to know, but she couldn't understand me. She kept saying "What? . . . Ha? . . . What? . . ." and then she said, "Never mind. It's OK" and went to ask different people. She never came back to talk to me after this happened. This experience made me nervous to talk to American people and hurt my feelings. Another example happened when my host family had a party and introduced me to their friends. When one guy came to ask me some questions, I tried to have a fun conversation with him, but he didn't want to stay and talk to me. I felt my English was too basic and boring, but I didn't really know what I was doing wrong. I was frustrated because I felt that I was out of place even though I wanted to fit in these circles and have fun just like native Americans.

Adapting to American culture caused me to discover difficulty in my own country. When I went back to Japan, it was hard for me to communicate with my family and my friends because they didn't accept me since I had become a different person. I discovered that I liked speaking English better than Japanese even though I didn't speak perfect English. I was confused because I felt awkward speaking my native language, Japanese, to my family and my friends. I do not know why, but it just didn't feel right to me to speak Japanese anymore. I was uncomfortable because I was forced to speak Japanese, and I felt that people did not accept me if I did not speak Japanese as my native language. I also found difficulty in my own culture when my family didn't accept my looks: my new clothes, my makeup, and my new hairstyle. They made funny comments about my new American appearance to make me feel uncomfortable. For example, my mom told me "Stop wearing those American clothes and makeup in Japan because you look funny. I do not have an American daughter." Another time my sister told me "Sis, you look like you are copying American style. You put makeup on just like your host sister, Lisa." I felt that I no longer fit in my own society any more. I found out that I liked myself more in America and American culture because I could express the best of me with English language, clothes, makeup and hair style.

My last painful experience while adapting to American society was when my roommate Natalie and I took a trip to visit her family in Montana. I discovered that some places in America are close minded and prejudice to different races. People in Montana treated me differently than American people and that hurt my feelings. One example is when I went into a restaurant in Montana with Natalie and her family. The waitress took orders from Natalie, her mom Ruth, her brother Jed, and then me. I never had to wait to be the last person to order, especially when a guy was with me. I felt uncomfortable and started to worry about my different culture appearances. I was sad and felt awkward because I was the last one to order after all the American people had ordered. Likewise, when Ruth introduced Natalie and me to Ruth's friends from work, her friends paid attention only to Natalie and didn't even look at me to introduce themselves. I know that people in California would have said something to me even if it was just to be polite. I felt out of place being there because of the way I looked was a different look from the American people. These are some of the experiences that hurt my feelings and left me confused.

In this essay I gave some examples of the painful experiences I had faced in American culture. Some of the experiences were dealing with the students in my class who did not understand my speech, not fitting in to the Japanese culture when I returned because of my actions and looks, and not being treated the same as Americans. Even though I fit into American culture, I still feel confused by the way the closed minded people treat me.

Student Essay 3

Mimi Avins writes in "*The Bachelor*: Silly, Sexist, and, to Many, Irresistible," about her own and many others' addiction to the TV show *The Bachelor*. She says that although many other shows never got her interest, this show did. Many of her smart and sophisticated female friends enjoyed the show, and soon enough she was addicted too. One of the reasons she enjoyed the show was because she enjoyed "analyzing how cleverly a drama was constructed." In addition, she says that the world liked the show because of its shallow aspect. By just skimming the personality of each person we are able to fill in the blanks on the rest of their lives and personalities. Another factor in why we enjoy seeing the show is because people make mistakes and we like to know that they're not that far from our own reality. Her sub-heading "Champagne wishes and caviar dreams" suggests that it's more entertaining to watch the rich and stylish and imagine ourselves in those situations than anything else. America also watched because it was a guide to "find a mate." One major complaint was that the show was sexist. She says that "in fact the show is as much about the quest for fame as the search for love." One of her major points about why America liked to watch the show was because everyone is a voyeur. I believe this is so true in many aspects of human nature.

Everyone secretly enjoys watching other people. This is evident in everyday life. How many people slow down when an accident happens and become "looky-loos," even though I'm sure the drivers know that looking will probably cause another accident. The accident can be so minor or a major serious fender bender and everyone slows down to watch. When anyone in public raises their voices don't we all turn and watch what is happening. We watch just because something might happen and it might be juicy. We don't want to be ridiculed for being nosey so we watch secretly from the corner of our eyes.

America enjoyed watching the show *The Bachelor* because they liked watching people make idiots of themselves. These moments of mistakes made it easier for us to watch because we knew that the people on TV weren't robots. It made us feel normal and not so idiotic ourselves. We laugh at those men who approach women who are obviously way out of their league trying to impress them. We laugh under our breath when someone trips over a rock or the sidewalk when they are walking. We enjoy sophisticated men and women on TV embarrassing themselves because they are supposed to be above such things. Men and women who jump through loops and run through mud to impress someone is a hilarious factor.

I think that human nature also prompts us to watch when other people hit emotional roads. We take pleasure in watching human nature at its most raw form. When we see someone crying and sobbing we want to know why, even if we don't know the whole story or who the person is. *The Bachelor* had many emotional ups and downs during it's duration on TV. The different women leaving each week and the cat fights that made for such excellent TV are just some rare moments of emotional roads that we loved to watch. We also liked to see the emotional highs that the show had. When the "bachelor" chose his "soul mate" on the season finale, we all watched as the couple cried and it made our own heart feel with joy. These moments are so enjoyable because its in our nature to be emotional.

Mimi Avins writes that she was addicted and the rest of America was addicted too. She gave many good examples of why she was addicted and many reasons of why America was addicted. I believe that she was right and I think a major reason was that everyone is a voyeur and we secretly and openly enjoy it. Human nature makes us more apt to watching others whether it's on TV or in real life.

SENTENCE COMBINING: APPOSITIVES

As you know from the earlier sentence-combining sections of this text, in English there are many ways to add information to the basic sentence. So far, you have practiced using adjectives, prepositional phrases, main clauses, subordinate clauses, and verbal phrases in your sentences. The **appositive** is yet another way to add interest and depth to your writing. Like most of the other sentence-combining methods you have studied, the appositive allows you to consolidate ideas into one sentence that otherwise might be expressed in two or more separate sentences.

At its simplest level, an appositive is simply a noun or a pronoun renaming or identifying another noun or pronoun. Usually the appositive is set off by commas, and it normally follows the noun or pronoun it is renaming. Here are some examples from the articles you have read in this chapter:

> Lam Ton, from Viet Nam, is already a U.S. citizen, and he did well with a restaurant, **the Mekong,** at the intersection of Broadway and Argyle Street in Chicago.

> Cash recently released a single called "Delia's Gone" from his latest album, **American Recordings.**

Notice that in each of the above examples a noun renames a noun. The noun *the Mekong* renames *restaurant* in the first sentence, and *American Recordings* renames *album* in the second. As is usually the case, each appositive follows and is set off by commas from the noun it renames.

Another characteristic of the appositive is that it usually includes modifiers of its own—adjectives, adverbs, or other modifiers that add information to the appositive word. Notice the modifiers of the appositive word in the following examples from "Serve or Fail " and "Killing Women: A Pop-Music Tradition":

> Alternatively, colleges could limit the service requirement to a student's junior year—**a time when the students are settled and have more hours and stability in their schedules.**

> The Beatles provide harsh and frightening imagery in "Run for Your Life," **a song which features premeditation along the traditional blues line.**

Punctuating Appositives

Most appositives are set off with commas. However, occasionally they are set off with dashes or with a colon. In general, follow these guidelines:

1. Use commas to set off most appositives.

   Two dogs, **an Irish setter and a German shepherd,** ran into the lobby of the hotel.

2. Use dashes to set off an appositive that consists of a series, that already uses internal commas, or that seems to require a strong break.

   Only three people—**a real estate agent, the manager of the local grocery store, and the town's only banker**—attended the Chamber of Commerce mixer.

3. Use a colon to set off an appositive at the end of a sentence if you want to establish a formal tone.

   Last Christmas, Jason visited only one person: **his father.**

   (Note that the above appositive could also have been set off with a comma or with a dash.)

RECOGNIZING WHEN TO USE APPOSITIVES

You have the opportunity to use an appositive almost any time you have a sentence consisting of a form of the verb *be* followed by a noun or pronoun. If you omit the verb, set off the resulting phrase with commas, and then continue with your sentence, you have created an appositive.

ORIGINAL SENTENCE WITH FORM OF BE

Alex Haley was the author of *Roots.*

OMIT THE VERB AND SET OFF THE RESULTING PHRASE WITH COMMAS

Alex Haley, the author of *Roots,*

COMPLETE THE SENTENCE

Alex Haley, the author of *Roots,* died in 1992.

If you watch for them, you will find many opportunities to create appositives when you have written sentences using a form of the verb *be* followed by a noun or pronoun. Notice, for example, how two of the following three sentences use *was* and *is* to introduce a noun.

Mr. Erickson **was** the winner of the Florida lottery. He gave all of his money to Helping Hands. Helping Hands **is** a small orphanage in New York.

Now notice how those same three sentences can be written as one sentence with two appositives.

Mr. Erickson, **the winner of the Florida lottery,** gave all of his money to Helping Hands, **a small orphanage in New York.**

EXERCISE 5.5

Use appositives and appropriate punctuation to combine the following sentences. In each case, the words to be made into an appositive are underlined.

EXAMPLES

Robert Louis Stevenson was <u>a British novelist</u>. He wrote *Treasure Island.*
Robert Louis Stevenson, a British novelist, wrote *Treasure Island.*

Johann von Goethe lived from 1749 to 1832. He was a <u>poet, dramatist, and novelist</u>.
Johann von Goethe—a poet, dramatist, and novelist—lived from 1749 to 1832.

1. Anyone who looked at Medusa was immediately turned into stone. Medusa was <u>the mythological Gorgon with a head full of snakes</u>.
2. Perseus was <u>the son of the god Zeus and the human princess Danae</u>. He used a reflecting shield to avoid looking at Medusa while he cut off her head.

3. From blood of the severed head of Medusa came Pegasus. Pegasus was <u>a beautiful winged horse</u>.

4. Pegasus was ridden by the Greek muses as well as by Apollo. He was <u>a symbol of the poetic imagination.</u>

5. Athena was <u>the Greek goddess of wisdom</u>. Perseus gave the severed head of Medusa to Athena, who placed it on her own shield.

CHANGING ADJECTIVE CLAUSES TO APPOSITIVES

Another opportunity to use an appositive arises whenever you write an adjective clause containing a form of the verb *be* followed by a noun or pronoun. In such cases, you can omit the relative pronoun that starts the adjective clause and the verb. The result will be an appositive.

EXAMPLE

USING AN ADJECTIVE CLAUSE

Amoxil, **which was** the most frequently prescribed drug in 1991, is an antibiotic.

USING AN APPOSITIVE

Amoxil, the most frequently prescribed drug in 1991, is an antibiotic.

EXERCISE 5.6

Use appositives and appropriate punctuation to combine the following sentences or to change adjective clauses to appositives. In each case, the words to be made into an appositive are underlined.

1. Benedict Arnold, who was <u>an infamous American general of the Revolutionary War</u>, plotted to betray the American fort at West Point, New York, to the British.

2. The Boston Tea Party was <u>a well-known act of defiance toward the British government prior to the Revolutionary War</u>. It was instigated by American colonists protesting Britain's attempt to undercut the price of tea set by American merchants.

3. "Stonewall" Jackson received his nickname when he and his army "stood like a stone wall" at Bull Run. Jackson was <u>a general in the Confederate army during the Civil War</u>.

4. Abraham Lincoln was assassinated by John Wilkes Booth, who was <u>an actor devoted to the Confederate cause in the Civil War.</u>

5. In the 1840s many Americans justified the acquisition of Oregon and much of the southwest, including California, by referring to "manifest destiny." It was <u>a concept suggesting that the United States was destined by God to expand across North America.</u>

EXERCISE 5.7

Use appositives and appropriate punctuation to combine the following sentences or to change adjective clauses to appositives.

1. The Great Pyramid of Khufu contains 2.3 million blocks of limestone averaging $2\frac{1}{2}$ tons each. It is the largest of all the pyramids.

2. Both Hansel and Gretel looked politely at the little old lady's new appliance, which was an extra-large General Electric oven.

3. More than 75% of the world's 850 active volcanoes lie within the "Ring of Fire." It is a zone running along the west coast of the Americas and down the east coast of Asia.

4. Medusa could not do a thing with her hair, but Perseus, who was the son of Zeus, soon solved that problem.

5. The first toothbrush was the "chew stick." It was a twig with one end frayed to a soft, fibrous condition.

6. Achilles stared in irritation at his heel, which was the only sore spot on his body.

7. Mercury is the nearest planet to the sun. It is the smallest of the planets known to be orbiting the sun.

8. Henry watched the battle between two armies of tiny combatants while he ate his favorite food. The combatants were red ants and black ants, and the food he ate was freshly baked bread.

9. Paul was uncomfortable around his father, who was a rough, drunken coal miner, but not around his mother. She was a woman who now regretted her marriage.

10. Amanda recalled the high point of her life while Laura stared at her favorite possession, which was a small glass unicorn. Amanda's high point was the time she had seventeen gentlemen callers.

EXERCISE 5.8

Combine the following sentences, using coordination, subordination, verbal phrases, or appositives.

1. The "Trail of Tears" refers to one of the many forced "removals" of Native Americans from their native lands.
   These "removals" resulted in the deaths of thousands of men, women, and children.

2. In the 1830s, these so-called removals focused on what are generally referred to as the Five Civilized Tribes of the Southeast.
   These were the Choctaw, Chickasaw, Creek, Cherokee, and Seminole nations.

3. Each of these Native American societies had developed a culture.
   The culture was compatible with white society.
   It even emulated European styles in many respects.

4. There was a problem, however.
   It was that these tribes resided in valuable territory.
   The territory was cotton-growing land.
5. The Indian Removal Act was passed in 1830.
   Thousands of Choctaws, Chickasaws, and Creeks were forced to move.
   They moved from the Southeast to territory west of Arkansas.
6. The forced move caused many hardships.
   Hundreds and eventually thousands of Native Americans died.
   They suffered from pneumonia, cholera, and other diseases.
7. Gold was discovered in Cherokee country in Georgia.
   The state of Georgia tried to force the Cherokee to leave.
   The Cherokee took their case to the United States Supreme Court.
8. At this time, the Cherokee were not nomads.
   They were a nation of Native Americans.
   They had built roads, schools, and churches.
   They even had a system of representative government.
9. The Supreme Court ruled against them.
   Seventeen thousand Cherokee were forced to travel the "Trail of Tears" to Oklahoma.
10. Along the way, 4,000 of the 17,000 died.
    Another 1,000 escaped.
    They hid in the Great Smoky Mountains.
11. In the following years, the Cherokee eventually won back 56,000 acres.
    Seven million acres of land had been taken from them.

Exploring **ONLINE**

Go to www.thomsonedu.com/devenglish/mcdonald for more information about writing appositives. Under "Chapter Resources" for Chapter 5, click on "Exploring Online."

Evaluating Reading Selections

6

The students in the Trudeau cartoon seem to be doing an excellent job of recording what their instructor has to say. Since they are listening carefully, their notes will probably be accurate summaries of the lecture. However, wouldn't you agree that something is missing from the students' activities in this cartoon? Shouldn't they have some reaction to the statements "Jefferson was the Antichrist! Democracy is Fascism! Black is White! Night is Day!"? The problem, of course, is that taking careful notes is just not enough. These students need to **evaluate** as well as record.

Evaluating what you read (or hear) is a valuable skill. We have all heard the old saying "Don't believe everything that you read," and certainly most people follow that advice. Unfortunately, what we do or do not believe is often not based on careful evaluation. Instead, many people merely accept material that confirms what they *already* believe and reject material that does not confirm their previously held beliefs.

Evaluation demands that you approach an idea with an open mind—that you be willing to consider its validity on the basis of the evidence presented, not on the basis of any preconceptions you may have. It demands that you be willing to change your ideas if the evidence suggests that you should. And it demands that you make an effort to understand the purpose of what you are reading so that you don't criticize something for failing to do what it was not intended to do.

AUDIENCE AND PURPOSE

Perhaps the first step in evaluating anything that you read is to determine the audience and the purpose of the article. The **audience** of an article is its intended readers. Obviously, an article in *Ms.* magazine on the sexual exploitation of women will have a different audience from an article on the same subject published in *Playboy,* and those different audiences may influence the authors' choices of ideas to be covered. Of course, no matter who the audience is, a writer must still provide reasonable support for his or her points.

An evaluation should also consider the **purpose** of any article that you read. Clearly it would be unfair to criticize a writer for failing to discuss the responsibilities of parenthood if that writer's purpose was to entertain you with humorous stories about the frustrations of living with a teenager. Here are four common purposes that you should consider whenever you read.

To Inform

This type of writing is often called *expository.* It generally consists of facts rather than opinions or arguments. Most newspaper reporting has *informing* as its purpose, as does most of the material that you read in textbooks.

To Entertain

Generally, nonfiction *entertainment* writing tends to be humorous and often focuses on situations that are common to the average person. Dave Barry, for example, is a nationally syndicated entertainment columnist.

To Persuade

Persuasive writing tends to focus on controversial issues, presenting opinions and arguments that are supported (effectively or ineffectively) with facts, examples, explanations, statistics, and/or references to authority. Editorials in newspapers and magazines are common examples of persuasive writing.

To Raise an Issue or Provoke Thought

This type of writing is similar to persuasive writing in that it examines controversial issues, but its purpose is not necessarily to persuade the reader that the writer's particular argument is the correct one. Instead, its intent is often to unsettle the reader, to raise questions that need to be answered but that are not fully answered in the article itself. Such articles are often found in newspaper and magazine editorials.

In this chapter, you will write evaluations of articles designed to persuade, to raise an issue, or to provoke thought. As you read each article in this chapter, you must ask yourself if the article's purpose is to convince you of a particular argument or if it is merely to get you to think about the issue at hand. Of course, at times, the purpose may be a little of both, so you should consider that possibility too.

EVALUATING SUPPORT

In addition to considering the audience and the purpose of what you read, you need to examine the evidence or support that is presented to you. For example, if a writer claims that we should do away with the minimum wage, you should look to see not only what reasons he gives but also what facts, statistics, examples, or references to authority he offers to explain his reasons.

When you do look closely at a written argument—especially an editorial in a newspaper or magazine—you will often find that the support is quite sketchy. Much of the argument may consist of opinions or explanations rather than facts or other specific types of support. In such cases, you must decide whether more support is needed or whether the argument is reasonably convincing as it stands. However, an argument without sufficient support should be looked at skeptically, no matter how well it is written.

FACTS

Facts are tricky things. Most people consider a fact to be something "true" or "correct" or "accurate." But not everyone agrees about what is or is not true. For example, is it a fact that drinking coffee is bad for your health? Some people might *claim* that such a statement is accurate, but just as many others would say it is not. And science itself has provided few answers about the long-term effects of coffee drinking. So is it or is it not true that coffee is bad for your health? Surely such a statement cannot be treated as a fact if there is so much disagreement about it.

The best way to define a fact is to move away from the idea of "truth" or "correctness" and toward the idea of objective, physical verification. Treat as a fact any statement that has been objectively verified through direct experience, measurement, or observation. Statistics, then, are facts, as are historical or current events, scientific observations, and even personal experience. If it has been verified that caffeine increases a person's blood pressure, then such a statement is a fact. If you visited a Toyota dealership yesterday and felt uncomfortable talking to the salesperson, your statement that such an event occurred and that you reacted the way you did are facts. If the distance between the sun and the earth has been measured as 92,900,000 miles, such a statement is a fact.

Of course, even using objective verification, you cannot assume all facts are always accurate. For many years, people believed it was a fact that the sun circled the earth, not vice versa. After all, anyone could see that each day the sun rose in the east and set in the west. In this case, objective verification was not accurate enough to lead us to the fact that the earth circled the sun. So how do you know which facts have been accurately verified and which have not? Often you must consider the source. If the writer of an article says that 24,700 murders were committed in the United States in 1991, you will probably accept that statement as a fact if the writer is a professional reporter or columnist whose career is riding on his or her accuracy. Of course, that does not mean that you should accept the writer's *conclusions,* especially if the writer is trying to persuade you to accept his or her particular point of view.

EXERCISE **6.**1

Discuss which of the following statements can and which cannot be objectively verified as facts.

1. In California, bicycle riders under the age of eighteen are required by law to wear a bicycle helmet.
2. If I had not eaten any sugar at the fair yesterday, I would have had a better time.
3. No loyal American would ever burn the American flag.
4. I saw a man with red hair run out of Bank of America yesterday.
5. Former President Gerald Ford's middle name is Rudolph.
6. Betsy Ross sewed the first American flag.
7. During the 2002 World Series, Barry Bonds of the San Francisco Giants hit four home runs.
8. Frankenstein was the name of the monster in the famous novel by the same name.
9. Most homeless people won't work even if you offer them jobs.
10. Cashews taste better than peanuts.

As you can see from the above sentences, some statements are more clearly facts than others. That Barry Bonds of the San Francisco Giants hit four home runs during the 2002 World Series could easily be verified if you had to do so, but how would you verify the statement that most homeless people won't work even if they are offered jobs? You would need to find a study of all homeless people in America; they would all have to have been offered jobs, and most would have to have refused. How likely is it that you will find such a study?

For that matter, how would you verify that cashews taste better than peanuts? Such a statement would be a fact only if it were worded this way: "I like cashews better than peanuts." Do you see the difference? The second statement refers only to the speaker's personal preference, which the speaker verifies merely by making the statement. By the way, one of the ten sentences above has long been accepted as a fact by most people even though scholars know that it has never been verified and is probably not a fact at all. Which sentence is it?

OPINIONS

When people say something like "That's just my opinion," they usually mean that they don't want to argue about the point. In fact, "That's just my opinion" is often a way of saying that you don't have any facts to support your idea. Of course, at one time or another we all hold opinions without having examined the facts behind them. Perhaps we hold them because people we respect—our parents, friends, or teachers—hold them or because they reinforce what we already believe to be true about the world or the society in which we live.

Clear, responsible thinking, however, demands that we examine our opinions and discard those that are not well supported. Although it is true that we are all entitled to our own opinions, certainly the unexamined, unsupported opinion is not as valuable as the opinion formed after one has carefully considered the facts. When you think about opinions, consider these three distinctions.

Personal Opinion

The term *personal opinion* is often used when the speaker really means *unsupported* or *unexamined opinion*. If you hear someone say (or if you yourself say) "Well, that's just my personal opinion," be aware that such a statement probably means the opinion has not been very thoroughly examined. In addition to referring to an unexamined opinion, a personal opinion may also refer to matters of personal taste, such as "Suspense novels are more fun to read than science fiction novels."

Considered Opinion

A *considered opinion* is one reached after you have considered the relevant facts and other types of support. If, for example, you have read various articles on the pros and cons of handgun control, you can be said to have developed a considered opinion of your own. Remember, however, that any considered opinion should be open to change if new evidence or support demands it.

Expert Opinion

As you learned in Chapter 3, one type of support is *reference to authority*. For the most part, you should be able to accept an opinion held by experts in a particular field as long as their opinion is related to their field of expertise. For example, you would probably accept an orthopedic surgeon's opinion about the usefulness of a particular knee brace, but there would be no reason to accept that surgeon's opinion about a particular political issue. In addition, even an expert's opinion about an issue in his or her own field must be questioned if other experts in the same field disagree.

EXERCISE 6.2

Indicate which of the following opinions you would take more seriously than others. Which of these opinions are more likely to be personal opinions, considered opinions, or expert opinions?

1. Your neighbor says that the Los Angeles Lakers are more fun to watch than the New York Knicks.

2. A person at a party says that capital punishment discriminates against those who cannot afford expensive attorneys.

3. A palm reader advises you not to take that trip to Hawaii.

4. One homeless person tells another that a particular police officer will not care if he sleeps on the park bench.

5. A Marine Corps colonel says that only a coward would refuse to fight for his country.

6. A local business owner says that the state lottery takes money from the people who can least afford to spend it.

7. A state senator says that restricting handgun sales will not help to reduce crime.

8. A member of the city council says that crime will not be reduced until we start locking up criminals and throwing away the key.

9. Your girlfriend (or boyfriend, or wife, or husband) says that you are no longer as romantic as you used to be.

10. A Honda salesperson says that Hondas have better maintenance records than Buicks.

 Exploring ONLINE

Go to www.thomsonedu.com/devenglish/mcdonald for more information about distinguishing fact from opinion. Under "Chapter Resources" for Chapter 6, click on "Exploring Online."

GENERALIZATIONS VERSUS SPECIFIC STATEMENTS

Much of your ability to evaluate what you read will depend on how well you can distinguish between a generalization and a specific statement. A *specific statement* will refer to specific people, places, events, or ideas, usually giving names and dates as it does, while a *generalization* will refer to groups of people, places, events, or ideas.

SPECIFIC STATEMENT

Yesterday, John McIntyre, a homeless man in San Diego, California, went the entire day without eating anything.

GENERALIZATION

Many homeless people often go an entire day without eating anything.

Both specific statements and generalizations can be facts or opinions, depending on what they say. For example, one of the following specific statements is clearly a fact, and one is clearly an opinion.

FACT

This morning Samantha spilled a cup of coffee on Angelo.

OPINION

> This morning Samantha's carelessness caused her to spill a cup of coffee on Angelo.

As you can see, both of the above statements are specific, but only one can be called a fact.

Like specific statements, generalizations may be either facts or opinions. Generalizations that are based on obviously verified facts rarely require support and are usually treated as facts, while generalizations requiring further support are treated as opinions. Of the following generalizations, which should be treated as a fact and which should not?

> People who smoke face a higher risk of developing lung cancer than people who don't smoke.

> Students' sloppy style of dress today reflects a general "I don't care" attitude toward all of society.

As you can see, both specific statements and generalizations can express facts, so both can be used to support a writer's ideas. However, most writing instructors will ask you to provide specific statements as often as possible, primarily because specific statements are more interesting to read and are more persuasive than generalizations. It is simply more compelling to hear that someone's best friend, who smoked two packs of cigarettes a day, died two days ago after a painful battle with lung cancer than it is to hear the generalization that people who smoke die of lung cancer more often than people who don't.

EXERCISE **6.3**

First, explain whether each of the following statements is a generalization or a specific statement. Then explain whether each statement should be considered a fact or an opinion. If it is an opinion, discuss whether or not it could be reasonably supported with facts.

1. Throughout most of civilized history, people have relied on animals or on their own feet for transportation.
2. The Chevrolet Malibu was the tenth best selling car in the United States in 2001.
3. The cartoon characters Beavis and Butthead caused my sister's son to set fire to the First Interstate Bank.
4. Today's social problems are indicators of our immoral society.
5. Many people today do not discipline their children very effectively.
6. Jerry has AIDS because God is punishing him for being a homosexual.
7. SpongeBob SquarePants is a cartoon character who lives in a pineapple under the Pacific Ocean with his pet snail, Gary.
8. The gang problem has become a serious concern in many high schools throughout the United States.

9. Uneducated people are crass and insensitive.

10. Lee Harvey Oswald was not the only person who fired shots when John F. Kennedy was assassinated.

CONSIDERING YOUR OWN KNOWLEDGE AND EXPERIENCE

Evaluating the support in a text demands that you also think about what *you* know to be true and compare it to what you are reading. For example, if you are a single mother who is successfully raising a happy, well-adjusted child, your experience will certainly contradict an article that asserts that single mothers cannot provide a healthy home environment for their children. You must then consider whether the argument in the article is flawed or overgeneralized or whether your own experience is an unusual exception. Whatever you decide, remember that your own knowledge and experience are important sources of information that you should consult before accepting the support offered by any writer.

CONSIDERING UNSTATED OBJECTIONS

A final step to take as you evaluate an argument is to determine whether the writer has ignored ideas that might contradict or otherwise weaken his or her position. For instance, if you are reading a newspaper editorial arguing that competition in school sports damages our children, consider what objections may not have been addressed by the writer. Do school sports benefit children in any ways that the writer has ignored? Is competition a valuable quality in any way?

Of course, a writer does not have to cover every—or any—objection to write an interesting, thought-provoking paper. If the purpose of the article is to raise issues that the reader should think about, you may not find any objections considered at all. However, the more a paper is intended to convince or persuade the reader, the more thoroughly the writer must consider and respond to major objections.

STEPS IN EVALUATING A TEXT

1. Read the text actively.
   - Determine its purpose and intended audience.
   - Identify its thesis.
   - Identify its main points.
2. Determine how well the main points are supported.
   - Distinguish between facts and opinions.
   - Distinguish between specific support and generalizations.
   - Identify statistics, examples, and references to authority.
3. Test the article's points against your own knowledge and experience.
4. Consider any obvious objections that have been ignored.

READINGS

Appearances Are Destructive   MARK MATHABANE

Mark Mathabane has appeared on The Oprah Winfrey Show, Today, CNN, NPR, The Charlie Rose Show, Larry King, *and numerous TV and radio programs across the country. His articles have appeared in* The New York Times, Newsday, *and* U.S. News & World Report. *Born and raised under apartheid in South Africa, he spent the first eighteen years of his life as the eldest of seven children in a one-square-mile ghetto that was home to more than 200,000 blacks. In the following selection from* The New York Times, *Mathabane describes his reaction to the open dress codes in the public schools of the United States.*

BEFORE YOU READ

1. Do you think students should be required to wear uniforms in public schools? Why or why not?
2. What problems might be caused by requiring students to wear uniforms in public schools? What problems are caused by not requiring such uniforms?

As public schools reopen for the new year, strategies to curb   1
school violence will once again be hotly debated. Installing metal detectors and hiring security guards will help, but the experience of my two sisters makes a compelling case for greater use of dress codes as a way to protect students and promote learning.

Shortly after my sisters arrived here from South Africa I   2
enrolled them at the local public school. I had great expectations for their educational experience. Compared with black schools under apartheid, American schools are Shangri-Las, with modern textbooks, school buses, computers, libraries, lunch programs, and dedicated teachers.

But despite these benefits, which students in many parts of   3
the world only dream about, my sisters' efforts at learning were almost derailed. They were constantly taunted for their homely outfits. A couple of times they came home in tears. In South Africa students were required to wear uniforms, so my sisters had never been preoccupied with clothes and jewelry.

They became so distraught that they insisted on transferring   4
to different schools, despite my reassurances that there was nothing wrong with them because of what they wore.

I have visited enough public schools around the country to   5
know that my sisters' experiences are not unique. In schools in

many areas, Nike, Calvin Klein, Adidas, Reebok, and Gucci are more familiar names to students than Zora Neale Hurston, Shakespeare, and Faulkner. Many students seem to pay more attention to what's on their bodies than in their minds.

Teachers have shared their frustrations with me at being unable to teach those students willing to learn because classes are frequently disrupted by other students ogling themselves in mirrors, painting their fingernails, combing their hair, shining their gigantic shoes, or comparing designer labels on jackets, caps, and jewelry.   6

The fiercest competition among students is often not over academic achievements, but over who dresses most expensively. And many students now measure parental love by how willing their mothers and fathers are to pamper them with money for the latest fads in clothes, sneakers, and jewelry.   7

Those parents without the money to waste on such meretricious extravagances are considered uncaring and cruel. They often watch in dismay and helplessness as their children become involved with gangs and peddle drugs to raise the money.   8

When students are asked why they attach so much importance to clothing, they frequently reply that it's the cool thing to do, that it gives them status and earns them respect. And clothes are also used to send sexual messages, with girls thinking that the only things that make them attractive to boys are skimpy dresses and gaudy looks, rather than intelligence and academic excellence.   9

The argument by civil libertarians that dress codes infringe on freedom of expression is misleading. We observe dress codes in nearly every aspect of our lives without any diminution of our freedoms—as demonstrated by flight attendants; bus drivers; postal employees; high school bands; military personnel; sports teams; Girl and Boy Scouts; and employees of fast-food chains, restaurants, and hotels.   10

In many countries where students outperform their American counterparts academically, school dress codes are observed as part of creating the proper learning environment. Their students tend to be neater, less disruptive in class, and more disciplined, mainly because their minds are focused more on learning and less on materialism.   11

It's time Americans realized that the benefits of safe and effective schools far outweigh any perceived curtailment of freedom of expression brought on by dress codes.   12

AFTER YOU READ

Work with other students to develop responses to these questions or to compare responses that you have already prepared.

1. State the thesis of the article in your own words. What sentences in the article, if any, best express the idea?

2. This article was originally published in *The New York Times.* Who would you say is Mathabane's audience? What is the purpose of his essay?

3. Divide the article into sections according to each major point that Mathabane makes.

4. Consider the support that Mathabane provides for each of his points. Does he use generalizations or specific statements? Facts or opinions? Are his opinions reasonably supported?

5. Consider your own experience or the experiences of people you know. Do they confirm or contradict Mathabane's points?

6. Are there any objections to Mathabane's points that you should consider?

Why Competition?   ALFIE KOHN

Have you ever wondered why our society is as competitive as it is? Does competition seem a natural element of human behavior to you? In the following reading selection, Alfie Kohn presents a thesis regarding competition that he admits is extreme. Consider you own reactions as you examine his reasoning. Alfie Kohn writes and speaks widely on human behavior, education, and social theory. He has been described by Time *magazine as "perhaps the country's most outspoken critic of education's fixation on grades [and] test scores." His criticisms of competition and rewards have helped to shape the thinking of educators—as well as parents and managers—across the country and abroad.*

BEFORE YOU READ

1. What do you consider to be the benefits and the drawbacks of competition? List as many benefits and drawbacks as you can think of.

2. Which list seems stronger—benefits or drawbacks?

3. Explain how your attitude toward competition might be a result of the culture in which you live.

"W-H-I-T-E! White Team is the team for me!" The cheer is   1
repeated, becoming increasingly frenzied as scores of campers, bedecked in the appropriate color, try to outshout their Blue opponents. The rope stretched over the lake is taut now, as determined tuggers give it their all. It looks as if a few will be yanked into the cold water, but a whistle pierces the air. "All right, we'll call this a

draw." Sighs of disappointment follow, but children are soon
scrambling off to the Marathon. Here, competitors will try to win
for their side by completing such tasks as standing upside-down in
a bucket of shampoo or forcing down great quantities of food in
a few seconds before tagging a teammate.

As a counselor in this camp over a period of several years, I   2
witnessed a number of Color Wars, and what constantly amazed
me was the abrupt and total transformation that took place each
time one began. As campers are read their assignments, children
who not ten minutes before were known as "David" or "Margie"
suddenly have a new identity; they have been arbitrarily designated as members of a team. The unspoken command is understood by even the youngest among them: Do everything possible
to win for your side. Strain every muscle to prove how superior
we are to the hostile Blues.

And so they will. Children who had wandered aimlessly   3
about the camp are suddenly driven with a Purpose. Children
who had tired of the regular routine are instantly provided with
Adventure. Children who had trouble making friends are unex-
pectedly part of a new Crowd. In the dining hall, every camper
sits with his or her team. Strategy is planned for the next battle;
troops are taught the next cheer. There is a coldness bordering on
suspicion when passing someone with a blue T-shirt—irrespective
of any friendship B.C. (Before Colors). If anyone has reservations
about participating in an activity, he needs only to be reminded
that the other team is just a few points behind.

"Why Sport?" asks Ed Cowan (*The Humanist,* November/   4
December 1979). When the sports are competitive ones, I cannot
find a single reason to answer his rhetorical query. Mr. Cowan's discussion of the pure—almost mystical—aesthetic pleasure that is
derived from athletics only directs attention away from what is, in
actuality, the primary impetus of any competitive activity: winning.

I would not make such a fuss over Color War, or even   5
complain about the absurd spectacle of grown men shrieking and
cursing on Sunday afternoons, were it not for the significance of
the role played by competition in our culture. It is bad enough
that Americans actually regard fighting as a sport; it is worse that
the outcome of even the gentlest of competitions—baseball—can
induce fans to hysteria and outright violence. But sports is only
the tip of the proverbial iceberg. Our entire society is affected
by—even structured upon—the need to be "better than."

My thesis is admittedly extreme; it is, simply put, that *competition by its very nature is always unhealthy.* This is true, to begin with, because competition and cooperation are mutually exclusive orientations. I say this fully aware of the famed camaraderie that is supposed to develop among players—or soldiers—on the same side. First, I have doubts, based on personal experience, concerning the depth and fullness of relationships that result from the need to become more effective against a common enemy.

Second, the "realm of the interhuman," to use Martin Buber's phrase, is severely curtailed when those on the other side are excluded from any possible community. Worse, they are generally regarded with suspicion and contempt in any competitive enterprise. (This is not to say that we cannot remain on good terms with, say, tennis opponents, but that whatever cooperation and meaningful relationship is in evidence exists in spite of the competitiveness.) Finally, the sweaty fellowship of the locker room (or, to draw the inescapable parallel again, the trenches) simply does not compensate for the inherent evils of competition.

The desire to win has a not very surprising (but too rarely remarked upon) characteristic: it tends to edge out other goals and values in the context of any given competitive activity. When I was in high school, I was a very successful debater for a school that boasted one of the country's better teams. After hundreds and hundreds of rounds of competition over three years, I can assert in no uncertain terms that the purpose of debate is not to seek the truth or resolve an issue. No argument, however compelling, is ever conceded; veracity is never attributed to the other side. The only reason debaters sacrifice their free time collecting thousands of pieces of evidence, analyzing arguments, and practicing speeches, is to win. Truth thereby suffers in at least two ways.

In any debate, neither team is concerned with arriving at a fuller understanding of the topic. The debaters concentrate on "covering" arguments, tying logical knots, and, above all, sounding convincing. Beyond this, though, there exists a tremendous temptation to fabricate and distort evidence. Words are left out, phrases added, sources modified in order to lend credibility to the position. One extremely successful debater on my team used to invent names of magazines which ostensibly printed substantiation for crucial arguments he wanted to use.

6

7

8

9

With respect to this last phenomenon, it is fruitless—and a   10
kind of self-deception, ultimately—to shake our heads and de-
plore this sort of thing. Similarly, we have no business condemning
"overly rough" football players or the excesses of "overzealous"
campaign aides or even, perhaps, violations of the Geneva Convention in time of war (which is essentially a treatise on How to
Kill Human Beings Without Doing Anything *Really* Unethical). We
are engaging in a massive (albeit implicit) exercise of hypocrisy to
decry these activities while continuing to condone, and even encourage, the competitive orientation of which they are only the
logical conclusion.

The cost of any kind of competition in human terms is   11
incalculable. When my success depends on other people's failure,
the prospects for a real human community are considerably di-
minished. This consequence speaks to the profoundly antihumanis-
tic quality of competitive activity, and it is abundantly evident in
American society. Moreover, when my success depends on my being *better than,* I am caught on a treadmill, destined never to enjoy
real satisfaction. Someone is always one step higher, and even the
summit is a precarious position in light of the hordes waiting to
occupy it in my stead. I am thus perpetually insecure and, as psychologist Rollo May points out, perpetually anxious.

. . . individual competitive success is both the dominant   12
goal in our culture and the most pervasive occasion for anxiety.
. . . [This] anxiety arises out of the interpersonal isolation and
alienation from others that inheres in a pattern in which self-
validation depends on triumphing over others (*The Meaning of
Anxiety,* rev. ed.).

I begin to see my self-worth as conditional—that is to say,   13
my goodness or value become contingent on how much better I
am than so many others in so many activities. If you believe, as I
do, that unconditional self-esteem is a singularly important requirement for (and indicator of) mental health, then the destruc-
tiveness of competition will clearly outweigh any putative benefit,
whether it be a greater effort at tug-of-war or a higher gross national product.

From the time we are quite small, the ethic of competi-   14
tiveness is drummed into us. The goal in school is not to grow
as a human being or even, in practice, to reach a satisfactory
level of intellectual competence. We are pushed instead to become brighter than, quicker than, better achievers than our

classmates, and the endless array of scores and grades lets us know at any given instant how we stand on that ladder of academic success.

If our schools are failing at their explicit tasks, we may rest assured of their overwhelming success regarding this hidden agenda. We are well trained to enter the marketplace and compete frantically for more money, more prestige, more of all the "good things" in life. An economy such as ours, understand, does not merely permit competition: *it demands it.* Ever greater profits becomes the watchword of private enterprise, and an inequitable distribution of wealth (a polite codeword for human suffering) follows naturally from such an arrangement.   15

Moreover, one must be constantly vigilant lest one's competitors attract more customers or conceive some innovation that gives them the edge. To become outraged at deceptive and unethical business practices is folly; it is the competitiveness of the system that promotes these phenomena. Whenever people are defined as opponents, doing everything possible to triumph must be seen not as an aberration from the structure but as its very consummation. (I recognize, of course, that I have raised a plethora of difficult issues across many disciplines that cry out for a more detailed consideration. I hope, however, to at least have opened up some provocative, and largely neglected, lines of inquiry.)   16

This orientation finds its way into our personal relationships as well. We bring our yardstick along to judge potential candidates for lover, trying to determine who is most attractive, most intelligent, and . . . the best lover. At the same time, of course, we are being similarly reduced to the status of competitor. The human costs are immense.   17

"Why Sport?", then, is a good question to begin with. It leads us to inquire, "Why Miss Universe contests?" "Why the arms race?" and—dare we say it?—"Why capitalism?" Whether a competition-free society can actually be constructed is another issue altogether, and I readily concede that this mentality has so permeated our lives that we find it difficult even to imagine alternatives in many settings. The first step, though, consists in understanding that rivalry of any kind is both psychologically disastrous and philosophically unjustifiable, that the phrase "healthy competition" is a contradiction in terms. Only then can we begin to develop saner, richer lifestyles for ourselves as individuals, and explore more humanistic possibilities for our society.   18

AFTER YOU READ

Work with other students to develop responses to these questions or to compare responses that you have already prepared.

1. State the thesis of the article in your own words. What sentences in the article, if any, best express the idea?

2. This article was originally published in *The Humanist*. Who would you say is Kohn's audience? What is the purpose of his essay?

3. Divide the article into sections according to each major point that Kohn makes.

4. Consider the support that Kohn provides for each of his points. Does he use generalizations or specific statements? Facts or opinions? Are his opinions reasonably supported?

5. Consider your own experience or the experiences of people you know. Do they confirm or contradict Kohn's points?

6. Are there any objections to Kohn's points that you should consider?

History 101: Pass the Popcorn, Please   ELAINE MINAMIDE

Elaine Minamide, a freelance writer who lives in southern California, is an adjunct instructor at Palomar Community College. In the following article, first published in the San Diego Union-Tribune, *she raises questions about the use and misuse of films in the classroom.*

BEFORE YOU READ

1. What do you think about the use of movies in the classroom? Do movies help students learn the subject matter?

2. Make a list of both the advantages and disadvantages of using movies in a classroom setting.

3. Which seems stronger, the advantages or the disadvantages?

On the face of it, the arguments make sense: 1

"Films provoke students to not only think about history, but   2
to experience it to its fullest."

"Movies give educators a priceless opportunity to connect to   3
young students bored by textbooks."

"Anything that gets the kids thinking and talking can only   4
be positive."

It's difficult to argue with success. Opening to chapter eight 5
in a history book rarely evokes the kind of hand-flailing, call-on-me-
teacher response most educators only dream about. Switching on
the VCR is a different story. From the opening credits, kids are
hooked, involved, and—dare we say it?—learning.

That's the bottom line, isn't it? So what if *Amistad* has, as   6
some critics have charged, "rewritten history"? Who cares if *Titanic*
is merely a backdrop for a hyped-up, modern love story? Does it
matter, as long as kids are thinking about the grander issues, like
slavery or the tragic arrogance of man?

The debate over the use of contemporary films in the   7
classroom may be stimulating, but something else is at stake that
has nothing to do with blurring the line between fact and fiction.
Any competent teacher can address head-on disputes over historical accuracy or propaganda. That's what education is all about, after all: guiding students into becoming discriminating, critical
thinkers.

The greater issue has to do with declining literacy and can   8
be traced back to the days when the letter "b" first danced across
the television screen. While older siblings sweated through math
problems and penmanship at school, the preschool set of the '70s
sat cross-legged on their carpets, mesmerized by Bert and Ernie
singing catchy jingles about the alphabet. Parents, of course, were
delighted: What better way for your precocious 3-year-old to
learn her ABCs than to plop her in front of the TV while you
made a few phone calls? *Sesame Street* was a godsend.

Wouldn't you know it—most educators didn't agree. By the   9
time those preschoolers entered kindergarten, not only did they already know their ABCs, but they sat in their little chairs, waiting for
the song and dance to begin. The Entertain Me pupils were in their
seats, and they're seated still. Today's high schoolers are yesterday's
Sesame Street watchers, clamoring to be entertained.

Evidently, teachers are accommodating them. A recent   10
feature article in the *San Diego Union-Tribune* focused on local
teachers who frequently supplement classroom instruction with
contemporary films. One eighth-grade history teacher, for example, has a must-see list of flicks that she either encourages her students to see or brings to the classroom herself.

A high school social-studies teacher uses movies to   11
introduce new subjects to his students. And they're not alone.
Some film companies (notably, the producers of *Amistad*) now
supply schools across the nation with study guides to accompany
their current releases.

It's been argued that since students spend so much more   12
time watching TV and movies than reading books, it's best to meet
them on common ground if you want them to learn. Furthermore

(the argument goes), since movies motivate students to further inquiry (researching the sinking of the *Titanic* is currently in vogue),
their use in the classroom is not only justifiable but highly innovative.

Their arguments contradict sound educational philosophy.   13
The purpose of education is to challenge students, not cater to
them. Children may prefer cookies and candy, but wise parents
still serve fruits and vegetables. The issue should be explored from
a broader perspective. To what degree do the apparent short-
term gains become long-term liabilities?

As time goes by, will students' dependency upon audio-   14
visual learning make it difficult, if not impossible, for them to extract meaning from books alone? In our quest to capture the wayward attention of kids raised on song and dance, do we handicap
them instead? It doesn't take much mental acumen to be inspired
and even informed by a well-made Hollywood movie. The question is not do movies enhance learning, but rather, are they becoming a substitute for actual learning?

That's not to say movies shouldn't be utilized in the   15
classroom. By all means, use them, but as dessert, not the main
course. Incorporate film into the curriculum after the historical
subject matter is fully grasped, not before, and only then as part
of a broader process of research and analysis. Use films to teach
critical thinking, to train students to look for bias, propaganda,
commercial exploitation, historical accuracy. Allow students' knowledge of a subject to influence their appreciation of a movie, rather
than the reverse.

More to the point, however, require that they read. If one of   16
the goals of education is to foster literacy, it seems counterproductive to assign movies as a supplement to learning when historical fiction may be just as effective. Assigning books like *Les Miserables* or *Gone with the Wind* has the added benefit of broadening
students' literary background. Teachers should be providing students with a must-read book list rather than a must-see movie list.

Why should kids read *Les Miserables* when they can see the   17
movie instead? Answer: They probably won't. That's why acquiescing
to the "entertain me" style of learning serves little purpose other
than to reinforce students' reluctance to read. Movie-watching is one
more marshmallow in the sugar-laden diet of popular curricula. We
have no one to blame but ourselves if all kids know about history or
culture is what they learned from their VCRs. After all, they came to
us expecting a song and dance. And we haven't disappointed.

AFTER YOU READ

Work with other students to develop responses to these questions or to compare responses that you have already prepared.

1. State the thesis of the article in your own words. What sentences in the article, if any, best express the idea?
2. This article was originally published in a San Diego newspaper. Who would you say is Minamide's audience? What is the purpose of her essay?
3. Divide the article into sections according to each major point that Minamide makes.
4. Consider the support that Minamide provides. Does she use generalizations or specific statements? Facts or opinions? Explain why you do or do not find her support convincing.
5. Consider your own experience or the experiences of people you know. Do they confirm or contradict Minamide's points?
6. Are there any objections to Minamide's points that you should consider?

Hell Is Other iPods: The Aural Loneliness of the Long-Distance Shuffler

CASPAR MELVILLE

Caspar Melville is editor of New Humanist *magazine, one of the world's continuously published magazines (starting life as* The Literary Review *in 1885).* New Humanist *describes itself as "a world leader in supporting and promoting humanism and rational inquiry and opposing religious dogma, irrationalism and bunkum wherever it is found." In the following selection, Melville considers the popularity of the iPod and its effect on what he calls "our already denuded culture."*

BEFORE YOU READ

1. Consider the title. What does it suggest will be the point of this reading selection?
2. If you own an iPod or other MP3 player, discuss in what way it has or has not affected your interactions with other people.

I don't have an iPod, but it's only a matter of time. I can feel the   1
pressure building up around me—the groovy TV ads, the smug
folks with the telltale white headphones on the subway making
me feel unhip, the proliferating choice of colors. And yet something in me resists, and it's not just the inner cheapskate. Something feels not quite right, and it's not only that the iPod comes in
a special red and black U2 collector's edition.

I read an article recently in *USA Today* about the new "gospel   2
of iPod," the emergence of "the iPod nation." Well, okay, the piece
is gently parodying Apple's conventionally hyped-up marketing and
loyal, if not to say fanatical, user base. (There is no zeal like the
zeal of an Apple Mac user; just try asking one innocently, as I once
did, if there really is any substantial difference between a Mac and
a PC.) So perhaps we shouldn't take it too seriously, but try these
statements on for size: "My friends all have [an iPod], and I just felt
it was time to catch up." Fair enough, typical teenage logic, and if
not for such sentiments, where would the hula hoop or the Rubik's
cube ever have got?

But how about this? "The iPod has changed my life," says   3
Andrea Kozek, perhaps revealing a lack of robustness in her life in
the first place. "When I need to block out the rest of the world, I
turn it on." And let's face it, the one thing we really need to do is
block out the rest of that pesky old world. But why not just listen
to the radio, Andrea? "Do I really want to hear Britney Spears doing Bobby Brown's 'My Prerogative'? It wasn't a good song in the
first place," she answers, revealing some talent for music criticism
but poor taste in radio stations, which I wonder if her iPod can really resolve. (By the way, Andrea has nicknamed her iPod "My Pre-
cious," a tribute to Gollum in *The Lord of the Rings* trilogy.)

It's easy to mock. So let's continue. One choice statement   4
explains how iPod can calm the turbulent waters of family life by
resolving the thorny subject of who gets to choose the music;
"We'll all be listening to music at the same time," says an iPod
mom from Williamsburg, New York. "I'll be connected to iTunes
on my laptop, my kids will have their iPods on, and my husband
likes to listen to his while he's surfing around on eBay." Remind
me not to accept an invitation to dinner at their place, or at least
to bring a good book with me.

Here's my real objection. The iPod is an example of a beautifully   5
designed, convenient, and desirable object that promises to make
our lives better, but whose promise, on reflection, as is so often
the case, turns out to reinforce the worst in our already denuded
culture. In an age of atomization and social fragmentation it reinforces solipsism and places the individual and that dreaded value
"choice" at the heart of experience; it suggests connection—always
the implicit promise of the digital age—while enforcing separation;
it encourages people to "tune out" while they're occupying social

space with others, as if the others were mere irritations; and it
reduces the experience of music, which in my view is an inherently social and collaborative art and medium, to a preselected relationship with the self.

The iPod shares this severe limitation with all post-Walkman   6
personal stereos. They personalize, indeed privatize, music, which
really comes to life only when it is public, shared, and collaborative. A large part of the joy of discovering good new music is
simultaneously anticipating the pleasure of sharing it with someone else. Anything else is masturbation. Overstated? Try this statement from one user: "With the iPod the Buddha is in the details.
The finish and the feel are such that you want to caress it. And
when you do, wonderful things happen."

Legal scholar Cass Sunstein has a theory about the internet   7
that he calls "The Daily We." The argument is that rather than
broaden our access to information, ideas, and experiences, the Internet, precisely because it offers such dizzying, disorienting choice
and possibility, reinforces the tendency to filter out what is unknown, stick to what you like, and congregate with others who
like the same thing.

A similar argument could be made for the "iPod jukebox."   8
Unlike listening to (good) radio, which could infuriate and surprise
you in equal measure, the iPod jukebox protects you from the
shocks, both highs and lows; it offers you a safe experience that
flatters, because every good track was one you chose, every familiar song reminds you of an emotion of memory: yours. Never
did I think I'd find myself sounding so much like that old Frankfurt
school philosopher-grump Theodor Adorno, but his argument that
pop music and its predictable structure deliver back to the user a
cheap thrill because he or she recognizes how it will end seems
to work for the iPod.

iPodistas like to talk up the social benefits of iPod-jacking: Total   9
strangers swap iPods for a moment to listen to each other's selections. Well, okay. The utter hell of having to listen to strangers' music
collections while standing close to them without talking in public
notwithstanding, such an idea proceeds from the premise that it is
the iPod that has offered this epochal opportunity for social interac-
tion. It was, I am given to understand, entirely possible even before
the iPod to approach a stranger on the street and attempt to swap
words, names, or even ideas in a form of "tuning in" known as a

conversation. A celebration of the joys of iPod-jacking seems a final acceptance that the possibility of actually communicating is gone for good, and we are left with a pale facsimile: You play me yours and I'll play you mine.

"This is all part of the shift from mass media to personalized   10
media," says Paul Saffo, a technology forecaster and director of the Institute of the Future. No doubt this is true, but is it, I wonder, a good thing? For all the cachet and control implied by the iPod, the laptop, the BlackBerry, the digital camera, and Wi-Fi, in the end what seems to be on offer are particular kinds of distraction and avoidance, and a peculiar kind of 21st-century digital loneliness.

Or am I just grumpy because no one bought me an iPod for Christmas?

AFTER YOU READ

Work with other students to develop responses to these questions or to compare responses that you have already prepared.

1. State the thesis of the article in your own words. What sentences in the article, if any, best express the idea?
2. This article was originally published in *New Humanist*. Who would you say is Melville's audience? What is the purpose of his essay?
3. Divide the article into sections according to each major point that Melville makes.
4. Consider the support that Melville provides. Does he use generalizations or specific statements? Facts or opinions? Explain why you do or do not find his support convincing.
5. Consider your own experience or the experiences of people you know. Do they confirm or contradict Melville's points?
6. Are there any objections to Melville's points that you should consider?

WRITING ASSIGNMENT

Choose one of the reading selections from this chapter or a selection assigned by your instructor. After a discussion with other members of your class, determine whether or not you find the reading selection convincing by identifying which points seem particularly weak or particularly strong. Then write a paper in which you evaluate the reading selection. Focus each body paragraph of your paper on a separate point from the article, explaining why it is or is not convincing to you.

As you read and evaluate the following essays, consider these areas.

Evaluation Essay

1. Introduction

   Does the introduction accurately and clearly state the central idea and purpose of the article? Does it smoothly and easily move the reader into the paper?

   1   2   3   4   5   6

2. Thesis

   Does the introduction end in a clear statement of evaluation of the effectiveness of the article?

   1   2   3   4   5   6

3. Unity

   Does each paragraph have a clear and specific topic sentence that accurately introduces and states an evaluation of one of the main points of the article? Is the material in each paragraph clearly related to its topic sentence?

   1   2   3   4   5   6

4. Development

   Is each topic sentence supported with clear references to the article as well as to details and examples from the writer's own knowledge and experience? Are references to ideas from the article accurately explained?

   1   2   3   4   5   6

5. Coherence

   Are transitions used between paragraphs? Where needed, are transitions used between sentences within each paragraph?

   1   2   3   4   5   6

6. References to the Text

   Are direct quotations and paraphrases correctly introduced and smoothly incorporated into the text? Do they reflect the writer's point accurately?

   1   2   3   4   5   6

7. Subordination and Sentence Variety

   Do the sentences combine ideas that are related, using coordination, subordination, or verbal or appositive phrases when appropriate? Are there too many brief, choppy main clauses?

   1   2   3   4   5   6

8. Grammar and Mechanics

   Does the paper contain fragments, comma splices, fused sentences, errors in subject-verb agreement, pronoun use, modifiers, punctuation, or spelling?

   1   2   3   4   5   6

9. Overall Ranking of the Essay

   1   2   3   4   5   6

Student Essay 1

In his essay "Why Competition?" Alfie Kohn attacks a trait embedded in the very fabric of American society, competition. By concluding that relationships between both teammates and rivals are undesireable and illustrating the pitfalls competition holds for both individuals and American society, Kohn tries to prove that "competition by its very nature is always unhealthy." Although Kohn uses several strong personal examples to support his claims, the essay contains little substantiated support. However, since Kohn's purpose was "to at least have opened up some provocative, and largely neglected, lines of inquiry," he was successful.

I disagree in part with Kohn's first point which concerns relationships between both teammates and rivals. Kohn believes that the relationships between teammates lack depth and fullness and also observes that rivalry causes the teammates to not only exclude their rivals from "any possible community," but often to regard them with "suspicion and contempt." Kohn supports this two pronged attack with his personal experiences as a camp counselor and also compares teammates to soldiers. After attending scores of high school football games, I cannot disagree with Kohn's observations about rivals, but, as an athlete, I always played on teams with people who were my true friends and not just "comrades."

Kohn's second point is that "the desire to win . . . tends to edge out other goals and values in the context of any given competitive activity." He claims that when people are competing, winning becomes all important, and values fly out the window. His support is another personal experience which consists of his participation on a debate team. Perhaps these "debaters" are just overzealous, or they just take themselves too seriously. When I compete recreationally, whether I'm arguing a point or dribbling a basketball, I'm concerned with having fun first and winning second.

After making it clear that none among us is above behaving competitively, Kohn states his third and most convincing argument, that the cost of competition in human terms is immeasurable. With individual success, says Kohn, comes anxiety. A person's self worth starts becoming conditional. Kohn says, "my . . . values become contingent on how much better I am than so many others in so many activities." With this kind of pressure on us, Kohn continues, we can never be satisfied. Kohn doesn't rely solely on personal experiences to support this argument, but also includes a quote from a psychologist. I agree with this final argument because during my eight years of ballet school, I often felt the envy competition breeds and also found myself measuring my own accomplishments in terms of other, more experienced, dancers.

Although Kohn does bring up some interesting points, his support is mainly from personal experience. The basis of the argument is strong and, with further development, could be pretty convincing. Despite its weaknesses, this essay definitely made me rethink the term "healthy competition."

Student Essay 2

Everyone agrees that children cannot afford to be uneducated. It is simply the means of educating children that provokes a controversy. In the article "History 101: Pass the Popcorn, Please," Elaine Minamide quotes those with opposing views in saying, "Movies give educators the priceless opportunity to connect to young students bored by textbooks." However, Minamide believes that watching contemporary films in class makes students dependent on audio-visual learning instead of books. She points out that students get used to the "song-and-dance" routine from *Sesame Street*. Unlike Minamide, I feel that kids need a more intriguing, interactive approach in order to learn and retain the material. I did not find Minamide's arguments very effective. Watching movies in the classroom is beneficial to the student because it is a more interesting way of presenting the material.

Minamide asks, "As time goes by, will students' dependency upon audio-visual learning make it difficult, if not impossible, for them to extract meaning from books alone?" To answer her question, I would say that's unlikely, but even if it that were the case, the students would still be learning, only in a more interesting fashion. In fact, one of the educational advantages of audio-visual learning is the interest it sparks in students. Most kids can't get an education from dry textbooks and boring lectures. Kids learn in many different ways, so the material must be presented in an interesting fashion. While I was doing an internship in a seventh-grade classroom at Diegueno Junior High School, the students were learning about Chinese dynasties. The teacher divided them into groups that would rotate through five stations. They would watch a movie about the dynasties, research it on the Internet, read from the text, listen to a lecture, and discuss it in groups. The kids ended up enjoying the movie most because it gave them a true sense about the different Chinese dynasties, and it provided a mental picture as well. Another example of audio-visual learning being successful is when my eleventh-grade history class watched *Schindler's List*. We had read about the Holocaust in the textbook, but none of us had a clear picture, and the fragments of the history we had learned were not put together. As we watched the movie, most everyone was in tears, and I must say that I've never seen quite such a reaction from reading a textbook.

Besides the benefit of providing more interesting ways to educate by using movies, the so-called song-and-dance routine, which Minamide thinks will handicap students, is really an effective way to learn. In order to learn the material, the students must enjoy themselves. Did you every wonder why kids in kindergarten have smiles on their faces while many high school students wear frowns? It's because the younger students are intrigued by the teacher's presentation, causing them to learn more. My history teacher sings songs to our class with his guitar. We listen to the lyrics and get lost in true history. As we all look pleasantly at our teacher, we find ourselves experiencing history instead of reading it. We must be involved; it is essential. As Benjamin Franklin put it, "Tell me and I forget. Teach me and I remember. Involve me and I learn."

Minamide writes, "More to the point, require that they read." Unlike the "song-and-dance" routine, reading is only beneficial if you enjoy it. Unless a student has an astounding imagination, he/she probably cannot absorb as much knowledge from textbooks as they would from historical films. When I was in fifth grade, my class was learning about the American presidents. Our class was split into two groups, the "readers" and the "watchers." Half of us reading the textbook, the other half watching a film. The next day, both groups were tested on the material, and the "watchers'" average test scores were double that of the "readers." Need I say more?

I most definitely believe that using audio-visual technology is beneficial to the students. It allows the student to learn from whatever means of education helps them the most. As Minamide quoted her critics, "Films provoke students to not only think about history, but to experience it to the fullest." Maybe students do need to be entertained, but is that such a bad thing? It's human nature to be interested in interesting things. As time goes on, we must move and advance along with it. Why keep students in the past with only reading books when they can learn from so many different methods? Children cannot afford to be uneducated. It is our job to spark their interests, which will soon grow into bright, luminous flames.

Student Essay 3

The reading selection "Teenagers in Dreamland" can be found in Part Four.

In "Teenagers in Dreamland," Robert J. Samuelson states that children live in a dreamland, curious and disorienting "mixture of adult freedoms and childlike expectations." Children are becoming more and more independent at an earlier age and adult authority is becoming less. He also explains the difference of children's attitudes if they attend private and public schools. Children are also working while they are attending school which causes problems with their schoolwork. Working while going to school makes kids think they are more independent and have more freedom. Society thinks the kids are growing up fine, but statistics show differently. I feel that Samuelson's argument about private schools educating students better than public school is weak; however, I agree with his arguments that students want more responsibility and freedom, and that students have jobs that demand more time than they have to do schoolwork.

I disagree with Samuelson's idea that private schools educate students better than public schools. He states that private schools give 50% more homework and have "rigorous courses in math, English, and history." When I was in high school, I felt that I had the same amount of homework as my friends in private schools. I also feel that they were more rebelling than I was because they had more authority watching over them. Private schools may provide better education for a small group, but Samuelson overlooks the fact that private schools have fewer students so they can focus more on their students. On the other hand, public schools can't limit their attendance so they have to focus on students with more needs. I feel that if I went to a private school, I would have turned out totally different. I think I would be more rebelling and not willing to go to college.

Samuelson states that children are growing up too soon. For example, they want to own their own cars and want to have more freedom to do what they please and do it when they want. Students move out of their parent's houses earlier than when their parents were their age. I see youths getting married really young and depending on others for support. When I was a high school student, I saw pregnancy within the high school population. Most of the girls were just about to finish high school and now they have a long road ahead of them. For example, one of my friends is 17 and pregnant. Her boyfriend is 25 and they thought they had all this freedom to do what they wanted. Now he is going off to Okinawa, and she will have to depend on others to help take care of the child. This is a case of a young woman growing up too fast.

Students are running into the dilemma of going to school and having a job. They feel that the only way to get freedom is to have a job. I had a job when I was going to high school, and it took away time from my schoolwork. It was hard to budget my time so I had time for schoolwork and still be able to spend time with my friends. My job was demanding more of my time from my friends and schoolwork. I liked the money because I was able to buy what I wanted, but my grades were bad.

I feel that Samuelson has a strong point that when children work while they are going to school, it takes away from their education. I also agree that children are growing up too soon. They want to be adults while in some ways they want to be kids. However, I disagree that private schools are better than public schools because he has not concerned the size of the populations in the school.

SENTENCE COMBINING: PARALLELISM

You were introduced to the concept of parallelism in Chapter 2 when you used coordination to combine sentences. At that time, you learned that ideas joined with coordinating conjunctions should be worded similarly. For example, two words joined with a coordinating conjunction, such as *and,* should both be nouns, or both adjectives, or both adverbs—the point is that they should both be the same type of word.

The same is true of two phrases or clauses joined with a coordinating conjunction. You can join two prepositional phrases or two participial phrases with a coordinating conjunction, but you should not join a prepositional phrase to a participial phrase with one.

ITEMS IN A SERIES

When you write three or more ideas in a series, you should word them similarly, just as you do when you join two ideas with a coordinating conjunction. The key is to use similar types of words, phrases, or clauses as you write the series. *The principle of parallelism requires that you use similar grammatical constructions when you join two ideas with coordinating conjunctions or when you join several ideas in a series.*

The following sentences are drawn from the reading selections in this text. Note that each sentence uses parallel sentence structure.

Parallel Words

nouns   Our culture stresses <u>freedom</u>, <u>individuality</u>, and <u>choice</u>.

adjectives, nouns But it will be <u>easier</u> and <u>happier</u> for us knowing that our grandson will be spared the continued <u>explanation</u> and <u>harassment</u>, the <u>doubts</u> and <u>anxieties</u>, of being a child of unmarried parents.

Parallel Phrases

infinitives   To be a hero you have <u>to stand out</u>, <u>to excel</u>, <u>to take risks</u>. . . .

verb phrases   Like millions of Americans, the cabdriver was probably a decent human being who had never <u>stolen anything</u>, <u>broken any law</u>, or <u>willfully injured another</u>. . . .

participial phrases The only reason debaters sacrifice their free time <u>collecting thousands of pieces of evidence</u>, <u>analyzing arguments</u>, and <u>practicing speeches</u>, is to win.

Parallel Clauses

subordinate clauses A fellow commits a crime <u>because he's basically insecure</u>, <u>because he hated his stepmother at nine</u>, or <u>because his sister needs an operation</u>.

main clauses   <u>Strategy is planned for the next battle</u>; <u>troops are taught the next cheer</u>.

As you can see from the above examples, you can use parallelism to join all kinds of sentence parts, as long as they are the same type of sentence part. You can join nouns to nouns, infinitives to infinitives, and subordinate clauses to subordinate clauses.

ITEMS JOINED BY CORRELATIVE CONJUNCTIONS

Correlative conjunctions are pairs of words that combine related ideas. The most common correlative conjunctions are *either . . . or, neither . . . nor, not only . . . but also,* and *both . . . and.* Follow the principles of parallel sentence structure when you use these correlatives. Each word, phrase, or clause joined to another by a correlative conjunction should be worded similarly to the other. The following examples illustrate both correct and incorrect usage.

INCORRECT

The timber wolf will **either** <u>adapt to its new environment</u> **or** <u>it will die a slow death</u>. (verb phrase combined with main clause)

CORRECT

The timber wolf will **either** <u>adapt to its new environment</u> **or** <u>die a slow death</u>. (verb phrase combined with verb phrase)

CORRECT

Either <u>the timber wolf will adapt to its new environment</u> **or** <u>it will die a slow death</u>. (main clause combined with main clause)

EXERCISE 6.4

Use parallel sentence structure to combine each group of sentences into one sentence.

EXAMPLE

Chelsea was startled by the sudden applause. She was also confused by the bright lights. She stuttered a few words. Then she ran from the stage.
Startled by the sudden applause and confused by the bright lights, Chelsea stuttered a few words and then ran from the stage.

1. The swan was waddling out of the lake. It was heading toward Leda. It had a strange look in its eye.

2. Last week's storm caused mudslides in the foothills. The storm also caused traffic jams on the freeways. Power outages throughout the city were another result.

3. The winning skier slipped. She broke her ankle. It happened after the race had ended. It was before the medal was awarded.

4. The horse was wandering down the freeway. It was stopping all the traffic. It was soon captured by the police officer.

5. Spiderman climbed out of the window. He scaled the side of the building. He fired his spider web at the thief.

6. Carmen could not decide whether she wanted to risk the earthquakes on the West Coast. Another possibility was that she could risk the hurricanes on the East Coast.

7. The produce manager knew it. The price of the oranges was too high. The quality of the oranges was too low.

8. Senator Milkwood proposed his new legislation. He was determined to preserve the disappearing forests. He was also determined to promote the lumber industry.

9. The Sphinx looked at Oedipus and asked, "What creature goes on four feet in the morning? The same creature goes on two feet at midday. It also goes on three feet in the evening."

10. By the time the play was over, Hugo was thoroughly disgusted. The play had made him completely depressed. He decided to buy a gallon of vanilla ice cream. He planned to cover it with chocolate sauce. Then he was going to eat it all by himself.

EXERCISE **6.5**

Revise the following sentences to correct any errors in parallelism.

EXAMPLE

The farmer knew that for the rest of his life he would be planting seeds, his crops needed tending, and prayers for a good harvest.

> The farmer knew that for the rest of his life he would be planting seeds, tending his crops, and praying for a good harvest.

1. In the early 1800s, John Palmer, a farmer with a long white beard, stood by his principles and refusing to be intimidated.

2. When the people in his town told him that he should be not only ashamed of his beard but also that he should cut it off, he refused.

3. Children jeered at him, stones were heaved through his windows by grown men, and women crossing to the opposite side of the street.

4. Saying that he was a vain man and with the insistence that he cut his beard, the local pastor denounced him.

5. When several men tried to grab him, hold him down, and shave him, he fought back.

6. As a result, he was arrested, a trial was held, and jailed for "unprovoked assault."

7. He was told either that he could cut his beard or stay in jail.

8. When Henry David Thoreau and Ralph Waldo Emerson heard of his plight, they persuaded people to support his cause and his release was arranged with their help.

9. John Palmer refused to leave his jail cell, saying that his jailers must admit that they were not only wrong but also must publicly state that he had a right to wear a beard.

EXERCISE **6.6**

Use parallel sentence structure to combine each group of sentences into one sentence.

1. Mark Twain, one of America's greatest writers, grew up in Hannibal, Missouri. Then he spent several years as a riverboat pilot on the Mississippi. Later he worked on newspapers in Nevada and California.

2. His literary career took him from the shores of the Mississippi. He traveled to the silver-mining boomtowns of Nevada. He lectured in the literary salons of Boston.

3. He was born Samuel Clemens, but he used many psuedonyms. One that he used was Thomas Jefferson Snodgrass. He also wrote as W. Epaminandos Adrastus Blab. Another was Sergeant Fathom. He finally settled on Mark Twain.

4. In Hannibal, Missouri, Twain was surrounded by the soft drawls of Virginia transplants. He also listened to the hard twangs of immigrants from Arkansas. There were many other accents that he heard.

5. As a boy, Mark Twain would love to load his pockets with small knives and his favorite marbles. His pockets would hold extra fishhooks and string. He would even carry toads in them. Later in life he was always interested in what people had in their pockets.

6. In Hannibal, Samuel Clemens would listen intently to ghost stories. He also would listen to Bible narratives. Adults would tell tall tales that he enjoyed hearing. Then he would retell them to his friends.

7. Both Mark Twain and Tom Sawyer, his famous literary double, cut school to play with friends. They sneaked out of the house at night to roam the streets of his town. They both played practical jokes on parents and siblings.

8. Mark Twain's clear, economical style is one of his strengths. So is his ability to reproduce the informal sounds of ordinary American speech. His unique sense of humor is also a strength. These are the chief characteristics of works like *The Adventures of Huckleberry Finn.*

9. Twain would edit his work ruthlessly. He would rework passages. He would change wording He would cut out entire sections if they didn't add to the story or the humor.

10. In the later years of his life, Twain experienced bankruptcy. He also suffered through the death of his favorite daughter. He also faced illness and death of his wife.

EXERCISE 6.7

Combine the following sentences, using coordination, subordination, verbal phrases, appositives, and parallel sentence structure where appropriate.

1. Of the five senses, many animals possess at least one that is special.
   That one is much more highly developed than it is in other animals.
   The five senses are sight, hearing, touch, smell, and taste.

2. A buzzard will be flying hundreds of feet in the air.
   It can see a beetle on the ground.
   An owl can hear the slight rustle of a mouse.
   It can home in on the rustle.
   That sound is inaudible to the human ear.

3. Most animals that hunt have many rod cells in their eyes.
   Rod cells are sensitive to movement.
   Animals that gather stationary food have many cone cells.
   Cone cells are sensitive to colors.

4. Dogs have over 200 million olfactory cells.

Humans have 5 million olfactory cells.

Dogs are literally millions of times better at detecting odors than are humans.

5. A female butterfly carries only 1/10,000 of a milligram of perfume.

She releases that perfume into the air.

A male butterfly can detect her scent up to seven miles away.

6. The sense of hearing is spectacularly developed in bats.

Bats emit high-frequency squeaks.

They use the echoes to find their way in the dark.

They also use them to hunt fast-flying insects.

7. Bats often fly in groups of thousands.

They are always able to recognize the echoes of their own squeaks.

They never confuse them with those of another bat.

8. Scientists have tried to "jam" the bats' signals.

They have broadcast on the same wavelength.

They have broadcast at 2,000 times the volume of a bat's squeak.

The bats were still able to recognize their own echoes.

9. Bees seem to have a sixth sense.

It is a sensitivity to the earth's magnetic field.

It enables them to navigate at great distances from their hive.

10. There are two dimples on each side of a rattlesnake's head.

They serve as heat-sensing organs.

They allow the snake to locate its prey.

They also allow it to determine the size of its prey.

And they help the snake determine the shape of its prey.

Go to www.thomsonedu.com/devenglish/mcdonald for more practice with parallel sentence structure. Under "Book Resources," click on "Grammar Review." Then click on "Parallelism." Also, under "Chapter Resources" for Chapter 6, click on "Exploring Online."

The Small Society. © King features syndicate

Synthesizing Ideas from Reading Selections

7

One of the goals of a college education is to learn to search out new ideas and to consider those that are different from our own. After all, we really can't claim to be educated about an issue if we know only one side of it. Many college assignments will ask you to discuss or explain the various issues involved in a particular topic. A philosophy instructor, for example, might ask you to explain the concept of love as it is developed by a number of philosophers; a health instructor might ask you to discuss different theories about the best way to prevent high cholesterol; and a political science instructor might ask you to write about the arguments involved in the debate over the powers delegated to the Department of Homeland Security.

People who are able to consider ideas from a number of sources, to see the relationships among those ideas, and to pull those ideas together into one coherent whole possess a valuable skill. They are the people who will be able to consider all sides of an issue and then reach reasonable, considered judgments about how they should vote, where they should work, or why they should accept one idea rather than another. They are also the people who will not oversimplify a complex issue, who will recognize that sometimes there is no one "correct" answer but merely one alternative that is only slightly better than other possible alternatives.

A **synthesis** is a paper or report that pulls together related ideas. In one sense, a synthesis is similar to a summary in that both papers require careful reading and accurate reporting. However, writing a synthesis is often more difficult than writing a summary because a synthesis requires that you read a number of sources, identify the related ideas, and then explain how those ideas are related. Sometimes several sources on the same topic will discuss very different points yet reach the same conclusion, and your synthesis will need to reflect that. Sometimes related sources will discuss the same points but reach quite different conclusions. And sometimes sources will simply repeat ideas you have already read in other sources.

PREPARING YOUR SOURCES AND NOTES

CLARIFY YOUR PURPOSE

The first step in writing a synthesis is to make sure you understand what you are and are not being asked to do. As you prepare this paper, think of yourself as a teacher. Your job is to educate those who read your paper about the issue at hand—*not to convince them to hold a particular opinion about it.* In other words, in this paper you will explain all sides of the issue, but you will *not* take a stand on the issue. (You will do that in Chapter 8.)

READ AND HIGHLIGHT YOUR SOURCES

Active, careful reading is very important when you write a synthesis. Read your source material with a pen, pencil, or highlighter in hand. Mark whatever seems like it might be important even on your first reading of the article. You can decide later whether you want to use everything you have marked.

TAKE NOTES

- Use a separate sheet of paper for each source.
- Write the title or author's name at the top of the page to keep each set of notes clearly separate from the others.
- Now start rereading the places you marked in the article, briefly summarizing or paraphrasing those ideas on your sheet of paper.
- Write the page number next to each note.
- If you write a direct quotation, be sure to put quotation marks around it.
- In addition to important ideas, make a note of any striking examples, statistics, or facts.

ORGANIZING YOUR MATERIAL

GROUP RELATED IDEAS

Once you have listed the ideas that each writer discusses, look for the relationships among those ideas. Take time with this step. Deciding which ideas are related requires careful reading.

Sometimes the relationships are easy to see. For instance, let's say you have read articles discussing the potential effects of television on its viewers. (Four reading selections on the effects of television appear in Part Four.) While reading the articles, you will have noticed that several of them are concerned with television's ability to educate. You might group those ideas under the heading "Is Television Educational?"

As you continue to read your notes, you might observe that some writers discuss the idea that television affects our character, influencing who we are or how we act. You might group those ideas under the heading "Does Television Make Us Better People?"

As you continue to group ideas, you might find it difficult to decide which ideas should be grouped together. Perhaps some ideas seem only somewhat related to others. In such cases you will have to decide whether or not to group them. You might also discover that one article discusses an important idea that is not discussed anywhere else. In such a case, create a separate category for that idea. You may or may not decide to use it in your synthesis.

Finally, you will probably discover that you need to go back and reread parts of some of the articles. Perhaps you remember that one of them discussed the educational value of television even though you had not made a note of it. Now is the time to quickly reread the article to find that idea.

Below is a sample grouping of ideas from the four reading selections. Notice that the entries have been divided into columns to keep opposing ideas clearly separated. Also notice that each entry includes the author's last name in parentheses.

Is Television Educational?

Yes	No
• TV can provide learning.	• TV cannot provide the time
(Henry)	needed to learn.
	(Robinson)
• Children learn alphabet from	
Sesame Street.	• Learning requires time to absorb facts.
(Henry)	It requires reading.
	(Robinson)
• High school students learn about	
toxic waste on beaches.	
(Henry)	

- A study by psychologist Daniel Anderson says children learn to think and draw inferences as they watch TV.
  (Drexler)
- Same study—TV does not replace reading; it replaces other recreational activities.
  (Drexler)
- Same study—TV watching does not lower IQ, although people with lower IQ do tend to watch more TV.
  (Drexler)

- A documentary about Marin County cannot really be accurate because it does not have the time to cover the complexities of life there.
  (Robinson)
- Educational TV is the worst kind—it makes people think they know something when they really don't.
  (Robinson)

Does Television Make Us Better People?

Yes
- TV's characters embody human truths.
  (Henry)
- They epitomize what we feel about ourselves.
  (Henry)
- They teach behavior and values. The character of Mary Richards summed up the lives of a whole generation of women.
  (Henry)
- Without TV we might be less violent, have more respect for institutions, be healthier, but we also might be less alert, less informed, less concerned about world matters, lonelier.
  (Henry)

No
- Opinion of psychologist Daniel Anderson—The violence, sexism, and materialism on TV are having a major social impact on our children.
  (Drexler)
- TV is often used as a form of escapism.
  (Drexler)
- TV causes confusion between reality and illusion.
  (Woolfolk Cross)

Is Television Valuable as Entertainment?

Yes
- TV is very good at entertaining. Jack Benny and Art Carney would not be nearly as funny in print. You need to see them and watch their timing.
  (Robinson)

No
- Many times watching TV is a default activity because there is nothing else to do.
  (Woolfolk Cross)

- A study by psychologist Daniel Anderson says when parents and kids watch together, kids tend to think about what they see.

  (Drexler)

- TV entertainment mesmerizes viewers. Kids prefer videos to real life.

  (Woolfolk Cross)

- Boys on raft were disappointed because it was more fun on TV.

  (Woolfolk Cross)

- Children preferred to watch a video of a fight rather than the real thing.

  (Woolfolk Cross)

- UPI reported children watching TV next to the corpse of their dead father.

  (Woolfolk Cross)

- Former DA Mario Merola says a jury wants the drama of TV and is less likely to convict if it doesn't get it.

  (Woolfolk Cross)

- In a Univ. of Nebraska study, over half of children chose TV over their fathers.

  (Woolfolk Cross)

DEVELOP A ROUGH OUTLINE OF THE ISSUES

Now that you have divided your notes into separate groups, arrange them in an order that will help your readers to understand the issue. You will probably devote one paragraph to each group, but which group should you present first? Does the reader need to understand one particular idea first? Does one idea lead to another, suggesting it should be placed before the other one? Does one idea seem more significant than the others? These are all questions you should consider as you experiment with different possible paragraph arrangements.

Try writing out a few rough outlines—nothing formal, just some possible paragraph arrangements. Choose the one that seems to present your ideas in the most understandable order.

WRITING THE DRAFT

WRITE A PRELIMINARY THESIS STATEMENT

You have been developing thesis statements the entire semester, so this step will seem obvious to you by now. Your thesis states the central idea of your paper and should appear as the last sentence of your introductory paragraph. But what is the central idea of a synthesis? Your papers up to this point have asserted your own ideas about your life, experiences, or reading. The synthesis paper, however, asks you *not* to assert your opinions but to report on the ideas and opinions of others.

Let's consider the discussion about the effects of television. A reading of several articles on the topic might result in the following rough outline:

- the educational value of television
- the entertainment value of television
- the social or behavioral value of television

Although there are many ways to write a successful thesis for such a paper, two common techniques are the **open thesis** and the **closed thesis.** The open thesis makes it clear to the reader that the paper will explain the issues, but it does not list them. The closed thesis, on the other hand, lists the material to be covered in the order that it will be covered.

OPEN THESIS

Although most would agree that television has had a profound effect on many of its viewers, there is little agreement about whether that effect has been for the better or the worse.

CLOSED THESIS

In the debate over the effects of television on its viewers, three particularly interesting questions involve television's ability to educate its audience, its value as a source of entertainment, and its effects upon our behavior.

Which type of thesis should you use? They both have advantages. The open thesis is more concise and does not lock you into a specific organization. The closed thesis clearly forecasts the direction of the paper, a clarity that you might prefer. (If you write a closed thesis, be sure to present the points in the body of your paper in the same order that they appear in the thesis.)

WRITE THE FIRST DRAFT

As with most first drafts, you want to get your ideas onto paper without worrying too much about how well you have written them. So try to *write* as much as possible at this point, not *correct.* (You can correct and improve later.)

Perhaps the most difficult task of writing a synthesis is to present the ideas in your own words, not as a list of quotations. Use the skills of paraphrasing and summarizing (discussed in Chapter 5 as well as in the Appendix) as you write each paragraph. Remember that your purpose is to explain the issues, not to argue one way or the other.

DOCUMENTING YOUR SOURCES

Whenever you use someone else's words or ideas in your writing, you must let the reader know the source of those words or ideas. It really doesn't matter whether you have paraphrased, summarized, or quoted—in each case, you must let the reader know whose material you are using.

Up to this point, your writing assignments have focused on one reading selection at a time. In them you have used simple transitions to tell the reader when you were using material from the reading selection. (See Chapter 5 as well as the Appendix for a discussion of transitions with paraphrases, summaries, and quotations.) There are, however, more formal methods of documentation that you will need to learn to use as you write in college classes.

The two most common methods of documentation are the MLA (Modern Language Association) method, used primarily in the humanities, and the APA (American Psychological Association) method, used mostly in the social sciences. Both methods use parentheses within the paper to identify the author and page number of a particular passage that is paraphrased, summarized, or quoted. They also both use a separate page at the end of the paper to give more detailed and complete identification of the sources used. In most classes, your instructor will tell you which method to use and will suggest a documentation guide that you should purchase.

Because this text includes its own reading selections, you do not need to write a separate page (called a Works Cited page) that gives detailed identification about the sources you use. However, the papers you write for Chapters 7 and 8 will be clearer if you learn to use parentheses to identify the particular article you are referring to at any given time. Use these guidelines to help you:

- Each paraphrase, summary, and quotation should be identified by author and page number in parentheses. Do not use the author's first name within the parentheses.

  According to one writer, "Educational TV corrupts the very notion of education and renders its victims uneducable" (Robinson 432).

  In defense of television, another writer claims that many schoolchildren learn the alphabet from *Sesame Street* and that high school students learn about the problems that our planet faces (Henry 428).

- If the author's name is already included in the transition, it does not need to be repeated in the parentheses.

  According to Paul Robinson, "Educational TV corrupts the very notion of education and renders its victims uneducable" (432).

  In defense of television, William Henry III claims that many schoolchildren learn the alphabet from *Sesame Street* and that high school students learn about the problems that our planet faces (428).

- When your source quotes or paraphrases someone else and you want to use that material, indicate it by using "qtd. in" as is done in the following example. (Here the quotation of Daniel Anderson comes from an article by Madeline Drexler.)

  According to Daniel Anderson, a psychologist at the University of Massachusetts at Amherst, children watching TV "muse upon the meaning of what they see, its plausibility and its implications for the future—whether they've tuned in to a news report of a natural disaster or an action show" (qtd. in Drexler 437).

- No punctuation is placed between the author's last name and the page number (see above examples).
- The parenthetical citation is placed at the end of the borrowed material but before the period at the end of the sentence (see above examples).

 Note   Further instruction in the use of parenthetical documentation as well as in the writing of a Works Cited page (if your instructor requires one) can be found in the Appendix.

REVISING AND REFINING THE SYNTHESIS

As with all papers, the difference between the average and the superior essay is often determined by the time and effort put into the revising and refining of it. Consider these suggestions as you revise.

REFINE THE THESIS STATEMENT

Once the first draft is finished, reread your thesis. Does it still accurately introduce what you have written? Would a rewriting of the thesis improve it?

ADD OR REFINE TOPIC SENTENCES

As you know, each paragraph in an academic essay should open with a clear topic sentence. Do your topic sentences clearly introduce the topic of each paragraph? Do they contain transitions that move them smoothly away from the topic of the preceding paragraph?

RETHINK WEAK PARAGRAPHS

Do any of your paragraphs seem weak to you? Perhaps one is much shorter than the others. The ideas in that paragraph might need more explanation. Consider rereading the sections of the articles that discuss the ideas in that paragraph and adding more explanation to it. Or perhaps the ideas in that paragraph should be grouped within another paragraph.

Does any paragraph read as if it jerks along from one confusing idea to the next? Consider taking out a new sheet of paper and completely rethinking it. Sometimes you need to rewrite a rough paragraph from start to finish.

PROOFREAD FOR ERRORS IN GRAMMAR, SPELLING, AND PUNCTUATION

Use but do not rely only on grammar and spelling checkers. Consider having someone whose judgment you trust read your final draft. Many colleges have free tutors available to students. Make use of them.

READINGS: PHYSICIAN-ASSISTED SUICIDE

BEFORE YOU READ

1. Should physician-assisted suicide be permitted? Why, or why not?
2. Make a list of reasons you would expect to hear both for permitting physician-assisted suicide and for prohibiting it.

In Defense of Voluntary Euthanasia   SIDNEY HOOK

Sidney Hook (1902–1989) was considered by many to be one of America's most controversial public philosophers. Beginning his career as the first American scholar of Marxism, a leading disciple of John Dewey, and an early supporter of Soviet Communism, Hook eventually renounced Marxism and came to be one of the most vehement supporters of the Cold War. An outspoken participant in many of the principal political debates of this century, he was best known for his vigorous defense of political and academic freedom and his stand against totalitarianism in all forms. The following essay was published in The New York Times *in 1987.*

A few short years ago, I lay at the point of death. A congestive heart failure was treated for diagnostic purposes by an angiogram that triggered a stroke. Violent and painful hiccups, uninterrupted for several days and nights, prevented the ingestion of food. My left side and one of my vocal cords became paralyzed. Some form of pleurisy set in, and I felt I was drowning in a sea of slime. At one point, my heart stopped beating; just as I lost consciousness, it was thumped back into action again. In one of my lucid intervals during those days of agony, I asked my physician to discontinue all life-supporting services or show me how to do it. He refused and told me that someday I would appreciate the unwisdom of my request. 1

A month later, I was discharged from the hospital. In six months, I regained the use of my limbs, and although my voice still lacks its old resonance and carrying power I no longer croak like a frog. There remain some minor disabilities and I am restricted to a rigorous, low sodium diet. I have resumed my writing and research. 2

My experience can be and has been cited as an argument against honoring requests of stricken patients to be gently eased out of their pain and life. I cannot agree. There are two main reasons. As an octogenarian, there is a reasonable likelihood that I may suffer another "cardiovascular accident" or worse. I may not even be in a position to ask for the surcease of pain. It seems to 3 me that I have already paid my dues to death—indeed, although time has softened my memories, they are vivid enough to justify my saying that I suffered enough to warrant dying several times over. Why run the risk of more?

Secondly, I dread imposing on my family and friends another grim round of misery similar to the one my first attack occasioned.   4

My wife and children endured enough for one lifetime. I know that for them the long days and nights of waiting, the disruption of their professional duties and their own familial responsibilities counted for nothing in their anxiety for me. In their joy at my recovery they have been forgotten. Nonetheless, to visit another prolonged spell of helpless suffering on them as my life ebbs away, or even worse, if I linger on into a comatose senility, seems altogether gratuitous.   5

But what, it may be asked, of the joy and satisfaction of living, of basking in the sunlight, listening to music, watching one's grandchildren growing into adolescence, following the news about the fate of freedom in a troubled world, playing with ideas, writing one's testament of wisdom and folly for posterity? Is not all that one endured, together with the risk of its recurrence, an acceptable price for the multiple satisfactions that are still open even to a person of advanced years?   6

Apparently those who cling to life, no matter what, think so. I do not.   7

The zest and intensity of these experiences are no longer what they used to be. I am not vain enough to delude myself that I can in the few remaining years make an important discovery useful for mankind or can lead a social movement or do anything that will be historically eventful, no less event-making. My autobiography, which describes a record of intellectual and political experiences of some historical value, already much too long, could be posthumously published. I have had my fill of joys and sorrows and am not greedy for more life. I have always thought that a test of whether one had found happiness in one's life is whether one would be willing to relive it—whether, if it were possible, one would accept the opportunity to be born again.   8

Having lived a full and relatively happy life, I would cheerfully accept the chance to be reborn, but certainly not to be reborn again as an infirm octogenarian. To some extent, my views reflect what I have seen happen to the aged and stricken who have   9 been so unfortunate as to survive crippling paralysis. They suffer, and impose suffering on others, unable even to make a request that their torment be ended.

I am mindful too of the burdens placed upon the   10
community, with its rapidly diminishing resources, to provide the adequate and costly services necessary to sustain the lives of those whose days and nights are spent on mattress graves of pain. A better use could be made of these resources to increase the opportunities and qualities of life for the young. I am not denying the moral obligation the community has to look after its disabled and aged. There are times, however, when an individual may find it pointless to insist on the fulfillment of a legal and moral right.

What is required is no great revolution in morals but an   11
enlargement of imagination and an intelligent evaluation of alternative uses of community resources.

Long ago, Seneca observed that "the wise man will live as   12
long as he ought, not as long as he can." One can envisage hypothetical circumstances in which one has a duty to prolong one's life despite its costs for the sake of others, but such circumstances are far removed from the ordinary prospects we are considering. If wisdom is rooted in the knowledge of the alternatives of choice, it must be reliably informed of the state one is in and its likely outcome. Scientific medicine is not infallible, but it is the best we have. Should a rational person be willing to endure acute suffering merely on the chance that a miraculous cure might presently be at hand? Each one should be permitted to make his own choice—especially when no one else is harmed by it.

The responsibility for the decision, whether deemed wise or   13
foolish, must be with the chooser.

Promoting a Culture of Abandonment   TERESA R. WAGNER

Teresa Wagner is a legal analyst specializing in human rights and right-to-life issues at Family Research Council, a Washington-based organization with the following mission statement: "The Family Research Council champions marriage and family as the foundation of civilization, the seedbed of virtue, and the wellspring of society. We shape public debate and formulate public policy that values human life and upholds the institutions of marriage and the family. Believing that God is the author of life, liberty, and the family, we promote the Judeo-Christian worldview as the basis for a just, free, and stable society."

The death toll in Oregon will really begin to rise now. Attorney 1
General Janet Reno has decided that a federal law regulating drug
usage (the Controlled Substances Act) somehow does not apply
to the use of lethal drugs in Oregon, the only state in the country
to legalize assisted suicide. The evidence will begin pouring in on
how deadly assisted suicide can be, not just for the individuals
subject to it, of course, but for the culture that countenances it.

There are frightening and compelling policy reasons to 2
oppose assisted suicide. Foremost is the risk of abuse. Proponents
of assisted suicide always insist that the practice will be carefully
limited: It will be available, they claim, only for those who request
it and only for those who are dying anyway (the terminally ill).

Such limitations are virtually impossible. People will 3
inevitably be killed without knowing or consenting to it. Several
state courts have already ruled as a matter of state constitutional
law that any rights given to competent patients (those who can
request death) must also be given to incompetent ones (those
who cannot). Third parties make treatment decisions for this latter
group. Now legal, assisted suicide will be just another treatment
option for surrogate decision makers to select, even if the patient
has made no indication of wanting to die.

What's more, the cost crunch in medicine virtually 4
guarantees that hospitals and doctors will eventually pressure, and
then coerce, patients to avail themselves of this easy and cheap alternative.

Similarly, the confinement of this right to the terminally ill 5
is impossible. As many groups opposing assisted suicide have
noted, the term itself is hardly clear. The Oregon law defines terminal disease as that which will produce death within six
months. Is that with or without medical treatment? Many individuals will die in much less than six months without very simple
medical treatment (insulin injections, for example). They could be
deemed terminal under this law and qualify for this new right to
death.

More importantly, the rationale for providing this new right 6
almost demands its extension beyond limits. After all, if we are
trying to relieve pain and suffering, the non-terminal patient, who
faces years of discomfort, has a more compelling claim to relief
than the terminal patient, whose hardship is supposed to be
short-lived. Courts will quickly recognize this and dispense with
any terminal requirement.

So much for limits.   7

The tragedy, of course, is that we have the ability right now   8
to relieve the suffering of those in even the most excruciating
pain. Anesthesiologists and others in pain centers around the
country claim that we can provide adequate palliation 99 percent
of the time.

Unfortunately, certain obstacles prevent patients from   9
getting the pain relief they need: Many in medicine fear, mistakenly,
that patients will become addicted to analgesic medications;
overzealous regulatory agencies penalize doctors who prescribe
the large doses needed (or they penalize the pharmacies that
stock them); and medical professionals generally are not trained
adequately in pain and symptom management.

The more important reasons to oppose assisted suicide,   10
however, are moral: We must decide what type of people we are
and how we will care for the weak and sick among us, for it is
only to these dependents, not to all individuals, that we are offering this new right. Is this because we respect their autonomy (allegedly the basis of the right to die) more than our own? Or do
we unconsciously (or consciously) believe their lives are of less
worth and therefore less entitled to make demands of care (not
to mention money) on us?

Make no mistake: Despite incessant clamor about rights,   11
ours is actually a culture of abandonment. The acceptance of assisted suicide and euthanasia in this culture is almost inevitable.
Abortion, of course, was the foundation. It taught (and still
teaches) society to abandon mothers, and mothers to abandon
their children. Divorce (husbands and wives leaving or abandoning
each other) sends the same message. The commitment to care
for others, both those who have been given to us and those we
have selected, no longer exists. We simply do not tolerate those
we do not want.

What to do about the advance of this culture? Replace it   12
with a culture of care, a culture of commitment.

This is obviously no easy task, for it is neither easy to   13
administer care nor easy to receive it. (Indeed, the elderly cite the
fear of dependence most often when indicating why they might
support assisted suicide.) But it is precisely within this context of
care, of giving and receiving, that we enjoy the dignity particular to
human beings. Otherwise we would simply shoot the terminal patient as we do the dying horse.

The assisted suicide question is really the battle between   14
these two cultures. We can follow the way of Jack Kevorkian or of
Mother Teresa. The life of Mother Teresa was a witness to nothing
if not to commitment and care. She was simply there to care for
the sick and the old, to assure them of their worth. Jack Kevorkian
and our culture of abandonment, epitomized by assisted suicide
and all the abuses to follow, surely will not.

The Right to Choose Death   KENNETH SWIFT

Kenneth Swift, the director of finance at a multinational technology company in Orange County, California, is a regular contributor to the Los Angeles Times. *In the following selection from the June 25, 2005, issue, he argues in support of California's proposed Assembly Bill 654, which "is intended to expand the range of care for dying patients to 'include choices for those relatively few whose suffering is extreme and cannot be palliated despite the best efforts.'"*

We were finally able to bring our little girl home, a joyful event   1
that seemed unlikely just a short time before. She had developed
an infection that turned out to be quite virulent, threatening her
internal organs and, potentially, her life. After weeks of hospitaliza-
tion, including a few days when her prognosis was particularly
grim, she showed the same resolve and fortitude that had often
been on display throughout her 14 years of life. With the help of
a wonderful staff of doctors and a state-of-the-art facility, she
beat the odds, overcame her affliction, and our family is whole
once again.

I can't say that I am afraid of death, but I do find the prospect   2
of dying quite frightening, especially for loved ones like my Megan.
Actually, when living turns into dying, when the quality of life becomes instead a daily struggle with pain and hopelessness, death
can be a relief.

There were a few days when we wondered if Megan had   3
crossed that invisible line between living and dying and whether
we would be strong enough to help her find that relief. During
her hospital stay, we saw others who had confronted the same issue, their decision easily discerned by the puffy eyes, glistening
cheeks and empty collar in their hands, leash still attached.

Yes, Megan is a dog, though for my wife and me, that is a fact   4
relevant only for health insurance purposes (she is not covered).
Although she does not qualify as our legal dependent, she more

than qualifies as a full-fledged, loved and loving member of our family. Yet, being "just a dog" and therefore no more than property under the law, she is afforded a right denied to most of her fellow mammalians of the bipedal variety: the right to die with dignity, spared of pain and suffering if that should be her fate.

Only residents of Oregon are able to exercise a similar right.   5
However, a bill in the Assembly, AB 654, would provide the same right to Californians that Oregonians have had since 1998.

This is not the first time that assisted suicide has been   6
considered by the California Legislature. Bills were introduced in 1995 and 1999 but never presented for a floor vote. In addition, Proposition 161 was on the ballot in 1992 but rejected by 54% of the voters. According to information on the Assembly's website, AB 654 is intended to expand the range of care for dying patients to "include choices for those relatively few whose suffering is extreme and cannot be palliated despite the best efforts." Makes sense to me.

Life is a precious gift. Yet when a life turns tragic through   7
disease or injury and the joy of living yields to the pain of interminable suffering, surely an enlightened society such as ours can accept that from death there can be peace.

Critics make the usual "slippery slope" argument that the right   8
to die is just the first step toward an eventual policy of euthanasia. In fact, the Assembly website notes the fear of the critics that "the right to die may become a responsibility to die" for those considered "socially disadvantaged," such as the elderly and the disabled.

In response to those fears, AB 654 is narrowly written to   9
apply only to the terminally ill and only after ascertaining the competence of the patient. Also, it requires two doctors to attest to the condition of the patient and the fact that the patient is acting voluntarily.

The bill is modeled on the law in Oregon, where, in the   10
seven years since the measure was passed, just over 200 residents have exercised their right to end their suffering and none of the concerns of the critics have been realized.

The more religious of the critics would argue that assisted   11
suicide attempts to usurp an authority that can only be the province of God. Yet even the religious support the taking of life for capital crimes and even the use of war when the cause is considered "just". So what could be more just than allowing a person

to choose to end a life that is bereft of hope and consumed with pain? It is time for compassion to replace unfounded fears.

If life is for the living, then surely death should be an option   12
for the dying. Megan shouldn't be the only one with that right.

Death and the Law: Why the Government Has an Interest in Preserving Life

LAWRENCE RUDDEN AND
GERARD V. BRADLEY

Lawrence Rudden is director of research for the Graham Williams Group in Washington, D.C. He writes on politics and culture. Gerard V. Bradley is a professor of law at the University of Notre Dame. In this selection from the May 2003 issue of World and I, *they argue that government must take "an unyielding stand in favor of life."*

Attorney General Ashcroft wants to stop doctors who kill.   1
He has good reason: doctors have a special responsibility to show by word and deed, in season and out, that intentionally killing another person is simply wrong. Yes, even if that person is, like Evelyn, terminally ill.

A doctor's calling is always to heal, never to harm. A doctor's   2
calling is special, though not unique. None of us possesses a license, privilege, or permission to kill, but the healer who purposely kills puts into question, in a unique way, our culture's commitment to the sanctity of life. The scandal created by doctors who kill is great, much like that caused by lawyers who flout the law, or bishops—shepherds—who do not care about their flocks. Whenever someone whose profession centers upon a single good—healing or respect for law or caring for souls—tramples that good, the rest of us cannot help but wonder: is it a good after all? Maybe it is for some, but not for others? Who decides? Is all the talk of that good as supremely worthwhile idle chatter or, worse, cynical propaganda?

Do not intentionally kill. This is what it means—principally   3
and essentially—to revere life. Making intentional killing of humans a serious crime is the earmark of society's respect for life. All our criminal laws against homicide (save for Oregon) make no exception—none whatsoever—for victims who say they want to die. Our law contains no case or category of "public service homicides," of people who should be dead. People hunting season is never open. Our laws against killing (except Oregon's) make no exception for those who suffer, even for those near death. None.

When someone commits the crime of murder, all we can   4
say is that the victim's life was shortened. We know not by how much; the law does not ask, or care. After all, no one knows how

much longer any of us shall live. Many persons who are the picture of health, in the bloom of youth, will die today in accidents, by another's hand, or of natural causes. Yes, we can say with confidence that someone's death, maybe Evelyn's, is near at hand. But so long as she draws breath, she has the same legal and moral right that you and I have not to be intentionally killed.

It is not that life is the only good thing which we, and our laws, 5 strive to protect. Life is not always an overriding good; we accept certain risks to life. What is the alternative? Do nothing at all that creates some (even a small) chance of death? Would we get up in the morning? Drive our cars? Take medicine? Go swimming? Fly in airplanes? Some risk to life is acceptable where the risk is modest and the activities that engender it are worthwhile.

Sometimes the risk can be great and still worth accepting. We 6 might instinctively step in front of a car, or jump into a freezing lake to save a loved one, or a stranger's wandering toddler. We might do the same upon reflection, but we do not want to die. We do not commit suicide.

Religious martyrs may face certain death, but they do not 7 want to die. They submit to death as the side effect of their acts, whether these be described as witnessing to the truth, or, in the case of Saint Thomas More, avoiding false witness. The axman, the lion tamer, the firing squad—they kill. They intend death.

This distinction between intending and accepting death is not 8 scholarly hairsplitting. This distinction is real, as real as space shuttles. The Columbia crew knew all along that they risked death by flying into space. That which they risked came to be, but they were not suicides.

Of course doctors may—even must—prescribe analgesics. 9 Doctors should try to relieve the suffering of their terminal patients, up to and even including toxic doses. Not because they want to kill, any more than they want to kill patients in exploratory surgery. Doctors who prescribe strong painkillers want to help, even to heal. Given how ill some patients are, the risk of death is worth running, just as some very risky surgeries are a risk worth taking.

Evelyn wants to let go, and she needs help to do so. Yet, none 10 of us walks into a doctor's office and demands a certain treatment. Doctors do not fetch medicines upon demand. They are not workmen at our service. Yes, doctors work toward our health in cooperation with us. They have no right to impose treatment we do not want. But we have no right to drugs, surgery, or anesthesia.

Or to lights out—even for Evelyn. 11

Why? Because autonomy, or self-rule, is not an all-consuming   12
value. It is not a trump card. Evelyn honestly wishes to bring down
the curtain. We may find her condition hideous, as she evidently
does, but our feelings (of repulsion, sympathy, or whatever) are
unreliable guides to sound choosing. Feelings certainly do not always, or even usually, mislead us. Often, though, they do.

Pause a moment and you will, if you try, think of something   13
attractive and pleasing you did not choose today, because it would
have been wrong, and something unappealing, even repulsive, you
chose to do because it was right. For me, some days, it has to do
with my mother, who suffers from advanced Alzheimer's. Enough
said.

On what basis does a society and its governing authorities   14
decide that life is a great common good? Because it is true: life is
good. The law is a powerful teacher of right and wrong. Like it or
not, what our laws permit is thought by many to be good, or at
least unobjectionable. What the law forbids is believed to be, well,
forbidden.

Why should our government take such an unyielding stand   15
in favor of life? Because we are all safer where everyone's life is
prized, not despised.

AFTER YOU READ

Work with other students to develop responses to the following suggestions or to compare responses that you have already prepared.

1. Identify the thesis of each article. Then divide each article into major
   sections.
2. To clarify the arguments presented by each article, ask yourself, "What
   are this writer's reasons for his position?" Examine each major division,
   and make a list of the different reasons offered.
3. Once you have developed such a list, consider ways the various writers' points can be grouped. Which points from different articles would
   you put together? Why?

READINGS: THE MINIMUM LEGAL DRINKING AGE

BEFORE YOU READ

1. What reasons might someone give to lower the drinking age? What
   reasons might one give to maintain it at twenty-one?
2. Where do you stand? Why?

Should the Legal Drinking Age Be Lowered to Eighteen or Nineteen? Yes.

RUTH C. ENGS

A professor of Applied Health Sciences at Indiana University in Bloomington, Ruth Engs is the author of seven books and many scientific papers on alcohol. She is an internationally recognized authority on drinking patterns and problems of college students.

The legal drinking age should be lowered from 21 to about 18   1
or 19, and young people should be allowed to drink in the presence of adults in such settings as restaurants, taverns and pubs
and at official school and university functions. Allowing young people to consume alcohol in such controlled environments would
enable them to learn mature and sensible drinking behaviors. The
flaunting of current drinking-age laws is readily apparent among
university students. Those under age 21 are more likely to be
heavy, or "binge," drinkers—consuming over five drinks at one sitting at least once a week; 22 percent of students under age 21
classify themselves as heavy drinkers, compared with 18 percent
of students over age 21.

Research has documented a decrease in problems associ-   2
ated with drinking and driving that has paralleled a decrease in
per capita consumption of alcohol. However, these declines
started in 1980, before Congress passed the law that required
states that had not already done so to raise the drinking age to
21 if they wanted to continue receiving federal highway funds. The
decrease in drinking and driving problems is the result of many
factors, including education programs concerning drunk driving,
designated-driver programs, increased seat belt and air bag usage,
safer automobiles and lower speed limits.

While drunk driving problems have declined over the past   3
two decades, there has been an increase in other problems related to heavy and irresponsible drinking among college-age
youth. These include vomiting after drinking, missing classes, getting
lower grades and getting into fights.

Our current approach to controlling underage drinking is   4
not working, and we need to try alternatives based on the experiences of other cultures that do not have these problems. Ethnic
groups that have few drinking-related problems tend to share
some common characteristics: They see alcohol as neither a poi-
son nor a magic potion; there is little or no social pressure to

drink; irresponsible behavior is never tolerated; young people
learn from their parents and other adults how to handle alcohol
in a responsible manner; there is a societal consensus on what
constitutes responsible drinking.

Because the laws making 21 the legal drinking age are not   5
working, and, in fact, are counterproductive, it behooves us as a
nation to change our current policy and instead concentrate on
teaching responsible drinking techniques for those who choose to
consume alcoholic beverages.

Should the Legal Drinking Age Be Lowered to Eighteen or Nineteen? No.

CHARLES A. HURLEY

*Charles Hurley was Executive Director of Public Affairs for the National Safety
Council when he wrote this article for the* Congressional Quarterly. *In it, he responds to those who argue that we should lower the minimum legal drinking age.*

Binge drinking on college campuses and elsewhere is a very   1
serious problem that recently has caused a number of highly pub-
licized tragedies. It also has triggered several calls for consideration
of lowering the drinking age from campus officials and the alcohol
industry. The National Safety Council welcomes this debate for
two reasons: The real causes of binge drinking must be addressed,
and the case for maintaining the current drinking age is overwhelming.

There are no simple answers to campus binge drinking, but   2
a number of promising strategies are being developed by a consortium led by the Harvard School of Public Health and others
through the Higher Education Center for Alcohol and Other
Drug Prevention. The consortium fosters a broad campus approach to change the underlying culture and environment that
condones irresponsible behavior.

As far as lowering the drinking age, I do not believe you   3
solve a problem by expanding it. Binge drinking did not start with
the uniform drinking age of 21. In fact, we may be in danger of
seeing history repeat itself. During the Vietnam War, drinking ages
were lowered based on the adage "old enough to fight, old
enough to drink." The results were horrific. The surgeon general of
the U.S. found in the early 1980s that longevity was increasing for
all age groups except one—those under 21—and the leading
cause of their deaths was drunk driving. As states individually
moved to correct this by raising their drinking ages, they often

were penalized severely by border states trying to attract under-age drinkers to travel across state lines, then try to make it home. The enactment by the Congress of the uniform drinking age legislation in 1984 was a direct outcome of those tragedies.

What has been the outcome of the uniform age-21 drinking   4
law? One thousand young lives are being saved every year, making it one of the more effective things that Congress has done in recent memory. Has it magically eliminated underage or binge drinking? No, but it has sharply reduced the late-night, bar-to-bar, across-state-lines patterns that had proved so fatal in the early 1980s. It has also saved nearly 1,000 families per year, some 15,000 to date, the senseless devastation that was occurring with lower drinking ages. Those who propose a return to the days when young people were being killed on our highways in record numbers must shoulder the burden of proving that lowering the drinking age would benefit anyone but the alcohol industry.

The Perils of Prohibition   ELIZABETH M. WHELAN

Elizabeth M. Whelan is president and a founder of the American Council on Science. She holds masters and doctoral degrees in public health from the Yale School of Medicine and the Harvard School of Public Health. She is the author or co-author of more than two dozen books, including Panic in the Pantry, Preventing Cancer, Toxic Terror, *and* A Smoking Gun—How the Tobacco Industry Gets Away with Murder.

My colleagues at the Harvard School of Public Health, where I   1
studied preventive medicine, deserve high praise for their recent study on teenage drinking. What they found in their survey of college students was that they drink "early and . . . often," frequently to the point of getting ill.

As a public-health scientist with a daughter, Christine,   2
heading to college this fall, I have professional and personal concerns about teen binge drinking. It is imperative that we explore *why* so many young people abuse alcohol. From my own study of the effects of alcohol restrictions and my observations of Christine and her friends' predicament about drinking, I believe that today's laws are unrealistic. Prohibiting the sale of liquor to responsible young adults creates an atmosphere where binge drinking and alcohol abuse have become a problem. American teens, unlike their European peers, don't learn how to drink gradually, safely and in moderation.

Alcohol is widely accepted and enjoyed in our culture.   3
Studies show that moderate drinking can be good for you. But we
legally proscribe alcohol until the age of 21 (why not 30 or 45?).
Christine and her classmates can drive cars, fly planes, marry, vote,
pay taxes, take out loans and risk their lives as members of the
U.S. armed forces. But laws in all 50 states say that no alcoholic
beverages may be sold to anyone until that magic 21st birthday.
We didn't always have a national "21" rule. When I was in college,
in the mid-'60s, the drinking age varied from state to state. This
posed its own risks, with underage students crossing state lines to
get a legal drink.

In parts of the Western world, moderate drinking by   4
teenagers and even children under their parents' supervision is a
given. Though the per capita consumption of alcohol in France,
Spain and Portugal is higher than in the United States, the rate of
alcoholism and alcohol abuse is lower. A glass of wine at dinner is
normal practice. Kids learn to regard moderate drinking as an enjoyable family activity rather than as something they have to sneak
away to do. Banning drinking by young people makes it a badge of
adulthood—a tantalizing forbidden fruit.

Christine and her teenage friends like to go out with a   5
group to a club, comedy show or sports bar to watch the game.
But teens today have to go on the sly with fake IDs and the fear
of getting caught. Otherwise, they're denied admittance to most
places and left to hang out on the street. That's hardly a safer alternative. Christine and her classmates now find themselves in a
legal no man's land. At 18, they're considered adults. Yet when they
want to enjoy a drink like other adults, they are, as they put it,
"disenfranchised."

Comparing my daughter's dilemma with my own as an   6
"underage" college student, I see a difference—and one that I
think has exacerbated the current dilemma. Today's teens are far
more sophisticated than we were. They're treated less like children and have more responsibilities than we did. This makes the
21 restriction seem anachronistic.

For the past few years, my husband and I have been   7
preparing Christine for college life and the inevitable partying—
read keg of beer—that goes with it. Last year, a young friend with
no drinking experience was violently ill for days after he was introduced to "clear liquids in small glasses" during freshman orientation. We want our daughter to learn how to drink sensibly and

avoid this pitfall. Starting at the age of 14, we invited her to join us for a glass of champagne with dinner. She'd tried it once before, thought it was "yucky" and declined. A year later, she enjoyed sampling wine at family meals.

When, at 16, she asked for a Mudslide (a bottled chocolate-milk-and-rum concoction), we used the opportunity to discuss it with her. We explained the alcohol content, told her the alcohol level is lower when the drink is blended with ice and compared it with a glass of wine. Since the drink of choice on campus is beer, we contrasted its potency with wine and hard liquor and stressed the importance of not drinking on an empty stomach. 8

Our purpose was to encourage her to know the alcohol content of what she is served. We want her to experience the effects of liquor in her own home, not on the highway and not for the first time during a college orientation week with free-flowing suds. Although Christine doesn't drive yet, we regularly reinforce the concept of choosing a designated driver. Happily, that already seems a widely accepted practice among our daughter's friends who drink. 9

We recently visited the Ivy League school Christine will attend in the fall. While we were there, we read a story in the college paper about a student who was nearly electrocuted when, in a drunken state, he climbed on top of a moving train at a railroad station near the campus. The student survived, but three of his limbs were later amputated. This incident reminded me of a tragic death on another campus. An intoxicated student maneuvered himself into a chimney. He was found three days later when frat brothers tried to light a fire in the fireplace. By then he was dead. 10

These tragedies are just two examples of our failure to teach young people how to use alcohol prudently. If 18-year-olds don't have legal access to even a beer at a public place, they have no experience handling liquor on their own. They feel "liberated" when they arrive on campus. With no parents to stop them, they have a "let's make up for lost time" attitude. The result: binge drinking. 11

We should make access to alcohol legal at 18. At the same time, we should come down much harder on alcohol abusers and drunk drivers of all ages. We should intensify our efforts at alcohol education for adolescents. We want them to understand that it is perfectly OK not to drink. But if they do, alcohol should be consumed in moderation. 12

After all, we choose to teach our children about safe sex,   13
including the benefits of teen abstinence. Why, then, can't we—
schools and parents alike—teach them about safe drinking?

The Minimum Legal Drinking Age: Facts and Fallacies

TRACI L. TOOMEY, CAROLYN
ROSENFELD, AND ALEXANDER WAGENAAR

The following selection, which appears on the website of the American Medical Association, is adapted from an article that originally appeared in Alcohol Health & Research World. In it, the authors summarize the scientific research related to the minimum legal drinking age.

Brief History of the MLDA

After Prohibition, nearly all states restricting youth access to   1
alcohol designated 21 as the minimum legal drinking age (MLDA).
Between 1970 and 1975, however, 29 states lowered the MLDA
to 18, 19, or 20. These changes occurred when the minimum age
for other activities, such as voting, also were being lowered
(Wechsler & Sands, 1980). Scientists began studying the effects of
the lowered MLDA, focusing particularly on the incidence of motor vehicle crashes, the leading cause of death among teenagers.
Several studies in the 1970s found that motor vehicle crashes increased significantly among teens when the MLDA was lowered
(Cucchiaro et al., 1974; Douglas et al., 1974; Wagenaar, 1983, 1993;
Whitehead, 1977; Whitehead et al., 1975; Williams et al., 1974).

With evidence that a lower drinking age resulted in more   2
traffic injuries and fatalities among youth, citizen advocacy groups
pressured states to restore the MLDA to 21. Because of such advocacy campaigns, 16 states increased their MLDAs between September 1976 and January 1983. Resistance from other states, and
concern that minors would travel across state lines to purchase
and consume alcohol, prompted the federal government in 1984
to enact the Uniform Drinking Age Act, which mandated reduced
federal transportation funds to those states that did not raise the
MLDA to 21. Among alcohol control policies, the MLDA has been
the most studied: since the 1970s, at least 70 studies have examined the effects of either increasing or decreasing the MLDA.

Research Findings

A higher minimum legal drinking age is effective in preventing   3
alcohol-related deaths and injuries among youth. When the MLDA

has been lowered, injury and death rates increase, and when the MLDA is increased, death and injury rates decline (Wagenaar, 1993).

A higher MLDA results in fewer alcohol-related problems   4
among youth, and the 21-year-old MLDA saves the lives of well over 1,000 youth each year (Jones et al., 1992; NHTSA, 1989). Conversely, when the MLDA is lowered, motor vehicle crashes and deaths among youth increase. At least 50 studies have evaluated this correlation (Wagenaar, 1993).

A common argument among opponents of a higher MLDA is   5
that because many minors still drink and purchase alcohol, the policy doesn't work. The evidence shows, however, that although many youth still consume alcohol, they drink less and experience fewer alcohol-related injuries and deaths (Wagenaar, 1993).

Research shows that when the MLDA is 21, people under   6
age 21 drink less overall and continue to do so through their early twenties (O'Malley & Wagenaar, 1991).

The effect of the higher MLDA occurs with little or no   7
enforcement. Historically, enforcement has focused primarily on penalizing underage drinkers for illegal alcohol possession and/or consumption. For every 1,000 minors arrested for alcohol possession, only 130 merchants have actions taken against them, and only 88 adults who supply alcohol to minors face criminal penalties (Wagenaar & Wolfson, 1995).

Researchers conducted an in-depth review of enforcement   8
actions in 295 counties in Kentucky, Michigan, Montana, and Oregon. The review showed that in a three-year period, 27 percent of the counties took no action against licensed establishments that sold alcohol to minors, and 41 percent of those counties made no arrests of adults who supplied alcohol to minors. Although the majority of the counties took at least one action against alcohol establishments and/or adults who provided alcohol to minors, many did not take such actions frequently (Wagenaar & Wolfson, 1995).

Regarding Europeans and alcohol use among youth,   9
research confirms that Europeans have rates of alcohol-related diseases (such as cirrhosis of the liver) similar to or higher than those in the U.S. population (Single, 1984). However, drinking and driving among youth may not be as great a problem in Europe as in the U.S. Compared to their American counterparts, European youth must be older to obtain their drivers' licenses, are less likely to have a car, and are more inclined to use public transportation (Wagenaar, 1993).

De-Demonizing Rum: What's Wrong with "Underage" Drinking?

ANDREW STUTTAFORD

The following selection appeared in National Review *in 2001. Its author, Andrew Stuttaford, has been contributing to* National Review *since 1993. He has written on subjects ranging from post-Soviet Russia to Xena, Warrior Princess. Based in New York since 1991, Andrew's day job is in the financial sector.*

It was a day of shame for the Bushes, an incident made all the more embarrassing by the family's previous well-publicized diffi-culties with alcohol. I refer, of course, to the regrettable 1997 deci-sion by then-governor George W. Bush to approve legislation further toughening the penalties for underage drinking. In Texas, the legal drinking age is 21. A typical Texan of 19—let's call her "Jenna"—is judged to be responsible enough to vote, drive, marry, serve in the military, and (this is Texas) be executed, but she is not, apparently, suf-ficiently mature to decide for herself whether to buy a margarita. The 1997 legislation made things worse: Miller Time could now mean hard time, a possible six months in jail for a third offense.   1

It is a ludicrous and demeaning law, but it has been policed with all the gung-ho enthusiasm that we have come to expect in a land where the prohibitionist impulse has never quite died. In Austin, there is now a special squad of undercover cops dedicated to fighting the scourge of teenage tippling. In other words, they hang around in bars.   2

The crusade does not stop there. The Texas Commission on Alcohol and Drug Abuse boasts a campaign called "2young2drink," which features billboards, a hotline (Denounce your friends!), and a program enticingly known as "Shattered Dreams." Other efforts in-clude the Texas Alcoholic Beverage Commission's sting operations (Make your kid a snoop!) and, for those parents 2stupid2think, a helpful series of danger signs compiled by the Texas Safety Net-work. One early indicator that your child is drinking may be the "smell of alcohol on [his] breath." Who knew?   3

But it's unfair to single out Texas. The legal drinking age has been raised to 21 in every state, a dreary legacy of Elizabeth Dole's otherwise unremarkable tenure as President Reagan's transporta-tion secretary. She is not apologizing; her only regret is that the age of barroom consent was not increased to 24. In her Jihad against gin, Mrs. Dole forgot that the guiding principle of the Reagan admin-istration was supposed to be a reduction in the role of the state.   4

And, as usual, government is not going to do any good. The 5
only circumstances in which the approach taken by the zero-
tolerance zealots could have the faintest chance of success would
be in a society where alcohol was a rarity. Zero tolerance has
been a disastrous failure in the case of young people and illegal
drugs; how can it be expected to work with a product that is
available in every mall or corner store? Sooner or later, your child
will be confronted with that seductive bottle. The only question is
how he is going to deal with it.

Not well, if the Dole approach continues to hold sway. 6
Demonizing alcohol—and thus elevating it to the status of forbidden fruit—is counterproductive. Adult disapproval magically trans-
forms that margarita from a simple pleasure into an especially
thrilling act of rebellion.

My parents avoided this error. Growing up in more tolerant 7
England, I could always ask them for a drink, and, fairly frequently, I
would even be given one. At least partly as a result, I went through
adolescence without feeling any need to drink a pint to make a
point. My drinks were for the right reasons. The only recollection I
have of any real parental anxiety in this area was when, at the age of
about 13, I accepted a brandy from a friend of the family (an alleged
murderer, as it happens, but that's another story). The worry was not
the drink, but the uninsured glass containing it: antique, priceless, and,
as our host explained to my trembling mother, quite irreplaceable. In
the event, the glass survived me, and I survived the drink.

Parents, not bureaucrats, are the best judges of how and 8
when their offspring should be permitted to drink. Intelligent parents don't let alcohol become a big deal, a mystery or a battleground. They teach its perils, but its pleasures, too. Have a bottle
of wine on the table, and let the kids take a gulp; it will not, I
promise, turn them into Frenchmen. Treat a drink as a part of
growing up, as something to be savored within a family, rather
than guzzled down in some rite to mark passage from that family.

Furthermore, too much of the discussion about alcohol in 9
this country reflects prohibitionist fervor rather than scientific fact.
We act as if alcohol were a vice, a degenerate habit that can—at
best—be tolerated. In reality, it does not need to be apologized
for. Alcohol has been a valuable part of Western culture for thousands of years. It can be abused, sure, but it can inspire as well as
intoxicate, illuminate as well as irritate. In excess, the demon drink
merits its nickname; in moderation, it can be good for you.

Ah yes, some will say, but what about drunk driving? They   10
have a point. While it is possible to debate the numbers, there can
be little doubt that the higher drinking age has coincided with a
reduction in the number of highway deaths. But has the price
been worth paying? The question sounds callous, particularly given
the horrors of the individual tragedies that make up the statistics,
but all legislation is, in the end, a matter of finding a balance between competing rights, interests, and responsibilities. We could,
for example, save lives by denying drivers' licenses to those over
65, but we do not. We understand the trade-off: There is an interest in safer roads, but there is also an interest in allowing older
people to retain their independence.

In the case of the drinking age, the balance has shifted too   11
far in one direction, away from individual responsibility and towards government control. Raising the limit may have reduced
drunken driving, but the cost in lost freedom has been too high,
and, quite possibly, unnecessary: Alcohol-related auto accidents
seem to be falling in most age categories. The problem of teen
DWI is best dealt with directly, by strengthening the deterrents,
rather than obliquely, in the context of a wider attack on "underage" drinking—an attack that might, in fact, ultimately backfire on
those whose interest lies in combating the drunk at the wheel.

For the most striking thing of all about the minimum   12
drinking age of 21 is how unsuccessful it has been. A 19-year-old
in search of a drink will not have to hunt for long; just ask "Jenna."
Almost impossible to police effectively, our current policy sends a
signal to the young that our legal system is capricious, weak, occasionally vindictive, and not to be respected. In the interest of enforcing important laws—such as those against drunk driving—we
should do what we can to make sure our young people see the
police not as interfering busybodies, but as representatives of a
mature, broadly respected moral order, who are prepared to treat
them as adults. Those who believe government should be in the
message-sending business should pay a little more attention to the
message they are really sending, when they ask the police to en-
force unenforceable—and frankly indefensible—taboos.

AFTER YOU READ

Work with other students to develop responses to the following suggestions or to compare responses that you have already prepared.

1. Identify the thesis of each article. Then divide each article into major
   sections.

2. To clarify the arguments presented by each article, ask yourself, "What are this writer's reasons for his position?" Examine each major division, and make a list of the different reasons offered.

3. Once you have developed such a list, consider ways the various writers' points can be grouped. Which points from different articles would you put together? Why?

WRITING ASSIGNMENTS

Note Working with several sources can be substantially more difficult than working with only one source. As you respond to one of these assignments, consider working with other students to clarify and organize your ideas.

1. Write a synthesis of the ideas presented in the articles involving "Physician-Assisted Suicide" or "The Minimum Legal Drinking Age." After taking careful notes of each article, divide related ideas into separate groupings and then decide on a logical organization of those groups. Remember that your purpose is to explain the issues, not to take a stand.

2. Write a synthesis of related articles assigned by your instructor from Chapter 8 or from Part Four.

EVALUATING SAMPLE PAPERS

Synthesis Essay

Use the following criteria to evaluate the student essays below.

1. Introduction

   Does the first paragraph introduce the topic and establish its complexity? Does the thesis make it clear that the point of the paper is to explain the issues discussed by a number of writers?

   1   2   3   4   5   6

2. Unity

   Does each paragraph have a clear and specific topic sentence that accurately introduces an idea discussed by one or more of the articles? Is the material in each paragraph clearly related to its topic sentence?

   1   2   3   4   5   6

3. Support

   Are all of the major points discussed? Is each point accurately and fully explained?

   1   2   3   4   5   6

4. Coherence

   Are transitions used between paragraphs? Are they used within paragraphs, especially when the writer is moving from what one article says to what is said in another?

   1   2   3   4   5   6

5. References to the Text

   Are direct quotations and paraphrases correctly introduced and smoothly incorporated into the text? Do they reflect the articles' points accurately?

   1   2   3   4   5   6

6. Sentence Structure

   Do the sentences combine ideas that are related, using coordination, subordination, verbal phrases, or parallelism when appropriate? Are there too many brief, choppy main clauses?

   1   2   3   4   5   6

7. Mechanics, Grammar, and Spelling

   Does the paper contain a distracting number of errors of these kinds?

   1   2   3   4   5   6

8. Overall Ranking of the Essay

   1   2   3   4   5   6

Evaluate the following student essays. Use the criteria above to determine which essay is most effective.

Student Essay 1 (See Part Four for the reading selections used for this synthesis)

Should the burning of the American flag be protected by the First Amendment? Should Americans pass an amendment to outlaw the burning of the American flag? These questions stir a heated controversy in the hearts of most Americans. Some people will argue that the burning of the flag is a form of freedom of speech and therefore protected by law, while others will argue that the flag is a symbol so sacred to Americans that there should be a law passed to protect it from harm. The issue is a complicated one. Although there are no easy answers here, understanding the arguments involved will at least allow one to take a position based on a careful consideration of the issues.

One issue that is discussed involves freedom of speech. Those who oppose an amendment to protect the flag claim that burning the American flag is a form of speech protected by the First Amendment. It is speech because it expresses a strong disagreement with the federal government and its policies (Levendosky 442). It is also protected by the First Amendment because that amendment applies not just to oral speech but to "writing, sign language, Morse code, auction gestures, etc.—any way we encode meanings in language" (Kaplan 447). Levendosky points out that since the Supreme Court recognizes other acts such as "raising a red flag to show support for worker unity," wearing "black armbands to protest our role in Vietnam," and sitting silently "to protest racial segregation" as symbolic speech protected under the First Amendment, flag burning should also be considered under those guidelines (442). According to this argument, the free speech guarantee applies to conduct when it functions as communication. Conduct may be considered communication when it involves meaning, requires an audience, and is intended to have a meaning—all of which is true for flag burning (Kaplan 447–448).

Arguments supporting the "flag amendment" take issue with the idea that the act of burning the flag is a form of *speech*. Although proponents of the flag amendment agree that the Supreme Court gave First Amendment protection to flag burning, they say that the court's decision was misguided and came on a divided 5-4 vote (Dole 445). According to this argument, any ordinary person can tell the difference between an action and a speech, and all the arguing about what is or is not speech causes people to lose sight of the obvious—that burning the flag is an action (Greenberg 439), In addition, even if flag burning were considered speech, not all speech is protected by the First Amendment. Just as obscenity, "fighting words," or yelling "fire!" in a crowded theater is not protected, burning the flag should not be either (Dole 445).

Symbolism is another issue that arises when discussing burning of the flag. What does the American flag stand for? Many people believe the American flag is a symbol worth protection by law. They believe that there are some symbols, such as the American flag, that are "so rooted in history and custom, and in the heroic imagination of a nation, that they transcend the merely symbolic; they become presences" (Greenberg 440). Robert Dole says that the flag represents the courage of the American people, that it is a symbol of their strength of character, principles, and ideals, and that it must therefore be protected by law (444). Opponents of the flag amendment do not deny the symbolism of the flag. Instead, they say that by protecting the symbol we harm what it symbolizes—which is freedom, liberty, and justice (Kaplan 448–449). They claim that the flag amendment will "protect the symbol of our liberties—at the expense of those liberties" (Levendosky 444).

In addition to freedom of speech and symbolism, there are other issues that should also be considered. Greenberg notes that "vandalizing a cemetery, or scrawling slogans on a church or synagogue, or spray-painting a national monument" are all acts, not forms of speech, that are prohibited by law, and he feels the act of flag-burning should be treated the same as these other forbidden acts. He feels these types of laws teach respect (441). He worries that the intellectuals who oppose an amendment to outlaw burning the flag are confusing physical acts with speech, thus having lost touch with their common sense (441). Since it is very difficult to draw the line on what desecrating the flag would be, Levendosky is concerned where the amendment to ban flag-burning would take us if it were passed. He asks if one could be arrested while wearing a flag bikini or eating a cake with a frosting flag (443–444). And Dole, in support of the flag amendment, claims that the flag goes beyond the symbolic, that it has almost a sacred quality to it, and that quality must be protected by law (446).

The arguments involved in this issue deserve serious consideration. There are strong points supporting the amendment to prohibit flag-burning as well as opposing it. Perhaps the most complicated idea involves the concept of the flag-burning as freedom of speech, but the most emotional one focuses on the flag as a symbol of our country. Each American will need to evaluate his or her own devotion to the flag and to the principles by which all Americans live.

Student Essay 2 (See Part Four for the reading selections used for this synthesis)

Have you ever been in a heated discussion over whether the effects of television are helpful or harmful? I have argued with my sister about this issue many times, especially when I see the kinds of television shows that she lets her children watch. It is clear to me that many people have strong opinions about whether or not television is educational, has any values, or confuses reality and illusion.

First, many people disagree on whether tv is or is not educational. According to Paul Robinson, tv is not at all educational. In fact, he says "Educational TV corrupts the very notion of education and renders its victims uneducable" (432). Robinson explains that television programs are not enough to rely on for real knowledge, and that even ignorance is better "because ignorance at least preserves a mental space that might someday be filled with real knowledge . . ." (432). Other people, on the other hand, say that television can provide useful learning. For instance, William Henry III mentions that there are probably children who learn the alphabet from *Sesame Street,* and some older students who "through TV have grasped some basic truths about the planet" (428). Henry also points out that television makes us aware of occurrences such as beaches being closed to bathers because of toxic wastes on shore. Furthermore, he recognizes the importance of television as a source of news for editors and reporters during elections (428).

Another point of discussion concerns whether television is significant or valuable. According to Robinson, television, such as soap operas like *All My Children,* attempts to be similar to the great American novel and therefore of literary value. He doesn't think television has any literary value, but he says it does have entertainment value and is "superbly fit to amuse" (433). Henry points out that television is strongly influential on our behavioral values, and says its deepest power is "the way its innocuous-looking entertainment reaches deep into the national mind" (428). Henry goes on to say that the characters on television portray how the nation feels about itself and that "they teach behavior and values" (428). Henry contradicts Robinson by noting a relationship of power between television and literature, and even sees television as going one step further than literature's ability to be philosophical. He says, "Television simply does this more effectively, more touchingly, than any kind of art that went before" (429).

The third issue that is discussed is the tendency for television to cause people to confuse reality and illusion. Almost everyone seems to agree that television mixes reality and illusion, but people disagree about whether the effect of that mixing is a problem. Robinson, as he explains that television is entertaining, yet not educational, implies negativity when he states that television "at the very least provides an escape from the world and from ourselves" (433). Henry says that unlike stage and movies, "the episodic TV series does not end in catharsis" (429). The characters return, and therefore television is more representative of ordinary life, and for some, he claims, this is barely distinguishable from reality. Cross has more of an emphasis on this issue throughout her article than Robinson and Henry. She uses two reports to prove her point that people's confusion of reality and illusion caused by television is bad. The first example is of behavior in the courtroom. She says that juries often expect real-life courtroom activities to be identical to television's version of courtroom activities. She adds a contributor's story of watching a jury that was confused because the defendant didn't follow the expected role of a defendant (as seen on television), and the result was a hung jury (436). The second example she used was a crime report that UPI filed explaining that a father was killed. His dead body was found within feet of his children who were watching television and were clearly oblivious to the killing (435).

As you can see, people hold many differing opinions about the overall effect of television. Most of the writers I have discussed see television as a mixed blessing. Even William Henry III, who praises television's ability to educate, recognizes that it also causes problems that affect us all.

SENTENCE COMBINING: SENTENCE VARIETY

Have you ever listened to someone talk who never varies the pitch or tone of his or her voice? Have you ever had to listen to a speaker (perhaps an instructor?) who drones on and on with no changes in the sound of her voice to help emphasize the important points or just to make what she is saying more interesting? If you have heard such a person, you know—as we do—how *boring* such a voice can be. Even if you aren't sleepy to begin with, you are ready to nod off within five minutes, right?

Writers have the same problems as speakers. They need to express their ideas in ways that will prevent their readers from taking a big yawn, closing their eyes, and starting to snore. **Sentence variety** is one technique that writers use to add interest to what they write. As the term implies, *sentence variety* means that the sentences in your paragraph or essay are somehow different from each other—they are *varied*—just as a good speaker's voice is frequently varied to keep the attention of the audience.

Actually, you have been practicing sentence variety throughout the sentence-combining sections of this text. When you embedded adjectives, adverbs, and prepositional phrases in Chapter 1, when you practiced using main and subordinate clauses in Chapters 2 and 3, when you used verbal phrases in Chapter 4 and appositives in Chapter 5, and when you practiced parallelism in Chapter 6—in each case, you were learning ways to vary the kinds of sentences that you write. In this section, you will work on writing sentences that are varied both in length and in structure.

SENTENCE LENGTH

One of the chief causes of monotonous writing is a series of relatively brief sentences, one after the other. Take a look at the following paragraph:

It was a warm, miserable morning last week. We went up to the Bronx Zoo. We wanted to see the moose calf. We also needed to break in a new pair of black shoes. We encountered better luck than we had bargained for. The cow moose and her young one were standing near the wall of the deer park. The wall was below the monkey house. We wanted a better view. We strolled down to the lower end of the park. We were by the brook. The path there is not much traveled. We approached the corner where the brook trickles under the wire fence. We noticed a red deer getting to her feet. Beside her was a spotted fawn. Its legs were just learning their business. The fawn was small and perfect. It was like a trinket seen through a reducing glass.

Wouldn't you agree that this writing is rather lackluster? The constant repetition of separate, short sentences makes the writing seem childlike and overly simple. However, with just a little work, many of the ideas in the excessively short sentences can be combined into longer sentences. Here is how the passage was actually written by the well-known essayist E. B. White:

> On a warm, miserable morning last week we went up to the Bronx Zoo to see the moose calf and to break in a new pair of black shoes. We encountered better luck than we had bargained for. The cow moose and her young one were standing near the wall of the deer park below the monkey house, and in order to get a better view we strolled down to the lower end of the park, by the brook. The path there is not much traveled. As we approached the corner where the brook trickles under the wire fence, we noticed a red deer getting to her feet. Beside her, on legs that were just learning their business, was a spotted fawn as small and perfect as a trinket seen through a reducing glass.
>
> —*E. B. White, "Twins"*

What do you think? Isn't the difference dramatic? E. B. White's paragraph is so effective not just because he is a master of descriptive detail (both paragraphs contain the same details) but because his sentences have a rhythm and flow that result from his ability to vary the lengths of his sentences.

EXERCISE 7.1

1. Count the number of sentences in E. B. White's paragraph, and compare that to the number of sentences in the choppy paragraph.
2. Now look at the lengths of the sentences in E. B. White's paragraph, and point out where the lengths vary. Try to explain the effect of the shorter and longer sentences.
3. Point out where details from the choppy paragraph are embedded in the E. B. White paragraph as prepositional phrases.
4. Point out where E. B. White's paragraph uses coordination and subordination to combine ideas that were separate sentences in the choppy paragraph.

SENTENCE STRUCTURE

Although a series of short, choppy sentences can be quite distracting, a more common cause of lifeless writing is a repetitive sentence structure. Perhaps the most commonly repeated sentence structure—and the easiest to vary—is the sentence that opens with the subject and verb of its main clause. Here are some examples of this common sentence pattern:

        S   V

Television has been blamed for a number of problems in our society.

>   S   V
>
> The house slid into the ravine after the rain weakened the cliffs below it.
>
>   S   V
>
> The committee voted to reduce the homeowners' fees.

As you can see, each of the above sentences opens with a main clause, and the subject and verb of each main clause are quite close to the start of the sentence. To add some variety to your writing, try opening many of your sentences with something other than the main clause. Here are some possibilities:

1. Open your sentence with a subordinate clause.

   <u>After the rain weakened the cliffs below it</u>, the house slid into the ravine.

2. Open your sentence with a prepositional phrase.

   <u>Over the past forty years</u>, television has been blamed for a number of problems in our society.

3. Open your sentence with a verbal phrase.

   <u>Responding to the complaints from a majority of the owners</u>, the committee voted to reduce the homeowners' fees. (present participial phrase)

   <u>Concerned about the rising cost of living</u>, the committee voted to reduce the homeowners' fees. (past participial phrase)

   <u>To prevent people from having to sell their homes</u>, the committee voted to reduce the homeowners' fees. (infinitive phrase)

Of course, another way to vary your sentence structures is to use subordinate clauses, prepositional phrases, verbal phrases, and appositives within as well as at the ends of sentences. The trick is to avoid using the same sentence pattern from one sentence to another to another.

EXERCISE 7.2

Rewrite the following paragraphs to improve their sentence variety. In both the original and revised versions, compute the average number of words in each sentence by counting all the words and dividing by the number of sentences. In each revised copy, underline any words, phrases, or subordinate clauses that open sentences before the appearance of the main clause.

1. Silly Putty was one of the most popular toy items of the '50s and '60s. It was originally developed as a possible substitute for rubber. In the 1940s, the U.S. War Production Board was looking for an inexpensive replacement for synthetic rubber. It wanted to use the replacement in jeep and airplane tires. It also wanted to use it in gas masks and other military gear. It asked General Electric to try to develop such a product. James Wright was the engineer who worked on the project. He eventually developed a rubbery goo. It stretched farther than rubber.

It rebounded 25 percent more than the best rubber ball. It was impervious to molds and decay. It withstood a wide range of temperatures without decomposing. It delighted children everywhere. It was pressed against the color print of newspaper comic pages. It lifted the image right onto itself. The new product really had no special advantages over synthetic rubber. It was never used commercially. It was not long before a man operating a toy store realized its possibilities. He began to market it inside colored plastic eggs. In its first year, Silly Putty outsold every item in the toy store. For the next two decades it was one of the most popular small toys in the country.

Average number of words per sentence: _____
Average number of words per sentence in your revision: _____

2. It was in the early years of our country. It was common for both soldiers and officers to wear long hair. They tied the hair back in a ponytail. In 1803 a Tennessee commander ordered all his officers to cut off their ponytails. Colonel Thomas Butler refused. He was a career officer with a distinguished record dating back to the Revolution. Butler was not about to cut his hair so easily. He was arrested and charged with insubordination. Friends of Butler rallied to his defense. Those friends included Andrew Jackson. They petitioned even President Jefferson to intervene on Butler's behalf. The President would not do so. On July 10, 1805, Butler was found guilty of mutinous conduct. He was sentenced to a year's suspension without pay. He died shortly after his conviction. He left a will requesting that a hole be drilled in his coffin. It requested that his ponytail be allowed to hang through it. He wanted everyone to see that, even when dead, he had not obeyed the order to cut it.

Average number of words per sentence: _____
Average number of words per sentence in your revision: _____

Exploring ONLINE

Go to www.thomsonedu.com/devenglish/mcdonald for a further discussion of sentence variety. Under "Chapter Resources" for Chapter 7, click on "Exploring Online."

Arguing from Several Reading Selections

8

WHAT IS AN ARGUMENT?

Well, an argument is probably *not* what Calvin proposes in the cartoon on the facing page ("I say, either agree with me or take a hike!"). Attitudes like Calvin's usually lead to quarrels and angry confrontations, which are, unfortunately, what many people think of when they hear the word *argument*.

The "argument" that you will write in this chapter will not be a quarrel in which you beat your reader into submission. Instead, it will be exactly the kind of writing you have been practicing all semester—a reasonable presentation of facts, statistics, examples, and other support in an attempt to convince your reader that your thesis makes sense. To a degree, you have been arguing every time you have written a paper this semester, for in each assignment you have attempted to support a thesis statement with reasonable and convincing evidence.

The difference between the earlier assignments and what is normally called an "argumentative" paper is that an argumentative thesis takes a stand on a *debatable* subject. As a result, your readers may already have opinions about your subject. Your job is to convince them that the opinion you express in your thesis is reasonable and worthy of their serious consideration. That's easier said than done.

To write a convincing argument, you will need to draw upon the writing skills you have been practicing so far:

- You will need to choose an appropriate topic, one that you can support with facts, examples, statistics, and statements from authority.
- You will need to organize your support into unified paragraphs that are introduced by clear and accurate topic sentences.
- You will need to summarize, paraphrase, and quote accurately when you draw material from reading selections.
- You will need to distinguish between facts and opinions as well as between specific and general statements.

THE ATTITUDE OF THE EFFECTIVE ARGUER

When you argue a position, no matter what the situation, your *attitude* can make all the difference in the world. Obviously, if your attitude, like Calvin's, is "I'm right, period! End of discussion!" you will not have much success. But even if you present evidence to support your ideas, you probably will not have much success if you are close-minded and show no understanding of your opposition's point of view. In fact, on many debatable issues, you should not expect to write a completely convincing argument; after all, an issue is debatable precisely *because* there are convincing arguments on both sides of it. As you approach any complicated, debatable issue, keep in mind the following points.

Keep an open mind until you have looked closely at the issue.   Perhaps the biggest mistake that many people make is *first* to decide what they think and *then* set out to prove that they are right. This is probably a natural thing to do—after all, nobody likes to be wrong—but will not lead to clear thinking and well-written arguments.

Whatever your beliefs are, set them aside until you have completed your study of the issue. As you read articles, talk to people, and consider your own experience, *be willing to change your mind* if the evidence suggests that you should—that willingness is one of the characteristics of a clear thinker.

Don't write as if your evidence completely resolves the issue.   Debatable topics exist because the "one, true" answer is not at all clear, so don't take the attitude that your support proves your opinion is right and all others are wrong. It probably doesn't. What it *may* prove, if your support is effective enough, is that your opinion is *reasonable* and should be considered by reasonable people. Too often people approach arguments as battles in which the other side must be thoroughly destroyed and discredited. But the "other side" is usually a figment of our imagination. There may be two or three or four or more ways of approaching a debatable issue—not one right way (yours) and one wrong way (theirs).

Don't misunderstand us. You *should* support your argument as well as you can, and you *should* be willing to take a stand. But you should also be willing to recognize points that might weaken your argument and to qualify your position if you need to.

PREPARING THE ARGUMENT

COLLECTING INFORMATION

As you have already read, the first step is *not* to take a stand or write a thesis statement. Even though you may already have an opinion on your topic, remember that the sign of a good thinker is the willingness to modify, qualify, or change an opinion once the information has been collected and examined. For example, suppose you think that watching too much television can cause serious problems, especially for children, so you decide to make television viewing the subject of your essay. Your *first* step is to try your best to set aside your personal opinion, keep an open mind, and start collecting information related to *both sides* of your topic. Your goal should be to come to an understanding of the opposing arguments related to television viewing and *only then* to draw a conclusion of your own. For the most part, the information you collect will come from material you read, from people you talk to, and from your own experiences.

LISTING AND EVALUATING INFORMATION

As you collect information, organize it into lists that reflect opposing attitudes toward the subject. For instance, a writer investigating the benefits and drawbacks of television viewing might develop the lists presented below after examining the articles in Part Four of this book under the heading "The Effects of Television" and after considering her personal experiences and the experiences of people she knows. If you have worked through the synthesis assignment in Chapter 7, you will recognize this list. Although an argument paper takes a stand while the synthesis does not, both assignments require that you understand all sides of the issue before you write the paper. (When you list an item, remember to identify its source so you can return to the article for more information when you evaluate the arguments.)

Is Television Educational?

Yes	No
• TV can provide learning. (Henry)	• TV cannot provide the time needed to learn. (Robinson)
• Children learn alphabet from *Sesame Street*. (Henry)	• Learning requires time to absorb facts. It requires reading. (Robinson)

- High school students learn about toxic waste on beaches.
  (Henry)
- A study by psychologist Daniel Anderson says children learn to think and draw inferences as they watch TV.
  (Drexler)
- Same study—TV does not replace reading; it replaces other recreational activities.
  (Drexler)
- Same study—TV watching does not lower IQ, although people with lower IQ do tend to watch more TV.
  (Drexler)
- Personal experience—I have used movies like *Gone with the Wind to* discuss history with my kids. A special about Bill Cosby led to questions about typical lifestyle of African-Americans.

- A documentary about Marin County cannot really be accurate because it does not have the time to cover the complexities of life there.
  (Robinson)
- Educational TV is the worst kind—it makes people think they know something when they really don't.
  (Robinson)

Does Television Make Us Better People?

Yes
- TV's characters embody human truths.
  (Henry)
- They epitomize what we feel about ourselves.
  (Henry)
- They teach behavior and values. The character of Mary Richards summed up the lives of a whole generation of women.
  (Henry)
- Without TV we might be less violent, have more respect for institutions, be healthier, but we also might be less alert, less informed, less concerned about world matters, lonelier.
  (Henry)

No
- Opinion of psychologist Daniel Anderson—The violence, sexism, and materialism on TV are having a major social impact on our children.
  (Drexler)
- TV is often used as a form of escapism.
  (Drexler)
- TV causes confusion between reality and illusion.
  (Woolfolk Cross)
- Personal knowledge—I have seen news reports about children imitating violent acts on television.

Is Television Valuable as Entertainment?

Yes
- TV is very good at entertaining. Jack Benny and Art Carney would not be nearly as funny in print. You need to see them and watch their timing.
  (Robinson)

No
- Many times watching TV is a default activity because there is nothing else to do.
  (Woolfolk Cross)

- Personal experience—I use TV to relax and entertain myself.
- A study by psychologist Daniel Anderson says when parents and kids watch together, kids tend to think about what they see.

(Drexler)

- Personal experience—My children have never confused TV with reality as far as I know, but we watch TV together and talk about what we see.

- TV entertainment mesmerizes viewers. Kids prefer videos to real life.

(Woolfolk Cross)

- Boys on a raft were disappointed because it was more fun on TV.

(Woolfolk Cross)

- Children preferred to watch a video of a fight rather than the real thing.

(Woolfolk Cross)

- UPI reported children watching TV next to the corpse of their dead father.

(Woolfolk Cross)

- In a Univ. of Nebraska study, over half of children chose TV over their fathers.

(Woolfolk Cross)

- Former DA Mario Merola says a jury wants the drama of TV and is less likely to convict if it doesn't get it.

(Woolfolk Cross)

As you can see, there is quite a bit of material to consider before you decide exactly where you stand, and not all of the material can be neatly divided into pro/con arguments. This writer, however, has attempted to divide the points she has found into three general groupings. The first focuses primarily on the educational value of television; the second seems to concern itself with television's impact on our behavior and values; and the third discusses both television's entertainment ability and the fear that television blurs the distinction between what is real and what is not.

At this point, you are in a position to evaluate the evidence. You have before you several major arguments about the benefits and drawbacks of television, some of which seem to directly contradict each other. Which seem more convincing? Consider which arguments use facts, examples, and expert testimony and which seem to rely more on unsupported opinions. Compare your own personal experiences to the arguments presented to see if they support or refute them.

As you evaluate the arguments, do not fall into the trap of thinking that one side must be right and the other must be wrong. Often that is just not the case. Do you see, for example, that it is possible that television has some benefits *and* some drawbacks, that the question is not necessarily a black-or-white, right-or-wrong issue? Such complexity is exactly why debatable, controversial issues *are* debatable and controversial. Both sides usually have points that need to be taken seriously. If you recognize the valid points on both sides of an issue and are willing to admit it when your opposition makes a good argument, then you have a better chance of convincing your reader that your own stand is a reasonable one that you have carefully thought out.

TAKING A STAND

Perhaps the most important point to note here is that taking a stand is the *final* step in preparing an argument, not the first step. Once you have collected, listed, and evaluated the various arguments related to your topic, you need to decide exactly what your opinion is. Remember that you do not have to prove that everything your opposition says is wrong for you to hold a differing opinion. Nor do you have to pretend that the reasons you give for your opinion should convince a reasonable person that you are right. What you *will* have to do is take a stand that you can reasonably support with the evidence available and that does not require you simply to ignore evidence that refutes your opinion.

OUTLINING AND ORGANIZING THE ARGUMENT

Several methods can be used to organize the material in an effective argument, but they all involve presenting points in support of your position and responding to points that seem to refute your position. *Before* you write the first draft of your paper, you should outline the points you intend to cover and the organizational pattern that will best serve your argument.

Below are some possible organizational patterns you can use. For shorter essays, each Roman numeral indicates a separate paragraph, but for longer essays, each numeral might indicate two or more paragraphs. In either case, you must remember to support each point with facts, examples, statistics, and references to authority, drawn either from your reading or from your own experiences or the experiences of people you know.

    I. Introduction and thesis
   II. First point in support of your thesis
  III. Second point in support of your thesis
  IV. Third point in support of your thesis
      (more points as needed)
    V. Major objection to your thesis and your response to it
  VI. Concluding paragraph

As you can see, this organization focuses primarily on presenting points that support your thesis, saving your discussion of any major objection until the end of the essay. Some topics, however, work better if the major objection is covered first, as in an organization like this:

    I. Introduction and thesis
   II. Major objection to your thesis and your response to it
  III. First point in support of your thesis
  IV. Second point in support of your thesis
    V. Third point in support of your thesis
      (more points as needed)
  VI. Concluding paragraph

Sometimes you may be taking a particularly unpopular stand, to which there are many obvious objections. In such a situation, consider this kind of organization:

   I. Introduction and thesis
  II. First objection and your response to it
 III. Second objection and your response to it
  IV. Third objection and your response to it
      (more objections and responses as needed)
   V. First point in support of your thesis
  VI. Second point in support of your thesis
      (more points as needed)
 VII. Concluding paragraph

Obviously, the organization and length of your argument can vary greatly, depending on how many objections you need to respond to and how many points you intend to cover. Here is an outline for a possible paper on the benefits of television:

   I. Introduction and thesis
      - Open with example of when I came home and kids were watching *The Simpsons.*
      - Tentative thesis: TV has more benefits than drawbacks.
  II. One benefit: It's entertaining and relaxing.
      - Support with personal experience of how it helps me after a long day as a student, employee, and mom.
      - Use Robinson's point about importance of entertainment.
 III. Another benefit: It can educate us and make us better thinkers.
      - Use examples from Henry article.
      - Use personal examples of *Gone with the Wind* and the special about Bill Cosby.
  IV. Another benefit: It makes people more aware of the world they live in.
      - Use personal examples of my kids asking questions about reruns of *I Love Lucy* and *Roseanne.*
      - Use Drexler's article about psychologist who says children think when helped by parents.
   V. Major objection: Woolfolk Cross says TV blurs reality and fantasy.
      - If TV is used incorrectly, she is right.
      - Refer to Drexler article again about parents guiding their children.
  VI. Another objection: TV hinders education because it replaces reading.
      - Use personal experience of my kids to show this isn't so.
 VII. Conclusion

WRITING THE ARGUMENT

If you have outlined and organized your points, writing the first draft of your paper should be no more difficult than writing the first drafts of every other paper you have written so far. Consider these points as you write:

1. Open your paper with an interesting lead-in. See Chapter 3 for a discussion of the many possibilities available to you.

2. Write a thesis statement that takes a clear position, but do not hesitate to qualify it if you need to. Notice, for example, how the qualification before this thesis helps the writer to sound like a reasonable person: "*I know that the television can be abused and misused, but so can any good thing.* On the whole, it seems to me that television watching has far more benefits than drawbacks."

3. Write clear topic sentences that refer to the central idea expressed in your thesis.

4. Support your topic sentences with facts, examples, statistics, and references to authority drawn either from your reading or from your own experiences or the experiences of people you know.

5. Respond to major objections in a reasonable manner. If the objection is simply inaccurate, explain why, giving support of your own. If the objection is reasonable yet does not change your point of view, explain why the reader should find your overall argument more persuasive.

6. See Chapter 3 for effective ways to conclude your essay.

PARAPHRASING, QUOTING, AND DOCUMENTING YOUR SOURCES

When you use material from the reading selections, identify the sources of all paraphrases, summaries, and quotations. Use clear transitions to introduce borrowed material as well as parentheses to identify the author and page number of each source. Refer to "Writing Paraphrases and Quotations" (pages 158–160), "Documenting Your Sources" (pages 234–236), and the Appendix (pages 464–468).

Exploring ONLINE

Go to www.thomsonedu.com/devenglish/mcdonald for more instruction in the writing of arguments. Under "Chapter Resources" for Chapter 8, click on "Exploring Online."

READINGS: SHOULD DRUGS BE LEGALIZED?

BEFORE YOU READ

1. What is your initial reaction to the suggestion that drugs be legalized? Would you call your reaction a personal opinion or a considered opinion?

2. What arguments do you expect to find in favor of and opposed to legalizing drugs?

3. As you read the following articles, set aside any personal opinions you may hold. Try to keep an open mind as you collect information about the issue.

The Case for Drug Legalization   GARY E. JOHNSON

Gary E. Johnson is the first governor in the history of New Mexico to be elected to two four-year consecutive terms. He is a conservative Republican, a businessman, and a triathlete. He also is a leading advocate in the movement to legalize drugs (starting with marijuana), regulating and taxing them like alcohol. Drug abuse, he says, should be treated as a health issue—not left to the police and the courts.

I am a "cost-benefit" analysis person. What's the cost and   1
what's the benefit? A couple of things scream out as failing cost-
benefit criteria. One is education. The other is the war on drugs. We
are presently spending $50 billion a year to combat drugs. I'm talk-
ing about police, courts, and jails. For the amount of money that
we're putting into it, I want to suggest, the war on drugs is an absolute failure. My "outrageous" hypothesis is that under a legalized
scenario, we could actually hold drug use level or see it decline.

Sometimes people say to me, "Governor, I am absolutely   2
opposed to your stand on drugs." I respond by asking them,
"You're for drugs, you want to see kids use drugs?" Let me make
something clear. I'm not pro-drug. I'm against drugs. Don't do
drugs. Drugs are a real handicap. Don't do alcohol or tobacco, either. They are real handicaps.

There's another issue beyond cost-benefit criteria. Should   3
you go to jail for using drugs? And I'm not talking about doing drugs
and committing a crime or driving a car. Should you go to jail for
simply doing drugs? I say no, you shouldn't. People ask me, "What
do you tell kids?" Well, you tell the truth: that by legalizing drugs, we
can control them, regulate and tax them. If we legalize drugs, we
might have a healthier society. And you explain how that might take
place. But you emphasize that drugs are a bad choice. Don't do
drugs. But if you do, we're not going to throw you in jail for it.

New Laws and Problems

If drugs are legalized, there will be a whole new set of laws. Let   4
me mention a few of them. Let's say you can't do drugs if you're
under 21. You can't sell drugs to kids. I say employers should be

able to discriminate against drug users. Employers should be able to conduct drug tests, and they should not have to comply with the Americans with Disabilities Act. Do drugs and commit a crime? Make it like a gun. Enhance the penalty for the crime in the same way we do today with guns. Do drugs and drive? There should be a law similar to one we have now for driving under the influence of alcohol.

I propose that we redirect the $50 billion that we're presently spending (state and federal) on the old laws to enforce a new set of laws. Society would be transformed if law enforcement could focus on crimes other than drug use. Police could crack down on speeding violations, burglaries, and other offenses that law enforcement now lacks the opportunity to enforce.   5

If drugs are legalized, there will be a new set of problems, but they will have only about half the negative consequence of those we have today. A legalization model will be a dynamic process that will be fine-tuned as we go along.   6

Does anybody want to press a button that would retroactively punish the 80 million Americans who have done illegal drugs over the years? I might point out that I'm one of those individuals. In running for my first term in office, I offered the fact that I had smoked marijuana. And the media were very quick to say, "Oh, so you experimented with marijuana?" "No," I said, "I smoked marijuana!" This is something I did, along with a lot of other people. I look back on it now, and I view drugs as a handicap. I stopped because it was a handicap. The same with drinking and tobacco. But did my friends and I belong in jail? I don't think that we should continue to lock up Americans because of bad choices.   7

And what about the bad choices regarding alcohol and tobacco? I've heard people say, "Governor, you're not comparing alcohol to drugs? You're not comparing tobacco to drugs?" I say, "Hell no! Alcohol killed 150,000 people last year. And I'm not talking about drinking and driving. I'm just talking about the health effects. The health effects of tobacco killed 450,000 people last year." I don't mean to be flippant, but I don't know of anybody ever dying from a marijuana overdose.   8

Less Lethal than Alcohol

I understand that 2,000 to 3,000 people died in 1998 from abusing cocaine and heroin. If drugs were legalized, those deaths would go away, theoretically speaking, because they would no longer   9 be counted as accidental. Instead, they'd be suicides, because in a legalized scenario drugs are controlled, taxed, and properly understood. I want to be so bold as to say that marijuana is never going to have the devastating effects on society that alcohol has had.

My own informal poll among doctors reveals that   10
75–80 percent of the patients they examine have health-related problems due to alcohol and tobacco. My brother is a cardiothoracic surgeon who performs heart transplants. He says that 80 percent of the problems he sees are alcohol and tobacco related. He sees about six people a year who have infected heart valves because of intravenous drug use, but the infection isn't from the drugs themselves. It's the dirty needles that cause the health problems.

Marijuana is said to be a gateway drug. We all know that,   11
right? You're 85 times more likely to do cocaine if you do marijuana. I don't mean to be flippant, but 100 percent of all substance abuse starts with milk. You've heard it, but that bears repeating. My new mantra here is "Just Say Know." Just know that there are two sides to all these arguments. I think the facts boil down to drugs being a bad choice. But should someone go to jail for just doing drugs? That is the reality of what is happening today. I believe the time has come for that to end.

I've been talking about legalization and not decriminaliz-   12
ation. Legalization means we educate, regulate, tax, and control the estimated $400 billion a year drug industry. That's larger than the automobile industry. Decriminalization is a muddy term. It turns its back to half the problems involved in getting the entire drug economy above the line. So that's why I talk about legalization, meaning control, the ability to tax, regulate, and educate.

We need to make drugs controlled substances just like   13
alcohol. Perhaps we ought to let the government regulate them; let the government grow or manufacture, distribute and market them. If that doesn't lead to decreased drug use, I don't know what would!

Kids today will tell you that legal prescription drugs are   14
harder to come by than illegal drugs. Well, of course. To get legal drugs, you must walk into a pharmacy and show identification. It's the difference between a controlled substance and an illegal substance. A teenager today will tell you that a bottle of beer is harder to come by than a joint. That's where we've come to today. It's where we've come to with regard to controlling alcohol, but it shows how out of control drugs have become.

Not Driving You Crazy

Drug Czar Barry McCaffrey has made me his poster child for   15
drug legalization. He claims that drug use has been cut in half and
that we are winning the drug war. Well, let's assume that we have
cut it in half. I don't buy that for a minute, but let's assume that it's
true. Consider these facts: In the late 1970s the federal government spent a billion dollars annually on the drug war. Today, the
feds are spending $19 billion a year on it. In the late 1970s, we
were arresting a few hundred thousand people. Today, we're arresting 1.6 million. Does that mean if drug use declines by half
from today's levels, we'll spend $38 billion federally and arrest
3.2 million people annually? I mean, to follow that logic, when
we're left with a few hundred users nationwide, the entire gross
national product will be devoted to drug-law enforcement!

Most people don't understand, as we New Mexicans do, that   16
the mules are carrying the drugs in. I'm talking about Mexican
citizens who are paid a couple hundred dollars to bring drugs
across the border, and they don't even know who has given
them the money. They just know that it's a king's ransom and that
there are more than enough Mexican citizens willing to do it. The
federal government is catching many of the mules and some of
the kingpins. Let's not deny that. But those who are caught, those
links out of the chain, don't make any difference in the overall
war on drugs.

I want to tell you a little bit about the response to what I've   17
been saying. Politically, this is a zero. For anybody holding office, for
anybody who aspires to hold office, has held office, or has a job
associated with politics, this is verboten. I am in the ground, and
the dirt is being thrown on top of my coffin. But among the public, the response is overwhelming. In New Mexico, I am being approached rapid-fire by people saying "right on" to my statements
regarding the war on drugs. To give an example, two elderly ladies
came up to my table during dinner the other night. They said,
"We're teachers, and we think your school voucher idea sucks.
But your position on the war on drugs is right on!"

What I have discovered, and it's been said before, is that the   18
war on drugs is thousands of miles long, but it's only about a
quarter-inch deep. I'm trying to communicate what I believe in
this issue. Drugs are bad, but we need to stop arresting and locking up the entire country.

Why Drug Legalization Should Be Opposed   CHARLES B. RANGEL

Congressman Charles B. Rangel is serving his eighteenth term as the Representative from the 15th Congressional District, comprising East and Central Harlem, the Upper West Side, and Washington Heights/Inwood. Congressman Rangel is the Ranking Member of the Committee on Ways and Means, Deputy Democratic Whip of the House of Representatives, a Co-Chair of the Democratic Congressional Campaign Committee, and Dean of the New York State Congressional Delegation.

In my view, the very idea of legalizing drugs in this country is counterproductive. Many well-meaning drug legalization advocates disagree with me, but their arguments are not convincing. The questions that I asked them twenty years ago remain unanswered. Would all drugs be legalized? If not, why?   1

Would consumers be allowed to purchase an unlimited supply? Are we prepared to pay the medical costs for illnesses that are spawned by excessive drug use? Who would be allowed to sell drugs? Would an illegal market still exist? Would surgeons, bus drivers, teachers, military personnel, engineers, and airline pilots be allowed to use drugs?   2

Drug legalization threatens to undermine our society. The argument about the economic costs associated with the drug war is a selfish argument that coincides with the short-sighted planning that we have been using with other social policies. With any legalization of drugs, related problems would not go away; they would only intensify. If we legalize, we will be paying much more than the $30 billion per year we now spend on direct health care costs associated with illegal drug use.   3

Drug legalization is not as simple as opening a chain of friendly neighborhood "drug" stores. While I agree that some drugs might be beneficial for medicinal purposes, this value should not be exploited to suggest that drugs should be legalized. Great Britain's experience with ·prescription heroin should provide a warning. Until 1968, British doctors were freely allowed to prescribe drugs to addicts for medicinal purposes. Due to the lack of rigorous controls, some serious problems became associated with this policy. Doctors supplied drugs to non-addicts, and addicts supplied legally obtained drugs to the general population resulting in an increased rate of addiction. There is plenty of evidence to show that drug legalization has not worked in other countries that have tried it. The United   4

States cannot afford such experiments when the data shows that drug legalization policies are failing in other countries.

In minority communities, legalization of drugs would be a nightmare. It would be a clear signal that America has no interest in removing the root causes of drug abuse: a sense of hopelessness that stems from poverty, unemployment, inadequate training and blight. Legalization of drugs would officially sanction the total annihilation of communities already at risk. Instead of advocating drug legalization, we should focus our efforts on rebuilding schools, strengthening our teachers, improving housing, and providing job skills to young people. 5

The issue should not be whether or not drugs should be legalized. Rather, we need to focus on changing the way the war on drugs is being fought. The real problems are our emphasis on incarceration, including mandatory minimum sentences, the unfair application of drug laws, the disparity in sentencing between crack cocaine and powder cocaine, and the failure to concentrate on the root causes of drug abuse. These shortcomings in our drug policy should not become a license for legalization. Many critics of the drug war have the knowledge and skills to improve our national drug control policy. Instead of supporting the Drug Czar, they use their resources to blast all efforts to eradicate drugs in this country. It is a shame that many educated and prominent people suggest that the only dangerous thing about drugs is that they are illegal. 6

If we are truly honest, we must confess that we have never fought that war on drugs as we have fought other adversaries. The promotion of drug legalization further complicates the issue. We must continue our efforts to stop the flow of illegal drugs into our country. Most importantly, we need to remove the root causes of drug abuse and increase our focus in the areas of prevention and treatment through education. Rather than holding up the white flag and allowing drugs to take over our country, we must continue to focus on drug demand as well as supply if we are to remain a free and productive society. 7

We're Losing the Drug War Because Prohibition Never Works

HODDING CARTER III

An award-winning journalist and commentator, Hodding Carter III has won four national Emmy Awards and the Edward R. Murrow Award for his public-television documentaries. He served in the presidential campaigns of Lyndon Johnson in 1960 and Jimmy Carter in 1976. He has been an opinion columnist for the Wall Street Journal *and a frequent contributor to* The New York Times, *the* Washington Post, *and many other newspapers and magazines.*

There is clearly no point in beating a dead horse, whether you are a politician or a columnist, but sometimes you have to do it just the same, if only for the record. So, for the record, here's another attempt to argue that a majority of the American people and their elected representatives can be and are wrong about the way they have chosen to wage the "war against drugs." Prohibition can't work, won't work, and has never worked, but it can and does have monumentally costly effects on the criminal justice system and on the integrity of government at every level.

Experience should be the best teacher, and my experience with prohibition is a little more recent than most Americans for whom the "noble experiment" ended with repeal in 1933. In my home state of Mississippi, it lasted for an additional thirty-three years, and for all those years it was a truism that the drinkers had their liquor, the preachers had their prohibition, and the sheriffs made the money. Al Capone would have been proud of the latitude that bootleggers were able to buy with their payoffs of constables, deputies, police chiefs, and sheriffs across the state.

But as a first-rate series in the *New York Times* made clear early last year, Mississippi's Prohibition-era corruption (and Chicago's before that) was penny ante stuff compared with what is happening in the United States today. From Brooklyn police precincts to Miami's police stations to rural Georgia courthouses, big drug money is purchasing major breakdowns in law enforcement. Sheriffs, other policemen, and now judges are being bought up by the gross. But that money, with the net profits for the drug traffickers estimated at anywhere from $40 billion to $100 billion a year, is also buying up banks, legitimate businesses and, to the south of us, entire governments. The latter becomes an increasingly likely outcome in a number of cities and states in this country as well. Cicero, Illinois, during Prohibition is an instructive case in point.

The money to be made from an illegal product that has about 23 million current users in this country also explains why its sale is so attractive on the mean streets of America's big cities. A street salesman can gross about $2,500 a day in Washington, which puts him in the pay category of a local television anchor, and this in a neighborhood of dead-end job chances.

Since the courts and jails are already swamped beyond   5
capacity by the arrests that are routinely made (44,000 drug dealers
and users over a two-year period in Washington alone, for instance),
and since those arrests barely skim the top of the pond, arguing that
stricter enforcement is the answer begs a larger question: Who is
going to pay the billions of dollars required to build the prisons, hire
the judges, train the policemen, and employ the prosecutors needed
for the load already on hand, let alone the huge one yet to come if
we ever get serious about arresting dealers and users?

Much is made of the costs of drug addiction, and it should   6
be, but the current breakdown in the criminal justice system is
not one of them. That breakdown is the result of prohibition, not
addiction. Drug addiction, after all, does not come close to the far
vaster problems of alcohol and tobacco addiction (as former Surgeon General Koop correctly noted, tobacco is at least as addictive as heroin). Hard drugs are estimated to kill 4,000 people a
year directly and several tens of thousands a year indirectly.
Alcohol kills at least 100,000 a year, addicts millions more and
costs the marketplace billions of dollars. Tobacco kills over
300,000 a year, addicts tens of millions, and fouls the atmosphere
as well. But neither alcohol nor tobacco threatens to subvert our
system of law and order, because they are treated as personal and
societal problems rather than as criminal ones.

Indeed, every argument that is made for prohibiting the use   7
of currently illegal drugs can be made even more convincingly
about tobacco and alcohol. The effects on the unborn? Stagger-
ingly direct. The effects on adolescents? Alcoholism is the addiction
of choice for young Americans on a ratio of about one hundred
to one. Lethal effect? Tobacco's murderous results are not a matter of debate anywhere outside the Tobacco Institute.

Which leaves the lingering and legitimate fear that   8
legalization might produce a surge in use. It probably would, although
not nearly as dramatic a one as opponents usually estimate. The fact
is that personal use of marijuana, whatever the local laws may say,
has been virtually decriminalized for some time now, but there has
been a stabilization or slight decline in use, rather than an increase,
for several years. Heroin addiction has held steady at about 500,000
people for some time, though the street price of heroin is far lower
now than it used to be. Use of cocaine in its old form also seems to
have stopped climbing and begun to drop off among young and old
alike, though there is an abundantly available supply.

That leaves crack cocaine, stalker of the inner city and   9
terror of the suburbs. Instant and addictive in effect, easy to use
and relatively cheap to buy, it is a personality-destroying substance
that is a clear menace to its users. But it is hard to imagine it being any more accessible under legalization than it is in most cities
today under prohibition, while the financial incentives for promoting its use would virtually disappear with legalization.

Proponents of legalization should not try to fuzz the issue,   10
nonetheless. Addiction levels might increase, at least temporarily, if legal sanctions were removed. That happened after the repeal of Prohibition, or so at least some studies have suggested. But while that
would be a personal disaster for the addicts and their families, and
would involve larger costs to society as a whole, those costs would
be minuscule compared with the costs of continued prohibition.

The young Capones of today own the inner cities, and the   11
wholesalers behind these young retailers are rapidly buying up the
larger system which is supposed to control them. Prohibition gave
us the Mafia and organized crime on a scale that has been with us
ever since. The new prohibition is writing a new chapter on that
old text. Hell-bent on learning nothing from history, we are witnessing its repetition, predictably enough, as tragedy.

Should Drugs Be Legalized?   WILLIAM J. BENNETT

*William J. Bennett served as Secretary of Education and Chairman of the National
Endowment for the Humanities under President Ronald Reagan, and as Director of
the Office of National Drug Control Policy under President George H. W. Bush. Currently he co-chairs, with former New York Governor Mario Cuomo, the Partnership
for a Drug-Free America. The following article was written while he served as the
National Drug "Czar" under former President George H. W. Bush.*

Since I took command of the war on drugs [as director of   1
National Drug Control Policy in Washington, D.C.], I have learned
from former secretary of state George Shultz that our concept of
fighting drugs is "flawed." The only thing to do, he says, is to "make
it possible for addicts to buy drugs at some regulated place." Conservative commentator William F. Buckley, Jr., suggests I should be
"fatalistic" about the flood of cocaine from South America and
simply "let it in." Syndicated columnist Mike Royko contends it
would be easier to sweep junkies out of the gutters "than to fight

a hopeless war" against the narcotics that send them there. Label-ing our efforts "bankrupt," federal judge Robert W. Sweet opts for legalization, saying, "If our society can learn to stop using butter, it should be able to cut down on cocaine."

Flawed, fatalistic, hopeless, bankrupt! I never realized   2
surrender was so fashionable until I assumed this post.

Though most Americans are overwhelmingly determined to   3
go toe-to-toe with the foreign drug lords and neighborhood pushers, a small minority believe that enforcing drug laws imposes greater costs on society than do drugs themselves. Like addicts seeking immediate euphoria, the legalizers want peace at any price, even though it means the inevitable proliferation of a prac-tice that degrades, impoverishes, and kills.

I am acutely aware of the burdens drug enforcement places   4
upon us. It consumes economic resources we would like to use elsewhere. It is sometimes frustrating, thankless, and often danger-ous. But the consequences of *not* enforcing drug laws would be far more costly. Those consequences involve the intrinsically de-structive nature of drugs and the toll they exact from our society in hundreds of thousands of lost and broken lives . . . human po-tential never realized . . . time stolen from families and jobs . . . pre-cious spiritual and economic resources squandered.

That is precisely why virtually every civilized society has   5
found it necessary to exert some form of control over mind-al-tering substances and why this war is so important. Americans feel up to their hips in drugs now. They would be up to their necks under legalization.

Even limited experiments in drug legalization have shown   6
that when drugs are more widely available, addiction skyrockets. In 1975 Italy liberalized its drug law and now has one of the highest heroin-related death rates in Western Europe. In Alaska, where marijuana was decriminalized in 1975, the easy atmosphere has in-creased usage of the drug, particularly among children. Nor does it stop there. Some Alaskan schoolchildren now tout "coco puffs," marijuana cigarettes laced with cocaine.

Many legalizers concede that drug legalization might   7
increase use, but they shrug off the matter. "It may well be that there would be more addicts, and I would regret that result," says Nobel laureate economist Milton Friedman. The late Harvard Med-ical School psychiatry professor Norman Zinberg, a longtime propo-nent of "responsible" drug use, admitted that "use of now-illicit drugs would certainly increase. Also casualties probably would increase."

In fact, Dr. Herbert D. Kleber of Yale University, my deputy   8
in charge of demand reduction, predicts legalization might cause a
"five-to-sixfold increase" in cocaine use. But legalizers regard this as
a necessary price for the "benefits" of legalization. What benefits?

1. Legalization Will Take the Profit Out of Drugs

The result supposedly will be the end of criminal drug pushers   9
and the big foreign drug wholesalers, who will turn to other enterprises because nobody will need to make furtive and dangerous trips to his local pusher.

But what, exactly, would the brave new world of legalized   10
drugs look like? Buckley stresses that "adults get to buy the stuff at
carefully regulated stores." (Would you want one in *your* neighborhood?) Others, like Friedman, suggest we sell the drugs at "ordinary retail outlets."

Former City University of New York sociologist Georgette   11
Bennett assures us that "brand-name competition will be prohib-
ited" and that strict quality control and proper labeling will be
overseen by the Food and Drug Administration. In a touching
egalitarian note, she adds that "free drugs will be provided to government clinics" for addicts too poor to buy them.

Almost all legalizers point out that the price of drugs will   12
fall, even though the drugs will be heavily taxed. Buckley, for example, argues that somehow federal drugstores will keep the price
"low enough to discourage a black market but high enough to ac-
cumulate a surplus to be used for drug education."

Supposedly, drug sales will generate huge amounts of   13
revenue, which will then be used to tell the public not to use
drugs and to treat those who don't listen.

In reality, this tax would only allow government to share the   14
drug profits now garnered by criminals. Legalizers would have to
tax drugs heavily in order to pay for drug education and treatment programs. Criminals could undercut the official price and still
make huge profits. What alternative would the government have?
Cut the price until it was within the lunch-money budget of the
average sixth-grade student?

2. Legalization Will Eliminate the Black Market.

Wrong. And not just because the regulated prices could be   15
undercut. Many legalizers admit that drugs such as crack or PCP
are simply too dangerous to allow the shelter of the law. Thus
criminals will provide what the government will not. "As long as

drugs that people very much want remain illegal, a black market will exist," says legalization advocate David Boaz of the libertarian Cato Institute.

Look at crack. In powdered form, cocaine was an expensive indulgence. But street chemists found that a better and far less expensive—and far more dangerous—high could be achieved by mixing cocaine with baking soda and heating it. Crack was born, and "cheap" coke invaded low-income communities with furious speed.

16

An ounce of powdered cocaine might sell on the street for $1200. That same ounce can produce 370 vials of crack at $10 each. Ten bucks seems like a cheap hit, but crack's intense ten- to fifteen-minute high is followed by an unbearable depression. The user wants more crack, thus starting a rapid and costly descent into addiction.

17

If government drugstores do not stock crack, addicts will find it in the clandestine market or simply bake it themselves from their legally purchased cocaine.

18

Currently crack is being laced with insecticides and animal tranquilizers to heighten its effect. Emergency rooms are now warned to expect victims of "sandwiches" and "moon rocks," life-threatening smokable mixtures of heroin and crack. Unless the government is prepared to sell these deadly variations of danger-ous drugs, it will perpetuate a criminal black market by default.

19

And what about children and teenagers? They would obviously be barred from drug purchases, just as they are prohib-ited from buying beer and liquor. But pushers will continue to cater to these young customers with the old, favorite come-ons—a couple of free fixes to get them hooked. And what good will antidrug education be when these youngsters observe their older brothers and sisters, parents, and friends lighting up and shooting up with government permission?

20

Legalization will give us the worst of both worlds: millions of *new* drug users and a thriving criminal black market.

21

3. Legalization Will Dramatically Reduce Crime

"It is the high price of drugs that leads addicts to robbery, murder, and other crimes," says Ira Glasser, executive director of the American Civil Liberties Union. A study by the Cato Institute concludes: "Most, if not all 'drug-related murders' are the result of drug prohibition."

22

But researchers tell us that many drug-related felonies are   23
committed by people involved in crime *before* they started taking
drugs. The drugs, so routinely available in criminal circles, make the
criminals more violent and unpredictable.

Certainly there are some kill-for-a-fix crimes, but does any   24
rational person believe that a cut-rate price for drugs at a government outlet will stop such psychopathic behavior? The fact is that
under the influence of drugs, normal people do not act normally,
and abnormal people behave in chilling and horrible ways. DEA
agents told me about a teenage addict in Manhattan who was
smoking crack when he sexually abused and caused permanent
internal injuries to his one-month-old daughter.

Children are among the most frequent victims of violent,   25
drug-related crimes that have nothing to do with the cost of acquiring the drugs. In Philadelphia in 1987 more than half the child-
abuse fatalities involved at least one parent who was a heavy drug
user. Seventy-three percent of the child-abuse deaths in New York
City in 1987 involved parental drug use.

In my travels to the ramparts of the drug war, I have seen   26
nothing to support the legalizers' argument that lower drug prices
would reduce crime. Virtually everywhere I have gone, police and
DEA agents have told me that crime rates are highest where
crack is cheapest.

4. Drug Use Should Be Legal since Users Only Harm Themselves

Those who believe this should stand beside the medical   27
examiner as he counts the thirty-six bullet wounds in the shattered corpse of a three-year-old who happened to get in the way
of his mother's drug-crazed boyfriend. They should visit the babies
abandoned by cocaine-addicted mothers—infants who already
carry the ravages of addiction in their own tiny bodies. They
should console the devastated relatives of the nun who worked in
a homeless shelter and was stabbed to death by a crack addict
enraged that she would not stake him to a fix.

Do drug addicts only harm themselves? Here is a former   28
cocaine addict describing the compulsion that quickly draws even
the most "responsible" user into irresponsible behavior: "Everything is about getting high, and any means necessary to get there
becomes rational. If it means stealing something from somebody
close to you, lying to your family, borrowing money from people

you know you can't pay back, writing checks you know you can't cover, you do all those things—things that are totally against everything you have ever believed in."

Society pays for this behavior, and not just in bigger   29
insurance premiums, losses from accidents, and poor job perform-ance. We pay in the loss of a priceless social currency as families are destroyed, trust between friends is betrayed, and promising careers are never fulfilled. I cannot imagine sanctioning behavior that would increase that toll.

I find no merit in the legalizers' case. The simple fact is that   30
drug use is wrong. And the moral argument, in the end, is the most compelling argument. A citizen in a drug-induced haze, whether on his backyard deck or on a mattress in a ghetto crack house, is not what the founding fathers meant by the "pursuit of happiness." Despite the legalizers' argument that drug use is a matter of "personal freedom," our nation's notion of liberty is rooted in the ideal of a self-reliant citizenry. Helpless wrecks in treatment centers, men chained by their noses to cocaine—these people are slaves.

Imagine if, in the darkest days of 1940, Winston Churchill   31
had rallied the West by saying, "This war looks hopeless, and be-sides, it will cost too much. Hitler can't be *that* bad. Let's surren-der and see what happens." That is essentially what we hear from the legalizers.

This war *can* be won. I am heartened by indications that   32
education and public revulsion are having an effect on drug use. The National Institute on Drug Abuse's latest survey of current users shows a 37 percent *decrease* in drug consumption since 1985. Cocaine is down 50 percent; marijuana use among young people is at its lowest rate since 1972. In my travels I've been en-couraged by signs that Americans are fighting back.

I am under no illusion that such developments, however   33
hopeful, mean the war is over. We need to involve more citizens in the fight, increase pressure on drug criminals, and build on an-tidrug programs that have proved to work. This will not be easy. But the moral and social costs of surrender are simply too great to contemplate.

AFTER YOU READ

Work with other students to develop responses to these questions or to compare responses that you have already prepared.

1. As in most debates, you should be able to find reasonable arguments on both sides of the issue. Make a list of the arguments for and against the legalization of drugs.

2. As you evaluate the arguments and take a stand, consider also your own experiences or the experiences of people you know. How would the arguments you have read in these articles affect them?

READINGS: SCHOOL, TEENAGERS, AND PART-TIME JOBS

BEFORE YOU READ

1. Consider whether or not you think it is a good idea for teenagers to work part-time while they are going to school. What are the advantages and/or disadvantages involved?

2. Did you work as a teenager? If you did, explain in what ways your experience benefited you. Did your experience have any negative results?

The Fast-Food Factories: McJobs Are Bad for Kids   AMITAI ETZIONI

Amitai Etzioni received his PhD from University of California, Berkeley, in 1958. He served as Professor of Sociology at Columbia University for twenty years, as a professor at The George Washington University, and as Senior Advisor to the White House from 1979 to 1980. In 2001, he was named as being among the top 100 American intellectuals as measured by academic citations. Dr. Etzioni is married and has five sons.

McDonald's is bad for your kids. I do not mean the flat patties and the white-flour buns; I refer to the jobs teen-agers undertake, mass-producing these choice items.   1

As many as two-thirds of America's high-school juniors and seniors now hold down part-time paying jobs, according to studies. Many of these are in fast-food chains, of which McDonald's is the pioneer, trend-setter and symbol.   2

At first, such jobs may seem right out of the Founding Fathers' educational manual for how to bring up self-reliant, work-ethic-driven, productive youngsters. But in fact, these jobs undermine school attendance and involvement, impart few skills that will be useful in later life, and simultaneously skew the values of teen-agers—especially their ideas about the worth of a dollar.   3

It has been a long-standing American tradition that   4
youngsters ought to get paying jobs. In folklore, few pursuits are
more deeply revered than the newspaper route and the sidewalk
lemonade stand. Here the youngsters are to learn how sweet are
the fruits of labor and self-discipline (papers are delivered early in
the morning, rain or shine) and the ways of trade (if you price
your lemonade too high or too low . . .).

Roy Rogers, Baskin-Robbins, Kentucky Fried Chicken, et al.,   5
may at first seem nothing but a vast extension of the lemonade
stand. They provide very large numbers of teen jobs, provide regular employment, pay quite well compared to many other teen
jobs and, in the modern equivalent of toiling over a hot stove, test
one's stamina.

Closer examination, however, finds the McDonald's kind of job   6
highly uneducational in several ways. Far from providing opportunities for entrepreneurship (the lemonade stand) or self-discipline,
self-supervision and self-scheduling (the paper route), most teen
jobs these days are highly structured—what social scientists call
"highly routinized."

True, you still have to have the gumption to get yourself over   7
to the hamburger stand, but once you don the prescribed uniform, your task is spelled out in minute detail. The franchise prescribes the shape of the coffee cups; the weight, size, shape and
color of the patties; and the texture of the napkins (if any). Fresh
coffee is to be made every eight minutes. And so on. There is no
room for initiative, creativity or even elementary rearrangements.
These are breeding grounds for robots working for yesterday's assembly lines, not tomorrow's high-tech posts.

There are very few studies of the matter. One is a 1984 study   8
by Ivan Chamer and Bryna Shore Fraser. It relies mainly on what
teen-agers write in response to questionnaires rather than actual
observations of fast-food jobs. The authors argue that the employees develop many skills, such as how to operate a food-preparation
machine and a cash register. However, little attention is paid to how
long it takes to acquire such a skill, or what its significance is. What
does it matter if you spend 20 minutes learning to use a cash register and then "operate" it? What "skill" have you acquired? It is a long
way from learning to work with a lathe or carpenter tools in the
olden days or to program computers in the modern age.

A 1980 study by A. V. Harrell and P. W. Wirtz found that,   9
among those students who worked at least 25 hours per week

while in school, their unemployment rate four years later was half of that of seniors who did not work. This is an impressive statistic. It must be seen, though, together with the finding that many who begin as part-time employees in fast-food chains drop out of high school and are gobbled up in the world of low-skill jobs.

Some say that while these jobs are rather unsuited for college-bound, white, middle-class youngsters, they are "ideal" for lower-class, "non-academic," minority youngsters. Indeed, minorities are "over-represented" in these jobs (21 percent of fast-food employees). While it is true that these places provide income, work and even some training to such youngsters, they also tend to perpetuate their disadvantaged status. They provide no career ladders and few marketable skills, and they undermine school attendance and involvement.   10

The hours are often long. Among those 14 to 17, a third of fast-food employees (including some school drop-outs) labor more than 30 hours per week, according to the Charner-Fraser study. Only 20 percent work 15 hours or less. The rest: between 15 and 30 hours. Often the restaurants close late, and after closing one must clean up and tally up. In affluent Montgomery County, where child labor would not seem to be a widespread economic necessity, 24 percent of the seniors at Walt Whitman High School in 1985 worked as much as five to seven days a week; 27 percent, three to five. There is just no way such amounts of work will not interfere with school work, especially homework. In an informal survey published in the most recent Walt Whitman yearbook, 58 percent of the seniors acknowledged that their jobs interfere with their school work.   11

The Charner-Fraser study sees merit in learning teamwork and working under supervision. The authors have a point here. However, it must be noted that such learning is not automatically educational or wholesome. For example, much of the supervision in fast-food places leans toward teaching one the worst kinds of compliance: blind obedience, or shared alienation with the "boss."   12

Supervision is often both tight and woefully inappropriate. Today, fast-food chains and other such places of work (record shops, bowling alleys) keep costs down by having teens supervise teens, often with no adult on the premises. There is no father or mother figure with which to identify, to emulate, to provide a role model and guidance. The work-culture varies from one place to another: Sometimes it is a tightly run shop (must keep the cash   13 registers ringing); sometimes a rather loose pot party interrupted by customers. However, only rarely is there a master to learn from, or much worth learning. Indeed, far from being places where solid adult work values are being transmitted, these are places where all too often delinquent teen values dominate. Typically, when my son Oren was dishing out ice cream for Baskin Robbins in upper Manhattan, his fellow teen-workers considered him a sucker for not helping himself to the till. Most youngsters felt they were entitled to $50 severance "pay" on their last day on the job.

The pay, oddly, is the part of the teen work-world which is most difficult to evaluate. The lemonade stand or paper route money was for your allowance. In the old days, apprentices learning a trade from a master contributed most, if not all, of their income to their parents' household. Today, the teen pay may be low by adult standards, but it is often, especially in the middle class, spent largely or wholly by the teens. That is, the youngsters live free at home ("after all, they are high school kids") and are left with very substantial sums of money.   14

Where this money goes is not quite clear. Some use it to support themselves, especially among the poor. More middle class kids set some money aside to help pay for college, or save it for a major purchase—often a car. But large amounts seem to flow to pay for an early introduction into the most trite aspects of American consumerism: Flimsy punk clothes, trinkets and whatever else is the last fast-moving teen craze.   15

One may say that this is only fair and square; they are being good American consumers, working and spending their money on what turns them on. At least, a cynic might add, these funds do not go into illicit drugs and booze. On the other hand, an educator might bemoan that these young, yet unformed individuals, so early in life are driven to buy objects of no intrinsic educational, cultural or social merit, learn so quickly the dubious merit of keeping up with the Jones' in ever-changing fads promoted by mass merchandising.   16

Many teens find the instant reward of money, and the youth status symbols it buys, much more alluring than credits in calculus courses, European history, or foreign languages. No wonder quite a few would rather skip school—and certainly homework—and instead work longer at a Burger King. Thus, most teen work these days is not providing early lessons in work ethic; it fosters escape from school and responsibilities, quick gratification and a short cut to the consumeristic aspects of adult life.   17

Thus, ironically, we must add youth employment, not merely   18
unemployment, to our list of social problems. And, like many
other social ills, the unfortunate aspects of teen work resist easy
correction. Sure, it would be much better if corporations that
employ teens would do so in conjunction with high schools and
school districts. Educators could help define what is the proper
amount of gainful work (not more than "X" hours per school
week), how late kids may be employed on school nights (not
later than 9 p.m.), encourage employer understanding during
exam periods, and insist on proper supervision. However, corporations are extremely unlikely to accept such an approach which,
in effect, would curb their ability to draw on a major source of
cheap labor. And, in these laissez-faire days, Congress is quite dis-
inclined to pass new social legislation forcing corporations to be
more attentive to the education needs of the minors they so
readily employ.

Schools might extend their own work-study programs   19
(starting their own franchises?!) but, without corporate help, these
are unlikely to amount to much. Luckily, few school (less than
10 percent) provide any credit for such work experience. But
schools that do should insist that they will provide credit for work
only if it meets their educational standards; only if they are con-
sulted on matters such as supervision and on-the-job training; and
only if their representatives are allowed to inspect the places of
employment. School counselors should guide the youngsters only
to those places of work that are willing to pay attention to educational elements of these jobs.

Parents who are still willing to take their role seriously may   20
encourage their youngsters to seek jobs at places that are proper
work settings and insist that fast-food chains and other franchises
shape up or not employ their kids. Also an agreement should be
reached with the youngsters that a significant share of teen earnings should be dedicated to the family, or saved for agreed-upon
items.

Above all, parents should look at teen employment not as   21
automatically educational. It is an activity—like sports—that can
be turned into an educational opportunity. But it can also easily
be abused. Youngsters must learn to balance the quest for income
with the needs to keep growing and pursue other endeavors
which do not pay off instantly—above all education.

Go back to school.

The Dead-End Kids   MICHELE MANGES

In the following reading selection, Michele Manges, a writer for the Wall Street Journal, *suggests that part-time jobs today are not teaching teenagers any worthwhile skills or attitudes. Instead, as she says, ". . . youngsters hustle at monotonous, dead-end jobs that prepare them for nothing." As you read the selection, consider her points in light of your own knowledge or experience.*

If just showing up accounts for 90 percent of success in life, as Woody Allen claims, then today's teenagers ought to make great recruits for tomorrow's permanent work force.   1

Well over half of them are already showing up in the part-time work force doing after-school and summer jobs. In times past, this kind of youthful zeal was universally applauded; the kids, we thought, were getting invaluable preliminary training for the world of work. But now a lot of people are *worried* about the surge in youth employment. Why?   2

Because a lot of today's eight million working teens—55 percent of all 16- to 19-year-olds—aren't learning anything much more useful than just showing up.   3

Taste of Adulthood

Not that long ago many youngsters could get part-time or summer jobs that taught them the rudiments of a trade they could pursue later. If this wasn't the case, they at least got a taste of the adult world, working closely with adults and being supervised by them. Also, in whatever they did they usually had to apply in a practical way at least some of the skills they'd learned in school, thus reinforcing them.   4

Today, however, a growing majority of working youngsters hustle at monotonous, dead-end jobs that prepare them for nothing. They certainly make up one of the largest groups of underemployed people in the country.   5

Many work in adolescent ghettos overseen by "supervisors" barely older than they are, and they don't need to apply much of anything they've learned in school, not even the simplest math; technology has turned them into near-automatons. Checkout scanners and sophisticated cash registers tot up bills and figure the change for them. At fast-food joints, automatic cooking timers remove the last possibility that a teen might pick up a smidgen of culinary skill.   6

Laurence Steinberg, a Temple University professor and   7
co-author of a book on teenage employment, estimates that at least
three out of every four working teenagers are in jobs that don't give
them any meaningful training. "Why we think that wrapping burgers
all day prepares kids for the future is beyond me," he says.

In a study of 550 teens, Prof. Steinberg and his colleagues   8
found that those working long hours at unchallenging jobs tended
to grow cynical about work in general. They did only their own
defined tasks and weren't inclined to help out others, their sense
of self-respect declined, and they began to feel that companies
don't care about their employees. In effect, they were burning out
before they even joined the permanent work force.

A lot of teenaged workers are just bone-tired, too. Shelley   9
Wurst, a cook at an Ohio franchise steakhouse, got so worn out
she stopped working on school nights. "I kept sleeping through my
first-period class," she says. "If it wasn't for the crew I'm working
with, I wouldn't want to work there at all."

This sort of thing is all too common. "Some kids are   10
working past 2 a.m. and have trouble waking up for morning
classes," says Larry Morrison, principal of Sylvania (Ohio)
Northview High School. Educators like him are beginning to wonder whether teenage work today is not only irrelevant to future
careers but even damaging to them; the schoolwork of students
who pour so much time and energy into dead-end jobs often suffers—thus dimming their eventual prospects in a permanent job
market that now stresses education.

As for the teens themselves, a great number would much   11
rather be working elsewhere, in more challenging or relevant jobs.
Some, like Tanya Paris, have sacrificed to do so.

A senior at Saratoga (Calif.) High School, she works six   12
hours a week with a scientist at the National Aeronautics and
Space Administration, studying marine algae, for no pay and no
school credit. The future biologist hopes that her NASA work will
help her decide which area of biology to pursue.

But most others either are lured by the money they can   13
make or can't find what they're looking for. Jay Jackson, a
senior at Northview High, says he'd take a pay cut from his
$3.40-an-hour job as a stock boy if he could find something allied
to psychology, his prospective career field. He hasn't been able to.
Schoolmate Bridget Ellenwood, a junior, yearned for a job that had
something to do with dentistry but had to settle for slicing up

chickens at a local Chick-fil-A franchise—a job, she says, "where you don't learn much at all."

And More to Come

Expect more teen jobs where you don't learn much at all. The   14
sweeping change in the economy from making things to service,
together with the growth of computerized service-industry technology that leaves almost nothing to individual skill and initiative, is
expected to accelerate.

So the mindless and irrelevant part-time jobs open to teens   15
in the near future will probably increase, while the better jobs
continue to decline. On top of that, a growing labor shortage,
which would drive up pay, figures to draw more kids into those
jobs—against their interests. "Teen-agers would be much better
off doing a clerical-type job or studying," says Prof. John Bishop of
Cornell University's Industrial and Labor Relations Center.

Efforts have been under way to cut back the number of   16
hours teens can work, but the worsening labor shortage is under-
cutting them. Many educators are instead urging the states to start
or expand more high-school cooperative education programs. These
plans tie school and outside work to future career goals and provide
more structure and adult supervision than ordinary outside work.

Employers also prefer students with this kind of experience.   17
A recent study by the Cooperative Work Experience Education
Association found that 136 of 141 businesses in Arkansas would
hire a young applicant who had been in such a program over one
who had worked independently. "The goal is not to get kids to
stop working," says Prof. Bishop of Cornell. "It's to get them to
learn more."

Part-Time Work Ethic: Should Teens Go for It?   DENNIS MCLELLAN

Dennis McLellan is a staff writer for the Los Angeles Times. *As you read the following article, note his attempt to consider the issue of teenage employment from an objective point of view, considering all sides of the issue. How well do you think he succeeds?*

John Fovos landed his first part-time job—as a box boy at Alpha   1
Beta on West Olympic—the summer after his sophomore year at
Fairfax High School in Los Angeles. "I wanted to be independent,"
he said, "and I felt it was time for me to see what the world was
really like."

Now an 18-year-old senior, Fovos works the late shift at the 2
supermarket stocking shelves four nights a week. He saves about
$50 a week, but most of his paycheck goes to his car payment
and membership at a health spa. "The rest is for food—what I
don't eat at home—and clothes."

Shelley Staats went to work part-time as a secretary for a 3
Century 21 office when she was 15. Since then, she has worked
as a cashier for a marine products company, scooped ice cream at
a Baskin-Robbins, cashiered at a Video Depot and worked as a
"floater" at May Co.

The Newport Harbor High School senior currently works 4
about 25 hours a week in the lingerie department at the new
Broadway in Costa Mesa. Although she saves about $200 a month
for college, she said she works "to support myself: my car and
clothes and just stuff I do, like going out."

Working also has helped her to learn to manage both her 5
time and money, Staats said, and her work in the department
store is providing experience for a future career in fashion
merchandising.

But, she acknowledged, there are times when working while 6
going to school has taken its toll.

"Last year I was sleeping in my first-period class half the 7
time," admitted Staats, who occasionally has forgone football
games and school dances because of work. "After a while, it just
wears you out."

Nathan Keethe, a Newport Harbor High School senior who 8
works more than 20 hours a week for an exterminating service,
admits to sometimes feeling like the odd man out when he sees
that fellow students "are out having a good time after school and
I'm working. But then I think there's a lot of other kids out there
working, too, and it doesn't seem so unusual."

Indeed, what clearly was the exception 40 years ago is now 9
the rule.

Fovos, Staats and Keethe are riding the crest of a wave of 10
part-time student employees that began building at the end of
World War II and has steadily increased to the present. In 1981,
according to a study by the National Center for Education Statistics, 80% of high school students have held part-time jobs by the
time they graduate.

Part-time work during the school years traditionally has 11
been viewed as an invaluable experience for adolescents, one that

builds character, teaches responsibility and prepares them for entering the adult world.

But the authors of a provocative new book challenge conventional wisdom, contending that an over-commitment to work during the school years "may make teenagers economically wealthy but psychologically poor. . . ." 12

The book, *When Teenagers Work: The Psychological and Social Costs of Adolescent Employment,* is by Ellen Greenberger, a developmental psychologist and professor of social ecology at the University of California, Irvine, and Laurence Steinberg, a professor of child and family studies at the University of Wisconsin. 13

Based on national research data and on the authors' own study of more than 500 working and non-working students at four Orange County [California] high schools, the book reports that: 14

Extensive part-time employment during the school year may undermine youngsters' education. Students who work long hours are more likely to cut back on courses at school, taking easier classes and avoiding tougher ones. And, say the authors, long hours of work begun early in the school years increase the likelihood of dropping out. 15

Working leads less often to the accumulation of savings or financial contributions to the family than to a higher level of spending on cars, clothes, stereos, concerts and other luxury items. 16

Working appears to promote, rather than deter, some forms of delinquent behavior. About 30% of the youngsters in their first part-time job have given away goods or services; 18% have taken things other than money from work; $5\frac{1}{2}$% have taken money from work; and 17% have worked under the influence of drugs or alcohol, according to the Orange County study. 17

Working long hours under stressful conditions leads to increased alcohol and marijuana use. 18

Teen-age employment—typically in dull or monotonous jobs for which the sole motivation is the paycheck—often leads to increased cynicism about working. 19

Moreover, the authors contend that adolescents who work long hours may develop the superficial social skills of an adult, but by devoting too much time to a job they severely curtail the time needed for reflection, introspection and identity experimentation that is required to develop true maturity. 20

Such findings lead Greenberger and Steinberg to conclude "that the benefits of working to the development of adolescents 21

have been overestimated, while the costs have been underestimated."

"We don't want to be read as saying that kids shouldn't work   22
during the school year," Greenberger said in an interview. "Our
argument is with over-commitment to work: That working long
hours may interfere with other very important goals of the growing years."

The authors place the blame partly on the types of jobs   23
available to young people today. By working in unchallenging, monotonous jobs in fast-food restaurants or retail shops, they contend, teen-agers learn few new skills, have little opportunity for
meaningful contact with adults and seldom gain work experience
that will lead to future careers.

"Parents and schools," Greenberger said, "should wake up   24
from the dream that having a kid who works 30 hours a week is
promoting his or her transition to adulthood."

Greenberger and Steinberg's findings, not surprisingly, do   25
not sit well with the fast-food industry.

"The fast-food industry is probably the largest employer of   26
young people in the United States," said Paul Mitchell, spokesperson for Carl Karcher Enterprises, which employs thousands of
teen-agers in its Carl's Jr. restaurants.

"For most of those young people," Mitchell said, "it's their   27
first job, the first time they are told that you make a product a
certain way, the first time they work with money, the first time
they are made aware to be there on time and do it right . . . and
it's just a tremendous working experience."

Terry Capatosto, a spokeswoman for McDonald's, calls   28
Greenberger and Steinberg's findings "absurd, to say the least."

"Working at McDonald's contributes tremendously to   29
[young people's] personal development and work ethic," said Capatosto, noting that countless McDonald's alumnae have gone on
to professional careers and that about half of the people at all
levels of McDonald's management, including the company's president and chairman of the board, started out as crew people.

"The whole idea of getting students out in the community   30
during the time they're also a student is a very productive thing to
do," said Jackie Oakes, college and career guidance specialist at
Santa Ana High School.

Although she feels most students work "for the extras kids   31
want," Oakes said they worked for a variety of reasons, including

earning money to go on a trip with the school band and saving
for college.

As for work taking time away from studying, Oakes said,   32
"I think if a kid isn't interested in studying, having a job doesn't impact that."

Newport Harbor High School's Nathan Keethe, who usually   33
earns Bs, doesn't think he'd devote more time to schoolwork if he
weren't working. "Not really, because even when I wasn't working
I wasn't too devoted to school," he said, adding that "for somebody who is, I wouldn't recommend working too much. I do think
it would interfere."

Fairfax High's John Fovos, who works about 27 hours a   34
week, however, said his grade-point average actually has risen since
he began working part time. The motivation? "My parents told me if
my job hindered my grades, they'd ask me to quit," he said.

Although she acknowledges that some teen-age workers   35
may experience growth in such areas as self-reliance and improved work habits, Greenberger said, "It's not evident that those
things couldn't be realized in other settings as well. There's no evidence that you have to be a teen-age drone in order to grow in
those areas."

As for the notion that "it would be great to get kids out into   36
the workplace because they'll learn," Greenberger said that "the
news is not so good. On the one hand we find that relatively little
time on the job is spent using anything resembling higher-order
cognitive skills," she said. "Computation nowadays is often done
automatically by the cash register; so much for practicing arith-
metic. Kids do extremely little writing and reading [on the job].
There's also very little job training. In fact, most of the youngsters
in our survey reported their job could be done by somebody
with a grade-school education or less."

Balancing Act: High School Students Making the Grade at Part-Time Jobs

MAUREEN BROWN

In this selection from the Los Angeles Times, *Maureen Brown interviews several
teenagers who work at part-time jobs. Keep the points from the previous two articles
in mind as you read these interviews. Do these students confirm or contradict the
ideas in the previous articles?*

First jobs have a way of permanently etching themselves in our   1
memories. Often, more than a paycheck was gained from that initial working experience.

Many of today's teens, like teens a generation ago, cut their   2
working teeth at fast-food restaurants. I always find it of interest
to learn that a successful executive, attorney, physician or teacher
was once a member of this business sector—and in a position
well below management.

A teen-ager's first job is one of many rites of passage   3
children and parents must go through. A dialogue of limits is appropriate when the subject of taking a job arises.

It's important to determine what are acceptable hours of   4
employment and how many hours a week are permitted so that
the student can maintain studies and other school-related activities. What about transportation? Job safety? How will the earnings
be spent?

For some families, the discussion of employment is   5
frequently not initiated by the child but rather by the parent. "I
think it's time we discuss the possibility of a job," has been uttered
in numerous households after a weekend of distributing funds to
teen-agers for entertainment and clothing.

While not feigning to have the answers to the question of   6
employment and teen-agers, a recent discussion with a group of
Mira Mesa teen-agers proved that more than money is gained
from a job.

Charlotte Iradjpanah, 17, a senior at Mira Mesa High, has   7
been working 10 to 20 hours a week at a Mira Mesa Burger King
since September.

"The job is close to my house and I needed the money for   8
senior activities," says Charlotte. "I'm also saving for college and
working keeps me out of trouble. A job is an opportunity to
know what it's like to hold responsibility. Sometimes I have to face
the fact that I have to go to work today and put aside my personal preferences."

Working at Burger King does not exclude Charlotte from   9
participating in extracurricular activities at school. She is a member of the speech and debate team and president of the photog-
raphy club.

"The job has actually strengthened my GPA since I've taken   10
on additional responsibilities," said Charlotte.

Jenni Hada, 18, a senior at Mira Mesa Summit High has   11
been at Burger King for 3 months. "I owe my parents some
money and want to buy a car, but working actually gives me
something constructive to do with my free time," she says.

Mike Vo, 17, a junior at Mira Mesa High, who has been at   12
Burger King for the past month, has held a part-time job since he
turned 16. "I didn't like living off of my parents," he says.

Mike's parents were skeptical when their son first brought   13
up the subject of having a part-time job in addition to school.
"Once they saw that I could still bring home good grades and
have a job, they felt differently," says Mike.

As well as school and a part-time job, Mike is a participant   14
in the junior tennis circuit.

Charlotte, Jenni and Mike work with a manager who   15
perceives the commitment and organization it demands to have a
part-time job while in high school. Manager Wade Palmer, 28,
started work at Burger King at age 17 while in high school and
senses the importance of allowing for flexibility in scheduling.

"We can work around your schedule," Palmer assures the   16
students.

Palmer views "listening to these teen-agers" as an important   17
facet of his role as a manager. Believing that "there are many valuable qualities one can develop on the job," Palmer delights in seeing former student-workers from his decade of work in North
County who have gone on into other fields.

"One is a banker in Mira Mesa, another is a paralegal, and   18
another is an assistant manager with Dixie line," proudly claims
Palmer.

Before In-N-Out Burger in Mira Mesa opened its doors in   19
August last year, the company sent out employment flyers and so-
licited workers in the local high schools and colleges.

"We had over 800 applications for employment," says Bill   20
Mayes, 31, the manager of the store on Mira Mesa Boulevard. "Of
those 800 applicants, we selected 50."

Like Wade Palmer, Mayes started working with In-N-Out   21
Burger at age 17 while still in high school. He continued part-time
in college, and eventually went into management.

"I think students, with their great amount of energy, work   22
out very well in our restaurant," Mayes says. "At In-N-Out, we're
looking for bright, friendly, outgoing people to meet our customers."

Ba Hog, 17, a Mira Mesa High student, is one of the 50 applicants who met Mayes' criteria.   23

"At first, my parents doubted I could get a job here—lots of people were applying," recalls Ba. "After I passed the first interview, they cautioned me to not get my hopes up. When I passed the second interview, I could not wait to go home and tell them!"   24

"Since I've had this job, my parents have been giving me a little more freedom—like staying out later," says Ba, who is trilingual—speaking Chinese, Vietnamese and English. "Now they feel I can better decide between what is right and wrong. Plus, my grades have not been affected since I started this job."   25

One other advantage of working, according to Ba, is that he has been able to delegate some of his previous home responsibilities to his older brother, Nghia, 18, who now carries out the trash and rakes leaves for the employed Ba.   26

Michelle Gust, 17, a senior at Mt. Carmel High, has been working 10 to 15 hours a week at In-N-Out since its opening. Balancing school and a part-time job with senior class council, peer counseling groups, cross-country running and the Girl Scouts, which recently awarded her the "Silver Award," has made Michelle aware of meticulous time scheduling. In addition to these activities, Michelle also spent her fall learning about deadlines as she filled out college applications.   27

"Working has taught me the importance of communicating with people," says Michelle. "The management wants you to communicate well with them and the customer. I've learned to be flexible."   28

When the lead part of Corie in the school play "Barefoot in the Park" was won by Kimberley Belnap, 17, of Mt. Carmel High, her work schedule at In-N-Out required adjustment.   29

"My mom also talked to Bill, the manager, and we were able to work out a schedule where I could still continue to work, be in the play and maintain my grades," she said.   30

"I've learned to budget my time. I'm the type of person who, when I have more to do, I find more time," she said.   31

In addition to organizing her schedule, Kimberley notes that since starting work at In-N-Out, she is painfully conscious of the service she receives in other restaurants. "I take a critical look at how others serve the public."   32

AFTER YOU READ

Work with other students to develop responses to these questions or to compare responses that you have already prepared.

1. As you can see, there are conflicting ideas about whether or not part-time work benefits teenagers who are attending school. To come to terms with the issues involved, list the advantages or disadvantages that are discussed in each article.

2. Look for different ways in which these writers say part-time work affects school performance. Do they discuss positive as well as negative points?

3. Not all of the ideas in these articles are related to school performance. Make a list of the ideas that are not necessarily related to school but that are important to the thesis of each article.

WRITING ASSIGNMENT

 Working with several sources can be substantially more difficult than working with only one source. As you respond to one of these assignments, consider working with other students to clarify and organize your ideas.

1. Write an essay in which you argue for or against the legalization of drugs. To support your thesis, use arguments and evidence from the articles you have read and from whatever relevant experiences you or people you know may have had.

2. What is your position regarding the benefits or drawbacks of high school students working while attending school? Write an essay in which you argue for or against such a practice. To support your thesis, use arguments and evidence from the articles you have read and from whatever relevant experiences you or people you know may have had.

3. Develop an argument based on reading selections in Chapter 7 or those in Part Four. Use arguments and evidence from those articles as well as from your own experiences or observations to support your position.

EVALUATING SAMPLE PAPERS

ARGUMENT ESSAY

Use the following criteria to evaluate the student essays below.

1. Introduction
   Does the first paragraph employ an effective lead-in to introduce the topic? Does the thesis take a definite stand and make it clear that the author intends to support a debatable point?

   1   2   3   4   5   6

2. Unity

Does each paragraph have a clear and specific topic sentence that in-troduces an argument in support of the thesis? Does the material in each paragraph clearly relate to its topic sentence?

1   2   3   4   5   6

3. Support

Is the argument within each paragraph supported with facts, examples, statistics, and/or references to authority?

1   2   3   4   5   6

4. Coherence

Are transitions used between paragraphs? Are they used within para-graphs, especially when the writer is moving from one type of support to another?

1   2   3   4   5   6

5. References to the Text

Are direct quotations and paraphrases correctly introduced and smoothly incorporated into the text? Do they reflect the articles' points accurately?

1   2   3   4   5   6

6. Tone and Attitude

Has the writer recognized that other responses to this topic are possi-ble? Has he or she raised and responded to obvious objections?

1   2   3   4   5   6

7. Sentence Structure

Do the sentences combine ideas that are related, using coordination, subordination, verbal phrases, or parallelism when appropriate? Are there too many brief, choppy main clauses?

1   2   3   4   5   6

8. Mechanics, Grammar, and Spelling

Does the paper contain a distracting number of errors of these kinds?

1   2   3   4   5   6

9. Overall Ranking of the Essay

1   2   3   4   5   6

Student Essay 1 This student essay contains references to two articles not in-cluded in this text.

Drugs, alcohol, and tobacco are all substances that can manipulate the body and mind. Out of those three substances, most people feel that one out of the three substances should be illegal even though they all have similar effects to the body. That one substance is drugs. Drugs today are seen as a big threat to soci-ety, even though it only kills 4,000 people per year compared to alcohol's 100,000 per year and tobacco's 300,000 per year rate. Knowing the death rates of all three substances, which one do you feel should be illegal? I feel that drugs should be legalized because the war on drugs will never be won, it will destroy the black market, and the value of drugs will decrease.

By legalizing drugs, we would be able to control the quality of drugs. William J. Bennett states that if the government does not stock crack in government drugstores, the crack junkies would go elsewhere to get it (286). Where else would they go? None other than the dealers that sell crack cocaine that has been "laced with insecticides and animal tranquilizers to heighten its effect" (Bennett 286). Would you be able to sleep at night knowing that if we do not legalize drugs to control its quality, we will allow these types of drugs to infest our cities, suburbs, and homes. If we legalize drugs, we can control its quality and produce drugs that are weaker. By making weaker drugs, we would help drug addicts gradually kick the habit.

In order to destroy the black market of drug sales, we need to legalize drugs. In "Should Drugs Be Legalized?" William J. Bennett states that if we legalize drugs, the black market will remain (285–286). The black market remaining may be true, but the value of drugs will decrease causing the profits that the drug cartels make to be not worth selling through the black market. For example, back in the prohibition days of the late 1920's, alcohol was the moneymaker for the Mafia and other organized crime groups. For years the Mafia profited off of alcohol which most Americans felt was illegal and immoral during that time period. But as soon as prohibition was repealed in 1933, the black market of alcohol was destroyed. Hodding Carter III states in "We're Losing the Drug War Because Prohibition Never Works," "Prohibition can't work, won't work, and never worked" (281). Today these words still hold some truth. The prohibition of drugs is only resulting in a rapidly growing black market. Unless we finally come to realize that prohibition is not the answer, the black market will remain.

Finally, the war on drugs is a complete waste of time. Why fight a war that will never be won? In fact, Van Deerlin states in "Police and Jails Have Failed" that "Mounting evidence that the campaign against drugs has proved no more successful than the ill-remembered Prohibition law aimed at alcohol in an earlier day" (198). For example, waiting in their car from a distance, two undercover police officers tape a drug sale that is about to go down between a junkie and a dealer. The junkie approaches the dealer, checks the merchandise, pays the dealer, and in an instant wrestles the dealer to the ground. While this is happening, the two police officers taping the sale, rush to the junkie's side, who is also another undercover police officer. They handcuff the dealer, book him, and lock him up. Twenty-four hours later, the dealer is released because the court system is booked for the next year or so. Within hours, the dealer restocks his supply and goes back to the same corner to sell the same drugs. This is the type of war that our justice department has been fighting for years. So how can we win the war? In "Best Remedy: Crack Down on User," Joseph Perkins states that the only way to bring down the drug cartels is to deprive them of their customers and, thus, their tremendous profits" (310). Do you really want to pay more taxes to build more jails, train more police officers, and train more judges? Statistics have shown that housing an inmate for one-year can cost as much as $50,000. I feel that the only way to win this war, is to stop treating users as criminals by giving them jail time, and start treating them as addicts by giving them therapy, a more effective and cheaper treatment.

A lot of time and money has been put into war on drugs and the education on how to say no to the use of them. But neither has been proven successful. We are wasting time trying to eliminate drugs from our world; therefore, we should open our eyes and legalize them.

Student Essay 2

Is it really meaningful for a person to work while attending school? Many students have a part time job while going to high school or college. Some enjoy the experience while others completely hate it. The pros and cons of working while going to school were discussed in Michele Manges' "The Dead End Kids," Dennis McLellan's "Part-Time Work Ethic:Should Teens Go For It?" and Maureen Brown's "Balancing Act:High School Students Making the Grade at Part-Time Jobs." After reading all three articles I came to the conclusion that working while going to school is not just okay, but better than not having a job.

Although I feel working is a plus while going to school, I do feel there are some disadvantages. One point against working is that while working nights one may not get home until late and he may still have homework to complete. Michele Manges says, "A lot of teenage workers are just bone-tired" (295), and one of the teenage workers that she interviewed explained that to do her job so late at night "I kept sleeping through my first period class" (295). Another negative effect that working may have on students is the stress that both the job and school bring to the student. Based on national research data and her own study of more than 500 students in Orange County, Ellen Greenberger found that working appears to promote forms of delinquent behavior and has also led students to increased alcohol and marijuana use (McLellan 298). All of these effects are being blamed on the jobs students are working while attending school. However, I feel there are many more positive effects from working than these few negative results.

One of the positive results from working a part-time job is the fact that a person learns how to manage their time and money. Shelley Staats, a senior at Newport Harbor High School, said that working has helped her to manage both her time and money, while her work in the department store is providing experience for a future career in fashion merchandising. Not only does she learn new responsibilities, she is gaining important information by working in the department store that will help her to decide what she likes and dislikes about her future careers (McLellan 197). Personally, I have run into a similar situation as Shelley's. As for my job, working at Eastview Community Center, I get to see all of the financial documents go through the office. Because I want to be an accountant after graduating from college, I enjoy seeing and observing the financial statements and balance sheets every month. After observing all the paperwork I have become aware of a few of the things my future job holds for me.

Not only do I not believe working causes a students grades to suffer, but I believe that in many instances getting a job has resulted in the student receiving better grades. John Fovos, a student at Fairfax High School, said as a result of getting a job his grade point average has actually risen due to the fact his parents told him if his grades dropped he would have to quit his job (McLellan 300). Following the same pattern, Charlotte Iradjpanah works 10 to 20 hours a week at a Mira Mesa

Burger King. She states, "The job has actually strengthened my GPA since I have taken on additional responsibilities" (Brown 301). I believe in these situations the students were aware that if their grades slipped the parents would place the blame on their new jobs. This fear of losing their jobs caused the students to work harder than they had before.

The biggest plus to working is that it puts one out into the real world. Michelle Gust, a senior at Mt. Carmel High, explained "Working has taught me the importance of communicating with people. The management wants you to communicate with them and the customer. I have learned to be flexible" (Brown 303). I believe these are very important skills young people need to learn and a job for many young people is usually the first experience they receive in the real world. Personally, I have also gained many essential traits while working. One of these experiences also came across the lines of communication. My job consists of enforcing the rules throughout the community center. One day about a month ago I let some teenage kids onto the tennis courts even though they were not wearing the appropriate shoes. As a result, I ended up cleaning all of their black marks off of the court as well as getting docked some points on my evaluation.

Don't get me wrong, for when it comes to school, I believe that school should come first. However, having a job while going to school brings many plus's along with the job. A young person learns how to manage his money as well as managing his time between school, homework, and work. Many times the job will also result in the student bringing home better grades for he wants his parents to let him keep his job. Most importantly, receiving a job while still young lets one know and understand how the real world operates.

Student Essay 3

> . . . a burglar . . . broke into a home and killed the father of three children, aged nine, eleven, and twelve. The crime went unnoticed until ten hours later, when police entered the apartment after being called by neighbors and found the three children watching television just a few feet away from the bloody corpse of their father. (Cross 435)

Doesn't this scene read like an unbelievable script for a bad movie? Unfortunately, according to Donna Woolfolk Cross in "Shadows on the Wall," it is a real-life situation, reported by United Press International. It illustrates the powerful hold that television has over young minds, and it points out how television can draw attention away from the real world, replacing reality with its own distorted fantasy world. I have to admit that I am one of the 1980's generation that grew up glued to the television, but I still think that in many ways the TV is one of the most dangerous devices invented in the last century.

One reason it's so dangerous is that it does exactly what the above quotation suggests—it replaces reality with illusion. Ms. Cross gives several studies to prove this point. One of them involved a group of children in a room where two people started to yell at each other and fight. The fight was projected on video screens, and rather than reacting to what was happening, the kids all sat and watched the screens. It was as if the video were more important than the people themselves (435). I've seen other situations that make me believe that television causes children to confuse reality and illusion. For instance, when I started high school, shows like *Beverly Hills 90210* had me thinking that all the kids there would look cool and be going to bed with each other. I was so worried that I would never fit in that for the first month I didn't even talk to anybody. Luckily, I finally figured out that real life was different from what I'd seen on TV, but I sure went through a lot of misery for nothing.

I think that TV is also dangerous because it pretends to be educational when it's really not. According to Paul Robinson in "TV Can't Educate," television cannot provide the time that is needed for a person to really think about an issue. Instead, all it can do is present bits and pieces of facts that ignore all sorts of more involved questions (431–432). I think this is really true. I remember watching *Sesame Street* as I grew up, and I can't remember ever really learning anything from it. I just liked Big Bird and Cookie Monster. I thought they were funny, but mostly I ignored or already knew all the things they did with the alphabet and numbers. Also, I practically never watch the news or shows like *Nightline* because I like to relax when I watch television, so for the most part the television is not really very educational for me.

The worst part about television is the violence and sex that are becoming so common, even during early evening hours. It seems to me that there is no way children can avoid being affected by all of the negative things they see every day and evening on television. Even the writers who argue in favor of TV admit how damaging this part of it can be. In "Don't Touch That Dial," Madeline Drexler refers to the "violence of primetime shows . . . the sexism of MTV . . . [and] the materialism of commercials" (428). Also, in "The Meaning of TV," William Henry III admits that without TV we might have a less violent society and a more restrained world where "premarital pregnancy and divorce were still treated with distaste rather than with sympathy" (429).

Some people think that TV doesn't cause as many problems as I have listed, but I don't see how they can really think that. Television is entertaining, and I have to admit that I watch it for that reason, but it's not educational, and it really does cause people to make bad judgments about what reality is like. When I have children, I don't think I'll want them to sit and stare at the TV all day, but I will let them watch shows that are entertaining and amusing.

SENTENCE COMBINING: A REVIEW

In the first seven chapters of this text, you have practiced using a variety of techniques to combine related ideas. In the paragraphs that follow, combine the related sentences using whichever techniques seem most appropriate. Here is a brief summary of the sentence-combining ideas you have studied.

Chapter 1: Embed adjectives, adverbs, and prepositional phrases in related sentences.

Chapter 2: Use coordination to combine sentences or parts of sentences that are grammatically alike.

Chapter 3: Use subordinate clauses to indicate the relative importance of related ideas.

Chapter 4: Use present participial phrases, past participial phrases, and infinitive phrases to combine related ideas.

Chapter 5: Use appositives when nouns or pronouns are used to rename other nouns and pronouns.

Chapter 6: Use parallel sentence structure to join items in a series or with correlative conjunctions.

Chapter 7: Vary the length and structure of your sentences to achieve sentence variety.

EXERCISE 8.1

1 Roger Williams was the great seventeenth-century religious emancipator. 2 He died in 1683. 3 He was buried in a poorly marked grave in the backyard of his home in Providence, Rhode Island. 4 Fifty-six years later, in 1739, a workman was excavating a nearby grave. 5 He accidentally broke into the coffin and exposed the bones. 6 Years after that, in 1860, a descendant of Williams ordered workmen to exhume the remains. 7 He wanted to transfer them to a more suitable tomb. 8 When the coffin was opened, no bones were found. 9 Instead, the coffin contained the root of a nearby apple tree. 10 It was exactly where the body should have been. 11 It was in the exact shape of Williams's body, from head to toe. 12 Apparently the root had entered the coffin when it was broken open in 1739. 13 It encountered Williams's skull. 14 Then it followed the path of least resistance. 15 It inched down the side of his head, backbone, hips, and legs. 16 It molded itself closely to the contours of his body. 17 The corpse itself was gone. 18 It had been absorbed into the tree through the roots. 19 The human-shaped root was removed for safekeeping. 20 Today it is on display at the Rhode Island Historical Society in Providence.

1 Many actors and actresses are superstitious people. 2 They rely not only on their talent, looks, and charm. 3 They also rely on rabbits' feet and a whole host of other superstitions. 4 Some stage superstitions are purely personal. 5 Others have been picked up from tradition. 6 They are treasured by those who have no idea how or why the superstitions originated. 7 For example, real flowers are welcome after a performance. 8 They are unlucky for stage decorations. 9 Of course, real flowers would fade and have to be replaced regularly. 10 The superstition probably derives from a very practical concern. 11 An artist might slip and fall if he stepped on a petal or leaf that had fallen from a vase. 12 There are other common stage superstitions. 13 A fall on stage is the sign of a long run. 14 Wishing an actor good luck will bring bad luck. 15 Performing or even quoting from Macbeth is unlucky. 16 Tradition also has it that something going wrong during dress rehearsal means the opening night's performance will be a success. 17 In fact, many actors have a firm belief. 18 A bad dress rehearsal heralds a smash opening night. 19 The list of superstitions goes on and on. 20 Flowers should be handed over the footlights instead of delivered backstage. 21 One should never mention the exact number of

lines he has in a show. 22 Congratulatory telegrams should not be read during a run. 23 One should not write on the dressing room mirror. 24 If someone whistles in the dressing room, one should go outside. 25 Then one should turn around three times and spit before re-entering.

1 Ever since 1966, a scientific controversy has raged. 2 The controversy is about whether apes actually exhibit signs of human intelligence. 3 In 1966, a chimpanzee named Washoe first began to use American Sign Language, or AMESLAN. 4 Apes that have been taught sign language have developed significantly large vocabularies. 5 They recognize nouns, like "fruit," "candy," and "banana." 6 They also recognize verbs, such as "give," "hug," and "take." 7 Sometimes they combine these words in creative ways. 8 One chimp did not know the term for citrus fruit. 9 It called them "smell fruit." 10 Others called watermelons "candy drink" and cucumbers "banana which is green." 11 Apes apparently recognize the meaning of certain words. 12 They seem able to string together some words into meaningful sentences. 13 Critics of ape research assert that supposed ape "language ability" is due solely to drill, imitation, or mere conditioned response. 14 These critics claim that ape trainers misinterpret ape "language." 15 They say that the trainers are too eager to believe that apes are truly displaying human-type intelligence. 16 In addition to language ability, researchers have discovered evidence that apes also possess self-awareness. 17 Self-awareness has long been considered an exclusive trait of the human race. 18 For example, apes can learn to recognize themselves in mirrors. 19 No primate other than humans seems able to do that. 20 It is suspected that other species with large brains, such as whales, porpoises, and elephants, may also be self-aware.

PART THREE

Editing Skills

Effective writing requires care and precision, much more so than speaking does. When speaking, we always have the opportunity to stop and explain ourselves further. When we write in college, business, and the professions, we make hundreds, even thousands, of separate choices, even in relatively brief pieces of writing. Some of the choices are large, such as those concerning the overall organization of our writing, and some of the choices are small, such as those concerning the placement of an apostrophe or comma. Other choices involve sentence patterns, words, and punctuation.

Skillful editing can enhance the quality of your writing and allow you to express yourself in the way that you desire. Not only does it allow you to write effectively, but it also gains you the confidence of your readers. Poor grammar and usage can cause your readers to feel that you have not thought carefully about either the form or the content of your writing. In this section, we will present the basic editing skills of a good writer. We begin with a few important definitions.

Some Basic Editing Terms

CLAUSE

A **clause** is a group of words that contains at least one subject and one verb. Here are some clauses:

> S   V
> Harvey cares about Beatrice.

> S   V
> The train was late.

> S   V
> Almost all cats hate dogs.

Here are some groups of words that are not clauses:

> To find out the cause of the problem.

> Trying out for the team.

To find out the cause of the problem is not a clause because it does not contain a subject and a verb. It does contain a form known as an infinitive ("to find"), but the infinitive is a **verbal,** and verbals cannot be used as the verb of a sentence.

Trying out for the team also lacks a subject and verb. This phrase contains another verbal—the "-ing" form of the verb. However, the "-ing" form cannot be used as the verb of a clause unless it is accompanied by a helping verb, as in the following clause:

> S V
> I <u>was trying</u> out for the team.

Clauses come in two types—main and subordinate.

MAIN CLAUSE

A **main clause** expresses a complete idea. Here are some main clauses:

>Cromwell was a serious man.
>
>Have some red beans and rice. (Here, the understood subject is <u>you</u>.)
>
>What have I done wrong?

SUBORDINATE CLAUSE

A **subordinate clause** begins with a word that prevents it from expressing a complete idea. Here are some subordinate clauses:

>   S   V
><u>When</u> I arrive at the airport . . .
>   S   V
>. . . <u>which</u> Joe kept for himself.
>   S   V
><u>After</u> you inspect the kitchen . . .

The words that begin the above subordinate clauses are called **subordinators.** They come in two types—**subordinating conjunctions** and **relative pronouns.**

Subordinating Conjunctions		**Relative Pronouns**	
after	so that	that	who(ever)
although	than	which	whom(ever)
as	though	(and sometimes *when* or *where*)	
as if	unless		
as long as	until		
because	when		
before	whenever		
even though	where		
if	wherever		
since	while		

Subordinate clauses may appear at the start, at the end, or in the middle of a sentence:

><u>After he had passed the bar exam</u>, Eduardo was ready to join a law firm.
>
>Sarah was angry at her coach <u>because he refused to listen to her excuses</u>.
>
>The movie <u>that I rented last night</u> was really boring.

(See pages 107–113 for a further discussion of subordinate clauses.)

SENTENCE

A **sentence** is a group of words that contains at least **one main clause.**

not a sentence	Just staring into the sky.
not a sentence	Because he was so angry.
sentence	He just stared into the sky.
sentence	Because he was so angry, he just stared into the sky.

EXERCISE 9.1

Indicate whether the following are main clauses (MC), subordinate clauses (SC), or neither (N):

1. Gordon forgot his sunscreen. _____
2. Shifting into warp speed. _____
3. Griffins are scary creatures. _____
4. If you say that one more time. _____
5. Why don't you understand? _____
6. To point his pistol at the intruder. _____
7. Charles and Ann are proud of the magazine. _____
8. Because Suzanne likes to ride horses. _____
9. Having already made up his mind. _____
10. He ordered a Spam-and-okra pizza. _____
11. Because Sam Lucas gave him such good advice. _____
12. Even though Jack had to use a cane. _____
13. He never missed one meeting. _____
14. Play it again, Sam. _____
15. When Brent fakes out the point guard. _____
16. To watch Charles and Louis comparing hatchets. _____
17. When Steve and Marste are chatting. _____
18. They do not want to be interrupted. _____
19. And I want an answer immediately. _____
20. It is a double pleasure to deceive the deceiver. _____

COORDINATING CONJUNCTION

The **coordinating conjunctions** are *and, but, or, nor, for, so,* and *yet.* An easy way to learn the coordinating conjunctions is to remember that their first letters can spell **BOYSFAN** (*But Or Yet So For And Nor*). These words join parts of a sentence that are grammatically equal. For example, they may join two subjects, two verbs, or two adjectives. They may also join two similar phrases, two subordinate clauses, or two main clauses.

two subjects	<u>Fred</u> **and** <u>Ethel</u> own this building.
two verbs	Lucy <u>stared</u> at the wallpaper **and** <u>started</u> to cry.
two adjectives	Alicia felt <u>awkward</u> **and** <u>uncomfortable</u> in the dentist's office.
two similar phrases	Jamie wanted <u>to win the marathon</u> **or** <u>to place in the top three finishers</u>.
two subordinates clauses	<u>After they ate the dessert</u> **but** <u>before they washed the dishes,</u> Dan and Roseanne yelled at the kids.
two main clauses	<u>I have mockingbirds in my backyard</u>, **and** <u>they mimic the sounds of the neighborhood's car alarms.</u>

(See pages 67–70 for a further discussion of coordinating conjunctions.)

CONJUNCTIVE ADVERB

A **conjunctive adverb** is a word or phrase that serves as a transition, usually between two main clauses. When a conjunctive adverb joins two main clauses, it is preceded by a semicolon and followed by a comma.

Percival enjoyed artichoke hearts; **however,** Consuela could not stand them.

Here is a list of the most commonly used conjunctive adverbs:

accordingly	however	next
as a result	indeed	otherwise
consequently	in fact	second
first	instead	still
for example	likewise	therefore
for instance	meanwhile	thus
furthermore	moreover	unfortunately
hence	nevertheless	

Do not use a semicolon before a conjunctive adverb that does not begin a main clause. For example, in the following sentences, the conjunctive adverbs are not immediately preceded by semicolons.

The man on the left, **meanwhile,** studied his bus schedule.

The cat yowled all night long; none of the neighbors, **however,** seemed to mind.

(See pages 70–71 for a further discussion of conjunctive adverbs.)

EXERCISE 9.2

In the following sentences, identify all main clauses by underlining them once and all subordinate clauses by underlining them twice. Identify all coordinating conjunctions by labeling them CC, all subordinating conjunctions by labeling them SC, all relative pronouns by labeling them RP, and all conjunctive adverbs by labeling them CA.

1. While Wally worked on his bicycle, Beaver watched television.
2. The CDs that I had bought were stolen from my car.
3. The pelicans skimmed the water as the sun came up.
4. The group of men kept shouting loudly; consequently, we moved to another part of the stadium.
5. The *Reader* comes out every Thursday, and it has a great deal of handy information.
6. Duke Ellington wrote many beautiful pieces, but my favorite is "Concerto for Cootie."
7. Cootie Williams played trumpet for the Duke Ellington orchestra; next, he formed his own band.
8. Some great blue herons have nested in some trees near our house, so we often see them flying majestically overhead.
9. My friend named his German shepherd Beethoven because he admired the composer so much.
10. If Ludwig were alive, he might be insulted.
11. The soldiers that fought for the South during the Civil War did not wear gray; in fact, they wore butternut.
12. Joseph Campbell taught us much about myth, but Louis Armstrong taught us to swing.
13. Although red beans and rice is my favorite dish, I would not mind some hushpuppies right now.
14. Homer is a heroic eater because he eats sushi; moreover, he eats snails.
15. Jazz may be the United States' only original art form although, according to some people, the short story was also developed here.

EXERCISE 9.3

In the following sentences, identify all main clauses by underlining them once and all subordinate clauses by underlining them twice. Identify all coordinating conjunctions by labeling them CC, all subordinating conjunctions by labeling them SC, all relative pronouns by labeling them RP, and all conjunctive adverbs by labeling them CA.

1 In April, 2005, people in Hamburg, Germany, reported that toads had begun to explode in a local pond. 2 The toads' intestines were being propelled up to three feet away, but no one knew why. 3 Because so many toads had begun to swell and burst apart, the residents started calling the place "The

Pond of Death." 4 Soon toads began to explode in a nearby lake across the border in Denmark. 5 Scientists who investigated the phenomenon wondered if the pond water contained a virus or fungus that was infecting the toads; however, tests revealed no evidence of disease in the toads or water. 6 Finally, a German scientist discovered the cause. 7 Hungry crows had developed a taste for toad livers. 8 They would attack a toad between its chest and abdominal cavity in order to peck out the liver; in addition, they were teaching other crows the trick. 9 When the toads would inflate their bodies in defense, the hole and missing liver led to a rupture of their blood vessels and lungs. 10 According to one veterinarian, such behavior is not unusual, although its occurrence in a populated area is not common.

The Writer's Response website includes links for more practice identifying main and subordinate clauses. Go to www.thomsonedu.com/devenglish/mcdonald. Under "Chapter Resources" for Chapter 9, click on "Exploring Online."

Sentence Fragments

10

The easiest way to identify a **sentence fragment** is to remember that *every sentence must contain a main clause.* If you do not have a main clause, you do *not* have a sentence. You can define a fragment, then, as follows: A **sentence fragment** occurs when a group of words that lacks a main clause is punctuated as a sentence.

Using this definition, you can identify almost any sentence fragment. However, you will find it easier to locate fragments in your own writing if you know that fragments can be divided into three basic types.

THE THREE TYPES OF SENTENCE FRAGMENTS

1. **Some fragments contain no clause at all.**   This type of fragment is simple to spot. It usually does not even sound like a sentence because it lacks a subject or a verb or both.

    The child in the park.

2. **Some fragments contain a verbal but still no clause.**   This fragment is a bit less obvious because a verbal can be mistaken for a verb. But remember, neither a participle nor an infinitive is a verb. (See Chapter 9 if you need to review this point.)

    participle   The child <u>playing</u> in the park.

    infinitive   <u>To play</u> on the swings in the park.

3. **Some fragments contain a subordinate clause but no main clause.**   This type of fragment is perhaps the most common because it does contain a subject and a verb. But remember, *a group of words without a main clause is* not *a sentence.*

    As the child played in the park.
    Because the swings in the park were wet.

REPAIRING SENTENCE FRAGMENTS

Once you have identified a fragment, you can repair it in one of two ways:

1. **Add words to give it a main clause:**

    fragment   The child in the park.

    sentence   The child <u>played</u> in the park.

    sentence   The child in the park <u>looked worried.</u>

    fragment   The child playing in the park.

    sentence   The child <u>was</u> playing in the park.

    sentence   The child playing in the park <u>ran toward the swings</u>.

    fragment   Because the swings in the park were wet.

    sentence   <u>The child played on the slide</u> because the swings in the park were wet.

2. **Join the fragment to a main clause written before or after it:**

    incorrect   I saw a ball rolling down the walk. And a child playing on the swings.

    correct   I saw a ball rolling down the walk and a child playing on the swings.

    incorrect   A dog chased a cat into the bushes. As a child played on the swings.

    correct   A dog chased a cat into the bushes as a child played on the swings.

Of the two possible ways to correct fragments shown above, try to use the second method of joining fragments to nearby main clauses as often as possible. Doing so will help you avoid writing a string of short, choppy sentences, and it will help clarify the relationship between the ideas you are joining.

One final point might help you identify and correct sentence fragments. Remember that we all speak in fragments every day. (If a friend asks you how you are, you might respond with the fragment "Fine.") Because we speak in fragments, you may find that your writing seems acceptable to you even though it contains fragments. When you work on the exercises in this chapter, do not rely on your "ear" alone. Look at the sentences. **If they do not contain main clauses, they are fragments, no matter how correct they may sound.**

EXERCISE 10.1

Underline any fragment you find. Then correct it either by adding new words to give it a main clause or by joining it to a main clause next to it.

1. Penelope worked on her weaving everyday. Thinking about Odysseus.
2. The dog that had been barking all night long.
3. After visiting the dentist. Zelda stopped at the ice cream store. Where she ate two hot fudge sundaes and a banana split.
4. Because Fabio had kissed her hand. Andrea did not wash it for three weeks.
5. Delighted by his arachnoid abilities. Which he had just discovered. Spiderman went on the Web to tell his friends.
6. To prevent Lois from discovering his true identity. Clark told her that he was afraid of heights.
7. A mouse scampered across the floor. Stopped to stare at the cat in the chair. And then disappeared into a crack in the wall.
8. From where she stood, Myna was able to hear every word. She kept repeating whatever the speaker said.
9. The vengeance of the whale had caused the *Pequod* to sink. And Ishmael to be left floating on a coffin.
10. Turning restlessly from side to side. Henry dreamed about Walden Pond. Which he knew would soon freeze over.
11. Even though Huck had never painted a fence before. Tom assured him that he could do a good job.
12. Dorothy stared at the Munchkins and then looked at the dead witch. She knew that she wasn't in Kansas anymore.
13. Tomorrow we will experience a full solar eclipse. For the last time in this decade. It should be rather exciting.
14. Whenever Sam and Ella visit a restaurant. All of the patrons scream and run away.
15. The deep blue skies. The rich green grass. The gentle afternoon breezes. The smell of the ocean. Karen missed them all.

EXERCISE 10.2

Underline any fragment you find. Then correct it either by adding words to create a main clause or by joining it to a main clause before or after it.

1 Floyd writes mystery novels about crimes against children. 2 His two main characters being Arturo and Felicia. 3 Who are pediatricians. 4 They have helped solve cases involving kidnapped children, child abuse, and child abandonment. 5 In their most recent case. 6 A young girl had been attacked and taken from her home. 7 When they found a piece of cloth with some blood on it. 8 They analyzed the cloth and blood in their laboratory. 9 Where they discovered that the cloth had come from the upholstery of a new BMW. 10 There were only two BMW dealerships in their town, so they talked to the owners. 11 In order to find out who had recently purchased a BMW with that upholstery. 12 The buyer of the BMW owning a cabin in the local mountains. 13 When the police surrounded the cabin. 14 They found the girl there. 15 Alive and well.

Fused Sentences and Comma Splices

11

The **fused sentence** and the **comma splice** are serious writing errors that you can correct with little effort. Either error can occur when you write a sentence that contains two or more main clauses.

FUSED SENTENCES

The **fused sentence** occurs when two or more main clauses are joined without a coordinating conjunction and without punctuation.

fused   Chelsea jumped into the pool she waved at her father.

As you can see, the two main clauses in the above fused sentence (*Chelsea jumped into the pool* and *she waved at her father*) have been joined without a coordinating conjunction and without punctuation of any kind.

COMMA SPLICES

The **comma splice** is a similar error. The comma splice occurs when two or more main clauses are joined with a comma but without a coordinating conjunction.

comma splice   The rain soaked all of the campers, they wondered when it would finally stop.

In this comma splice, the two main clauses (*The rain soaked all of the campers* and *they wondered when it would finally stop*) are joined by a comma, but a comma alone is not enough to join main clauses.

One of the most frequent comma splices occurs when a writer joins two main clauses with a comma and a conjunctive adverb rather than with a semicolon and a conjunctive adverb.

comma splice   I saved enough money to take a trip to Hawaii, however, at the last minute I had to change my plans.

REPAIRING FUSED SENTENCES AND COMMA SPLICES

Because both fused sentences and comma splices occur when two main clauses are joined incorrectly, you can correct either error using one of five methods. Consider these two errors:

fused   Leroy won the lottery he decided to buy a car.

comma splice   Leroy won the lottery, he decided to buy a car.

Both of these errors can be corrected in one of five ways:

1. **Use a comma and a coordinating conjunction.** (See page 68 for a list of coordinating conjunctions.)

   Leroy won the lottery, **so** he decided to buy a car.

2. **Use a semicolon.**

   Leroy won the lottery; he decided to buy a car.

3. **Use a semicolon and a conjunctive adverb.** (See page 71 for a list of conjunctive adverbs.)

   Leroy won the lottery; **therefore,** he decided to buy a car.

Do not use a semicolon before a conjunctive adverb that does not join two main clauses. For example, in the following sentence, *however* does not need a semicolon.

   The person in the blue raincoat, **however,** has not seen this movie.

4. **Change one of the clauses to a subordinate clause by beginning it with a subordinating conjunction or relative pronoun.** (See page 108 for a list of subordinating conjunctions and relative pronouns.)

   When Leroy won the lottery, he decided to buy a car.

5. Punctuate the clauses as two separate sentences.
Leroy won the lottery. He decided to buy a car.

Sometimes the two main clauses in a fused sentence or comma splice are interrupted by a subordinate clause. When this sentence pattern occurs, the two main clauses must still be connected in one of the five ways.

fused	Roberta sold her house even though she had thought she would always live there she could not afford the payments.
comma splice	Roberta sold her house even though she had thought she would always live there, she could not afford the payments.
possible correction	Roberta sold her house even though she had thought she would always live there; unfortunately, she could not afford the payments.

EXERCISE 11.1

Identify the following sentences as fused (F), comma splice (CS), or correct (C). Then correct each incorrect sentence using one of the five methods just discussed.

F 1. The marriage broker was afraid of the Duke of Ferrara, *because* he knew what was going to happen to the next duchess.

CS 2. The pilot said that he was not superstitious; nevertheless, he always avoided the Bermuda Triangle.

FC 3. Two alley cats climbed over the fence *and* then they began to yowl.

CM 4. As Lois questioned him, Clark became evasive.

CS 5. Suddenly a message appeared on the computer screen, *and* it said that the hard drive had crashed.

F 6. Don Quixote stared at the windmill. He raised his lance and attacked it.

FC 7. The miner threw his helmet into the air, and *or* gave a victorious shout, because he had finally found the Lost Dutchman's Mine.

CS 8. All of the wiring had been installed correctly; however, the lights still would not turn on.

CM 9. After visiting Earth, the extraterrestrials headed for home, disappointed by their failure to discover any intelligent life.

CS 10. The German shepherd down the street; however, is quite gentle.

CS 11. Although the mariner had shot the albatross, the sailors remained hopeful; then the wind stopped.

F 12. A deranged-looking man *however* claimed giant ants were living in the sewers of Los Angeles *and* nobody believed him.

CS 13. Leonardo's knock-knock jokes were rather dumb; consequently, all Mona Lisa would do was smile politely.

CS 14. The sun had reached its zenith Doc Holliday, and the Earp brothers entered the O.K. Corral.

_____**15.** After fifteen years of hard labor, Jackson wondered if he would ever again see his home and family, but little did he know that his brother, Seymour, had decided to rescue him and was about to make his move.

EXERCISE 11.2

Identify the following sentences as fused (F), comma splice (CS), or correct (C). Then correct each error using one of the five methods discussed in this chapter.

1 The Batiquitos Lagoon north of San Diego is an appealing place to visit on a mild day the trails present many attention-grabbing sights. 2 Visitors can walk or jog next to the lagoon, they can sit on the benches provided and enjoy the view. 3 While they are there, they might see a giant heron. 4 The sharp-eyed visitor will also see hummingbirds, hawks, finches, snowy egrets, in fact, he might even see an osprey family. 5 Crossing the trail is a small stream, where frogs and minnows live. 6 Beyond it, one might see a coyote looking for the small rodents and squirrels that live by the lagoon. 7 Of course, the lagoon contains many fish, sharks, halibut, bass, anchovies, and sardines are among the fish found there. 8 As visitors travel the trail, they will feel far from civilization, however, a golf course, a highway, and several houses are nearby. 9 The trail is wide and well-kept mothers or fathers with their babies in strollers use it often. 10 People from around the county love to visit the Batiguitos Lagoon, it's not difficult to see why.

Exploring
ONLINE

The Writer's Response website includes links for more practice correcting comma splices and fused sentences. Go to www.thomsonedu.com/devenglish/mcdonald. Under "Chapter Resources" for Chapter 11, click on "Exploring Online." In addition, under "Course Resources," click on "Online Grammar Quizzes" and then on "Correcting the Run-on."

Consistency in Verb Tense and Verb Voice

12

SHIFTS IN VERB TENSE

Like almost all English speakers and writers, you use verb tenses quite unconsciously. If you are discussing something that happened in the past, you use the past tense without giving it a second thought (I *ate that entire turkey!*). If you are writing about future events, you very naturally shift to future tense (I *will eat that entire turkey!*). Sometimes, however, writers accidentally shift from one tense to another when there is no reason to do so. Such unnecessary shifts occur most commonly between the past and present tenses:

> *past*
> When Joel <u>saw</u> the lion at the circus yesterday,
> *present*   *present*
> he <u>sits</u> right in front of its cage and <u>starts</u> to tease it.

Would you agree that there is no reason for the writer to shift to the present tense in the above example? All three actions occurred in the past, so all three should be written in the past tense. Of course, you *should* shift tenses if the meaning requires such a shift, as in the following example:

> *present*   *future*
> Alex <u>hopes</u> that he <u>will win</u> tonight's lottery because last weekend he
>
> *past*
> <u>lost</u> all of his rent money in Las Vegas.

PAST-TENSE VERBS ENDING IN *-D* AND *-ED*

Sometimes you might mistakenly write a past-tense verb in its present-tense form by leaving off a *-d* or *-ed* ending. This problem is particularly common for students who do not pronounce those endings when they speak. If such is the case in your writing, you need to look closely at each of your verbs as you proofread your papers. If you are discussing an event that occurred in the past, add *-d* or *-ed* where such endings are needed.

INCORRECT   After the party last night, Mark <u>thank</u> Fiona for giving him a ride home.

CORRECT   After the party last night, Mark <u>thanked</u> Fiona for giving him a ride home.

SUPPOSED TO, USED TO

Two verbs that are often incorrectly written without the *-d* ending are *suppose* and *use* when they are followed by the word *to*. Don't leave the *-d* off the ending just because you don't hear it. (It tends to be combined with the *t* in *to*.)

INCORRECT   Calvin is <u>suppose to</u> be on a diet, but he can't get <u>use to</u> skipping his usual dessert of chocolate chip ice cream.

CORRECT   Calvin is <u>supposed to</u> be on a diet, but he can't get <u>used to</u> skipping his usual dessert of chocolate chip ice cream.

VERB TENSE WHEN DISCUSSING SOMEONE ELSE'S WRITING

Throughout this text, you are asked to respond to what other writers have written. You should use the present tense when you write about someone else's writing—whether it be nonfiction, fiction, or poetry—or when you write about film. Be careful not to inadvertently shift to the past tense.

INCORRECT   In "Why I Won't Buy My Sons Toy Guns," Robert Shaffer <u>claims</u> toys are teachers. He <u>said</u> that toy guns will teach children to solve problems with violence.

CORRECT   In "Why I Won't Buy My Sons Toy Guns," Robert Shaffer <u>claims</u> toys are teachers. He <u>says</u> that toy guns will teach children to solve problems with violence.

EXERCISE 12.1

Revise the following paragraphs to correct any unnecessary shifts in verb tense:

1 In "The Thin Grey Line," Marya Mannes says that the difference between right and wrong is becoming blurred. 2 She wrote that today's society was losing its moral fiber. 3 I agreed with many of the points that Mannes makes.

4 One point I agree with was that the parents of today's children cross the "thin grey line" many times a day. 5 When I was a child, my parents use to hide my brother and me on the floor of our Pinto so they would not have to pay for us when we go to drive-in movies. 6 And when I am too old for a Kids' Meal at McDonald's, they would lie and get me one anyway. 7 As I grew older, these things do not seem wrong to me. 8 I thought that as long as I didn't get caught there is nothing wrong.

9 Mannes also wrote, "Your son's friend admitted cheating at exams because 'everybody does it.'" 10 I have to admit that I also have cheat on an exam or two and that many people I know have done the same. 11 In the eleventh grade a student I know manage to get a copy of the exam we were suppose to take the next day. 12 He then proceeds to distribute it to his friends, and no one ever was caught. 13 Did we all learn a lesson? 14 We sure did. 15 We learn how easy it is to cheat.

16 All in all, the morality of the nation was headed in the wrong direction. 17 And if this generation is bad, what will the next generation be like? 18 Mannes's solution was a good one. 19 We use to be a moral nation, and we can be one again if we educate people. 20 We should start with the children before they became corrupt in their thinking.

SHIFTS IN VERB VOICE

Verb voice refers to the relationship between the subject and the verb of a sentence. If the subject is *performing* ("doing") the action of the verb, the sentence is in the **active voice.** If the subject is *receiving* the action of the verb, the sentence is in the **passive voice.** Note that the subject is the "doer" in the following active-voice sentence:

active voice

              S   V

A red-tailed hawk seized the unsuspecting rabbit.

(The subject—the hawk—*performs* the action.)

Now compare the above active-voice sentence with its passive-voice counterpart:

passive voice

              S   V

The unsuspecting rabbit was seized by a red-tailed hawk.

(The subject—the rabbit—*receives* the action.)

IDENTIFYING VERB VOICE

To distinguish between active and passive voice, first identify the verb itself, and then ask the following questions:

1. Does the subject perform the action of the verb, or does it receive the action? If the subject performs the action, the sentence is in the active voice; if the subject receives the action, the sentence is in the passive voice.

2. Does the verb consist of a form of *to be* and a past participle? The forms of *to be* are *am, are, is, was, were, be, being,* and *been. Any* verb consisting of one of these verb forms *and* a past participle is in the passive voice. All of the following verbs, therefore, are automatically passive: *has been eaten, is passed, was purchased, might be seen, were stolen.*

CHOOSING THE ACTIVE VOICE

Most writers prefer the active voice, so they try not to shift to the passive voice unless there is a good reason to do so. One reason writers prefer the active voice is that it requires fewer words than the passive. In the above examples about the hawk and the rabbit, for instance, the active voice requires only seven words while the passive voice requires nine. Two extra words don't seem excessive, do they? But over the course of an entire essay, those needless words begin to add up, creating a sense of looseness and wordiness that can detract from the effectiveness of your writing.

Another reason writers choose active voice is that passive-voice verbs, as the word *passive* implies, lack the forcefulness of active-voice verbs. Because the subject in the passive voice *receives* the action rather than *performs* it, there is a sense that the sentence is not moving forward. In fact, too many passive-voice verbs can make your writing dull and lifeless.

Finally, the passive voice often obscures the real performer of the action, either by placing that performer in a prepositional phrase following the verb or by omitting the performer altogether. Who, for example, is the person who denies the building permit in the following sentence?

> After serious consideration, your request for a building permit has been denied.

Not all verbs must be either active or passive. For example, when a form of *to be (am, are, is, was, were, be, being, been)* is the main verb of a sentence, no action is shown at all, so the verb is neither active nor passive. Verbs of this type are called linking verbs. Although these verbs are not passive, you can often improve your writing by replacing them with active-voice verbs.

linking verb

                      S   V
Mrs. Mallard's driving <u>is</u> quite reckless.

active voice

                  S   V
Mrs. Mallard <u>drives</u> quite recklessly.

CHOOSING THE PASSIVE VOICE

If the above discussion has left you with the impression that you should write in the active voice, it has achieved its purpose. But don't be misled—the passive voice does have a place in good writing, particularly in the following situations:

1. Use the passive voice when the performer of an action is unimportant or when the receiver of the action needs to be emphasized.

   S   V
   All of the buildings had been inspected by noon yesterday.

   (Who did the inspecting is not important.)

2. Use passive voice when the performer of the action is unknown.

                          S   V
   Last night my car was stolen from the Wal-Mart parking lot.

   (Who stole the car is not known.)

3. Use the passive voice when the receiver of the action needs to be emphasized.

                              S   V
   During the Holocaust, Jewish people were executed by the hundreds of thousands.

   (The receiver of the action—Jewish people—is being emphasized.)

CHANGING THE PASSIVE VOICE TO THE ACTIVE VOICE

Some people write too many sentences in the passive voice merely because they cannot figure out how to change them to the active voice. Use these suggestions to help you revise your passive sentences to active ones:

1. If the performer of the action is an object (usually following the verb), reverse the subject and the object.

                          S   O
   passive voice   The CD-ROM drive was purchased by John for $200.

                          S   O
   active voice   John purchased the CD-ROM drive for $200.

2. If the performer of the action has been left out of the sentence, write it in as the subject.

                                  S   V
   passive voice   Every official transcript was destroyed last night.

                              S   V
   active voice   Last night's fire destroyed every official transcript.

3. Change the verb.

v

passive voice   Stephen Spielberg was given an Academy Award for directing *Schindler's List.*

v

active voice   Stephen Spielberg received an Academy Award for directing *Schindler's List.*

EXERCISE 12.2

Rewrite the following sentences so that they use the active voice. When necessary, supply the missing performer of the action. Some of the sentences may already use the active voice.

1. Alice was invited to play croquet by the Queen of Hearts.
2. The Daltons and the Clantons were never captured by the posse.
3. Mario had been training for the marathon for six months.
4. Janet was not allowed to watch the movie because her homework was not yet completed.
5. Members of the army were inoculated for scarlet fever by the government.
6. Airline passengers are routinely checked by security guards to make sure no weapons are being carried on board.
7. Many scenes of American life in the 1950s were painted by Norman Rockwell.
8. Fireworks are considered dangerous by many people and have been outlawed by many cities.
9. Emily Dickinson's poems had been rejected by publishers many times.
10. The Harry Potter movies were watched numerous times by Douglas and Jaime.
11. The strong wind bent the newly planted birch tree to the ground.
12. Blue skies and warm weather are hoped for by everyone who has been invited to the picnic.
13. Darnell is studying to be a doctor even though he does not know how his tuition will be paid.
14. Herman started to worry when he was told that wasps had been seen flying into his bedroom.
15. A llama and an aardvark were chased from one end of the park to the other by six worried zookeepers.

EXERCISE 12.3

Rewrite the following sentences so that they use the active voice. When necessary, supply the missing performer of the action. Some of the sentences may already use the active voice.

1 Over the last few years two major catastrophes have been experienced by the United States. 2 One was caused by human beings; the other was caused by nature. 3 On September 11, 2001, four airliners were hijacked by terrorists. 4 Box cutters were used as weapons by them to gain control of the four airliners. 5 Then two of the jets were flown into the Twin Towers, killing thousands of people. 6 A third plane was flown into the Pentagon, resulting in many deaths, injuries, and much destruction. 7 On the fourth plane, the terrorists were attacked by courageous passengers, but they all died when the airliner crashed. 8 Then, in late 2005, the southern part of the United States was devastated by Hurricane Katrina. 9 The levees separating Lake Pontchartrain from the city of New Orleans were breached by the storm surge. 10 As a result, 80% of the city of New Orleans was flooded and hundreds of people were killed by the fierce storm.

The Writer's Response website includes links for more practice identifying and correcting the misuse of passive voice. Go to www.thomsonedu.com/devenglish/mcdonald. Under "Chapter Resources" for Chapter 12, click on "Exploring Online."

Subject-Verb Agreement

13

Subject-verb agreement refers to the need for the form of the verb you have used in a sentence to match the form of its subject. If the subject of your sentence is singular, your verb must be singular. If the subject is plural, your verb must be plural.

You need to pay special attention to subject-verb agreement when you use present-tense verbs. **Most present-tense verbs that have singular subjects end in -*s*. Most present-tense verbs that have plural subjects do not end in -*s*.** Here are some examples:

Singular	Plural
The bird flie**s**.	The birds fly.
He sing**s**.	They sing.
It i**s**.	They are.
The child ha**s**.	The children have.
She doe**s**.	They do.

Notice that in each case the verb ends in -*s* when the subject is singular. This rule can be confusing because an *s* at the end of a *noun* almost always means that the noun is plural, but an -*s* at the end of a *verb* almost always means it is singular.

PROBLEM AREAS

Almost all subject-verb agreement errors occur for one of two reasons: Either the writer has identified the wrong word as the subject of the verb or the writer has mistaken a singular subject for a plural one (or vice versa). The following points address these two problems:

1. **Subjects are never part of a prepositional phrase.** Prepositional phrases often occur between the subject and the verb. Do not confuse the object of the prepositional phrase with the subject of the verb.

   S   V
   <u>One</u> of our neighbor's dogs <u>barks</u> every night.

   The subject is *One,* not *dogs,* because *dogs* is part of the prepositional phrase *of our neighbor's dogs.* Here is a list of common prepositions to help you identify prepositional phrases:

about	because of	except	of	toward
across	behind	from	onto	until
after	below	in	over	up
among	beside	in spite of	past	upon
around	between	into	through	with
as	by	like	till	without
at	during	near	to	

2. **The order of the subject and verb is reversed in sentences that begin with *there* or *here* and in questions.**

   V   S
   There were several people in the park this morning.

   V   S
   Here is the person with the keys.

   V   S
   Is the plane on time?

   V   S
   Was the photo album in the box in the attic?

3. **Only the subject affects the form of the verb.**

   S   V
   Our least concern is the people next door.

   The singular verb form is correct here because the subject is the singular noun *concern.* The plural noun *people* does not affect the form of the verb.

4. **Two subjects joined by *and* are plural.**

   S   S   V
   The puppet and the grasshopper were an unusual pair.

   S   S   V
   Steak and eggs sound good to me.

5. **If a subject is modified by *each* or *every*, it is singular.**

   S   S   V
   Every can and bottle on the beach was picked up.

   S   S   V
   Each driver and bicyclist is eligible to enter the contest.

6. **Indefinite pronouns are usually singular.** See page 345 for a list of indefinite pronouns.

   S   V
   Each of the contestants is on the stage.

   S   V
   Everyone in the stadium has a white flag.

7. **A few nouns and indefinite pronouns, such as *none, some, all, most, more, part,* and *half* (and other fractions), may sometimes be considered plural and sometimes singular, depending on the prepositional phrase that follows them.**

singular

   S   V
   Some of the food is missing.

plural

   S   V
   Some of the cars were stolen.

8. **When the subjects are joined by *either/or, neither/nor, not only/but also,* or *just or,* the verb agrees with the subject closer to it.**

   S   S   V
   Neither Maria nor her sisters want to leave the house.

   Of course, if you reverse the order of the subjects above, you must change the verb form.

   S   S   V
   Neither her sisters nor Maria wants to leave the house.

   This rule also applies to questions.

   V   S   S   V
   Does Maria or her sisters want to leave the house?

   V   S   S   V
   Do her sisters or Maria want to leave the house?

 When you have helping verbs in a sentence, as in the example above, the helping verb—not the main verb—changes form.

9. **Collective nouns usually take the singular form of the verb.** Collective nouns represent groups of people or things, but they are considered singular. Some common collective nouns are *audience, band, class, committee, crowd, family, flock, group, herd, jury, society,* and *team.*

   S   V
   The jury was told to reach its verdict as quickly as possible.

   S   V
   My family goes to Yellowstone National Park every summer.

10. **The relative pronouns** *that, which,* **and** *who* **may be either singular or plural.** When one of these pronouns is the subject of a verb, you will need to know which word it refers to before you decide whether it is singular or plural.

singular

                     S   V

       I bought the peach that was ripe.

plural

                     S   V

       I bought the peaches that were ripe.

plural

                                  S   V

       Colleen is one of the students who are taking flying lessons.

singular

                                        S   V

       Colleen is the only one of the students who is taking flying lessons.

11. **A few nouns end in** *-s* **but are considered singular; they take the singular form of the verb.** These nouns include *economics, gymnastics, mathematics, measles, mumps, physics,* and *politics.*

                     S   V

       International politics is not my favorite field of study.

                  S   V

       Mathematics has been difficult for me.

12. **When units of measurement for distance, time, volume, height, weight, money, and so on are used as subjects, they usually take the singular verb form.**

               S   V

       Two teaspoons of sugar was all that the cake recipe called for.

               S   V

       Five dollars is too much to pay for a hot dog.

EXERCISE 13.1

Circle the subjects, and underline the correct verb form (in parentheses) for each one.

1. Someone with too many children (has)(have) been turned away from the theater.

2. His dream of success and his fear of failure always (keep)(keeps) Joe feeling frustrated.

3. The audience attending last night's premiere (was)(were) disgusted by the performance.

4. A sofa with two matching chairs (cost)(costs) $1,000 at Jerome's Furniture.

5. Five hundred miles (is)(are) a long way from home.

6. Here (is)(are) the lawn food and snail bait that you ordered.

7. Every fan and player at recent Chargers and Raiders games (has)(have) been disgusted by the behavior of some of the people in the stadium.

8. Neither his sisters nor his wife (visit)(visits) Mr. Parker in the rest home very often.

9. One of the scientists who (works)(work) in that lab has cloned Jennifer Lopez.

10. A group of anti-lepidopterists (has)(have) recently started to demand equal rights for butterflies.

EXERCISE 13.2

Correct any subject-verb agreement errors in the following sentences. If a sentence is correct, do nothing to it. To check your answers, circle the subjects.

1. Either the telephone book or the encyclopedia have enough weight to press that flower.

2. Every book and magazine in the library has been attacked by bookworms.

3. In the past two weeks, there has been a fistfight and a mugging in the walkway near the cafeteria.

4. A herd of buffalo cross the stream behind my house every evening.

5. Does the Del Mar Fair or the Pomona County Fair make the most money?

6. Mr. Gadget is one of the people who applies for a new patent nearly every year.

7. On the roof of the business across the street stands a large wooden chicken and a gigantic ax.

8. Each of the fifteen applicants from the three different cities were presented with a bowl of fruit.

9. Elmer's main concern was the flies and bugs that kept invading his house.

10. Fifteen minutes have passed since we received our last telephone solicitation.

EXERCISE 13.3

Correct all subject-verb agreement errors. Not all sentences will contain errors.

1 The custom of offering a blessing or word of goodwill when someone sneezes derive from a number of historical causes. 2 First, there was the ancient beliefs that a person's life force reside in the head and that a sneeze can dislodge that vital force. 3 Each of these beliefs were reinforced whenever a person died after an illness involving bouts of sneezing. 4 Someone who heard a person sneeze would perform a short ritual which were meant to protect that person's life force. 5 Later, in the fourth century

B.C., Greek thinkers explained that sneezing is caused when the body tries to expel irritating material that have come in through the nostrils. 6 However, they also recognized that bouts of sneezing precedes many illnesses, so they gave a blessing to people who sneezed, such as "May you enjoy good health!" 7 Then Roman physicians added to the custom by claiming that a series of strong sneezes actually help rid the body of spirits that causes illnesses. 8 They encouraged people to sneeze by saying "Congratulations!" 9 Finally, the common "God bless you" of today derive from the sixth century, when a deadly plague ravaged Italy. 10 One of its most telling symptoms were severe sneezes. 11 Pope Gregory the Great ordered people to ask for God's help in the form of "God bless you." 12 As the plague spread throughout Europe, killing hundreds of thousands of people, the response of "God bless you" to any sudden sneezes were widespread.

The Writer's Response website includes links for more practice in subject-verb agreement. Go to www.thomsonedu.com/devenglish/mcdonald. Under "Chapter Resources" for Chapter 13, click on "Exploring Online." In addition, under "Course Resources," click on "Online Grammar Quizzes."

Pronoun Agreement and Reference

14

PRONOUN–ANTECEDENT AGREEMENT

Because pronouns stand for or take the place of nouns, it is important that you make clear in your writing which pronouns stand for which nouns. The noun that the pronoun takes the place of is called the **antecedent**. The term **pronoun–antecedent agreement** refers to the idea that a pronoun must match, or "agree with," the noun that it stands for in **person** and **number**.

PERSON

Person, in describing pronouns, refers to the relationship of the speaker (or writer) to the pronoun. There are three persons: **first person**, **second person**, and **third person**.

1. **First-person pronouns** refer to the person speaking or writing:

Singular	Plural
I	we
me	us
my, mine	our, ours

2. **Second-person pronouns** refer to the person spoken or written to:

Singular	**Plural**
you	you
you	you
your, yours	your, yours

3. **Third-person pronouns** refer to the person or thing spoken or written about:

Singular	**Plural**
he, she, it	they
him, her, it	them
his, her, hers, its	their, theirs

Because nouns are almost always in the third person, pronouns that refer to nouns should also be in the third person. Usually this rule poses no problem, but sometimes writers mistakenly shift from third to second person when they are referring to a noun.

> When <u>a person</u> first enters the Department of Motor Vehicles, you might feel overwhelmed by the crowd of people.

In this sentence, *you* has mistakenly been used to refer to *person.* The mistake occurs because the noun *person* is in the third person, but the pronoun *you* is in the second person. There are two ways to correct the sentence:

1. You can change the second-person pronoun *you* to a third-person pronoun.

> When <u>a person</u> first enters the Department of Motor Vehicles, <u>he or she</u> might feel overwhelmed by the crowd of people.

2. You can change the noun *person* to the second-person pronoun *you.*

> When <u>you</u> first enter the Department of Motor Vehicles, <u>you</u> might feel overwhelmed by the crowd of people.

Here is another incorrect sentence:

> Most <u>visitors</u> to the Wild Animal Park will have a good time if <u>you</u> follow the signs and do not stray off the marked path.

One way to correct this sentence is to change *you* to *they* so that it agrees with *visitors:*

> Most <u>visitors</u> to the Wild Animal Park will have a good time if <u>they</u> follow the signs and do not stray off the marked path.

NUMBER

Errors in number are the most common pronoun–antecedent errors. To make pronouns agree with their antecedents in **number,** use singular pronouns to refer to singular nouns and plural pronouns to refer to plural nouns. The following guidelines will help you avoid errors in number:

1. **When you use a pronoun to refer to words joined by *and*, you should use a plural pronoun unless the words are modified by *each* or *every*.**

   <u>Benjamin Franklin</u> and <u>Thomas Edison</u> were both known for <u>their</u> work with electricity.

   Every <u>dog</u> and <u>cat</u> in the kennel had lost <u>its</u> appetite.

2. **Because the following indefinite pronouns are singular, you should use singular pronouns to refer to them.**

anybody	either	neither	one
anyone	everybody	nobody	somebody
anything	everyone	no one	someone
each	everything	nothing	something

   <u>Everything</u> that he said seemed to have <u>its</u> own secret meaning.

   <u>Neither</u> of the contestants wanted to trade <u>her</u> prize for an unmarked door.

   <u>One</u> of the children was staring sadly at <u>his</u> broken toy.

 In spoken English, the plural pronouns *they, them,* and *their* are often used to refer to the antecedents *everyone* or *everybody*. However, in written English the singular pronoun is still more commonly used.

   <u>Everybody</u> on the men's hockey team was determined to do <u>his</u> best.

3. **You should use singular pronouns to refer to collective nouns.** Some common collective nouns are *audience, band, class, committee, crowd, family, flock, group, herd, jury, society,* and *team*.

   The <u>class</u> decided to skip <u>its</u> scheduled break in order to review for the test.

   The <u>family</u> next door spent <u>its</u> summer in the Grand Canyon last year.

4. **When antecedents are joined by the following words, you should use a pronoun that agrees with the closer antecedent.**

either/or	neither/nor	nor
or	not only/but also	

   Neither <u>Mr. Snead</u> nor the <u>golfers</u> remembered to bring <u>their</u> golf shoes.

The plural pronoun *their* agrees with the plural noun *golfers* because *golfers* is the closer noun.

Sexist Language

In the past it has been traditional to use masculine pronouns when referring to singular nouns whose gender could be either masculine or feminine. A good example is the sentence *A **driver** should slow down whenever **he** approaches a blind intersection.* Although the noun *driver* could be either masculine or feminine, traditionally only masculine pronouns like *he* or *his* have been used in a case like this one.

Because females make up over 50 percent of the English-speaking population, many of them have been justifiably dissatisfied with this tradition. The problem is that the English language does not contain a singular personal pronoun that can refer to either sex at the same time in the way that the forms of *they* can.

The solutions to this problem can prove awkward. One of the solutions is to use feminine pronouns as freely as masculine ones to refer to singular nouns whose gender could be masculine or feminine. Either of the following sentences using this solution is acceptable:

> A <u>driver</u> should slow down whenever <u>she</u> approaches a blind intersection.

> A <u>driver</u> should slow down whenever <u>he</u> approaches a blind intersection.

Another solution is to change the *he* to *he or she*. Then the sentence would look like this:

> A <u>driver</u> should slow down whenever <u>he or she</u> approaches a blind intersection.

As you can see, this solution does not result in a very graceful sentence. Still another alternative is to use *she/he*, but the result would be about the same as the one above. Sometimes a better solution is to change a singular antecedent to a plural one and use the forms of *they*, which can refer to either gender. Doing so would result in a sentence like this:

> <u>Drivers</u> should slow down whenever <u>they</u> approach a blind intersection.

This sentence is less awkward and just as fair. Finally, in some situations, the masculine pronoun alone will be appropriate, and in others the feminine pronoun alone will be. Here are two such sentences:

> <u>Each</u> of the football players threw <u>his</u> helmet into the air after the victory.
> (The football team is all male.)

> <u>One member</u> of the Arabian swim team passed <u>her</u> opponent ten yards before the finish line.
> (The swim team is all female.)

Whatever your solutions to this problem, it is important that you be logical and correct in your pronoun–antecedent agreement in addition to being fair.

EXERCISE 14.1

Choose the pronoun (in parentheses) that agrees with the antecedent. When you choose a pronoun, you may also need to change the verb.

1. If a motorcyclist rides without a helmet in California, (you)(he or she) (they) will be given a ticket.

2. Everybody who attended the Fourth of July party brought (their)(his or her) own food.

3. When a person is first learning to work with a computer, (you) (they) (he or she) might feel a little intimidated.

4. The committee returned to (its)(their) meeting room to discuss the senator's embarrassing remarks.

5. Neither Oliver nor Stanley visited (his)(their) mother on Mother's Day.

6. When a fan enters that ballpark, (you)(he or she)(they) will see a number of dramatic changes.

7. A noisy patron of that library will sometimes be asked to lower (their) (his or her) voice.

8. Each of the members of Footwear Anonymous vowed to throw all of (their)(his or her) shoes into the garbage.

9. After the humiliating defeat, the team boarded (their)(its) bus and headed for home.

10. Skinner could tell that either the pigeon or the mouse would soon learn to signal for (its)(their) food.

UNCLEAR PRONOUN REFERENCE

Sometimes, even though a pronoun appears to agree with an antecedent, it is not clear exactly which noun in the sentence is the antecedent. And sometimes a writer will use a pronoun that does not clearly refer to any antecedent at all. The following two points will help you to use pronouns correctly.

1. A pronoun should refer to a specific antecedent.

After <u>James</u> gave his brother the present, <u>he</u> began to cry.

In this sentence, *he* could refer to James or his brother. To correct this problem, you can eliminate the unclear pronoun.

After <u>James</u> gave <u>his brother</u> the present, <u>his brother</u> began to cry.

Or you can revise the sentence so the pronoun refers to one specific antecedent.

<u>James</u> began to cry after <u>he</u> gave his brother the present.

2. Pronouns should not refer to implied or unstated antecedents. Be especially careful with the pronouns *this, that, which,* and *it*.

The game was canceled even though we had driven five hundred miles to see it; <u>this</u> was unfair.

In Paul Goodman's "A Proposal to Abolish Grading," <u>it</u> says that grades do more harm than good.

In the first example, there is no antecedent to which *this* can refer. In the second example, *it* seems to refer to something inside the article, but there is no antecedent given. The following sentences clarify the pronoun references:

The game was canceled even though we had driven five hundred miles to see it; <u>canceling the game after we had driven so far</u> was unfair.

In "A Proposal to Abolish Grading," <u>Paul Goodman says</u> that grades do more harm than good.

Sometimes a pronoun refers to a noun that is only implied in the first part of the sentence.

Mr. Brouillard is a fisherman, <u>which</u> he does every weekend.

In this sentence, the *which* apparently refers to *fishing,* which is implied in the noun *fisherman;* however, there is no specific noun for the pronoun *which* to refer to. The faulty pronoun reference can be cleared up in several ways:

Mr. Brouillard is a fisherman, <u>and he goes fishing</u> every weekend.

Mr. Brouillard is a fisherman <u>who fishes</u> every weekend.

EXERCISE 14.2

Correct all errors in pronoun–antecedent agreement as well as in pronoun reference in the following sentences. If a sentence is correct, do nothing to it.

1. Macbeth hesitated to kill Duncan because he was a good man.
2. Ahab could not find the white whale, which frustrated him.
3. When someone is blindfolded and turned in a circle, you can easily lose your sense of direction.
4. Anybody who responds to this questionnaire will receive a free trip to the country of her choice.
5. Rats were recently found in a local restaurant, so the health department closed it down. This worried many people.
6. If a person is rude to retail clerks, you shouldn't be surprised if they are rude back.
7. Just as the police officer was about to write my mother a ticket for speeding, she fainted.
8. Will you please take either the grapes on the counter or the watermelon in the refrigerator and put it into the picnic basket?
9. On the news it said that last night's fire was started by an arsonist.
10. Pip knew that you were supposed to show respect for the crazy lady in the rotting wedding dress.

EXERCISE 14.3

Correct any errors in pronoun–antecedent agreement as well as in pronoun reference. Not all sentences contain errors.

1 Many everyday clothing fashions that appear to have no real purpose actually have a very practical cause for its existence. 2 For example, miners complained because the pockets of their blue jeans would split when you carried heavy tools in them. 3 This bothered Levi Strauss because miners were his best customers, so they added rivets. 4 As time passed, everyone had to own their own pair of "Levi's," complete with rivets. 5 Another curious clothing custom is that of a man buttoning their clothing from right to left and a woman from left to right. 6 This started in the fifteenth century. 7 At that time, men generally dressed themselves, and, since most people are right-handed, you preferred to button clothing from right to left. 8 However, a woman who could afford the expensive buttoned clothing of the day generally had a maid who helped them dress. 9 When a maid faced her mistress, the maid's right hand was on their mistress's left; hence buttons on women's clothing were sewn on the left side. 10 These are just a few of the many reasons a man or a woman dresses the way they do today.

The Writer's Response website includes links for more practice in pronoun agreement and reference. Go to www.thomsonedu.com/devenglish/mcdonald. Under "Chapter Resources" for Chapter 14, click on "Exploring Online."

Pronoun Case

15

Pronouns, like verbs, can appear in a variety of forms, depending on how they function in a sentence. For example, the pronoun that refers to the speaker in a sentence may be written as *I, me, my,* or *mine.* These different spellings are the result of what is called **pronoun case.**

The three pronoun cases for English are the **subjective,** the **objective,** and the **possessive.**

Subjective Case

Singular	**Plural**
I	we
you	you
he, she, it	they
who	who

Objective Case

Singular	**Plural**
me	us
you	you
him, her, it	them
whom	whom

Possessive Case

Singular	Plural
my, mine	our, ours
your, yours	your, yours
his, her, hers, its	their, theirs
whose	whose

SUBJECTIVE PRONOUNS

The **subjective pronouns** are *I, we, you, he, she, it, they,* and *who.* They are used in two situations:

1. **Subjective pronouns are used as subjects of sentences.**

    S
    <u>I</u> will take the test next week.

    S
    <u>They</u> have stolen my car.

2. **Subjective pronouns are used when they follow linking verbs.** Because the linking verb *identifies* the pronoun with the subject, the pronoun must be in the same case as the subject.

    S
    <u>It</u> was <u>he</u> who found the missing link.
    > The subjective pronoun *he* is identified with the subject *it* by the linking verb "was."

    S
    <u>That</u> was <u>I</u> you heard speaking on the phone.

    S
    <u>It</u> was <u>they</u> who won the final game of the series.

OBJECTIVE PRONOUNS

The **objective pronouns** are *me, us, you, him, her, it, them,* and *whom.* They are used in three situations:

1. **Objective pronouns are used as objects of prepositions.**

    Oliver stared at the birthday card that Stanley had given <u>to him</u>.

    The disagreement <u>between Shayla and me</u> was not really very serious.

2. **Objective pronouns are used as direct objects of action verbs.** The noun or pronoun that receives the action of the action verb is called the **direct object.** For example, in the sentence *Tuan visited Serena yesterday*, the verb is *visited*, an action verb. The direct object of *visited* is *Serena* because *Serena* receives the action of the verb *visited*. If you substitute a pronoun for *Serena*, it must be the objective pronoun *her: Tuan visited **her** yesterday.*

Tyrone insulted <u>her</u> at the party last night.

After we ate dinner, Juanita took <u>me</u> to the mall.

Mr. Kong picked up all of the banana peels and threw <u>them</u> out the window.

3. **Objective pronouns are used as indirect objects. The indirect object indicates to whom or for whom (or to what or for what) an action is directed,** but the prepositions *to* and *for* are left out.

Prepositional phrase   He gave the flowers <u>to her</u>.

Indirect object   He gave <u>her</u> the flowers.

In the first sentence, *her* is the object of the preposition *to*. In the second sentence, the *to* is omitted and the pronoun is moved, making *her* the indirect object. In both sentences, the direct object is *flowers*. Here are other examples:

She had already told <u>him</u> the secret password.

My sister showed <u>them</u> a baseball that had been autographed by Babe Ruth.

POSSESSIVE PRONOUNS

The **possessive pronouns** are *my, mine, our, ours, your, yours, his, her, hers, its, their, theirs,* and *whose.* They are used in two situations:

1. **Possessive pronouns are used as adjectives to indicate possession.**

Mrs. Cleaver could not believe what <u>her</u> ears had just heard.

Lumpy and Eddie looked sheepishly at <u>their</u> feet.

Wally looked at the car and wondered who had stolen <u>its</u> tires.

 The contraction *it's* means "it is." The word *its* is the only possessive form for *it.* (In fact, you do not use apostrophes with any of the possessive pronouns.)

2. **Some possessive pronouns indicate possession without being used as adjectives.** In this case, they may be used as subjects or objects.

I used my father's watch because <u>mine</u> was broken.
   Here the possessive pronoun *mine* is the subject of its clause.

Maria's room is neat, but <u>yours</u> is a mess.
   In this example, *yours* is the subject of its clause.

Arlo rented a car because he had sold <u>his</u>.
   Here the possessive pronoun *his* is a direct object.

COMMON SOURCES OF ERRORS IN PRONOUN CASE

COMPOUND CONSTRUCTIONS

Compound subjects and objects often cause problems when they include pronouns. If your sentence includes a compound construction, be sure you use the correct pronoun case.

compound subject	<u>Melissa and she</u> own a fifty-acre ranch.
compound after linking verb	That was <u>Leslie and I</u> whom you spoke to last night.
compound object of a preposition	After the fire, the police took statements from <u>my brother and me</u>.
compound direct object	Julio saw <u>Mark and him</u> at the racetrack.
compound indirect object	She gave <u>him and me</u> a reward when we found her lost dog.

In most cases, you can use a simple test to check whether you have chosen the right pronoun case when you have a compound construction. Simply remove one of the subjects or objects so that only one pronoun is left. For example, is this sentence correct? *Our host gave **Erin and I** a drink.* Test it by dropping **Erin and.** *Our host gave I a drink.* Now you can see that the *I* should be *me* because it is an object (an indirect object). The correct sentence should read: *Our host gave **Erin and me** a drink.*

WHO AND WHOM

When to use *who* or *whom* is a mystery to many writers, but you should have no problem with these pronouns if you remember two simple rules:

1. Use the subjective pronoun *who* or *whoever* if it is used as the subject of a verb.
2. Use the objective pronoun *whom* or *whomever* if it is not used as the subject of a verb.

   While standing in line at the bus depot, I saw someone <u>who</u> looked like my long-lost brother.
   Who is the subject of *looked*.

   The position will be given to the person <u>whom</u> the committee finds most qualified.
   Whom is not the subject of a verb.

   This wallet should be returned to <u>whoever</u> lost it.
   Whoever is the subject of *lost*.

COMPARISONS

When a pronoun is used in a comparison, you often need to supply the implied words to know what pronoun case to use. For example, in the sentence *My brother cannot skate as well as I,* the implied words are the verb *can skate: My brother cannot skate as well as I [can skate].*

   When we visited the petting zoo, the animals seemed to like my brother more than <u>me</u>.

You can tell that *me* is the correct case in this sentence when you supply the implied words:

When we visited the petting zoo, the animals seemed to like my brother more than [they liked] <u>me</u>.

APPOSITIVES

An appositive is a word group containing a noun or pronoun that renames another noun or pronoun. When the appositive contains a **pronoun** that does the renaming, be sure that the pronoun is in the same case as the word it renames. (For more discussion of appositives, see pages 188–190.)

Three employees—Miguel, Pierre, and <u>I</u>—were fired for insubordination.

Here *I* is in the subjective case because the appositive *Miguel, Pierre, and I* renames the word *employees,* the subject of the sentence.

This report is the responsibility of only two people, Mark and <u>her</u>.

Here *her* is in the objective case because the appositive *Mark and her* renames *people,* the object of the preposition *of.*

EXERCISE 15.1

In each sentence, underline the correct pronoun form (in parentheses).

1. Just between you and (I)(me), do you really think we should eat this entire gallon of ice cream?
2. A lone Hobbit was trying to find (its)(it's) way home.
3. The tram took Bill and (he)(him) on a ride through Universal Studios.
4. The Leonards next door bought many more fireworks for the Fourth of July than (we) (us).
5. Ask Amy and (she)(her) to water our lawn while we are on vacation.
6. Do Tiffany and (her)(she) have any extra money with them?
7. Two skiers, Alberto and (he)(him), have a chance to win the gold medal.
8. The prize goes to (whoever)(whomever) can explain what Willy was carrying in his black bags.
9. Sam wondered why his parents would not buy a new jet ski for his sister and (he)(him).
10. (It's)(Its) loud, grinding sound frightened Steve and (she)(her).

EXERCISE 15.2

Correct any errors in pronoun case in the following sentences. Some sentences may not contain errors.

1. Mr. Livingston loves to visit Africa, but his sister is much less fond of that country than him.
2. Where have Orville and he put the parachute?

3. Carla was sure that it was George Clooney who she saw in the emergency room.

4. On the camping trip, our guide told Armando and I a terrifying story.

5. Its too bad that your dog hurt it's neck when its chain became caught in the tractor.

6. Yvonne and Eunice, whom were passengers on the *Titanic*, feel uncomfortable whenever they take a bath.

7. Although Frank and Joe spoke to all of the neighbors, the Bobbsey twins still sold more tickets than them.

8. Between Ramona and he stood a huge marble column covered with mysterious inscriptions.

9. Both Julianne and Dennis are great actors, but the Oscar judges gave Julianne more points than him.

10. To the winners of the marathon, Hal and him, the judges gave blister ointment and bandages.

EXERCISE 15.3

Correct any errors in pronoun case in the following sentences. Some sentences may not contain errors.

1 The condominium complex where my wife and me live is home for a wide variety of people. 2 For example, our neighbors Charlie and Meredith are in their late twenties and have four small children. 3 Charlie recently told me that Meredith and him are able to save money for their children's college education by buying a "condo" instead of a house. 4 Charlie's sister, whom has fewer children than him, also lives in our complex. 5 She prefers condominium living because so many children live nearby who her own kids can play with. 6 Jorge, a single twenty-five-year-old attorney, lives behind my wife and I. 7 His business partners own houses, but Jorge says he prefers a condominium because of it's low maintenance requirements. 8 There are also many elderly residents in our community. 9 They provide a maturity and stability that sometimes us younger families don't have. 10 Often they act as surrogate grandparents who younger families come to for advice. 11 In many cases, the older residents are more active than us younger ones. 12 Clearly, the lifestyle offered by condominium living is attractive to many people who are different from my wife and me in many ways.

The Writer's Response website includes links for more practice in pronoun case. Go to www.thomsonedu.com/devenglish/mcdonald. Under "Chapter Resources" for Chapter 15, click on "Exploring Online." In addition, under "Course Resources," click on "Online Grammar Quizzes." Then click on "Choosing the Correct Pronoun Form."

Misplaced and Dangling Modifiers

16

MISPLACED MODIFIERS

Misplaced modifiers are exactly what their name says they are—modifiers that have been "misplaced" within a sentence. But how is a modifier "misplaced"? The answer is simple. If you remember that a modifier is nearly always placed just before or just after the word it modifies, then a misplaced modifier must be one that has been mistakenly placed so that it causes a reader to be confused about what it modifies. Consider the following sentence, for example:

> A police officer told us <u>slowly</u> to raise our hands.

Does the modifier *slowly* state how the officer told us, or does it state how we were supposed to raise our hands? Changing the placement of the modifier will clarify the meaning.

> A police officer <u>slowly</u> told us to raise our hands.
> Here the word modifies the verb *told*.

> A police officer told us to raise our hands <u>slowly</u>.
> Here the word modifies the infinitive *to raise*.

MISPLACED WORDS

Any modifier can be misplaced, but one particular group of modifiers causes quite a bit of trouble for many people. These words are *only, almost, just, merely,* and *nearly.* Consider, for example, the following sentences:

> By buying her new waterbed on sale, Maureen <u>almost</u> saved $100.

> By buying her new waterbed on sale, Maureen saved <u>almost</u> $100.

As you can see, these sentences actually make two different statements. In the first sentence, *almost* modifies *saved.* If you *almost* saved something, you did *not* save it. In the second sentence, *almost* modifies *$100.* If you saved *almost* $100, you saved $85, $90, $95, or some other amount close to $100.

Which statement does the writer want to make—that Maureen did *not* save any money or that she *did* save an amount close to $100? Because the point was that she bought her waterbed on sale, the second sentence makes more sense.

To avoid confusion, be sure that you place all of your modifiers carefully.

INCORRECT   Her coach told her <u>often</u> to work out with weights.

CORRECT   Her coach <u>often</u> told her to work out with weights.

INCORRECT   Kara <u>nearly</u> ate a gallon of ice cream yesterday.

CORRECT   Kara ate <u>nearly</u> a gallon of ice cream yesterday.

MISPLACED PHRASES AND CLAUSES

Phrases and clauses are as easily misplaced as individual words. Generally, phrases and clauses should appear immediately before or after the words they modify. Notice how misplaced phrases and clauses confuse the meaning of the following sentences:

> A bird flew over the house <u>with blue wings</u>.

> The irritated secretary slapped at the fly <u>typing the report</u>.

> They gave the food to the dog <u>left over from dinner</u>.

> Lucia smashed the car into a telephone pole <u>that she had borrowed from her sister</u>.

Obviously, misplaced phrases and clauses can cause rather confusing (and sometimes even humorous) situations. However, when such clauses are placed close to the words they modify, their meaning is clear:

> A bird <u>with blue wings</u> flew over the house.

> The irritated secretary <u>typing the report</u> slapped at the fly.

> <u>Typing the report</u>, the irritated secretary slapped at the fly.

> They gave the food <u>left over from dinner</u> to the dog.

> Lucia smashed the car that <u>she had borrowed from her sister</u> into a telephone pole.

Whether the modifier appears before or after the word it modifies, the point is that you should place a modifier so that it clearly refers to a specific word in the sentence.

DANGLING MODIFIERS

A **dangling modifier** is usually an introductory phrase (usually a verbal phrase) that lacks an appropriate subject to modify. Since these modifiers usually represent some sort of action, they need a **doer** or **agent** of the action represented.

For example, in the following sentence, the introductory phrase "dangles" because it is not followed by a subject that could be the "doer" of the action represented by the phrase:

> Singing at the top of his voice, the song was irritating everybody at the party.

The phrase *Singing at the top of his voice* should be followed by a subject that could logically perform the action of the phrase. Instead, it is followed by the subject *song*. Was the song *singing*? Probably not. Therefore, the modifying phrase "dangles" because it has no subject to which it can logically refer. Here are some more sentences with dangling modifiers:

> Completely satisfied, the painting was admired.
>   Was the *painting* satisfied?

> After reviewing all of the facts, a decision was reached.
>   Did the *decision* review the facts?

> To impress the judges, Cecil's mustache was waxed.
>   Did the *mustache* want to impress the judges?

As you can see, you should check for dangling modifiers when you use introductory phrases.

CORRECTING DANGLING MODIFIERS

You can correct a dangling modifier in one of two ways:

1. **Rewrite the sentence so that its subject can be logically modified by the introductory modifier.**

   Completely satisfied, <u>Vincent</u> admired the painting.
     Vincent was completely satisfied.

   After reviewing all of the facts, <u>I</u> reached a decision.
     I reviewed all of the facts.

   To impress the judges, <u>Cecil</u> waxed his mustache.
     Cecil wanted to impress the judges.

2. **Change the introductory phrase to a clause.**

   <u>When Vincent was completely satisfied</u>, he admired the painting.
   <u>After I reviewed all of the facts</u>, I reached a decision.
   <u>Because Cecil wanted to impress the judges</u>, he waxed his mustache.

Do not correct a dangling modifier by moving it to the end of the sentence. In either case, it will still "dangle" because it lacks a **"doer,"** or **agent,** that could perform the action of the modifier.

INCORRECT

<u>After missing three meetings</u>, the request was denied.
  There is no "doer" for *missing*.

STILL INCORRECT

The request was denied <u>after missing three meetings</u>.
  There is no "doer" for *missing*.

STILL INCORRECT

<u>After missing three meetings</u>, Alfredo's request was denied.
  Adding the possessive form *Alfredo's* does not add a "doer" of the action.

CORRECT

<u>After Alfredo had missed three meetings</u>, his request was denied.
  Here the "doer" of the action is clear.

CORRECT

After missing three meetings, Alfredo was told that his request was denied.
  Here *Alfredo* is clearly the person who missed the meetings.

EXERCISE 16.1

Identify and correct any misplaced or dangling modifiers in the following sentences. Some of the sentences may be correct.

1. Pulling quickly over to the curb, the drugstore appeared to be open.
2. The painting was found in a pawnshop that had been stolen from the museum.
3. Amber only decided to study after she had received poor grades on her first two tests.
4. Whistling under her breath, Julissa walked her dogs down the street and into the park.
5. Frustrated by his poor performance, the runner's fists were tightly clenched.
6. The dog groomer put the collie on the table with the shaggy tail and began to clip its fur.
7. After almost eating three strawberry pies, Oscar felt a bit woozy.
8. Slowly sinking toward the horizon, Bonnie and Clyde held hands and admired the sunset.
9. Butch Cassidy pulled out his pistol and shot at a coyote riding his favorite horse.

10. After robbing dozens of trains, Jesse James's luck finally ran out.
11. Sara Lee finally decided to serve the dessert to her guests that she had been keeping in the refrigerator.
12. The doctor performing the autopsy carefully recorded her findings.
13. Crossing the avenue, the light changed too quickly from green to red.
14. The SWAT team only captured one of the escaped convicts.
15. While camping in the desert, a snake crawled next to my sister with a triangular head.

EXERCISE 16.2

Correct any misplaced or dangling modifiers in the following paragraph. Some sentences may be correct.

1 To put up with Howard, my college roommate, a good deal of tolerance was necessary. 2 Howard was racist, violent, and selfish. 3 Hanging on the wall next to his bed, Howard proudly displayed a Nazi flag. 4 He almost belonged to every racist organization on or off campus. 5 He even had a swastika tattooed to advertise his beliefs on his neck. 6 Once, when he was angry at someone, he grabbed a baseball bat and took a swing at him, which he kept under his bed. 7 Refusing to calm down or apologize, the police were finally called. 8 And then, one day he took my car and nearly drove it all the way to San Francisco, two hundred miles away. 9 Asking him to pay for the mileage and gas, he just laughed at me. 10 Howard was finally asked to leave the school, who was failing all his classes, when he threw a garbage can at one of his professors.

The Writer's Response website includes links for more practice in pronoun case. Go to www.thomsonedu.com/devenglish/mcdonald. Under "Chapter Resources" for Chapter 16, click on "Exploring Online."

Comma Usage

17

The comma is probably more troublesome to writers than any other punctuation mark. Long ago commas were used to tell readers where to put in a slight pause. Although the placement of the comma does affect the rhythm of a sentence, today it also conveys many more messages than when to pause. Comma use can be broken down into four general rules:

1. Use commas before coordinating conjunctions that join main clauses.
2. Use commas between elements in a series.
3. Use commas after introductory elements.
4. Use commas before and after interrupting elements.

COMMAS BEFORE COORDINATING CONJUNCTIONS THAT JOIN MAIN CLAUSES

1. **Place a comma before a coordinating conjunction that joins two main clauses.**

   Richard Pryor is a hilarious comedian, **and** Robin Williams is also great in his own unique way.

   Hercules had to shovel a huge amount of horse manure, **or** he would never complete his task.

2. **Do not put a comma before a conjunction that joins other parts of a sentence, such as two words, two phrases, or two subordinate clauses.**

   Every morning Charlie shaves with his favorite cleaver **and** then goes down to breakfast with his family.

   (No comma is needed before *and* because it does not join two main clauses. It joins the verbs *shaves* and *goes*.)

   You can find good coffee **and** conversation at Kafana Coffee House **or** at Spill the Beans.

   (No comma is required before *and* because it joins the nouns *coffee* and *conversation*. No comma is required before *or* because it just joins the names of the coffee shops.)

COMMAS WITH ELEMENTS IN A SERIES

1. **Separate with commas three or more elements (words, phrases, clauses) listed in a series.** When the last two elements are joined by a coordinating conjunction, a comma before the conjunction is optional.

   WORDS

   The film *Vanilla Sky* was **intriguing, puzzling, and controversial.**

   PHRASES

   Omar enjoyed **cooking okra and Spam for his friends, competing in the Spam cooking contest at the fair, and betting on horses with strange names at the racetrack.**

   CLAUSES

   While shopping at the mall, **Quinlan bought pants that were much too big, his brother bought him a hat that he could wear backwards, and his girlfriend bought some Doc Marten black boots.**

2. **Separate with commas two or more adjectives used to modify the same noun if you can put** *and* **between the adjectives without changing the meaning or if you can easily reverse the order of the adjectives.**

The bear waded into the **shallow, swift** river after the salmon.

The **witty, gregarious** comedian kept us laughing for hours with her stories.

Note   You could use *and* between the adjectives. (The river is *shallow* and *swift;* the comedian is *witty* and *gregarious.*) You could also reverse the adjectives (the *swift, shallow* river or the *gregarious, witty* comedian).

3. **On the other hand, no commas are necessary if the adjectives cannot be joined by** *and* **or are not easily reversed.**

The computer technician wore **white cotton** gloves as she worked.

Notice how awkward the sentence would sound if you placed *and* between the adjectives (the *white and cotton* gloves) or if you reversed them (the *cotton white* gloves).

COMMAS WITH INTRODUCTORY ELEMENTS

1. **Use a comma after introductory words and phrases.**

Introductory Words

next	third	similarly	indeed
first	nevertheless	moreover	yes
second	therefore	however	no

Introductory Phrases

on the other hand	for example	in addition
in a similar manner	for instance	as a result
in other words	in fact	

Next, Persephone made the mistake of eating a pomegranate.

In addition, Charles purchased a remote electronic noise device to embarrass his colleagues.

2. **Use a comma after introductory prepositional phrases of five words or more.** However, you may need to use a comma after a shorter introductory prepositional phrase if not doing so would cause confusion.

Before the famous main attraction, a very good harmonica band entertained the audience.

In the film, actors kept changing into androids.

(Without the comma, this sentence might be read as *in the film actors.*)

3. **Use a comma after all introductory infinitive and participial phrases.**

infinitive phrase

To eat a hot dog, Ambrose had to forget his diet.

present participial
phrase

Running in the marathon, Sam finally achieved his goal.

past participial
phrase

Congregated in the student union, the students planned their protest.

(See pages 143–145 for a further discussion of infinitive and participial phrases.)

4. **Use a comma after a subordinate clause that precedes a main clause.**

Because Ulysses was bored, he wanted to go fishing again.

Although I am an English major, I sometimes say "ain't."

(See page 110 for a further discussion of punctuating subordinate clauses.)

COMMAS WITH INTERRUPTING ELEMENTS

Sometimes certain words, phrases, or clauses will interrupt the flow of thought in a sentence to add emphasis or additional information. These **interrupting elements** are enclosed by commas.

1. **Use commas to set off parenthetical expressions.** Common parenthetical expressions are *however, indeed, consequently, as a result, moreover, of course, for example, for instance, that is, in fact, after all, I think,* and *therefore.*

A new baseball glove was, **after all,** a luxury.

Her old one, **therefore,** would have to do for another season.

ote Whenever a parenthetical expression introduces a second main clause after a semicolon, the semicolon takes the place of the comma in front of it.

Colin was looking forward to his vacation; **moreover,** he was eager to visit his family in England.

2. **Use commas to set off nonrestrictive elements. Nonrestrictive** elements are modifying words, phrases, or clauses that are *not* necessary to identify the words they modify. On the other hand, **restrictive** elements are those that *are* necessary to identify the words they modify. Restrictive elements are not set off with commas. Adjective subordinate clauses, participial phrases, and appositives require that you decide whether they are nonrestrictive or restrictive.

Adjective subordinate clauses begin with one of the relative pronouns: *who, whom, whose, which, that,* and sometimes *when* or *where.* They follow the nouns or pronouns that they modify. An adjective clause is **nonrestrictive** when it *is not necessary to identify the word it modifies.* It is enclosed in commas.

nonrestrictive

Dizzy Gillespie, **who helped to develop the form of jazz known as bebop,** played an unusual trumpet.

> Because Dizzy Gillespie is named, the adjective clause *who helped to develop the form of jazz known as bebop* is nonrestrictive. It is not needed to identify Dizzy Gillespie.

restrictive

One of the people **who helped to develop the form of jazz known as bebop** was Dizzy Gillespie.

> Because *who helped to develop the form of jazz* is needed to identify the "people" you are referring to, it is restrictive and is not set off with commas.

Here is another example of a nonrestrictive clause:

nonrestrictive

My youngest sister, **who is a paleontologist,** showed me her collection of skulls.

> Because a person can have only one youngest sister, the adjective clause *is not needed to identify her,* making it nonrestrictive.

(See page 110 for a further discussion of punctuating adjective clauses.)

Participial phrases that *do not contain information necessary to identify the word they modify* are nonrestrictive and are therefore set off by commas. Restrictive participial phrases do not require commas.

nonrestrictive

Van Gogh, **seeking something to paint,** looked up into the night sky.

> Because Van Gogh is named, the participial phrase *seeking something to paint* is nonrestrictive. It is not needed to identify Van Gogh.

restrictive

The man **painting in the middle of the night** called the work *Starry Night.*

> Because the man is not named, the participial phrase *painting in the middle of the night* is restrictive.

(See pages 143–145 for a further discussion of participial phrases.)

An **appositive** is a noun or pronoun, along with any modifiers, that **renames** another noun or pronoun. The appositive almost always follows the word it refers to, and it is usually set off by commas.

The computer, **an extremely useful tool,** has advanced a long way in just a few years.

> The noun *tool* renames the noun *computer.*

On the street, the Yugo, **the one with the rusty doors,** is an eyesore.

> The pronoun *one* renames the noun *Yugo.*

(See pages 188–190 for a further discussion of appositives.)

3. **Use commas to set off words of direct address.** If a writer addresses someone directly in a sentence, the words that stand for that person or persons are set off by commas. If the words in direct address begin a sentence, they are followed by a comma. If they end a sentence, they are preceded by a comma.

What if, **Charlie,** you were to hurt someone with one of your weapons?

Brent, you are hogging the ball.

I am sorry if I hurt your feelings, **Aaron.**

4. **Use commas to set off dates and addresses.** If your sentence contains two or more elements of a date or address, use commas to set off these elements. The following sentences contain two or more elements:

We went to Magic Mountain on **Thursday, November 18, 2002,** because children were admitted free that day.

Concepcion had lived at 4590 **Portello Street, San Francisco, California,** for twelve years.

In 1992 she moved to 1754 **Pacific Court, Vista, California** 92083, to be near her mother.

Note The state is not separated from the zip code by a comma.

EXERCISE 17.1

Add commas to the following sentences where necessary.

1. Even though she was a great artist Frieda remained in the shadow of her husband for a long time.
2. I have always enjoyed driving up the coast of California so we will leave for Big Sur on Saturday.
3. Ringo on the other hand greatly admired Beethoven.
4. Tomorrow Oedipus intends to go to the foot doctor talk to the Sphinx eat lunch with his wife and ponder his fate.
5. The salesperson's considerate kind attention impressed Mr. Gutierrez.
6. Tony Soprano wanted the pasta dish yet feared that it was poisoned.
7. Sunday June 4 2006 was an important day in Jose's life.
8. Billie Holiday who is one of the greatest jazz singers lived a hard life.
9. King Lear a stupid old man finally saw the errors that he had committed.
10. Suzanne called Brent packed her belongings said her goodbyes and moved to her new place.

11. The man who corrupted Hadleyburg just disappeared.

12. Send the feathers and wax to 8965 Maze Way Minotaur Ohio 09999 and make it quick Otto.

13. To force the owners of factories to listen to their demands they threw shoes into the machinery.

14. Friar Laurence did you say that Juliet was just sleeping?

15. Beginning on July 1 1863 the Civil War battle that took place at Gettysburg Pennsylvania was probably the most decisive battle of the war.

EXERCISE 17.2

Add commas to the following sentences where necessary.

1. Yes Icarus flew like a bird but he lived to regret it.

2. Watch Ophelia as I kill your father my uncle and Laertes.

3. Ken's bicycle had a flat near Taos New Mexico so he camped there overnight.

4. On July 9 1898 Torvald refused to do the dishes or change the baby's diapers.

5. Nora enraged by his behavior told him how she felt; moreover she packed her bags and left.

6. Torvald a notoriously insensitive man did not understand her feelings.

7. The rugged dependable DC-3 passenger plane served in World War II and it is still in service all over the world.

8. Clapping loudly Heidi pointed to Beethoven who could not hear the applause because he was deaf.

9. In the middle of a serious speech on poverty the senator suddenly recited a tasteless poem a bawdy limerick.

10. Grabbing his wallet and sword Achilles headed for Troy New York to join his friends.

11. When he arrived they had already started building a large wooden horse.

12. New Orleans for instance is my favorite city because of the music the food the coffee and the wide variety of people who like to have fun.

13. June 24 1981 was a special day for Michelle for on that day she saw sunshine clouds and sky for the first time.

14. Persephone famished after so much time in hell finally decided to eat a pomegranate.

15. In fact Katie included most of the characters from *Alice in Wonderland* in her "Alice" paintings which are now being shown at the Museum of Modern Art.

EXERCISE 17.3

Add commas to the following sentences where necessary.

1 Mistletoe which is also known by the Latin name of *Vicsum album* has long been considered to have unusual characteristics. 2 Today it is known as the plant that provides an excuse to kiss someone but its reputation as a plant with special powers goes back to the Bronze Age. 3 Because it seems to appear out of nowhere the ancient Druids thought the plant was sent from heaven. 4 In fact it is a parasite that sinks its root-like feelers into the top of a tree and then it literally sucks the life juices out of it. 5 Growing slowly ruthlessly and patiently it does not die until the tree that it is attached to dies. 6 Druid priests would climb the tree and harvest the mistletoe which was believed to cure toothache epilepsy and even infertility. 7 Although researchers have recently found that mistletoe leaf extract might inhibit the growth of cancer cells we also know that mistletoe is poisonous. 8 During the days of the Roman empire mistletoe was regarded as a symbol of peace. 9 Standing under a sprig of the plant enemies would throw away their weapons declare a truce and embrace. 10 The origin of today's custom of kissing under the mistletoe is not clear; however it may derive from the Norwegian story of Frigga who kissed everyone who walked under the mistletoe when her son came back to life.

Exploring ONLINE

The Writer's Response website includes links for more practice in the use of commas. Go to www.thomsonedu.com/devenglish/mcdonald. Under "Chapter Resources" for Chapter 17, click on "Exploring Online."

Semicolons and Colons

18

THE SEMICOLON

1. **A semicolon is used to join two main clauses that are not joined by a comma and a coordinating conjunction.** Sometimes a conjunctive adverb follows the semicolon. (See page 71 for a list of conjunctive adverbs.)

   The generals checked Hitler's horoscope; it told them when to attack.

   Nancy wanted to check her horoscope; however, Ron advised against it.

2. **A semicolon can be used to join elements in a series when the elements require further internal punctuation.**

   By the time Guillermo reached home, he had worked for eighteen hours, which tired him out; he had had a car accident, which depressed him; he had drunk too much coffee, which made him jittery; and he had yelled at his partner, which made him remorseful.

3. **Do not use a semicolon to separate two phrases or two subordinate clauses.**

INCORRECT

Sonia is going to Little Vietnam because she likes the spring rolls; and because she likes the atmosphere.

CORRECT

Sonia is going to Little Vietnam because she likes the spring rolls and because she likes the atmosphere.

(See pages 70–71 for further discussion of semicolon usage.)

THE COLON

1. **A colon is used to join two main clauses when the second clause is an example, an illustration, or a restatement of the first clause.**

   The party had been a great success: everyone had had fun and had gotten safely home.

   This incident is the same as all of the others: Wolfgang never agrees with any of our ideas.

2. **A colon is used when a complete sentence introduces an example, a quotation, a series, or a list.**

   The magazine covered a number of subjects related to biking: racing bicycles, touring bicycles, mountain bicycles, and safety equipment.

   In "The Cautious and Obedient Life," Susan Walton made the following statement: "Some people are born to follow instructions."

   The list on the refrigerator included the following requests: clean the kitchen, wash the car, make reservations at Jake's, and take a shower.

3. **A colon is generally not used after a verb.**

   INCORRECT

   My favorite foods are: red beans and rice, catfish, and pasta carbonara.

   CORRECT

   My favorite foods are red beans and rice, catfish, and pasta carbonara.

EXERCISE 18.1

Add semicolons or colons where necessary. (Some commas may need to be replaced with semicolons or colons.)

1. Dizzy picked up his trumpet then he blew a scorching version of "Salt Peanuts."
2. Describe one of the following characters Hamlet, Captain Ahab, Emma, Roseanne, Joan of Arc, Holden Caulfield, or Iago.

3. The elves enjoyed the shade of the mushroom, however, they lamented the lack of dew.

4. Here is what the refugee carried the novel *Heart of Darkness*, the poem "Patterns," and the candy bar Baby Ruth.

5. The ingredients are pink beans, ham hocks, hominy, and okra.

6. The artist kept painting melted watches meanwhile, his friends told him that his paintings would never sell.

7. In "Why I Won't Buy My Sons Toy Guns," Robert Shaffer makes an interesting point "Any toy is a teacher."

8. Coltrane had been playing "My Favorite Things" for two hours it was time to quit.

9. Mark Twain once said, "The lack of money is the root of all evil."

10. Last summer we visited my cousin Alice, who lives in Monroe, South Dakota, my brother John, who lives in San Luis Obispo, California, and my best friend, Jim, who lives in Atlanta, Georgia.

EXERCISE 18.2

Add semicolons or colons where necessary. (Some commas may need to be replaced with semicolons or colons.)

1 Coffee is one of the most popular beverages in the United States, therefore, it is natural for people to wonder how the caffeine in coffee affects them. 2 To understand how caffeine works, one needs to understand the relationship between three chemicals adenosine, caffeine, and adrenaline. 3 Adenosine is one of the many chemicals in the brain it is the one that makes a person sleepy. 4 Caffeine's molecular structure is similar to adenosine's, as a result, caffeine binds to adenosine receptors when it enters the brain, but it doesn't activate the "sleepy" adenosine response. 5 Instead, caffeine works the opposite of adenosine it increases the neuron firing in the brain. 6 The nerve cells also speed up because caffeine has blocked the adenosine. 7 The pituitary gland senses an emergency situation, therefore, it tells the adrenal glands to release adrenaline. 8 The following reactions result the pupils dilate, the breathing tubes open up, the heart beats faster, the blood vessels on the surface constrict, the blood pressure rises, the blood flow to the stomach slows, and the muscles tighten. 9 In addition to all of these reactions, the liver releases sugar into the bloodstream the added sugar causes extra energy. 10 These complex bodily responses are what make coffee the popular drink it is today.

Exploring ONLINE

The Writer's Response website includes links for more practice in the use of semicolons and colons. Go to www.thomsonedu.com/devenglish/mcdonald. Under "Chapter Resources" for Chapter 18, click on "Exploring Online."

The Apostrophe

19

1. **Apostrophes are used to form contractions.**

   The apostrophe replaces the omitted letter or letters.

it is	it's
cannot	can't
I am	I'm
were not	weren't
they are	they're
is not	isn't
would have	would've
does not	doesn't

2. **Apostrophes are used to form the possessives of nouns and indefinite pronouns.**

   - Add *'s* to form the possessive of all singular nouns and indefinite pronouns.

singular nouns	The <u>boy's</u> bicycle was new.
	<u>Louis's</u> courage was never questioned.
indefinite pronouns	<u>Someone's</u> horn was honking
compound words	My <u>father-in-law's</u> car had a flat.
joint possession	<u>Julio and Maria's</u> mountain cabin is for rent.

• Add only an apostrophe to form the possessive of plural nouns that end in -*s*. However, add -'*s* to form the possessive of plural nouns that do not end in -*s*.

plural nouns that end is -*s*

Both <u>teams'</u> shoes were lined up on the field.

The <u>Smiths'</u> house was on fire.

plural nouns that do not end in -*s*

The <u>women's</u> cars were parked in front of the house.

• Expressions referring to time or money often require an apostrophe.

Sheila asked for a <u>dollar's</u> worth of candy.

The player was given three <u>days'</u> suspension.

3. **Do not use apostrophes with the possessive forms of personal pronouns.**

Incorrect	Correct
her's	hers
our's	ours
their's	theirs

 It's means "it is." The possessive form of *it* is *its*.

EXERCISE 19.1

Add apostrophes (or -*s*) to the following sentences where necessary.

1. That is Barrys baseball glove; he wont mind if you use it.
2. In twenty-four hours time, Oedipus found out that he had killed his father and married his mother.
3. Its customary for the female black widow spider to kill its mate.
4. Youre also aware, Im sure, that the female praying mantis bites off the head of her mate and eats it.
5. The childrens bicycles shouldnt have been left out in the rain.
6. My mother-in-laws visits to her five relatives homes were a pleasant surprise.
7. The dog could not find shelter, and its puppies cries were beginning to grow louder.
8. Hasnt the McDonalds house been painted yet?
9. Carlas mistake cost Woody three days pay.
10. A weeks vacation in the Bahamas had nearly erased the worry lines from my brothers face.

EXERCISE 19.2

Add apostrophes (or -'s) to the following sentences where necessary.

1 One of my mothers favorite stories is about the time she organized all of the quilting clubs in town to protest the Vietnam War. 2 The clubs members had always been politically active, so few people objected. 3 After just a few months work, they had made hundreds of quilts with slogans on them objecting to the war. 4 My aunts quilt had pictures and names of people killed in the war. 5 Knowing my family, I wasnt surprised to hear that both of my grandmothers also participated in the quilting. 6 On the day designated for the protest, my uncle Charles leased twelve buses to take the quilters to the mayors office. 7 Uncle Charles younger brother had died in the war several years earlier. 8 Once they were downtown, the women held up their quilts and chanted, "Its time to end the war!" 9 Newspapers from miles away covered the protest, and the local television stations daily schedule was interrupted to televise it. 10 My mother says, "We werent a big group of thousands of people, but even small protests like ours can make a difference."

The Writer's Response website includes links for more practice in the use of apostrophes. Go to www.thomsonedu.com/devenglish/mcdonald. Under "Chapter Resources" for Chapter 19, click on "Exploring Online."

Quotation Marks

20

1. **Quotation marks are used to enclose direct quotations and dialogue.**

   As Oscar Wilde once said, "Fashion is a form of ugliness so intolerable that we have to alter it every six months."

   Will Rogers said, "Liberty doesn't work as well in practice as it does in speeches."

2. **Quotation marks are not used with indirect quotations.**

   direct quotation   Tony said, "I'll play trumpet in the band."

   indirect quotation   Tony said that he would play trumpet in the band.

3. **Place periods and commas inside quotation marks.**

   Eudora Welty wrote the short story "A Worn Path."

   "I am a man more sinned against than sinning," cried Lear.

4. **Place colons and semicolons outside quotation marks.**

   The class did not like the poem "Thoughts on Capital Punishment": it was silly, sentimental, and insipid, and the rhythm was awkward and inappropriate.

   The local newspaper ran a story entitled "Mayor Caught Nude on the Beach"; it was just a joke for April Fools' Day.

5. **Place the question mark inside the quotation marks if the quotation is a question. Place the question mark outside the quotation marks if the quotation is not a question but the whole sentence is.**

   Homer asked, "What is for dinner, my dear Hortense?"

   Did Hortense really reply, "Hominy, okra, and barbecued Spam"?

6. **Place the exclamation point inside the quotation marks if the quotation is an exclamation. Place it outside the quotation marks if the quotation is not an exclamation but the whole sentence is.**

   "I have a dream!" yelled Martin Luther King, Jr.

   I insist that you stop calling me "dude"!

   (See pages 158–160 for a further discussion of quotation marks.)

EXERCISE 20.1

Add quotation marks to the following sentences where necessary.

1. Hal said, Squid tentacles are my favorite snacks.
2. Will you get the tickets for the concert? asked Georgette.
3. Did Bob Dylan really sing Moon River?
4. Mark Twain once muttered that a classic was a book that everyone praised, but no one read.
5. Biff, I wish you would stop calling me Happy, he said.
6. Did the Cyclops actually believe him when he said, My name is No Man?
7. According to Charles Levendosky, Burning the flag is the act of someone who has little or no political power.
8. Camilla said, I am going to write a short story about an aardvark in Ireland; afterwards, she changed her mind.
9. *Star Trek* fans used to say, Beam me up, Scotty.
10. Send in the clowns, sang the frustrated coach.

EXERCISE 20.2

Add quotation marks to the following sentences where necessary.

1 When Sophia spent the evening with her friend Alicia at Alicia's house, she was surprised at the family's conversation during dinner. 2 Alicia's brother Paulo, who was taking a literature course at his college, said that he had been reading a short story by Eudora Welty entitled Petrified Man. 3 I'd never read any short stories at all before I took this class, he said. 4 Sophia responded that she had never read Eudora Welty but that she enjoyed Flannery O'Connor. 5 Alicia's mother then asked Sophia, Have you ever read a poem called My Last Duchess? 6 Sophia nodded and said, I read it just last semester; Alicia's mother looked pleased. 7 Doesn't the Duchess die at the end? asked Alicia's father. 8 Later the discussion turned to newspaper articles they had read. 9 Paulo asked, Did anyone see yesterday's article entitled We Need to Do More about Global Warming? 10 After a long discussion of the need for ecological awareness, Sophia thanked the family for its hospitality, and, when asked if she would like to come back the following week, she replied, Definitely!

The Writer's Response website includes links for more practice in the use of quotation marks. Go to www.thomsonedu.com/devenglish/mcdonald. Under "Chapter Resources" for Chapter 20, click on "Exploring Online."

Titles, Capitalization and Numbers

21

TITLES

1. Underline or place in italics the titles of longer works, such as books, periodicals, plays, CDs, and television programs.

   - Books: *Moby Dick, Bartlett's Familiar Quotations*
   - Plays: *The Glass Menagerie, A Doll's House*
   - Pamphlets: *Grooming Your Labrador, Charleston's Ten Best Restaurants*
   - Long musical works: Mozart's *String Quartet in C Major,* Miles Davis's *Sketches of Spain*
   - Long poems: *Howl, The Faerie Queene*
   - Periodicals: *The Washington Post, Time*
   - Films: *Memoirs of a Geisha, Brokeback Mountain*
   - Television and radio programs: *American Idol, Masterpiece Theater*
   - Works of art: El Greco's *Saint Matthew, Nike of Samothrace*

2. Use quotation marks to enclose the titles of all shorter works, such as songs, poems, and short stories, as well as parts of larger works, such as articles in magazines and chapters in books.

383

- Songs: "The Sweetest Days," "Friends"
- Poems: "My Last Duchess," "Dover Beach"
- Articles in periodicals: "Three-Headed Snake Born As Two-Headed Brother Looks On," "The Last Stand"
- Short stories: "A Jury of Her Peers," "Resurrection"
- Essays: "Male Fixations," "A Custody Fight for an Egg"
- Episodes of radio and television shows: "What's in a Name?"
- Subdivisions of books: "The Cassock" (Chapter 29 of *Moby Dick*)

CAPITALIZATION

1. Capitalize the personal pronoun *I*.
2. Capitalize the first letter of every sentence.
3. Capitalize the first letter of each word in a title except for *a, an,* and *the,* coordinating conjunctions, and prepositions.

 The first letter of the first and last word of a title is always capitalized.

Dictionary of Philosophy and Religion

"A Good Man Is Hard to Find"

4. Capitalize the first letter of all proper nouns and adjectives derived from proper nouns.

- Names and titles of people: President Bush, William Shakespeare, Uncle Christopher, Ms. Hohman
- Names of specific places: Chicago, Smoky Mountains, Tennessee, The Armenian Cafe, Saturn, the South

Note Do not capitalize the first letter of words that refer to a direction, such as *north, south, east,* or *west.* Do capitalize such words when they refer to a specific region.

Alabama and Mississippi are among the states in the <u>South</u>.

Turn <u>south</u> on Hill Street and go four blocks to the end of the street.

- Names of ethnic, national, or racial groups: Native American, British, French, Canadian, Hispanic, Russian
- Names of groups or organizations: National Organization for Women, Girl Scouts of America, Methodists
- Names of companies: General Motors, Nordstrom, Pepsi-Cola Bottling Company, R. J. Reynolds
- Names of the days of the week and the months of the year but not the seasons: Saturday, April, winter, spring

- Names of holidays and historical events: the Gulf War, Christmas, the Battle of Concord
- Names of *specific* gods and religious writings: God, Zeus, Buddha, Koran, Yahweh, Bible

 The names of academic subjects are not capitalized unless they refer to an ethnic or national origin or are the names of specific courses. Examples include *mathematics, history, Spanish,* and *Physics 100.*

NUMBERS

The following rules about numbers apply to general writing rather than to technical or scientific writing.

1. **Spell out numbers that require no more than two words. Use numerals for numbers that require more than two words.**

   <u>Ninety-three</u> people attended the dean's retirement party.

   We have now gone <u>125</u> days without rain.

2. **Spell out numbers at the beginning of sentences.**

   <u>Two hundred thirty-five</u> miles is a long distance to rollerblade.

3. **Use numerals in the following situations:**

   - Dates: June 24, 1981; 55 B.C.
   - Sections of books or plays: Chapter 26, page 390; Act 5, scene 2, lines 78–90
   - Addresses: 3245 Sisyphus Street
     Stonewall, Nebraska 90345
   - Decimals, percentages, and fractions: 7.5; 75%, 75 percent; 1/8
   - Exact amounts of money: $10.86; $6,723,001
   - Scores and statistics: Padres 10, Reds 0; a ratio of 4 to 1
   - Time of day: 5:23; 12:45

 Round amounts of money that can be expressed in a few words can be written out: *thirty cents, twelve dollars, three hundred dollars.* Also when the word *"o'clock"* is used with the time of day, the time of day should be written out: *eight o'clock.*

4. **When numbers are compared, are joined by conjunctions, or occur in a series, either consistently use numerals or consistently spell them out.**

   For the birthday party we needed <u>one hundred fifteen</u> paper hats, <u>two hundred twenty</u> napkins, <u>one hundred fifteen</u> paper plates and forks, eight gallons of ice cream, three cakes, forty candles, and eight cases of soda.

or

For the birthday party we needed 115 paper hats, 220 napkins, 115 paper plates and forks, 8 gallons of ice cream, 3 cakes, 40 candles, and 8 cases of soda.

EXERCISE 21.1

The following sentences contain errors in the use of titles, capitalization, and numbers. Correct any errors you find.

1. The character of edgar in the play king lear and the character of iago in the play othello are two of shakespeare's worst Villains.
2. 375 cats were believed to have been killed in the city of pompeii when mount vesuvius erupted in seventy-nine A.D.
3. The Principal of imperial valley high school canceled classes when the Temperature reached 100 degrees.
4. Yesterday, the houston rockets beat the new york knicks eighty-six to 84.
5. My fine was three dollars and seventy-five cents when i returned the book the hero with a thousand faces to the Library.
6. Before he closed up, amador ordered 2 new computers, one hundred fifty reams of paper, 90 gallons of ink, and two hundred boxes of staples and paper clips for his copy shop.
7. Brent likes to listen to the radio program fresh air on national public radio.
8. On their album kiko, the band los lobos included a song called arizona skies.
9. A psychologist, dr. john gavion, claims that as many as fifty percent of the homeless people are vietnam veterans.
10. Andre took notes as professor guerra talked about south american art in his hispanic studies 120 class.

EXERCISE 21.2

In the following sentences, correct any errors in the use of titles, capitalization, and numbers.

1 When brad awoke that wednesday morning, he was one happy fellow. 2 The first thing he saw was a thick copy of leo tolstoy's novel war and peace. 3 The night before he had read the first 100 pages of it, and he was pleased to find he really enjoyed it. 4 Today he was going to meet his girlfriend grace after he went to the Dentist's office. 5 Later in the day they were

going to join his art class as it toured the chicago museum of art. 6 He was looking forward to seeing the famous painting by grant wood, american gothic. 7 He had heard that over Three Million Five Hundred Thousand people had traveled to chicago just to see this painting. 8 Grace met him at their favorite coffee shop, caffeinemania, where they listened to enya's popular song orinoco flow. 9 As they left the coffee shop, they saw a copy of time magazine with an article entitled prospects for end of war not good. 10 Wanting to stay in a good mood, brad and grace went for a slow 20-minute walk in the Winter air, and then they headed for the Museum to meet brad's Art Professor and the other members of his class.

Exploring ONLINE

The Writer's Response website includes links for more practice in the use of titles, capitalization, and numbers. Go to www.thomsonedu.com/devenglish/mcdonald. Under "Chapter Resources" for Chapter 21, click on "Exploring Online." In addition, under "Course Resources," click on "Online Grammar Quizzes." Then click on "Using Correct Capitalization and Punctuation," Self Tests 1 and 2.

Clear and Concise Sentences

22

If you are like most writers, your first drafts will have their share of confusing, murky sentences. Sometimes the point of a sentence can be completely lost in a maze of words that seems to lead nowhere. One sure way to improve such sentences is to learn to cut and rewrite and then to cut and rewrite again. Here are some areas to consider as you work toward clear, concise sentences.

REDUNDANCIES

Redundant wording consists of saying the same thing twice (or more than twice), using different words each time. Cut and rewrite redundancies.

redundant   We left for Los Angeles at 10:00 **p.m. at night.**

concise   We left for Los Angeles at 10:00 p.m.

redundant   My **brother is a man** who always pays his bills.

concise   My brother always pays his bills.

| redundant | Good baseball players know the **basic fundamentals** of the game. |
| concise | Good baseball players know the fundamentals of the game. |

NEEDLESS REPETITION

Repeating a word or phrase can weaken a sentence unless you are intentionally trying to emphasize the idea. Cut and rewrite needless repetition.

repetitive	My favorite **picture** is the **picture** of our house in Newport Beach.
concise	My favorite picture is the one of our house in Newport Beach.
repetitive	When my sister called me on the **telephone** at **two o'clock this morning,** I told her that **two o'clock in the morning** was too early **in the morning** for her to call on **the telephone.**
concise	When my sister phoned me at two o'clock this morning, I told her that she should not be calling so early.

ROUNDABOUT PHRASES

Replace phrases that say in four or five words what can be said in one or two.

Roundabout	Concise
at all times	always
at the present time	now
at this point in time	now
on many occasions	often
in this modern day and age	today
because of the fact that	because
due to the fact that	because
for the purpose of	for
until such time as	until
in spite of the fact that	although, even though
make reference to	refer to
be of the opinion that	think, believe
in the event that	if

EXERCISE 22.1

Revise the following sentences to eliminate redundancies, needless repetition, and roundabout phrases.

1. Due to the fact that it is it is raining, at this point in time all games are cancelled and will not be played.

2. In this modern day and age, no one should ever be homeless or not have a place to live.

3. The car that hit the pedestrian was the car weaving in and out of traffic a few seconds before it hit the pedestrian.

4. Please remain seated in your chairs until such time as the plane comes to a complete stop.

5. We ascended up the stairs and continued on until we descended down on the elevator.

6. Randy's new teak desk was very expensive in price, but he needed to buy it for the purpose of his growing business.

7. The death penalty is an unfair penalty because it is applied more often to poor people because poor people do not have the money to hire expensive attorneys to fight the death penalty.

8. I thought in my mind that he must be of the opinion that the earth is flat and not round.

9. At this point in time you know only the basic fundamentals of the game, so don't become overconfident.

10. In my memory I remember what my hometown, where I was born, looked like.

WEAK SUBJECTS AND VERBS

You can improve most writing by treating each sentence as if it told a story. Find the action of the story and make it the verb. Find the actor or "doer" of the action and make it the subject. Watch for the following situations in particular.

NEEDLESS *TO BE* VERBS

Replace *to be* verbs *(am, are, is, was, were, been, being, be)* with verbs that express an action.

weak	She **is** the one who **is** responsible for your damaged car.
improved	She **damaged** your car.
weak	His behavior **was** a demonstration of my point
improved	His behavior **demonstrated** my point.
weak	Sergio and Rene **were** the winners of the $10,000 raffle.
improved	Sergio and Rene **won** the $10,000 raffle.

NOMINALIZATIONS

Nominalizations are nouns formed from verbs. From *realize* we have *realization.* From *argue* we have *argument.* From *criticize* we have *criticism.* Nominalizations can hide both the action of the sentence as well as the performer of the action. When possible, change nominalizations to verb forms to clarify the actor and the action of the sentence.

weak	Mario's **realization** of his **betrayal** by his business partner occurred when he saw the bank statement.
improved	Mario **realized** that his business partner **had betrayed** him when he saw the bank statement.
weak	Shelley's **request** was that we conduct an **examination** of the finances of the city council members.
improved	Shelley **requested** that we **examine** the finances of the city council members.

UNNECESSARY INITIAL *IT* AND *THERE*

Sentences beginning with *it* and *there* often contain needless extra words. When possible, revise such sentences to focus on the actor and the action of the sentence.

wordy	There is a belief held by many people that we should lower taxes.
improved	Many people believe that we should lower taxes.
wordy	It is imperative that we leave in five minutes if we want to arrive on time.
improved	We must leave in five minutes if we want to arrive on time.

UNNECESSARY PASSIVE VOICE

See Chapter 12 for a discussion of active and passive voice. In general, use active voice verbs to emphasize the actor and the action of your sentences.

passive	The car **was driven** two hundred miles by Mr. Ogilvey before he **was found** by the police
active	Mr. Oglivey **drove** the car two hundred miles before the police **found** him.

EXERCISE 22.2

Revise the following sentences to strengthen weak subjects and verbs.

1. The promise of freedom in America has been a great attraction for many immigrants.
2. There were three people standing under the awning.
3. Sometimes lying is necessary in order to provide protection for innocent people.
4. The wish on the part of the child was that she would be given a bicycle by Santa.
5. It is John's loyalty that he gives to me that makes me have a favorable feeling toward him.

6. Because gay marriages are not approved of by John, he is the one who is not willing to talk to you.

7. The admission of the president of the company is that he was a participant in the act of the embezzlement of funds.

8. Music is used by many people as an experience in meditation and relaxation.

9. It is with great regret that we have reached the decision that it is necessary to terminate your employment.

10. Aside from Faulkner's story being an examination of family conflict, there are also considerations of racial conflict added to it.

EXERCISE 22.3

Revise the following sentences to make them clearer and more concise.

1 Each and every one of us in this great country of the United States of America should all pay attention to the air and water and plants and other people and creatures around us. 2 It is a fact the some of these things are being abused and harmed by too many of us. 3 As a result, there are many people in this country who are worried and concerned about a thing called global warming. 4 The layers of air above us that protect us from solar radiation are in the process of becoming thinner because of all the things that come out of our cars and factories and manufacturing places. 5 It is reported by scientists that this thinning causes the polar caps, which are all the ice and snow at the top and bottom of the world, to melt. 6 This melting can be the causative factor in all sorts of weather changes that cause damage and destruction.7 It is former Vice President Al Gore who has been warning us lately, and his words should be listened to by all of us about this problem. 8 But in addition all of us should each also try to do our own part. 9 If we all just drove our vehicles and cars fewer miles, that stuff that comes from our autos, called exhaust, would not thin or harm the atmosphere as much. 10 In conclusion of all this, it is necessary in this modern day and age that we pay attention to and think about how we treat our world and environment.

Exploring ONLINE

The Writer's Response website includes links for more practice in the writing of clear and concise sentences. Go to www.thomsonedu.com/devenglish/mcdonald. Under "Chapter Resources" for Chapter 22, click on "Exploring Online."

ESL Issues

23

If English is your second language, you know the confusion and frustration that can sometimes result when you try to apply the grammar rules and usage patterns of English. Of course, you are not alone. Anyone who has ever tried to learn a second language has encountered similar problems. This chapter reviews some of the more common issues faced by ESL writers.

COUNT AND NONCOUNT NOUNS

1. **Count nouns refer to nouns that exist as separate items that can be counted. They usually have singular and plural forms:** *one bottle, two bottles; one thought, two thoughts: one teacher, two teachers.*

2. **Noncount nouns refer to nouns that cannot be counted and usually do not take plural forms. Here** are some common noncount nouns:

- Food and drink: *meat, bacon, spinach, celery, water, milk, wine*
- Nonfood material: *equipment, furniture, luggage, rain, silver, gasoline*
- Abstractions: *anger, beauty, happiness, honesty, courage*

Note   **Noncount nouns** stay in their singular form. It would be incorrect to say *bacons, furnitures,* or *courages*.

3. **Some nouns can be either count or noncount, depending on whether you use them as specific, countable items or as a substance or general concept.**

NONCOUNT	The *fruit* in the bowl looks moldy.
COUNT	Eat all the *fruits* and vegetables that you want.
NONCOUNT	Time slows as you approach the speed of *light*.
COUNT	The *lights* in the stadium all went out.

ARTICLES WITH COUNT AND NONCOUNT NOUNS

INDEFINITE ARTICLES

1. **The indefinite articles are *a* and *an*. They are used with *singular count nouns* that are *general* or *nonspecific*. Usually, the noun is being introduced for the first time.**

   Yesterday I saw **a dog** chase **a car** down the street.
   An apple fell from the tree and rolled into the pool.

   In these sentences, *dog, car,* and *apple* are general count nouns that could refer to any dog, car, or apple at all, so the articles *a* and *an* are used with them.

2. **Do not use indefinite articles with noncount nouns.**

INCORRECT	He has had a diabetes since he was young.
CORRECT	He has had diabetes since he was young.

DEFINITE ARTICLES

1. **The word *the* is a definite article. It is used with *specific nouns*, both *count* and *noncount*.**
2. **You can usually tell if a noun is specific by its context.** In some cases, other words in a sentence make it clear that the noun refers to a specific thing or things. In other instances, the noun has been mentioned in a previous sentence, so the second reference to it is specific.

   I bought **the dog** that licked my hand.   (This singular count noun refers to a *specific* dog, the one that licked my hand.)

A car and a motorcycle roared down the street. **The car** sounded as if it had no muffler.	(This singular count noun refers to a *specific* car, the one in the previous sentence.)
The courage that he demonstrated impressed me.	(This noncount noun refers to the *specific* courage of one man.)

ARTICLES WITH PROPER NOUNS

1. Use *the* with plural proper nouns (*the United States, the Smiths*).

2. Do not use *the* with most singular proper nouns (*John, San Diego, Germany*).

3. Use *the* with some singular proper nouns, including names of oceans, seas, and rivers (*the Mississippi River, the Atlantic Ocean*), names using *of* (*the Republic of China, the University of Colorado*), and names of large regions, deserts, and peninsulas (*the Mideast, the Sahara Desert, the Iberian Peninsula*).

NO ARTICLES

1. **Articles are generally not used with noncount nouns or plural nouns that are making general statements.**

   Racism and *prejudice* should worry *parents* and *teachers.*

   In this sentence, the noncount nouns *racism* and *prejudice* as well as the plural count nouns *parents* and *teachers* do not use articles because they are general, referring to *any* racism or prejudice and *any* parent or teacher.

2. **Remember that all singular count nouns require an article, whether they are specific or general.**

   SPECIFIC   The *chicken* will look for some seed.

   GENERAL   A *chicken* will look for some seed.

EXERCISE 23.1

In the spaces provided, write the appropriate article (*a, an,* or *the*) whenever one is needed. If no article is needed, leave the space blank.

1. Oscar had never seen _____ penguin before he traveled to _____ Antartica.

2. I smiled at _____ woman who held _____ largest balloon.

3. Whenever we go to _____ football game, my father buys _____ bottle of beer.

4. Emilio has suffered from _____ amnesia ever since his accident on _____ Fourth of July.

5. Last year we took _____ trip to _____ Hawaii.

HELPING VERBS AND MAIN VERBS

1. If a verb consists of one word, it is a main verb (MV).

   MV
   My father **stared** at the waiter.

2. If a verb consists of two or more words, the last word of the verb is the main verb (MV). The earlier words are helping verbs (HV).

   HV MV
   My father **is staring** at the waiter.

HELPING VERBS

1. There are twenty-three helping verbs in English. Nine of them are called *modals*. They are always helping verbs.

Modals	can	will	shall	may
	could	would	should	might
				must

2. The other fourteen sometimes function as helping verbs and sometimes as main verbs.

   Forms of *do: do, does, did*
   Forms of *have: have, has, had*
   Forms of *be: am, is, are, was, were, be, being, been*

MAIN VERBS

1. All main verbs use five forms (except for be, which uses eight).

Base Form	**-S Form**	**Past Tense**	**Past Participle**	**Present Participle**
walk	walks	walked	walked	walking
call	calls	called	called	calling
eat	eats	ate	eaten	eating
ring	rings	rang	rung	ringing

2. **Regular verbs.** A regular verb forms its past tense and past participle by adding –d or –ed to the base form of the verb. In the above list, *call* and *walk* are regular verbs.

3. **Irregular verbs.** An irregular verb does not form its past tense and past participle by adding –d or –ed. Instead, it changes its spelling in a variety of ways. In the above list, *eat* and *ring* are irregular verbs.

COMBINING HELPING VERBS AND MAIN VERBS

When combining helping verbs and main verbs, pay careful attention to the verb forms that you use.

1. **Modal** + **base form.** After one of the nine modals (*can, could, will, would, shall, should, may, might, must*), use the base form of a verb.

   INCORRECT   He **will leaving** soon.

   CORRECT   He **will leave** soon.

2. *Do, does,* or *did* + **base form.** When forms of *do* are used as helping verbs, use the base form after them.

   INCORRECT   **Did** your daughter **asked** you for a present?

   CORRECT   **Did** your daughter **ask** you for a present?

3. *Have, has,* or *had* + **past participle.** Use the past participle form after *have, has,* or *had.* Check a dictionary if you are not sure how to spell the past participle.

   INCORRECT   The monkey **has eating** all of the fruit.

   CORRECT   The monkey **has eaten** all of the fruit.

4. **Forms of** *be* + **present participle.** To show continuous action, use the present participle (the *-ing* form) after a form of *be* (*am, is, are, was, were, be, been*).

   INCORRECT   I **reading** the book.

   CORRECT   I **am reading** the book.

5. **Forms of** *be* + **past participle.** To express passive voice (the subject receives the action rather than performs it), use a form of *be* followed by the past participle form.

   INCORRECT   The football **was threw** by the quarterback.

   CORRECT   The football **was thrown** by the quarterback.

EXERCISE 23.2

Correct any errors in the use of helping verbs and main verbs.

1. After dinner my brother will driving to work.
2. The man who is singing outside has refusing to go away.
3. Did his father walked to the store?
4. Someone from our neighborhood has call the police.
5. Esteban says that he does not wants any help.

ADJECTIVES IN THE CORRECT ORDER

1. **In a series of adjectives, place determiners first.** (Determiners consist of articles, possessives, limiting and quantity words, and numerals.) Examples of determiners: *the old car, Jim's empty wallet, her sad face, this heavy box, some scattered coins, three dead trees.*

2. **If one of the modifiers is usually a noun, place it directly before the word it modifies:** *the boring basketball game, the rusty trash can.*

3. **Evaluative adjectives** (*beautiful, interesting, courageous*) **usually come before descriptive adjectives** (*small, round, red, wooden*): *the <u>beautiful red</u> rose, an <u>interesting wooden</u> cabinet.*

4. **Descriptive adjectives indicating size usually appear before other descriptive adjectives: but after evaluative adjectives:** *my <u>huge</u> leather sofa, a strange <u>little</u> old man.*

 In general, avoid long strings of adjectives. More than two or three adjectives in a row will usually sound awkward to the native English speaker.

EXERCISE 23.3

Arrange the following groups of adjectives in the correct order.

1. (green, my, beautiful) lawn
2. (Thai, local, the) restaurant
3. (television, a, boring) show
4. (old, football, his, red) jacket
5. (favorite, father's, family, my) tradition

EXERCISE 23.4

Correct any errors in the use of articles, helping and main verbs, and adjective order in the following sentences.

1 Visitors who step through front door of Oscar's house are surprising at what they see. 2 On his wooden old coffee table is aquarium full of sawdust and the orange peels. 3 In the corner of the aquarium two miniature rats are play with dog biscuit. 4 Rats are name Vanilla Wafer and Marshmallow. 5 Vanilla Wafer is a black and white fat rat that is very friendly. 6 The Marshmallow is usually hide in the sawdust. 7 Once Marshmallow became very sick because he had eating the spoiled orange. 8 Oscar took him to the veterinarian who had open an office near grocery store on the corner. 9 Luckily, Marshmallow recovered, and he soon was play with Vanilla Wafer again. 10 Many people think that rats are disgusted, but Oscar has always love his happy two rats.

Exploring ONLINE   *The Writer's Response* website includes links for more practice in ESL issues. Go to www.thomsonedu.com/devenglish/mcdonald. Under "Chapter Resources" for Chapter 23, click on "Exploring online."

PART FOUR

Additional Readings for Writing

The reading selections on the following pages present ideas and opinions on a range of topics. The articles in the section entitled "Culture and Country" present the perspectives of writers from a variety of ethnic, racial, and cultural backgrounds. The selections in "Behavior" examine body piercing, the effects of "adolescent autonomy," and the tendency to live life mindlessly. The topics in "Education" discuss the problems of large lecture classes and the grading system. The final four sections—"The Effects of Television," "Flag Burning and Freedom of Speech," "Animal Experimentation," and "Same-Sex Marriage"—present related articles that can be used as multiple sources for synthesis or argument papers. As you read these selections, consider the "Steps in Evaluating a Text" from Chapter 6:

1. Read the text actively.
   a. Determine its intended audience and purpose.
   b. Identify its thesis.
   c. Identify its main points.
2. Determine how well the main points are supported.
   a. Distinguish between facts and opinions.
   b. Distinguish between specific support and generalizations.
   c. Identify statistics, examples, and references to authority.
3. Test the article's points against your own knowledge and experience.
4. Consider any obvious objections that have been ignored.

CULTURE AND COUNTRY

The Middle-Class Black's Burden   LEANITA McCLAIN

Leanita McClain was born in 1952 in a housing project on Chicago's South Side. She attended Chicago State University and Medill School of Journalism at North- western University. After graduate school she worked at the Chicago Tribune. *After suffering years of depression, she committed suicide in 1984. In the following selec- tion, McClain discusses the misconceptions held by both blacks and whites regarding the black middle class.*

I am a member of the black middle class who has had it with   1
being patted on the head by white hands and slapped in the face
by black hands for my success.

Here's a discovery that too many people still find startling: 2
when given equal opportunities at white-collar pencil pushing,
blacks want the same things from life that everyone else wants.
These include the proverbial dream house, two cars, an above-
average school, and a vacation for the kids at Disneyland. We may,
in fact, want these things more than other Americans because
most of us have been denied them so long.

Meanwhile, a considerable number of the folks we left   3
behind in the "old country," commonly called the ghetto, and the
militants we left behind in their antiquated ideology can't berate
middle-class blacks enough for "forgetting where we came from."
We have forsaken the revolution, we are told, we have sold out.
We are Oreos, they say, black on the outside, white within.

The truth is, we have not forgotten; we would not dare. We   4
are simply fighting on different fronts and are no less war weary,
and possibly more heartbroken, for we know the black and white
worlds can meld, that there can be a better world.

It is impossible for me to forget where I came from as long   5
as I am prey to the jive hustler who does not hesitate to exploit my
childhood friendship. I am reminded, too, when I go back to the old
neighborhood in fear—and have my purse snatched—and when I sit
down to a business lunch and have an old classmate wait on my table.
I recall the girl I played dolls with who now rears five children on welfare, the boy from church who is in prison for murder, the pal found
dead of a drug overdose in the alley where we once played tag.

My life abounds in incongruities. Fresh from a vacation in   6
Paris, I may, a week later, be on the milk-run Trailways bus in Deep

South back-country attending the funeral of an ancient uncle whose world stretched only 50 miles and who never learned to read. Sometimes when I wait at the bus stop with my attache case, I meet my aunt getting off the bus with other cleaning ladies on their way to do my neighbors' floors.

But I am not ashamed. Black progress has surpassed our greatest expectations; we never even saw much hope for it, and the achievement has taken us by surprise.

7

In my heart, however, there is no safe distance from the wretched past of my ancestors or the purposeless present of some of my contemporaries; I fear such a fate can reclaim me. I am not comfortably middle class; I am uncomfortably middle class.

8

I have made it, but where? Racism still dogs my people. There are still communities in which crosses are burned on the lawns of black families who have the money and grit to move in.

9

What a hollow victory we have won when my sister, dressed in her designer everything, is driven to the rear door of the luxury high rise in which she lives because the cab driver, noting only her skin color, assumes she is the maid, or nanny, or the cook, but certainly not the lady of any house at this address.

10

I have heard the immigrants' bootstrap tales, the simplistic reproach of "Why can't you people be like us?" I have fulfilled the entry requirements of the American middle class, yet I am left, at times, feeling unwelcome and stereotyped. I have overcome the problems of food, clothing and shelter, but I have not overcome my old nemesis, prejudice. Life is easier, being black is not.

11

I am burdened daily with showing whites that blacks are people. I am, in the old vernacular, a credit to my race. I am my brothers' keeper, and my sisters', though many of them have abandoned me because they think that I have abandoned them.

12

I run a gauntlet between two worlds, and I am cursed and blessed by both. I travel, observe, and take part in both; I can also be used by both. I am a rope in a tug of war. If I am a token in my downtown office, so am I at my cousin's church tea. I assuage white guilt. I disprove black inadequacy and prove to my parents' generation that their patience was indeed a virtue.

13

I have a foot in each world, but I cannot fool myself about either. I can see the transparent deceptions of some whites and the bitter hopelessness of some blacks. I know how tenuous my grip on one way of life is, and how strangling the grip of the other way of life can be.

14

Many whites have lulled themselves into thinking that race   15
relations are just grand because they were the first on their block to
discuss crab grass with the new black family. Yet too few blacks and
whites in this country send their children to school together, entertain each other, or call each other friend. Blacks and whites dining
out together draw stares. Many of my coworkers see no black faces
from the time the train pulls out Friday evening until they meet me
at the coffee machine Monday morning. I remain a novelty.

Some of my "liberal" white acquaintances pat me on the   16
head, hinting that I am a freak, that my success is less a matter of
talent than of luck and affirmative action. I may live among them,
but it is difficult to live with them. How can they be sincere about
respecting me, yet hold my fellows in contempt? And if I am silent
when they attempt to sever me from my own, how can I live with
myself?

Whites won't believe I remain culturally different; blacks   17
won't believe I remain culturally the same.

I need only look in a mirror to know my true allegiance,   18
and I am painfully aware that, even with my off-white trappings, I
am prejudged by my color.

As for the envy of my own people, am I to give up my   19
career, my standard of living, to pacify them and set my conscience
at ease? No. I have worked for these amenities and deserve them,
though I can never enjoy them without feeling guilty.

These comforts do not make me less black, nor oblivious to   20
the woe in which many of my people are drowning. As long as we
are denigrated as a group, no one of us has made it. In as much as
we all suffer for every one left behind, we all gain for every one
who conquers the hurdle.

The Future/El Futuro   RICHARD RODRIGUEZ

Richard Rodriguez is an editor at Pacific News Service and a contributing editor for Harper's Magazine, U.S. News & World Report, *and the Sunday "Opinion" section of the* Los Angeles Times. *He has published numerous articles in* The New York Times, The Wall Street Journal, The American Scholar, Time, Mother Jones, *and* The New Republic, *as well as other publications. He has also written three books:* Brown: The Last Discovery of America; Hunger of Memory; *and* Days of Obligation: An Argument with My Mexican Father, *as well as two BBC documentaries.*

Californians are afraid of the future and cannot imagine   1
themselves in the great world. To prove it, Gov. Pete Wilson last
week published an open letter to President Bill Clinton, urging a
constitutional amendment to deny citizenship to the children of illegal immigrants as well as the repeal of federal mandates requiring health and education services for illegal immigrants.

On the same day that the governor published his letter ("on   2
behalf of the people of California"), I was at a chic Los Angeles hotel.
All day, I saw Mexicans busily working to maintain California's behalf
legendary "quality of life." The common complaint of Californians is
that the immigrants, whether legally or illegally here, are destroying
our quality of life. But there the Mexicans were—hosing down the
tiles by the hotel swimming pool, gardening, everywhere gardening.
The woman who could barely speak English was making beds; at the
Yuppie restaurant, Mexican men impersonated Italian chefs.

Who could accuse Wilson of xenophobia? The governor was,   3
after all, only concerned with those immigrants illegally here. His
presumption was that the illegal immigrants are here only for the
umbrella of welfare services. Remove those benefits and they will
go back to Mexico, the governor reasoned. Here was a presumption in Wilson's letter that betrayed naivete about the desperation
of the Third World poor and their wild ambition for work.

"God, do they work," a friend confides over martinis in   4
Bel-Air. "I've never seen people work like those Mexicans."

What troubles us about Mexican immigrants is that they   5
work too hard. The myth California has advertised to the world is
that here is a place of leisure—the myth of blond beaches and
palm trees.

It is embarrassing to watch the Mexican work, like watching   6
a peasant eat. The Mexican, perhaps most especially the illegal immigrant, reminds us how hard life is; he reminds us that in much
of this world, one must work or die.

Work becomes life. The feel of work, the assurance of a   7
handle to hold, a hope. The peach is torn from the branch, the
knife slits open the fish; the stake is plunged into the earth faster
and faster. Work or die. The Mexican works.

Not only Mexicans are working, of course. There are also   8
Vietnamese, Koreans, Guatemalans, Salvadorans, Chinese. Wilson's
letter to the president was only concerned with Mexicans and
with Mexico, but many Californians probably are made more
uneasy with the Asian migration. If, as the governor believes,

Mexicans are a burden because they are poor, Asians are a threat because they are poised to take over the city. In San Francisco, people say it all the time: The Chinese are taking over the city.

During the Gold Rush, in the mid-19th century, Chinese   9
miners were chased off the fields by other prospectors. Mexicans (many of whom arrived from northern Mexico, bringing with them mining skills) were also chased away. But many generations later, now, the parent in Walnut Creek, a father of three, tells me that Asians are unfair. (His daughter has not been admitted to Berkeley.) "Asians are unfair because they work so hard."

Californians should be thinking of ways to join with Mexico   10
if we are as modern, as advanced, as we like to tell our fellow Americans we are. We would be imagining a global state. Instead, environmentalists are using the North American Free Trade Agreement as a way of keeping Mexico at bay, under our control. And Gov. Wilson urges the president to tie NAFTA to Mexico's policing of its northern border. Clean yourself, we tell Mexico, clean yourself and then we will embrace you.

Sen. Dianne Feinstein wonders if we shouldn't charge a toll   11
for entering California from Mexico. And her fellow liberal in the Senate, Barbara Boxer, wants to enlist the National Guard to protect our border. But, of course, millions of middle-class Californians assume that they can use Mexico whenever and however they want. They go to Mexico for a tan. They go to Mexico to adopt a baby. They retire to Mexico—get a condo in Cabo. They reach into Mexico for an inexpensive gardener or nanny.

Despite ourselves and because of the immigrants, California   12
is becoming a world society—an extraordinary meeting place of Asia and Latin America with white and black America.

Poor New York, thousands of miles away, senses that   13
something is going on in California but hasn't a clue. All summer, New York has been taken by the notion that the California dream is tarnished. *The New Yorker* dispatched Joan Didion from her upper East Side apartment. Regis Philbin confided to his viewers: "It's so sad—all those poor people going to L.A."

CBS News sent several correspondents to Los Angeles a few   14
weeks ago to view the apocalypse. Except for an eccentric Latino who predicted a Latino takeover of the Southland, the entire hour of *48 Hours* was given to white and black opinions. Lots of blond people said they were fed up with California—"it's not what we had in mind."

No correspondent bothered to ask the Guatemalan teen-ager 15
or the Chinese short-order cook why they had come to California.

Dear Regis Philbin: California does not have an immigrant 16
problem. California has a native-born problem.

Gov. Wilson, I think, would have done better addressing a 17
letter to his fellow Californians—rich, middle-class, poor. The governor might well have asked if, as Californians, we assume too
much about our right to leisure and the government's obligation
to our well-being.

Ross Perot may have it half right. Americans are going to 18
have to be harder on themselves. The government is running out
of money for savings-and-loan fat cats, Social Security grandmas
and welfare mothers. But Perot is wrong in thinking that we can
close ourselves from the world.

Neighbors should not live oblivious to one another. Any 19
coyote in Tijuana can tell you that illegal immigration is inevitable
as long as distinctions between rich countries and poor, developed countries and the Third World, are not ameliorated. If we
want fewer illegal Mexican immigrants, we must work with
Mexico, as Mexico must work with Guatemala.

In time, though, California will turn the Mexican and 20
Chinese teen-agers into rock stars and surfers. But I think the immigrants also will change California—their gift to us—reminding
us of what our German and Italian ancestors knew when they
came, hopeful, to the brick tenement blocks of the East Coast.

Life is work. 21

A Match Made in Heaven: Liberal Leftie Chats with a Promise Keeper

SUZANNE PHARR

A longtime activist from the South, Suzanne Pharr has written about injustice and oppression; the relationship of homophobia, sexism, and racism; and strategies for creating a just and caring society. She is the author of Homophobia: A Weapon of Sexism *and* In the Time of the Right: Reflections of Liberation.

In February, as I boarded a plane to Portland, Oregon, I 1
overheard a man say to a woman, "We're almost all Promise
Keepers on this flight. We are returning from an Atlanta meeting
of 43,000 pastors." "Forty-three thousand pastors," I thought.
"That's like 43,000 organizers because they have influence over
their congregations." I entered the plane thinking, "We're sunk."

For the last couple of years I have been watching the growth   2
of the Promise Keepers with fascination and fear. As a Southern
lesbian-feminist and anti-racist worker, I am keenly interested in
any group of white men organizing around issues related to
women and people of color.

As a long-time community organizer, I have to admire the   3
brilliance of the Promise Keepers' organizing strategy. How smart
it is to recognize not only the anger and confusion that men have
about this changing society, but also their desire for connection
and purpose.

How smart to bring them into sports stadiums around the   4
country to sing, touch, do the wave, and bond through physical
and emotional contact they rarely allow themselves.

I believe the Promise Keepers are the ground troops in an   5
authoritarian movement that seeks to merge church and state. It
does not matter that a rightwing agenda is not overt in the form-
ative stages of this movement; when the leaders are ready to
move their men in response to their agenda, they will have thousands disciplined to obey and command.

The plane was full of men dressed in casual clothes, many   6
sporting new Promise Keepers shirts. During the flight, they stood
in the aisles, talking excitedly. The scene reminded me of the 1987
March on Washington, which I attended along with thousands of
lesbians and gay men. For the first time in our lives, we were the
majority in airplanes, subways, buses, restaurants, and the streets.
The experience was exhilarating. The Promise Keepers on the
plane seemed to be having a similar experience, as though they
had found each other for the first time.

After trying to escape through reading, I finally gave up and   7
began chatting with the man next to me, dressed in a blue work
shirt and jeans and reading a Tom Clancy novel. He reminded me
very much of my brothers from rural Georgia. I asked if he was returning from Atlanta. "Yes," he replied. "I've just been to the Promise
Keepers meeting, and I'm returning to my small town in Oregon."

I told him that I was a feminist, a civil-rights worker, and   8
a lesbian, that I have very mixed feelings about the Promise Keepers, and that I wanted him to tell me about them.

He told me that he was pastor at a Baptist church, married,   9
father of a teenage son, and that he would enjoy talking about his
experience with the Promise Keepers. "You are the second homosexual I've ever met," he said, adding with a grin, "I think." With

that introduction, we launched into an hour-and-a-half-long conversation.

The pastor told me that the first thing the Promise Keepers   10
make clear is that men are responsible for all that's wrong with
the family; they are not victims.

I told him that was going a little too far for this feminist—I   11
think women might have some responsibility for the negative side
of the ledger, too.

He said the Promise Keepers were not to dominate their   12
wives but to lead them. When I asked what this meant, he said,
"Man's role is laid out in the Bible—'As God is to man, man is to
the family'—and it is to take charge of his family. This means listening to their needs and wishes, then deciding what is best for them."

I said, "As a feminist, I am deeply concerned about shared   13
decision-making, about equality."

"We share the conversations, but I make the decisions," he   14
said. "My job is to lead."

This talk about leadership made me feel that I was in a time   15
warp in which the women's movement had never occurred. I
thought about the current status of women struggling with families, jobs, and intimate relationships, I thought about stories I have
read that mention how pleased some Promise Keepers' wives are
to have their husbands taking a dominant role in the family. With
some sadness I considered how damning this is of many male–
female relationships: that men are often so absent emotionally
that women would be willing to give up autonomy in order to
gain their husbands' presence.

I suggested the Promise Keepers could make an enormous   16
contribution to women if they added an additional promise to
their credo: that they would not lift their hand against women, and
that they would stop other men from committing violence against
women and children.

The Promise Keepers are against harming women, he said.   17
They want to protect them. But adding an eighth promise would
have to be up to the leadership.

Of everything that happened to this pastor at the meeting,   18
the most life-changing, he said, was racial reconciliation. He said he
had never thought about himself as someone prejudiced or discriminatory, and he came to recognize it in himself: "I'm not an
emotional man, but I cried along with the audience when the men
of color were called to the stage and they could not get there

because they were intercepted by white pastors hugging them, shaking their hands, pounding them on the back."

The pastors were sent home, he said, to work to bring about   19
racial reconciliation in their churches.

Since my conversation with the pastor on the airplane,   20
Ralph Reed has been calling for racial reconciliation in the wake
of the recent rash of black church burnings in the South. At a
meeting with black pastors, Reed admitted that the Christian
Coalition has a history of being on the "wrong side" when it
comes to race. Now it wants to be on the right side, he says.
But why? Calls from the Christian Coalition and the Promise
Keepers for racial reconciliation do not include any effort to end
institutional racism, or to stop coded attacks on "welfare mothers" or immigrants or affirmative action. Rather, moving into
black churches gives the religious right a foothold in the black
community. In this way, the call for racial reconciliation is one of
the most insidious aspects of the Promise Keepers and their al-
lies on the Christian right. Just as the right is hungry for people
of color who are willing to denounce affirmative action and the
civil-rights struggles that have traditionally benefited their communities, the Promise Keepers' recruitment of black church leaders looks like a way to persuade the black community to act
against its own best interests.

I asked the pastor about the Promise Keepers' attitudes   21
toward lesbians and gays.

The pastor said it was not for a Promise Keeper to judge   22
homosexuals ("That is God's job") but that they believe homo-
sexuality is immoral because the Bible says it is.

"This is not judging?" I thought.   23

He said that he was sure there were many of us who were   24
fine people but that we suffered from being identified with our
"fringe" people who marched in those San Francisco parades.

I asked him if Jesus today would not be thought of as   25
gay—an unmarried thirty-three-year-old who spent almost all of
his time with twelve close male friends, one of whom in particular
was "beloved."

He said, "No doubt if Jesus returned today, he might not be   26
accepted in many churches."

We then talked about how few were the references in the   27
Bible to same-sex relationships and how many were the references
to sharing wealth, caring for those who have less, and opening one's

home and heart to others. Why, then, did fundamentalists not have a strong economic agenda for the redistribution of wealth?

It's true, he said. This is a contradiction.   28

In the end, I thought we had communicated honestly with   29
each other and that on some points, we had moved toward one
another in understanding. It seemed to me that a great difference
between us was his belief in the literal truth of the Bible, and my
belief that it is a historical document with great spiritual content. I
told him I thought that almost all of Christendom falls somewhere
between those two positions. He agreed.

I wondered, can people who have very different beliefs and   30
cultural practices live in peace with one another?

My final question to him was: Can you and I live in homes   31
side by side, borrow sugar from one another, and encourage our
children to play together? He said yes.

This conversation led me to think more deeply about the   32
difference between the right's leaders (those engaged in an
organizing strategy that threatens democracy) and its followers
(those searching for solutions to social and economic instability,
whose heartfelt beliefs make them easy targets for manipulation).
Many progressives write off the latter, discarding them as ignorant
or mean.

Our conversation stayed on my mind for weeks afterwards,   33
and I thought of this one Promise Keeper with respect and continued interest. Then one day he phoned me long distance from
his small town, saying he was just calling to keep in touch and to
say what a profound effect our conversation had had on him.

"It eliminated whole areas of ignorance for me," he said.   34

"Me too," I replied.   35

My conversations with this Promise Keeper made me   36
understand that progressive people must rethink their relation to
the American right.

How do we point out the differences between the generals   37
of this army and their recruits?

How do we talk to people who are different from ourselves?   38

How do we hold different beliefs and still live in harmony?   39

Is there any hope for preventing the merger of church and   40
state if we do not hold authentic conversations with those who
believe fervently in the inerrancy of the Bible?

How do we get closer to people's real needs and their values   41
in our organizing for change?

Finally, how do we carry on this conversation and organize   42
as progressives committed to equal rights for everyone—nothing
more, nothing less?

BEHAVIOR

The Modern Primitives   JOHN LEO

A self-proclaimed "social conservative," John Leo is a senior writer and columnist at
U.S. News & World Report. *He is the author of two books, including* How the
Russians Invented Baseball *and* Other Essays of Enlightenment. *His weekly
column appears in over 140 newspapers.*

The days when body piercers could draw stares by wearing   1
multiple earrings and a nose stud are long gone. We are now in the
late baroque phase of self-penetration. Metal rings and bars hang
from eyebrows, noses, nipples, lips, chins, cheeks, navels and (for that
coveted neo-Frankenstein look) from the side of the neck.

"If it sticks out, pierce it" is the motto, and so they do, with   2
special attention to genitals. Some of the same middle-class
folks who decry genital mutilation in Africa are paying to have
needles driven through the scrotum, the labia, the clitoris, or
the head or the shaft of the penis. Many genital piercings have
their own names, such as the ampallang or the Prince Albert.
(Don't ask.)

And, in most cases, the body heals without damage, though   3
some women who have had their nipples pierced report damage
to the breast's milk ducts, and some men who have been Prince
Albert-ed no longer urinate in quite the same way.

What is going on here? Well, the mainstreaming-of-deviancy   4
thesis naturally springs to mind. The piercings of nipples and genitals arose in the homosexual sadomasochistic culture of the West
Coast. The Gauntlet, founded in Los Angeles in 1975 mostly to do
master and slave piercings, now has three shops around the country that are about as controversial as Elizabeth Arden salons.
Rumbling through the biker culture and punk, piercing gradually
shed its outlaw image and was mass marketed to the impression-
able by music videos, rock stars and models.

The nasty, aggressive edge of piercing is still there, but now   5
it is coated in happy talk (it's just body decoration, like any other)

and a New Age-y rationale (we are becoming more centered, reclaiming our bodies in an anti-body culture). Various new pagans, witches and New Agers see piercing as symbolic of unspecified spiritual transformation. One way or another, as Guy Trebay writes in the Village Voice, "You will never find anyone on the piercing scene who thinks of what he's doing as pathological."

The yearning to irritate parents and shock the middle class 6
seems to rank high as a motive for getting punctured repeatedly. Some ask for dramatic piercings to enhance sexual pleasure, to seem daring or fashionable, to express rage, or to forge a group identity. Some think of it as an ordeal that serves as a rite of passage, like ritual suspension of Indian males from hooks in their chests.

Piercing is part of the broader "body modification" 7
movement, which includes tattooing, corsetry, branding and scarring by knife. It's a sign of the times that the more bizarre expressions of this movement keep pushing into the mainstream. The current issue of Spin magazine features a hair-raising photo of a woman carving little rivers of blood into another woman's back. "Piercing is like toothbrushing now," one of the cutters told Spin. "It's why cutting is becoming popular." Slicing someone's back is a violent act. But one of the cutters has a bland justification: People want to be cut "for adornment, or as a test of endurance, or as a sacrifice toward a transformation." Later on we read that "women are reclaiming their bodies from a culture that has commodified starvation and faux sex." One cuttee says: "It creates intimacy. My scars are emotional centers, signs of a life lived."

But most of us achieve intimacy, or at least search for it, 8
without a knife in hand. The truth seems to be that the sado-masochistic instinct is being repositioned to look spiritually high-toned. Many people have found that S&M play "is a way of opening up the body–spirit connection," the high priest of the body modification movement, Fakir Musafar, said in one interview.

Musafar, who has corseted his waist down to 19 inches and 9
mortified his flesh with all kinds of blades, hooks and pins, calls the mostly twentyish people in the body modification movement "the modern primitives." This is another side of the movement: the conscious attempt to repudiate Western norms and values by adopting the marks and rings of primitive cultures. In some cases this is expressed by tusks worn in the nose or by stretching and exaggerating holes in the earlobe or nipple.

Not everyone who pierces a nipple or wears a tongue stud is   10
buying into this, but something like a new primitivism seems to
be emerging in body modification, as in other areas of American
life. It plugs into a wider dissatisfaction with traditional Western ra-
tionality, logic and sexual norms, as well as anger at the impact of
Western technology on the natural environment and anger at the
state of American political and social life.

Two sympathetic analysts say: "Amidst an almost universal   11
feeling of powerlessness to 'change the world,' individuals are
changing what they have power over: their own bodies. . . . By giving visible expression to unknown desires and latent obsessions
welling up from within, individuals can provoke change."

Probably not. Cultural crisis can't really be dealt with by   12
letting loose our personal obsessions and marking up our bodies.
But the rapid spread of this movement is yet another sign that the
crisis is here.

Are You Living Mindlessly?   MICHAEL RYAN

In the following selection from Parade Magazine, *Michael Ryan interviews Ellen Langer, who wrote* Mindfulness *and* The Power of Mindful Learning. *As you read the article, consider how you live your own life. Do you live mindfully or mindlessly?*

Have you ever been mindless?   1

That's not thoughtless, it's mindless—and we all have been.   2
You've been mindless if you've ever "zoned out" and missed a
highway exit; if you've put the cereal in the refrigerator and the
milk in the cupboard; or if you've mumbled "you too" when the
airport cab driver wishes you a good flight—even though you
knew you were catching a plane and he wasn't. Psychologists call
this "automaticity"—putting your brain on autopilot and giving the
usual responses, even if you aren't in the appropriate situation.

"Being mindless means you're not there," said Ellen Langer,   3
a professor of psychology at Harvard who is the author of *Mindfulness* and *The Power of Mindful Learning.* "You're not in the moment and aware of everything going on around you." I had gone
to Cambridge, Massachusetts, to talk with Langer about mindlessness and its opposite, mindfulness, and how switching from one to
the other can enrich our lives.

The penalty for mindlessness—letting ourselves operate   4
without thinking in a situation we think we're familiar with—can be
as minor as missing our highway exit or finding warm milk in the
cupboard. But mindlessness also can lead to failure, frustration—
even tragedy.

Many of us learn to live mindlessly in our earliest school   5
days "Too often, we teach people things like, 'There's a right way
and a wrong way to do everything, regardless of the circumstances,'" Langer explained. "What we should be teaching them is
how to think flexibly, to be mindful of all the different possibilities
of every situation and not close themselves off from information
that could help them."

"I love tennis," Langer continued. "When I was younger, I   6
went to a tennis camp, and they taught me how to hold a racket
when I served. Years later, I was watching the U.S. Open, and I realized that not one of the players held the racket that way." Langer
saw that the world's best players had put thought and energy into
developing a grip and a serve best suited to their individual talents.

"The problem comes in the way we learn," Langer said.   7
"We are rarely taught conditionally: 'This might be a good grip for
you.' Usually, we're taught: 'This is the right grip.'" Being mindful—
using imagination and creativity to learn what works best for
you—is what makes the difference between an average player
and a champ.

Langer served up other examples, like the woman who   8
always cut one end off her holiday roasts before putting them
into the oven. The woman explained that her mother had always
done it that way. The mother, in turn, said it was what her own
mother did. When they approached the matriarch, the old woman
told them that, as a young bride, she had a very small oven and
had been forced to cook her meat in two parts. Mindlessly, the
habit had been passed down for generations, long after the need
for it had disappeared.

"If you ask most people, 'Is there more than one way to look   9
at anything?' they'll say, 'Of course,'" Langer said. "But it's remarkable
that so many go through life with a single-minded lens. It's not that
they wouldn't agree with other perspectives. It just doesn't occur
to them to look."

In one experiment, psychologists provided a group of   10
subjects with simple objects and asked them to explain their use.
The answers were straightforward: a screwdriver turned screws, a

sheet covered a bed, etc. But when they were asked what else the items could be used for, people's creativity burst forth: the sheet could be used as a tent for someone shipwrecked; the screwdriver could be a tent peg, and so on. "When people see that there's more than one way of looking at things, they become mindful," Langer said.

Langer and her colleagues have conducted a wide range of   11
experiments, which she documents in her two books. In one experiment, students were given a reading assignment: Half were told simply to learn the material, while the other half were told to think about what they were reading in ways that made it meaningful to their own lives. When they were tested later, the second group—the ones who thought about what they had read instead of just "learning" it the old-fashioned way—scored far higher.

"The way you cultivate mindfulness," Langer said, "is to   12
realize that information about the world around you is endlessly interesting, and it looks different from different perspectives." But many people operate mindlessly, pursuing routines rather than looking for new details around them. The results can be disastrous.

Investigations of both the Three Mile Island and Chernobyl   13
nuclear accidents found evidence that technicians—numbed into mindlessness by years of routine—had failed to respond in time to changes in instrument readings that would have told them accidents were about to happen. The most widely accepted theory of how Korean Air Lines Flight 007 went astray—it flew into Soviet airspace and was shot down by an air-to-air missile—holds that the pilots entered incorrect coordinates into their compass. Then, literally on autopilot, they ignored cues from the 747's computers to reconsider their course. Like a driver who has traveled the same highway a hundred times, they expected no problems and saw none.

At its worst, mindlessness can help to destroy people's lives,   14
as Langer found in 1974, when she was studying patients and workers in nursing homes. "I argued that we should go around nursing homes making life more complex, not easier," she said. "It's important for people to be in control of their lives, and the way to be in control is to be in the active process of mastering something. It's in the mastering that mindfulness comes in." Langer found that patients who lived in the wards where they were required to take charge of much of their daily routine—dressing themselves or choosing food—had lower mortality rates than

people in comparable health who lived in the wards where attendants and nurses saw to all their needs. Langer also found that
nursing-home workers who were taught to think mindfully about
their work were less likely to quit. "If the workers realize that
much of the burnout they experience is the result of mindless
over-rhythmization, turnover goes down by a third," she reported.

Langer told me that mindlessness is also at the root of   15
prejudice—but she said the way to solve it was with *more* discrimination, not less. "Prejudice comes from the mindless assumption that there are nonoverlapping categories," she explained.
"You're either black or white, Jew or non-Jew. Most people, if they
go far enough into their backgrounds, will find that they are not
purebreds. The mistake we make in dealing with prejudice is trying
to counter it by saying we're all one big human group, we're all
the same."

Langer reasoned that, if we are mindful of each other's   16
individual characteristics—not just race and religion but also
height, weight, talent, even hair color—we will understand that
each human being is unique.

We can be mindful in any situation, Langer said—even when   17
faced with huge challenges. "If all you think about is how you're
likely to fail at a challenge, you probably will," she said. "But if you
ask yourself, 'What are 10 ways I could succeed at this?' your
chances of success are much greater. Just noticing new things
keeps you alive."

Teenagers in Dreamland

ROBERT J. SAMUELSON

Robert J. Samuelson, a contributing editor of Newsweek *since 1984, has written a
column for* The Washington Post *since 1977. His columns are syndicated to about
40 U.S. and 20 foreign papers by The Washington Post Writers Group. In the following selection, he suggests that our schools have been crippled by an increase in
"adolescent autonomy."*

Meet Carlos. He's a senior at American High School in Fremont,   1
California. He's also a central character in a recent public television documentary on U.S. education. Carlos is a big fellow with a
crew cut and a friendly manner. We see him driving his pickup
truck, strolling with a girlfriend and playing in a football game. "I
don't want to graduate," he says at one point. "It's fun. I like it."

If you want to worry about our economic future, worry   2
about Carlos and all those like him. It is the problem of adolescence in America. Our teen-agers live in a dreamland. It's a
curious and disorienting mixture of adult freedoms and childlike
expectations. Hey, why work? Average high school students
do less than an hour of daily homework. Naturally, they're not
acquiring the skills they will need for their well-being and the
nation's.

Don't mistake me: I'm not blaming today's teen-agers. They   3
are simply the latest heirs of an adolescent subculture—we have
all been part of it—that's been evolving for decades. American
children are becoming more and more independent at an earlier
and earlier age. By 17, two-fifths of Americans have their own car
or truck. About 60 percent have their own telephones and televi-
sions. Adult authority wanes, and teen-age power rises. It's precisely this development that has crippled our schools.

Consider the research of sociologist James Coleman of the   4
University of Chicago. He found that students from similar economic and social backgrounds consistently do better at Catholic
high schools than at public high schools. The immediate explanation is simple: students at Catholic schools take more rigorous
courses in math, English and history, and they do nearly 50 percent more homework. But why do Catholic schools make these
demands when public schools don't?

The difference, Coleman concluded, lies with parents: 5
"Parents [of public school students] do not exercise as much authority over their high-school-aged students as they once did," he
recently told a conference at the Manhattan Institute. Since the
1960s, public schools have become less demanding—in discipline,
required course work and homework—because they can't en-
force stiffer demands. By contrast, parents of parochial school students impose more control. "The schools therefore [are] able to
operate under a different set of ground rules," Coleman said.

There are obviously many good public schools and hard-   6
working students. But the basic trends are well-established and
have been altered only slightly by recent "reforms." Change comes
slowly, because stricter academic standards collide with adolescent
reality. In the TV documentary, Tony—a pal of Carlos—is asked
why he doesn't take tougher math courses to prepare him as a
computer technician, which is what he wants to be. "It's my senior
year," he says, "and I think I'm going to relax."

Adolescent autonomy continues to increase. "Teens have   7
changed so dramatically in the past decade that more advertisers
. . . are targeting 'adults' as 15-plus or 13-plus rather than the typical 18-plus," notes Teenage Research Unlimited, a market research
firm. It estimates that the average 16-to-17-year-old has nearly
$60 a week in spending money from jobs and allowances. By jun-
ior year, more than 40 percent of high school students have jobs.

These demanding school-time jobs are held predominantly   8
by middle-class students. Popular wisdom asserts that early work
promotes responsibility, but the actual effect may be harmful. In a
powerful book (*When Teenagers Work*), psychologists Ellen Greenberger of the University of California (Irvine) and Laurence Steinberg of Temple University show that jobs hurt academic
performance and do not provide needed family income. Rather,
they simply establish teen-agers as independent consumers better
able to satisfy their own wants. Jobs often encourage drug use.

Our style of adolescence reflects prosperity and our values.   9
We can afford it. In the 19th century, children worked to ensure
family survival; the same is true today in many developing countries. Our culture stresses freedom, individuality and choice. Everyone has "rights." Authority is to be questioned. Self-expression is
encouraged. These attitudes take root early. My 4-year-old daughter recently announced her philosophy of life: "I should be able to
do anything I want to do."

Parental guilt also plays a role. The American premise is   10
that the young ought to be able to enjoy their youth. Schools
shouldn't spoil it, as if an hour and a half of daily homework (well
above the average) would mean misery for teen-agers. Finally, more
divorce and more families with two wage-earners mean that teen-
agers are increasingly left to themselves. They often assume some
family responsibilities—shopping or caring for younger children. Many
teen-agers feel harried and confused, because the conflicts among all
these roles (student, worker, child and adult) are overwhelming.

Americans, young and old, delude themselves about the   11
results of these changes. A recent study of 13-year-olds in six
countries placed Americans last in mathematics and Koreans first.
But when students were asked whether they were "good at
mathematics," 68 percent of the Americans said yes (the highest)
compared with only 23 percent of the Koreans (the lowest).

This was no quirk. Psychologist Harold Stevenson of the   12
University of Michigan, who has studied American and Asian

students for years, finds the same relationship. Americans score lower in achievement but, along with their parents, are more satisfied with their performance. "If children believe they are already doing well—and their parents agree with them—what is the purpose of studying harder?" he writes.

Good question. No one should be surprised that U.S.   13
businesses complain about workers with poor skills, or that a high school diploma no longer guarantees a well-paying job. More school spending or new educational "theories" won't magically give students knowledge or skills. It takes work. Our style of adolescence is something of a national curse. Americans are growing up faster, but they may not be growing up better.

EDUCATION

A Proposal to Abolish Grading   PAUL GOODMAN

Paul Goodman (1911–1972) wrote poetry, plays, and fiction, but he is best know for his many books and articles of social criticism in the 1960s. His critiques of schooling and society provided many in the 1960s and early 1970s with a more critical appreciation of education and its possibilities. The following selection is from his book Compulsory Miseducation.

Let half a dozen of the prestigious universities—Chicago,   1
Stanford, the Ivy League—abolish grading, and use testing only and entirely for pedagogic purposes as teachers see fit.

Anyone who knows the frantic temper of the present   2
schools will understand the transvaluation of values that would be effected by this modest innovation. For most of the students, the competitive grade has come to be the essence. The naive teacher points to the beauty of the subject and the ingenuity of the research; the shrewd student asks if he is responsible for that on the final exam.

Let me at once dispose of an objection whose unanimity is   3
quite fascinating. I think that the great majority of professors agree that grading hinders teaching and creates a bad spirit, going as far as cheating and plagiarizing. I have before me the collection of essays *Examining in Harvard College,* and this is the consensus. It is uniformly asserted, however, that the grading is inevitable; for how else will the graduate schools, the foundations, the corporations

know whom to accept, reward, hire? How will the talent scouts know whom to tap?

By testing the applicants, of course, according to the specific task requirements of the inducting institution, just as applicants for the Civil Service or for licenses in medicine, law, and architecture are tested. Why should Harvard professors do the testing *for* corporations and graduate schools?   4

The objection is ludicrous. Dean Whitla, of the Harvard Office of Tests, points out that the scholastic aptitude and achievement tests used for *admission* to Harvard are a super-excellent index for all-around Harvard performance, better than high-school grades or particular Harvard course grades. Presumably, these college entrance tests are tailored for what Harvard and similar institutions want. By the same logic, would not an employer do far better to apply his own job aptitude test rather than to rely on the vagaries of Harvard section men? Indeed, I doubt that many employers bother to look at such grades; they are more likely to be interested merely in the fact of a Harvard diploma, whatever that connotes to them. The grades have most of their weight with the graduate schools—here, as elsewhere, the system runs mainly for its own sake.   5

It is really necessary to remind our academics of the ancient history of examination. In the medieval university, the whole point of the grueling trial of the candidate was whether or not to accept him as a peer. His disputation and lecture for the Master's was just that, a master-piece to enter the guild. It was not to make comparative evaluations. It was not to weed out and select for an extramural licensor or employer. It was certainly not to pit one young fellow against another in an ugly competition. My philosophic impression is that the medievals thought they knew what a good job of work was and that we are competitive because we do not know. But the more status is achieved by largely irrelevant competitive evaluation, the less will we ever know.   6

(Of course, our American examinations never did have this purely guild orientation, just as our faculties have rarely had absolute autonomy; the examining was to satisfy Overseers, Elders, distant Regents—and they as paternal superiors have always doted on giving grades, rather than accepting peers. But I submit that this setup itself makes it impossible for the student to *become* a master, to *have* grown up, and to commence on his own. He will always   7 be making A or B for some overseer. And in the present atmosphere, he will always be climbing on his friend's neck.)

Perhaps the chief objectors to abolishing grading would be   8
the students and their parents. The parents should be simply disregarded; their anxiety has done enough damage already. For the students, it seems to me that a primary duty of the university is to deprive them of their props, their dependence on extrinsic valuation and motivation, and to force them to confront the difficult enterprise itself and finally lose themselves in it.

A miserable effect of grading is to nullify the various uses of   9
testing. Testing, for both student and teacher, is a means of structuring, and also of finding out what is blank or wrong and what has been assimilated and can be taken for granted. Review—including high-pressure review—is a means of bringing together the fragments, so that there are flashes of synoptic insight.

There are several good reasons for testing, and kinds of test.   10
But if the aim is to discover weakness, what is the point of downgrading and punishing it, and thereby inviting the student to conceal his weakness, by faking and bulling, if not cheating? The natural conclusion of synthesis is the insight itself, not a grade for having had it. For the important purpose of placement, if one can establish in the student the belief that one is testing *not* to grade and make invidious comparisons but for his own advantage, the student should normally seek his own level, where he is challenged and yet capable, rather than trying to get by. If the student dares to accept himself as he is, a teacher's grade is a crude instrument compared with a student's self-awareness. But it is rare in our universities that students are encouraged to notice objectively their vast confusion. Unlike Socrates, our teachers rely on power drives rather than shame and ingenuous idealism.

Many students are lazy, so teachers try to goad or threaten   11
them by grading. In the long run this must do more harm than good. Laziness is a character defense. It may be a way of avoiding learning, in order to protect the conceit that one is already perfect (deeper, the despair that one *never* can be). It may be a way of avoiding just the risk of failing and being downgraded. Sometimes it is a way of politely saying, "I won't." But since it is the authoritarian grown-up demands that have created such attitudes in the first place, why repeat the trauma? There comes a time when we must treat people as adult, laziness and all. It is one thing

courageously to fire a do-nothing out of your class; it is quite another thing to evaluate him with a lordly F.

Most important of all, it is often obvious that balking in doing the work, especially among bright young people who get to great universities, means exactly what it says: The work does not suit me, not this subject, or not at this time, or not in this school, or not in school altogether. The student might not be bookish; he might be school-tired; perhaps his development ought now to take another direction. Yet unfortunately, if such a student is intelligent and is not sure of himself, he *can* be bullied into passing, and this obscures everything. My hunch is that I am describing a common situation. What a grim waste of young life and teacherly effort! Such a student will retain nothing of what he has "passed" in. Sometimes he must get mononucleosis to tell his story and be believed. 12

And ironically, the converse is also probably commonly true. A student flunks, and is mechanically weeded out, who is really ready and eager to learn in a scholastic setting, but has not quite caught on. A good teacher can recognize the situation, but the computer wreaks its will. 13

College Lectures: Is Anybody Listening?   DAVID DANIELS

Almost every student has sat through at least one interminably long lecture delivered in an unchanging, impersonal voice. As you read the following selection, consider what David Daniels has to say regarding the drawbacks of and reasons for the "lecture system" of education.

A former teacher of mine, Robert A. Fowkes of New York University, likes to tell the story of a class he took in Old Welsh while studying in Germany during the 1930s. On the first day the professor strode up to the podium, shuffled his notes, coughed, and began, "*Guten Tag, Meine Damen und Herren*" ("Good day, ladies and gentlemen"). Fowkes glanced around uneasily. He was the only student in the course. 1

Toward the middle of the semester, Fowkes fell ill and missed a class. When he returned, the professor nodded vaguely and, to Fowkes's astonishment, began to deliver not the next lecture in the sequence but the one after. Had he, in fact, lectured to an empty hall in the absence of his solitary student? Fowkes thought it perfectly possible. 2

Today, American colleges and universities (originally   3
modeled on German ones) are under strong attack from many
quarters. Teachers, it is charged, are not doing a good job of teaching, and students are not doing a good job of learning. American
businesses and industries suffer from unenterprising, uncreative
executives educated not to think for themselves but to mouth
outdated truisms the rest of the world has long discarded. College graduates lack both basic skills and general culture. Studies
are conducted and reports are issued on the status of higher education, but any changes that result either are largely cosmetic or
make a bad situation worse.

One aspect of American education too seldom challenged is   4
the lecture system. Professors continue to lecture and students to
take notes much as they did in the thirteenth century, when
books were so scarce and expensive that few students could own
them. The time is long overdue for us to abandon the lecture system and turn to methods that really work.

To understand the inadequacy of the present system, it is   5
enough to follow a single imaginary first-year student—let's call
her Mary—through a term of lectures on, say, introductory psychology (although any other subject would do as well). She arrives
on the first day and looks around the huge lecture hall, taken a little aback to see how large the class is. Once the hundred or
more students enrolled in the course discover that the professor
never takes attendance (how can he?—calling the role would take
far too much time), the class shrinks to a less imposing size.

Some days Mary sits in the front row, from where she can   6
watch the professor read from a stack of yellowed notes that
seem nearly as old as he is. She is bored by the lectures, and so
are most of the other students, to judge by the way they are nodding off or doodling in their notebooks. Gradually she realizes the
professor is as bored as his audience. At the end of each lecture
he asks, "Are there any questions?" in a tone of voice that makes
it plain he would much rather there weren't. He needn't worry—
the students are as relieved as he is that the class is over.

Mary knows very well she should read an assignment before   7
every lecture. However, as the professor gives no quizzes and asks
no questions, she soon realizes she needn't prepare. At the end of
the term she catches up by skimming her notes and memorizing a
list of facts and dates. After the final exam, she promptly forgets
much of what she has memorized. Some of her fellow students,

disappointed at the impersonality of it all, drop out of college al-together. Others, like Mary, stick it out, grow resigned to the system and await better days when, as juniors and seniors, they will attend smaller classes and at last get the kind of personal attention real learning requires.

I admit this picture is overdrawn—most universities supplement lecture courses with discussion groups, usually led by graduate students, and some classes, such as first-year English, are always relatively small. Nevertheless, far too many courses rely principally or entirely on lectures, an arrangement much loved by faculty and administrators but scarcely designed to benefit the students. 8

One problem with lectures is that listening intelligently is hard work. Reading the same material in a textbook is a more efficient way to learn because students can proceed as slowly as they need to until the subject matter becomes clear to them. Even simply paying attention is very difficult: people can listen at a rate of four hundred to six hundred words a minute, while the most impassioned professor talks at scarcely a third of that speed. This time lag between speech and comprehension leads to day-dreaming. Many students believe years of watching television have sabotaged their attention span, but their real problem is that listening attentively is much harder than they think. 9

Worse still, attending lectures is passive learning, at least for inexperienced listeners. Active learning, in which students write essays or perform experiments and then have their work evaluated by an instructor, is far more beneficial for those who have not yet fully learned how to learn. While it's true that techniques of active listening, such as trying to anticipate the speaker's next point or taking notes selectively, can enhance the value of a lecture, few students possess such skills at the beginning of their college careers. More commonly, students try to write everything down and even bring tape recorders to class in a clumsy effort to capture every word. 10

Students need to question their professors and to have their ideas taken seriously. Only then will they develop the analytical skills required to think intelligently and creatively. Most students learn best by engaging in frequent and even heated debate, not by scribbling down a professor's often unsatisfactory summary of complicated issues. They need small discussion classes that demand the common labors of teacher and students rather than classes in which one person, however learned, propounds his or her own ideas. 11

The lecture system ultimately harms professors as well. It   12
reduces feedback to a minimum, so that the lecturer can neither
judge how well students understand the material nor benefit from
their questions or comments. Questions that require the speaker
to clarify obscure points and comments that challenge sloppily
constructed arguments are indispensable to scholarship. Without
them, the liveliest mind can atrophy. Undergraduates may not be
able to make telling contributions very often, but lecturing insu-
lates a professor even from the beginner's naive question that
could have triggered a fruitful line of thought.

If lectures make so little sense, why have they been allowed   13
to continue? Administrators love them, of course. They can cram
far more students into a lecture hall than into a discussion class,
and for many administrators that is almost the end of the story.
But the truth is that faculty members, and even students, conspire
with them to keep the lecture system alive and well. Lectures are
easier on everyone than debates. Professors can pretend to teach
by lecturing just as students can pretend to learn by attending lectures, with no one the wiser, including the participants. Moreover,
if lectures afford some students an opportunity to sit back and let
the professor run the show, they offer some professors an irresistible forum for showing off. In a classroom where everyone
contributes, students are less able to hide and professors less
tempted to engage in intellectual exhibitionism.

Smaller classes in which students are required to involve   14
themselves in discussion put an end to students' passivity. Students
become actively involved when forced to question their own
ideas as well as their instructor's. Their listening skills improve dramatically in the excitement of intellectual give and take with their
instructors and fellow students. Such interchanges help professors
do their job better because they allow them to discover who
knows what—before final exams, not after. When exams are given
in this type of course, they can require analysis and synthesis from
the students, not empty memorization. Classes like this require
energy, imagination, and commitment from professors, all of which
can be exhausting. But they compel students to share responsibility for their own intellectual growth.

Lectures will never entirely disappear from the university   15
scene both because they seem to be economically necessary and
because they spring from a long tradition in a setting that rightly
values tradition for its own sake. But the lectures too frequently

come at the wrong end of the students' educational careers—
during the first two years, when they most need close, even individual, instruction. If lecture classes were restricted to junior and
senior undergraduates and to graduate students, who are less in
need of scholarly nurturing and more able to prepare work on
their own, they would be far less destructive of students' interests
and enthusiasm than the present system. After all, students must
learn to listen before they can listen to learn.

THE EFFECTS OF TELEVISION

The Meaning of TV   WILLIAM HENRY III

At the time of his death in June 1994, William A. Henry III was a registered
Democrat, a card-carrying member of the ACLU, and a senior writer for Time *and*
a two-time winner of the Pulitzer Prize. He claimed that his book In Defense of
Elitism *is actually a defense of common sense: "the simple fact that some people are*
better than others—smarter, harder working, more learned, more productive,
harder to replace."

We tend to talk about television as though it has always been   1
there, as though it provides the same experience for everyone, as
though it were a single, living organism. In conversation almost
everyone speaks of "television" doing this or that, intending this or
that. A moment's thought is enough to recall that "television" is
made up of a score and more broadcast and cable networks,
some 1,300 local stations and countless production companies.
The medium is collaborative; there are few if any *auteurs*. Yet TV is
so potent a presence that it seems to have a mind, and personality, of its own.

If TV has changed over time, we take it mostly as a   2
reflection of how we who view it have changed, and in a sense
that is right. While TV may not sense our moods and respond to
them like a friend or family member, the people who administer,
advertise on and program television all devote themselves to research that tracks each zig and zag of national mood. Their goal is
to keep television exactly in step with mainstream taste, so that in
most homes it will resemble a family member or a congenial
neighbor. If television really were a personality, it would qualify as
almost everyone's closest friend.

The average American watches TV about four hours a day;   3
the average household has the set on for seven hours in all. Even
people who say they "don't watch much television" turn out to be
forgetting to count news, or sports, or Mister Rogers with the
toddlers, or old movies, or vintage reruns, or something or other
that they somehow consider to be not mere TV. Just why do people in all walks of life feel such guilt about watching TV, or assert
such superiority in pretending that they do not? Because, despite
their affection for TV, they think watching it is too passive, an inert
substitute for exercise or reading, or conversation—or study.

The reality is that TV can provide plenty of learning, and   4
not merely on *Sunrise Semester*. For every schoolchild whose
reading problems might be blamed on an excess of TV, there is
probably another who learned the alphabet from *Sesame Street*
and began see-and-say reading with the on-screen words of commercials. High school students may have trouble spotting South
America on a map, but through TV they have grasped some basic
truths about the planet. Wherever they live, they were shaken last
summer by images of beaches closed to bathers because the
sands were strewn with toxic hospital waste. Among television's
diehard critics, the print journalists, it is an open secret that the
most important source of news flow during any election night or
political crisis is the television set, around which editors and reporters cluster to stay abreast and to test their news judgment.
And the same scholars and opinion-makers who profess to view
television with disdain are nearly always avid to appear on it—fully
expecting that their friends will see them. Most of the nation's
elite seem to live by at least the latter half of Gore Vidal's reported dictum, "There are two things in life one must never refuse. One is sex, and the other is television."

Perhaps TV's deepest power is not the change it works on   5
sports or commerce or any other branch of reality, but the way
its innocuous-looking entertainment reaches deep into the national mind. TV has the ability to generate, or regenerate, national
mythology. The great characters of television embody human
truths as profound as the great characters in Moliere or Ibsen,
and for vastly bigger audiences. The viewership for even one modestly successful airing of a prime-time series would fill every theater on Broadway, eight performances a week, for a couple of
years. These characters linger in memory because they epitomize
what the nation feels about itself. They teach behavior and values.

They enter the language. Say the name Falstaff, and some minority of the population will know that you mean a vainglorious coward; say Ralph Kramden, and everyone will know what you mean. The Mary Richards character created by Mary Tyler Moore summed up their own lives for a whole generation of thirtysomething single women who could have any careers they wanted, but often at the expense of satisfaction at home. This is not new with television. The great civilizing effect of all literature is that it takes people's vision beyond the immediate, the clan and the tribe. It enables them to make the philosophical leap that Jean-Paul Sartre described as "seeing the other as another self." Television simply does this more effectively, more touchingly, than any kind of art that went before. Unlike the stage and movies, the episodic TV series does not end in catharsis. The characters come back week after week, evolving at the slow pace of ordinary life, exposing themselves more fully than most relatives or friends. Other literature provides occasional experiences. Television becomes an ongoing part of life and for some susceptible people is only barely distinguishable from real life itself.

6   It is hard to imagine a world without television, harder still to imagine what the world of the last half century would have been without those first flickering images from NBC and all that followed. We might have fewer terrorists, because there would be no worldwide pulpit for their propaganda. We might have a less violent society, because the typical child would not have been exposed to tens of thousands of actual and simulated violent crimes on news and entertainment by the time he or she reached adulthood. We might have a society in which people still felt respect for established institutions and their leaders, instead of one in which TV-bred skepticism had lowered the approval rating for Congress, business executives and even judges to between 20 and 40 percent. We might have a healthier society, one in which children played outside instead of watching the box hour after hour, one in which meals cooked from scratch at home had not been outdistanced by snacks and fast food loaded with sugar, salt and fat, all encingly advertised. We might have a more restrained, less libertine world, one in which virginity and marriage were still revered while premarital pregnancy and divorce were still treated with distaste rather than sympathy. All of these effects have been attributed, sometimes convincingly, to TV. But we might also have a less alert world, one in which citizens were not so widely informed about the economy, about medical

matters, about foreign military adventures that run the risk of war. We might have a less concerned world, one in which starvation in Ethiopia could never inspire Live Aid, one in which the homeless of Manhattan or Chicago might remain unseen by the rest of the nation. We might have a lonelier, more isolated world in which the old lived without much entertainment, without much company, without the sense of involvement in life that can be conferred even by watching Donahue.

Only one thing can be said for certain. Whatever world we   7
would have, it would be different in many and unimaginable ways from this one. Like fire and the wheel and the alphabet, television has changed the world that humans live in. And more, perhaps, than any invention or discovery before it, television has changed the definition of what it means to be human.

TV Can't Educate   PAUL ROBINSON

In the following selection, first published in The New Republic, *Paul Robinson argues that television and movies by their very nature cannot educate because they "are structurally unsuited to that process." Consider your own experiences with television—educational or otherwise—as you read this article.*

On July 20 [1978] NBC aired a documentary on life in Marin   1
County, a bedroom community just across the Golden Gate
Bridge from San Francisco. The program was called "I Want It All
Now" and its single theme was the predominance of narcissism in
Marin. The program's host, Edwin Newman, introduced viewers, in
his studied casual manner, to a variety of "consciousness-raising"
groups ensconced in Marin and insinuated that this new narcissis-
tic manner was leading to a breakdown not only of the family
(a divorce rate of 75 percent was mentioned three times) but
also of traditional civic virtue. The following day the *San Francisco
Chronicle* carried a long front-page article on the outraged reaction of Marin's respectable citizenry to what it considered a
grossly distorted portrait of itself. Several residents argued, per-
suasively, that Marin was in fact a highly political suburb—that it
had been a hot spot of the anti-Vietnam war movement, and that
only last year it had responded dramatically to the water crisis in
California, cutting back on water use much more than was required by law. Television journalism appeared to be up to its old
tricks: producers saw what they wanted to see, and they were not

about to pass up the chance to show a woman being massaged by two nude men and chirping about how delightful it was to "re-ceive" without having to "give."

I was reminded, however, improbably, of an experience in Berlin, where I had spent the previous six months teaching. The Germans are all exercised over a recent movie about Adolf Hitler (*Hitler: Eine Karriere*), which is based on a biography by the jour-nalist Joachim Fest. The charge leveled against the film is that it glorifies Hitler (though it uses nothing but documentary footage; there are no actors), and it has been linked with a supposed resurgence of Nazism in Germany, particularly among the young. I saw only parts of the film and therefore can't speak to the jus-tice of the charge. What I wish to report on—and what the Marin program brought to mind—is a lecture I attended by a young German historian from the Free University of Berlin, in which he took issue with the film because it had failed to treat Hitler's rela-tions with the German industrialists, who were crucial in support-ing the Nazi Party before it came to power and apparently benefited from its success.

The critics of the Newman program and my young scholar friend in Berlin were guilty of the same error. They both bought the assumption that television and movies can be a source of knowledge, that one can "learn" from them. By knowledge and learning I obviously don't mean an assortment of facts. Rather I have in mind the analytic process that locates pieces of informa-tion within a larger context of argument and meaning. Movies and TV are structurally unsuited to that process.

There is no great mystery here. It's a simple matter of time. Learning requires one kind of time, visual media are bound to an-other. In learning one must be able to freeze the absorption of fact or proposition at any moment in order to make mental com-parisons, to test the fact or proposition against known facts and propositions, to measure it against the formal rules of logic and evidence—in short, to carry on a mental debate. Television is a matter of seconds, minutes and hours, it moves inexorably for-ward, and thus even with the best will in the world (a utopian as-sumption), it can never teach. In the last analysis there is only one way to learn: by reading. That's how you'll find out about Hitler's relations with the German industrialists, if you can find out about them at all. Such a complex, many-layered phenomenon simply cannot be reduced to a scene (which would presumably meet my scholar-friend's objection) in which Hitler has dinner with Baron Krupp. Similarly, you will not find out about life in Marin county from an hour-long TV program or, for that matter, from a 24-hour-long one. What are the control populations? What statistical methods are being used? Is there more consciousness raising going on in Marin than in Cambridge? What is the correlation between narcissism and income level, educational background, employment, religious affiliation, marital status, sexual inclination and so forth? If these questions have answers, they are to be found in the books and articles of sociologists, not on TV.

I am prepared, indeed eager, to follow my argument to its   5
logical conclusion: the worst thing on TV is educational TV (and not just on educational stations). By comparison, the gratuitous violence of most commercial shows is a mere peccadillo. Educational TV corrupts the very notion of education and renders its victims uneducable. I hear grown-ups launching conversations with, "Mike Wallace says that . . ." as if Mike Wallace actually knew something. Viewers hold forth authoritatively about South Africa, or DNA, or black holes, or whatever because they have watched a segment about them on *60 Minutes* or some such program. Complete ignorance really would be preferable, because ignorance at least preserves a mental space that might someday be filled with real knowledge, or some approximation of it.

There is a new form of slumming popular among intellectuals: 6
watching "bad" (i.e., commercial) TV and even writing books about it (as Dan Wakefield has about the afternoon soap opera *All My Children*). I would like to think that the motive behind this development is revulsion against the intellectual pretensions of "good" TV. But, as often happens with academics, the reaction has been dressed up in phony theoretical garb. *All My Children*, we're supposed to believe, is the great American novel, heir to the tradition of Dickens and Trollope. Of course it's nothing of the sort. But it is very good entertainment. And that is precisely what TV is prepared to do: to entertain, to divert, above all to amuse. It is superbly amusing, ironically, for the same reason that it can't educate: it is tied to the clock, which has enormous comic potential. It is not accidental that one speaks of a comedian's "timing." Jack Benny would not be funny in print. He must wait just the right length of time after the robber threatens, "Your money or your life," before responding. (Imagine the situation in a novel: "The robber said, 'Your money or your life.' Jack took ten

seconds trying to make up his mind.'') Nor can you do a double-take in print, only on the screen. The brilliant manipulation of time made *The Honeymooners* so funny: Art Carney squandered it while Jackie Gleason, whose clock ran at double-time, burned. Audrey Meadows stood immobile, producing a magnificently sustained and silent obbligato to Gleason's frantic buffo patter.

Television, then, is superbly fit to amuse. And amusement is   7
not to be despised. At the very least it provides an escape from the world and from ourselves. It is pleasurable (by definition, one might say), and it gives us a sense of union with humanity, if only in its foibles. Herbert Marcuse might even contend that it keeps alive the image of an unrepressed existence. Television can provide all this. But it can't educate.

Movies are faced with the same dilemma. The desire to   8
educate accounts, I believe, for the increasingly deliberate pace of movies. It is as if the director were trying to provide room within his time-bound narrative for the kind of reflection associated with analysis. This was brought home to me recently when, during the same week, I saw the movie *Julia* in the theater and *Jezebel* on TV. The latter, made in 1938, portrays the tragedy of a strong-willed southern girl who refuses to conform to the rules of antebellum New Orleans society. The most striking difference between the two movies is their pace. *Jezebel* moves along swiftly (there is probably more dialogue in the first 15 minutes than in all of *Julia*), treats its theme with appropriate superficiality and entertains effortlessly. *Julia,* on the other hand, is lugubrious and obviously beyond its depth. It succeeds only with the character of Julia herself, who, like Jezebel, is powerful, beautiful, virtuous and unburdened by intellectual or psychological complexity. By way of contrast, the narrative figure, Lilli, tries vainly to deal with issues that movies can't manage: the difficulty of writing, a relationship with an older man who is at once lover, mentor, and patient-to-be, the tension between literary success and political commitment. All of these are wonderfully captured in Lillian Hellman's memoir, but not even two fine actors like Jane Fonda and Jason Robards can bring such uncinematic matters to life on the screen. The "issue" of the memoir—despite all those meaningful silences—inevitably eluded the movie.

Let us, then, not ask more of movies and TV than they can   9
deliver. In fact, let us discourage them from trying to "educate" us.

Shadows on the Wall
DONNA WOOLFOLK CROSS

Donna Woolfolk Cross is the author of two books on language, Word Abuse *and* Mediaspeak *(from which this selection is taken), and coauthor of* Speaking of Words. *In 1996 she published* Pope Joan, *a novel about a ninth-century woman who supposedly disguised herself as a man and for two years sat on the papal throne.*

> I see no virtue in having a public that cannot distinguish fact from fantasy. When you start thinking fantasy is reality you have a serious problem. People can be stampeded into all kinds of fanaticism, folly and warfare.
>
> —Isaac Asimov

> Why, sometimes I've believed as many as six impossible things before breakfast.
>
> —Queen to Alice in Lewis Carroll's Through the Looking Glass

In Book Four of *The Republic,* Plato tells a story about four   1
prisoners who since birth have been chained inside a cave, totally isolated from the world outside. They face a wall on which shadows flicker, cast by the light of the fire. The flickering shadows are the only reality they know. Finally, one of the prisoners is released and permitted to leave the cave. Once outside, he realizes that the shadows he has watched for so long are only pale, distorted reflections of a much brighter, better world. He returns to tell the others about the world outside the cave. They listen in disbelief, then in anger, for what he says contradicts all they have known. Unable to accept the truth, they cast him out as a heretic.

Today, our picture of the world is formed in great part from   2
television's flickering shadows. Sometimes that picture is a fairly accurate reflection of the real world; sometimes it is not. But either way, we accept it as real and we act upon it as if it were reality itself. "And that's the way it is," Walter Cronkite assured us every evening for over nineteen years, and most of us did not doubt it.

A generation of Americans has grown up so dependent on   3
television that its images appear as real to them as life itself. On a recent trip to a widely advertised amusement park, my husband, daughter, and I rode a "white-water" raft through manufactured "rapids." As we spun and screamed and got thoroughly soaked, I noticed that the two young boys who shared our raft appeared rather glum. When the ride ended, I heard one remark to the other, "It's more fun on television."

As an experiment, Jerzy Kosinski gathered a group of children,   4
aged seven to ten years, into a room to show them some televised film. Before the show began, he announced, "Those who
want to stay inside and watch the films are free to remain in the
classroom, but there's something fascinating happening in the cor-
ridor, and those who want to see it are free to leave the room."
Kosinski describes what happened next:

No more than 10 percent of the children left. I repeated,   5
"You know, what's outside is really fantastic. You have never seen it be-
fore. Why don't you just step out and take a look?"
And they always said, "No, no, no, we prefer to stay here   6
and watch the film." I'd say, "But you don't know what's outside."
"Well, what is it?" they'd ask. "You have to go find out." And they'd say,
"Why don't we just sit here and see the film first?" . . . They were al-
ready too corrupted to take a chance on the outside.

In another experiment, Kosinski brought a group of children   7
into a room with two giant video screens mounted on the side
walls. He stood in the front of the room and began to tell them a
story. Suddenly, as part of a prearranged plan, a man entered and
pretended to attack Kosinski, yelling at him and hitting him. The
entire episode was shown on the two video screens as it happened. The children did not respond, but merely watched the
episode unfold on the video screens. They rarely glanced at the
two men struggling in the front of the room. Later, in an interview
with Kosinski, they explained that the video screens captured the
event much more satisfactorily, providing close-ups of the participants, their expressions, and such details as the attacker's hand on
Kosinski's face.

Some children can become so preoccupied with television   8
that they are oblivious to the real world around them. UPI filed a
report on a burglar who broke into a home and killed the father
of three children, aged nine, eleven, and twelve. The crime went
unnoticed until ten hours later, when police entered the apartment after being called by neighbors and found the three children
watching television just a few feet away from the bloody corpse
of their father.

Shortly after this report was released, the University of   9
Nebraska conducted a national survey in which children were
asked which they would keep if they had to choose—their fathers
or their television sets. *Over half* chose the television sets!

Evidence of this confusion between reality and illusion 10
grows daily. Trial lawyers, for example, complain that juries have become conditioned to the formulas of televised courtroom dramas.

Former Bronx District Attorney Mario Merola says, "All they 11
want is drama, suspense—a confession. Never in all my years as a
prosecutor have I seen someone cry from the witness stand, 'I did
it! I did it—I confess!' But that's what happens on prime-time TV—
and that's what the jurors think the court system is all about." He
adds, "Such misconceptions make the work of a district attorney's
office much harder than it needs to be." Robert Daley describes
one actual courtroom scene in which the defendant was sub-
jected to harsh and unrelenting cross-examination: "I watched the
jury," he says. "It seemed to me that I had seen this scene before,
and indeed I had dozens of times—on television. On television
the murderer always cracks eventually and says something like 'I
can't take it any more.' He suddenly breaks down blubbering and
admits his guilt. But this defendant did not break down, he did not
admit his guilt. He did not blubber. It seemed to me I could see
the jury conclude before my eyes: ergo, he cannot be guilty—and
indeed the trial ended in a hung jury. . . . Later I lay in bed in the
dark and brooded about the trial. . . . If [television courtroom dra-
mas] had never existed, would the jury have found the defendant
guilty even though he did not crack?" . . .

Don't Touch that Dial   MADELINE DREXLER

*In the following selection, Madeline Drexler reports on the research of Daniel
Anderson, a psychologist at the University of Massachusetts at Amherst, who suggests that television does not affect a child's ability to think and learn. Anderson
claims that, although television has a major "social" impact on children, it has little "cognitive" impact.*

Television acts as a narcotic on children—mesmerizing them, 1
stunting their ability to think, and displacing such wholesome activities as book reading and family discussions. Right?

Wrong, says researcher Daniel Anderson, a psychologist at 2
the University of Massachusetts at Amherst. Anderson doesn't
have any particular affection for *Garfield and Friends*, MTV clips, or
Gilligan's Island reruns. But he does believe it's important to distinguish television's impact on children from influences of the family

and the wider culture. We tend to blame TV, he says, for problems it doesn't really cause. In the process, we overlook our own roles in shaping children's minds.

One conventional belief about television is that it impairs a child's ability to think and to interpret the world. But Anderson's own research and reviews of the scientific literature discredit this assumption. While watching TV, children do not merely absorb words and images. Instead, they muse upon the meaning of what they see, its plausibility, and its implications for the future— whether they've tuned in to a news report of a natural disaster or an action show. Because television relies on such cinematic techniques as montage and crosscutting, children learn early how to draw inferences about the passage of time, character psychology, and implied events. Even preschoolers comprehend more than just the information supplied on the tube.

Another contention about television is that it displaces reading as a form of entertainment. But according to Anderson, the amount of time spent watching television is not related to reading ability. For one thing, TV doesn't take the place of reading for most children; it takes the place of similar sorts of recreation, such as going to the movies, reading comic books, listening to the radio, and playing sports. Variables such as socioeconomic status and parents' educational background exert a far stronger influence on a child's reading. "Far and away," Anderson says, "the best predictor of reading ability, and of how much a child reads, is how much a parent reads."

Conventional wisdom has it that heavy television-watching lowers IQ scores and hinders school performance. Since the 1960s, SAT scores have dropped, along with state and national assessments of educational achievement. But here, too, Anderson notes that no studies have linked prolonged television exposure in childhood to lower IQ later on. In fact, research suggests that it's the other way around. Early IQ predicts how much TV an older child will watch. "If you're smart young, you'll watch less TV when you're older," Anderson says. Conversely, in the same self-selecting process, people of lower IQ tend to be lifelong television devotees.

When parents watch TV with their young children, explaining new words and ideas to them, the children comprehend far more than they would if they were watching alone. This is due partly to the fact that when kids expect that TV will require thought, they spend more time thinking. What's ironic is that most parents use an educational program as an opportunity to park their kids in front of the set and do something in another room. "Even for parents who are generally wary of television," Anderson says, "*Sesame Street* is considered a show where it's perfectly okay to leave a child alone." The program was actually intended to be viewed by parents and children together, he says.

Because our attitudes inform TV viewing, Anderson applauds   7
the nascent trend of offering high school courses that teach students how to "decode" television. In these classes, students learn to analyze the persuasive techniques of commercials, compare the reality of crime to its dramatic portrayal, inquire into the economics of broadcasting, and understand the mechanics of TV production. Such courses, Anderson contends, teach the kind of critical thinking central to the purpose of education. "Kids can be taught as much about television as about text or computers," he says.

If anything, Anderson's views underscore the fact that   8
television cannot be disparaged in isolation from larger forces. For years researchers have attempted to show that television is inherently dangerous to children, hypnotizing them with its movement and color, cutting their attention span with its fast-paced, disconnected images, curbing intellectual development, and taking the place of loftier pastimes.

By showing that television promotes none of these effects,   9
Anderson intends to shift the discussion to the real issue: content. That, of course, is a thornier discussion. How should our society judge the violence of primetime shows? The sexism of MTV? The materialism of commercials? "I feel television is almost surely having a major social impact on the kids, as opposed to a cognitive impact," Anderson says.

In this context, he offers some advice to parents: First,   10
"Parents should think of their kids as actively absorbing everything on television. They are not just passively mesmerized—in one eye and out the other. Some things on TV are probably good for children to watch, like educational TV, and some things are bad."

Second, "If you think your kid is spending lots of time   11
watching television, think about what alternatives there are, from the child's point of view." Does a youngster have too much free time? Are there books, toys, games, or playmates around? "A lot of the time, kids watch TV as a default activity: There's nothing else to do."

Finally, "If a child persists in watching too much television,   12
the question is why. It's rare that TV shows are themselves so entertaining." More often than not, the motive is escapism. A teenager may be uncomfortable with his or her peers; a child may
want to retreat from a home torn by marital strife; there may be
problems at school.

For children, as for adults, television can be a source of   13
enlightenment or a descent into mindlessness—depending mostly
on the choices of lucre-driven executives. But as viewers, we can't
ignore what we ourselves bring to the medium.

FLAG BURNING AND FREEDOM OF SPEECH

The American Flag: A Symbol We Should Protect   PAUL GREENBERG

*Pulitzer Prize–winning Paul Greenberg is the editor of the editorial pages of the
Arkansas Democrat-Gazette. A thoughtful essayist who can also be a devastating
critic, Greenberg describes himself as an "ideologically unreliable conservative." A
frequent critic of Bill Clinton when the former president was governor of Arkansas,
Greenberg coined the phrase, "Slick Willie."*

The flag amendment is back. And well on its way to becoming   1
the 28th Amendment to the Constitution of the United States.
What's this? It was supposed to be dead a couple of years ago,
remember?

But now the House of Representatives has voted in favor of   2
a simple declaration that, once upon a common-sense time,
would scarcely have attracted notice, let alone controversy: "The
Congress and the States shall have the power to prohibit the
physical desecration of the flag of the United States." The vote
was 312 to 120, easily more than the two-thirds' vote (280) required to propose a constitutional amendment. The prospect for
Senate approval is good, and the states are primed to ratify.

But didn't our intelligentsia explain to us yokels again and   3
again that burning the flag of the United States isn't an action, but
speech, and therefore a constitutionally protected right? That's
what the Supreme Court decided, too, if only in one of its confused and confusing 5-to-4 splits.

But the people don't seem to have caught on. They still   4
insist that burning the flag is burning the flag, not making a speech.

Stubborn lot, the people. Powerful thing, public opinion. Congress certainly seems to be reflecting it.

It isn't the *idea* of desecrating the flag that the American   5
people propose to ban. Any street-corner orator who takes a notion to should be able to stand on a soapbox and bad-mouth the American flag all day long—and apple pie and motherhood, too, if that's the way the speaker feels. It's a free country.

It's actually burning Old Glory, it's defacing the Stars and   6
Stripes, it's the physical desecration of the flag of the United States that ought to be against the law. And the people of the United States just can't seem to be talked out of that notion—or orated out of it, or lectured out of it, or condescended and patronized out of it.

Maybe it's because the people can't shut their eyes to homely   7
truths as easily as our Advanced Thinkers. How many legs does a dog have, Abraham Lincoln once asked, if you call its tail a leg? And he answered: still four. Calling a tail a leg doesn't make it one. Not even a symbolic leg. The people have this stubborn notion that calling something a constitutional right doesn't make it one, despite the best our theorists and pettifoggers can do.

The people keep being told that their flag is just a symbol.   8

Just a symbol.   9

"We live by symbols," said a justice of the United States   10
Supreme Court (Felix Frankfurter) when the standards for appointees, whether liberals or conservatives or neither, were considerably higher. And if a nation lives by its symbols, it also dies with them.

To turn aside when the American flag is defaced, with all   11
that the flag means—yes, all that it *symbolizes*—is to ask too much of Americans.

There are symbols and there are Symbols. There are some   12
so rooted in history and custom, and in the heroic imagination of a nation, that they transcend the merely symbolic; they become presences.

Many of us may not have the words to express it (which is   13
why nations wave flags instead of computer printouts), but we know it's right to protect the flag—by law. To do nothing when that flag, that presence, is desecrated is not simply to let the violent bear it away; it is to join the mob, to aid and abet it by our silence, our permission, our unnatural law. It is to become one more accessory to the general coarsening of society, to the desensitizing of America, to the death of the symbolic.

No, this is not an argument over who loves the flag more. Patriots can disagree; American ones almost have an obligation to. This Republic was not conceived as some kind of factory for manufacture of robots. And those on the other side of this issue have every right to resent it if somebody wants to turn this disagreement over law and the role of the symbolic in American life into some kind of loyalty test. No one political persuasion has a monopoly on the American flag. May it long wave over every kind of political rally. 14

But this also isn't a fight over who loves the Bill of Rights more. And those of us who favor a simple constitutional amendment to protect the flag have every reason to resent it when others try to monopolize the Bill of Rights, or confuse it with the Supreme Court's confused reading of the First Amendment where the flag is concerned. 15

Burning the flag is no more speech than vandalizing a cemetery, or scrawling slogans on a church or synagogue, or spray-painting a national monument—all of which are *acts* properly forbidden by the laws of a civilized country. Not to mention public decency. 16

Even if no flag were ever burned, or no cemetery or church ever defaced, laws against such acts would be proper, and should be constitutional. Because the law is a great teacher, and one thing it needs to teach a less-and-less-civil society is a little respect. 17

The great Italian—what? historian? philosopher? moralist? philosopher of history? proto-anthropologist?—Giambattista Vico spoke of a barbarism of the intellect that confuses concept with reality (speech with action?) and so loses touch with the *sensus communis,* the common-sense values of language and custom in which nations are rooted. Today's strange arguments from our best-and-brightest against protecting the national emblem are not symptomatic of any kind of treason-of-the-intellectuals, but of a different malady: an isolating intellectualism cut off from a sense of reverence, and so from the historical memory and heroic imagination that determines the fate of any nation. 18

Flag Burning and The First Amendment   CHARLES LEVENDOSKY

Charles Levendosky is editorial page editor of the Casper, Wyoming, Star-Tribune. *A poet and journalist, he speaks nationwide about the necessity and power of a free press and on the need to safeguard our freedom to read, learn, and speak without government intervention.*

Click on Internet's Flag Burning Page, and you can flick a virtual Bic and burn a virtual American flag. Is that desecration? 1

Members of the House of Representatives, in a stampede to show us just how super patriotic they are, overwhelmingly passed a proposed amendment to the Constitution which would allow Congress and the states "to prohibit the physical desecration of the flag of the United States." 2

As they rushed to vote, their heels stomped all over the core meaning of the First Amendment. Reason couldn't head them off. Argument couldn't. Not even the Constitution can halt a herd of congressmen when they want to prove to voters they are patriotic. 3

If the Senate doesn't stop this proposed amendment, free speech will have another exception carved out. One that impacts political speech. 4

The First Amendment is clear and decisive: "Congress shall make no law ... abridging the freedom of speech ..." But once again Congress is mucking about with our liberties. 5

Some say that flag burning isn't speech. Then why are these folks so upset about the flag being burned? Obviously, the act does communicate something. It expresses a profound disagreement with the policies of the federal government. 6

The "not speech" ploy is an attempt to persuade us that the proposed amendment would not limit the First Amendment. 7

Of course, there is symbolic speech. 8

And some acts are eloquent speech. 9

The U.S. Supreme Court recognized that more than 60 years ago when it ruled that raising a red flag to show support for worker unity was protected speech. And again 25 years ago, when the high court protected the right of students to wear black armbands to protest our role in Vietnam. 10

Even silent sit-ins to protest racial segregation were recognized as symbolic speech and thus protected by the court. 11

Burning the flag is the act of someone who has little or no political power. 12

It is an act of someone who desperately wants to communicate a disagreement with U.S. policy. It shocks us into paying attention to those who could not otherwise command the 13 interest of the media. It presents a grandstand forum in order to express political dissent. Our dissidents are then heard.

This is a profound First Amendment issue for the powerless.   14

It is easy for those in the power structure to ignore this side   15
of the issue. A member of Congress can call a news conference whenever he or she wishes. The media will be there. The little guy, the working class stiff, commands no such attention.

The flag proposal is another piece of elitism parading in the   16
guise of patriotism.

Nothing in our Constitution could be more significant than   17
protecting the right of the ordinary citizen to express his or her disagreement with the government—so that the dissent will be heard. This is a profound First Amendment issue for our nation.

Political speech must have the broadest protection—even to   18
include burning the American flag—for us to be able to contend that We the People govern ourselves.

We protect waving the flag or displaying it as a statement of   19
political assent. The First Amendment means that we must protect burning the flag as a counter-statement, a statement of political dissent. That is the essence of freedom of speech.

What your congressmen aren't telling you is that, if they   20
wished—even if the amendment is ratified—they could burn the American flag on the floor of either house of Congress during congressional debate and not be taken to court for it.

Read Article I, sec. 6 of the U.S. Constitution: they cannot   21
be held legally accountable for any speech while in debate on the floor of Congress.

So, We the People, who by inalienable right should have the   22
most expansive reading of the First Amendment, will have a narrower one, while our political servants have the greater. Seems backward, doesn't it?

That's because this amendment is flagrantly, deeply un-American. 23

And where will this erosion of liberty stop? Will a few   24
ministers begin a movement to stop people from burning the cross—after all, can't the cross be considered a more important symbol than the flag?

What does physical desecration of the flag mean?   25
Does it mean you can be arrested if you wear a bikini with a representation of the flag on it? The U.S. Code defines the American flag as "any substance" that shows the colors, stars and stripes, and could be considered a clear representation.

Will the flag be desecrated if you sit down while wearing your flag pants?   26

Will a frosting flag on a Fourth of July cake be desecrated if you eat the cake?   27

Is burning a virtual flag in the cyberspace of Internet desecration?   28

Confused? That's because we are dealing with a symbolism. Symbolism has few boundaries in the real world. But liberty is tangible in our daily lives.   29

Our Congress seems willing to protect the symbol of our liberties—at the expense of those liberties. Our representatives have sworn to protect the Constitution, yet in this proposal they violate the very essence of it.   30

Clearly, our stampeding congressmen have charged off the edge—just to prove they are patriotic. What sad irony.   31

May Americans Do Battle to Save Our Flag   ROBERT DOLE

Robert Dole served in Congress as the Senate majority leader and was the 1996 Republican presidential candidate. He is a veteran of World War II and now serves as chairman of the World War II Memorial Campaign. In the following selection he explains why he favors an amendment to protect the American flag.

On Dec. 7, 1941, exactly 54 years ago today, more than 2,300 brave Americans lost their lives during the attack on Pearl Harbor. As a testament to their great sacrifice, some of the dead are permanently entombed in the Arizona, one of the ships sunk during the morning raid.   1

As World War II raged on, thousands of other brave American soldiers followed their country's flag into battle. The great sacrifices made by our fighting men and women during this war and in subsequent conflicts—Korea, Vietnam, the Persian Gulf, Somalia—reflect the courage, the strength of character and the resilience of the American people.   2

Our flag is a unique and beloved symbol of these qualities. It also represents our principles and ideals as a nation. There is no other symbol that so captures the American spirit and experience. The flag, representing Americans of every race, creed and social background, is the one symbol that brings to life the phrase "e *pluribus unum*"—out of many, one.   3

Indeed, one of our most enduring national images is the   4
famous picture of the Marines raising Old Glory at the top of Iwo
Jima's Mount Suribachi. Nearly 6,000 Americans gave their lives
during their deadly ascent up that hill.

Yet, today, the act of burning the American flag is   5
constitutionally protected. In its misguided Texas vs. Johnson
decision, the Supreme Court effectively overturned 48 state
statutes and a federal law proscribing flag desecration. Most of
these statutes had been on the books for decades, without any
threat to our freedom, but five of the nine justices of the
Supreme Court somehow concluded in 1989 that flag burning
should be wrapped around the First Amendment's free-speech
guarantee. Although the First Amendment does not protect obscenity or "fighting words" or yelling "fire" in a crowded theater,
the court concluded that the act of desecrating our nation's symbol deserved such protection.

Like most Americans, I strongly disagree with the Johnson   6
decision. That's why I have joined with the Citizens' Flag Alliance, the
American Legion, and 113 other civic and patriotic organizations in
supporting a constitutional amendment that would overturn this
decision and restore to the American people the power to protect
our flag.

We must remember that the Framers of the Constitution in   7
tentionally made the amendment process a difficult one, requiring
the assent of two-thirds of each house of Congress and three-
fourths of the state legislatures before an amendment's ratifica-
tion. These sensible hurdles were designed to protect the
Constitution from frivolous changes. But once an amendment has
been ratified, clearing the hurdles built into the amendment
process itself, the American people have spoken.

The flag, of course, belongs to all of us—not just to veterans,   8
not just to native-born Americans, but also to those whom we
welcome to our shores as immigrants.

Stephan Ross is one of these immigrants. In 1940, at the age   9
of nine, the Nazis seized Ross from his home in Krasnik, Poland.
For five years, he was held in 10 different Nazi death camps, and
barely survived.

The U.S. Army eventually liberated Ross from the Dachau   10
death camp. As Ross headed to Munich for medical care, an
American tank commander jumped off his vehicle to lend his
help to Ross and to the other victims of Nazi brutality. As Ross

recounts: "He gave me his own food. He touched my withered body with his hands and heart. His love instilled in me a will to live, and I fell at his feet and shed my first tears in five years."

The American soldier then gave Ross what he thought was a   11
handkerchief, but he soon realized, "it was a small American flag, the first I had ever seen. It became my flag of redemption and freedom."

Even today, Stephan Ross still keeps that same cherished flag: 12

"It represents the hope, freedom and life that the American   13
soldiers returned to me when they found me, nursed me to health, and restored my faith in mankind."

Ross now works as a psychologist in Boston.   14

"Even now, 50 years later," Ross says, "I am overcome with   15
tears and gratitude whenever I see our glorious American flag, because I know what it represents not only to me, but to millions around the world.... Protest if you wish. Speak loudly, even curse our country and our flag, but please, in the name of all those who died for our freedoms, don't physically harm what is so sacred to me and to countless others."

Stephan Ross is right: We must protect that which is sacred   16
to us as citizens of this great country. Amid the rich diversity that is America, we must cherish the principles and ideals that bind us together as one people, one nation, and for which thousands of Americans have given their lives. As the unique symbol of these principles and ideals, the flag must receive the constitutional protection it so richly deserves.

Flag-Burning Ban: Protecting What It Symbolizes or the Symbol?

JEFFREY P. KAPLAN

Jeffrey Kaplan is a professor of linguistics at San Diego State University. In the following selection, which appeared in the San Diego Union-Tribune, *he uses his background in linguistics to argue that burning a flag is a form of political speech and should be protected by the First Amendment.*

Should we amend the Constitution to let Congress ban flag   1
desecration? Despite its defeat Tuesday in the Senate, the proposed amendment won't go away, its supporters vow, and polls indicate that up to 80 percent of Americans find such an amendment desirable. But the better term may be "seductive."

The word "speech" in the First Amendment covers speech, writing, sign language, Morse code, auction gestures, etc.—any way we encode meanings in language. More importantly, the Supreme Court has applied the free speech guarantee through the years not just to language, but to conduct: picketing, sitting-in, contributing money to political candidates, displaying a red banner as a symbol of opposition to government, wearing a military uniform in a manner calculated to discredit the military, wearing a black armband to protest the Vietnam War, civil rights boycotts of merchants and displaying a U.S. flag with a peace symbol attached.   2

What unites all these forms of conduct is that they function as communication. In fact, what the First Amendment really guarantees is freedom of communication, according to Loyola law professor (and linguist) Peter Tiersma in a 1993 article in the *Wisconsin Law Review*.   3

Is flag-burning communication? What is communication? First, it involves meaning. While sometimes a communicative act naturally resembles its meaning—as in pointing and beckoning— most human communication involves symbols, to which meaning attaches "conventionally." The word "road" means road, despite the fact that the sequence of sounds represented by "r," "oa," and "d" don't resemble a road at all.   4

In the same arbitrary way, a swastika represents Nazism, a black armband symbolizes mourning the dead, and a peace symbol means opposition to war. Meaningless vocalizations like "Gleeg!" aren't communicative; and conduct that doesn't encode a meaning—sleeping, eating a doughnut—generally isn't communicative either.   5

Flag-burning is meaningful. Ceremonial book- and effigy-burnings indicate that burning can carry the meaning of harsh condemnation. This meaning arises partly naturally: Burning is an effective way to destroy something we hate.   6

The meaning is partly conventional: Burning is just one of many ways to show strong revulsion (others: averting eyes, making illegal, smashing); and burning does not always operate as a symbol for condemnation (as when we burn trash). The symbolic function of burning arises only in ritual contexts.   7

Second, communication requires an audience. Talking to oneself isn't really communicative. The flag-burning addressed by the proposed amendment is effective, from the flag burner's perspective, only when carried out before an audience.   8

Third, to be communication, an instance of language must be intended by the speaker or actor to have a meaning. The monkey at the typewriter who fortuitously produces the text of "Hamlet" does not intend the words to have meaning, though they do. There is no communication because there is no intent.   9

Intentional meaningfulness is necessary also for communicative, nonverbal conduct. Placing lights in Boston's Old North Church any night but April 18, 1775, would probably not have manifested an intent to convey meaning, but that night, placing them there did, and Paul Revere understood the intended meaning.   10

Political flag-burners intend their act to have meaning, since the point is not to reduce fabric to ashes, but to dramatically express hatred toward what the flag symbolizes.   11

Actually, for communication, the essential intent is, subtly, more than just intending that words or acts have meaning. The speaker or actor must intend the audience to recognize, in the words or action, the intention to communicate.   12

Awaiting service in a tavern, you might clear your throat in order to get noticed. That's not communication. But if you clear your throat in an exaggerated way, it is; you intend to get the bartender to recognize not only that you seek attention but also that you are making a noise in order to signal that.   13

Flag-burners similarly intend to communicate by having their audience recognize the intention embodied in their act, and they fail if no one recognizes what they are doing. Imagine their personal frustration if an observer compliments them for disposing of a soiled flag.   14

Flag-burning is communication. Because it is so striking a form of communication, with such offensive content, many Americans want to empower the state to ban it.   15

But since its content is quintessentially political, it receives First Amendment protection, even though—and partly because—it is so offensive. The proposed amendment could trump the First Amendment, but only at the cost of gutting its fundamental protection of free political expression.   16

The flag itself is a symbol. The words of the Pledge of Allegiance "with liberty and justice for all" suggest that it symbolizes, beyond the nation, ideals of liberty, including, presumably, First Amendment liberties.   17

Those who would change the Constitution to permit   18
Congress to ban flag-burning must face two questions: Which is
more important to defend, the symbol, or what it symbolizes? Is it
rational to seek to shield the former at the cost of damaging the
latter?

ANIMAL EXPERIMENTATION

The Trials of Animals   CLEVELAND AMORY

*Self-described curmudgeon and author of several best-selling books, Cleveland
Amory devoted his life to promoting animal rights. He founded The Fund for Animals in 1967 and served without pay as its president until his death in 1998. From
1980 to 1998, Amory was senior contributing editor of* Parade *magazine.*

Ask an experimenter about the animals in his laboratory. Nine   1
times out of ten he will tell you that they are well cared for and
that he abides by the Animal Welfare Act passed by Congress in
1966.

What he will not say is that both he and his colleagues   2
fought the act and the amendments to it every step of the way;
that, under the act, his laboratory is inspected at most (if at all)
once a year; that when his animals are under experimentation, the
act doesn't apply. Nor will he say that many laboratories ignore the
act's most important amendment, passed in 1986, which mandates
that at least one member of the public vote on the laboratory's
animal-care committee.

Your experimenter is not a scofflaw. Having been for so long   3
sole judge and jury of what he does, he believes that he is above
the law. A prime example is that of the monkeys in Silver Spring,
Maryland.

The monkeys were used in experiments in which, first,   4
nerves in their limbs were removed and then stimuli—including
electrical shocks and flames—were applied to see if they could
still use their appendages.

Dr. Edward Taub, who ran the laboratory, was eventually   5
tried and found guilty, not of cruelty to animals but of maintaining
a filthy lab. Maryland is one of many states that exempts federally
funded experiments from cruelty charges.

Dr. Taub is today a free man. His monkeys, however, are   6
not. They are still in a laboratory under the jurisdiction of the National Institutes of Health, which first funded these cruel experiments. Three hundred members of Congress have asked the NIH
to release the monkeys; the NIH says it does not want them; two
animal sanctuaries have offered to take them. Why can't they live
what remains of their lives receiving the first evidence of human
kindness they have ever known?

In the overcrowded field of cat experimentation, researchers   7
at Louisiana State University, under an eight-year, $2 million De-
partment of Defense contract, put cats in vises, remove part of
their skulls, and then shoot them in the head.

More than two hundred doctors and Senator Daniel Inouye,   8
chairman of the Defense Appropriations Subcommittee, have
protested this cruelty. The experimenters say that their purpose is
to find a way to return brain-wounded solders to active duty.

"Basic training for an Army infantryman costs $9,000,"   9
one experimenter argues. "If our research allows only 170 additional men to return to active duty . . . it will have paid for itself."
But Dr. Donald Doll of Truman Veterans Hospital in Columbia,
Missouri, said of these experiments: "I can find nothing which supports applying any of this data to humans."

At the University of Oregon, under a seventeen-year, $1.5   10
million grant, psychologists surgically rotated the eyes of kittens, im-
planting electrodes in their brains, and forced them to jump onto a
block in a pan of water to test their equilibrium. These experiments resulted in a famous laboratory break-in in 1986, and the
subsequent trial and conviction of one of the animals' liberators.

During the trial, experimenters were unable to cite a single   11
case in which their research had benefited humans. Additional testimony revealed instances of cats being inadequately anesthetized
while having their eye muscles cut, untrained and unlicensed personnel performing the surgery, and mother cats suffering such
stress that they ate their babies.

The trial judge, Edwin Allen, stated that the testimony was   12
"disturbing to me as a citizen of this state and as a graduate of
the University of Oregon. It would be highly appropriate to have
these facilities opened to the public."

It would, indeed—and a judge is just what is needed. A   13
judge first, then a jury. The experimenters have been both long
enough.

A Scientist: I Am the Enemy

RON KLINE

*Dr. Ron Kline is a pediatric hematologist oncologist in Las Vegas, where he is a part-
ner in the Comprehensive Cancer Centers of Nevada, Pediatrics Division. In the following selection, he argues that the more radical members of the animal rights'
movement "will bring about a tragedy that will cost many lives" if they are allowed
to have their way.*

I am the enemy! One of those vilified, inhumane physician-
scientists involved in animal research. How strange, for I have never
thought of myself as an evil person. I became a pediatrician because of my love for children and my desire to keep them healthy.
During medical school and residency, however, I saw many children
die of leukemia, prematurity and traumatic injury—circumstances
against which medicine has made tremendous progress, but still
has far to go. More important, I also saw children, alive and healthy,
thanks to advances in medical science such as infant respirators,
potent antibiotics, new surgical techniques and the entire field of
organ transplantation. My desire to tip the scales in favor of the
healthy, happy children drew me to medical research.

My accusers claim that I inflict torture on animals for the
sole purpose of career advancement. My experiments supposedly
have no relevance to medicine and are easily replaced by computer simulation. Meanwhile, an apathetic public barely watches,
convinced that the issue has no significance, and publicity-conscious
politicians increasingly give way to the demands of the activists.

We in medical research have also been unconscionably
apathetic. We have allowed the most extreme animal-rights pro-
testers to seize the initiative and frame the issue as one of "animal
fraud." We have been complacent in our belief that a knowledge-
able public would sense the importance of animal research to the
public health. Perhaps we have been mistaken in not responding
to the emotional tone of the argument created by those sad
posters of animals by waving equally sad posters of children dying
of leukemia or cystic fibrosis.

Much is made of the pain inflicted on these animals in the
name of medical science. The animal-rights activists contend that
this is evidence of our malevolent and sadistic nature. A more reasonable argument, however, can be advanced in our defense. Life is
often cruel, both to animals and human beings. Teenagers get
thrown from the back of a pickup truck and suffer severe head

injuries. Toddlers, barely able to walk, find themselves at the bottom of a swimming pool while a parent checks the mail. Physicians hoping to alleviate the pain and suffering these tragedies cause have but three choices: create an animal model of the injury or disease and use that model to understand the process and test new therapies; experiment on human beings—some experiments will succeed, most will fail—or finally, leave medical knowledge static, hoping that accidental discoveries will lead us to the advances.

Some animal-rights activists would suggest a fourth choice,   5 claiming that computer models can simulate animal experiments, thus making the actual experiments unnecessary. Computers can simulate, reasonably well, the effects of well-understood principles on complex systems, as in the application of the laws of physics to airplane and automobile design. However, when the principles themselves are in question, as is the case with the complex biological systems under study, computer modeling alone is of little value.

One of the terrifying effects of the effort to restrict the use   6 of animals in medical research is that the impact will not be felt for years and decades: drugs that might have been discovered will not be; surgical techniques that might have been developed will not be; and fundamental biological processes that might have been understood will remain mysteries. There is the danger that politically expedient solutions will be found to placate a vocal minority, while the consequences of those decisions will not be apparent until long after the decisions are made and the decision making forgotten.

Fortunately, most of us enjoy good health, and the trauma   7 of watching one's child die has become a rare experience. Yet our good fortune should not make us unappreciative of the health we enjoy or the advances that make it possible. Vaccines, antibiotics, insulin and drugs to treat heart disease, hypertension and stroke are all based on animal research. Most complex surgical procedures, such as coronary-artery bypass and organ transplantation, are initially developed in animals. Presently undergoing animal studies are techniques to insert genes in humans in order to replace the defective ones found to be the cause of so much disease. These studies will effectively end if animal research is severely restricted.

In America today, death has become an event isolated from   8 our daily existence—out of the sight and thoughts of most of us.

As a doctor who has watched many children die, and their parents grieve, I am particularly angered by people capable of so much compassion for a dog or a cat, but with seemingly so little for a dying human being. These people seem so insulated from the reality of human life and death and what it means.

Make no mistake, however: I am not advocating the needlessly cruel treatment of animals. To the extent that the animal-rights movement has made us more aware of the needs of these animals, and made us search harder for suitable alternatives, they have made a significant contribution. But if the more radical members of this movement are successful in limiting further research, their efforts will bring about a tragedy that will cost many lives. The real question is whether an apathetic majority can be aroused to protect its future against a vocal, but misdirected, minority.

9

SAME-SEX MARRIAGE

Desecration? Dedication!

ANNA QUINDLEN

Anna Quindlen is the best-selling author of four novels, four nonfiction books, and two children's books. Her New York Times *column, "Public and Private," won the Pulitzer Prize in 1992. Her column now appears every other week in* Newsweek. *In the following selection, she argues that "gay couples are being held to a standard the denizens of Vegas chapels and divorce courts have never had to meet."*

And now for a short quiz:

1

- How many amendments are there in the Constitution?
- How many times may a senator be re-elected?
- Which president was the first commander in chief of the U.S. military?
- What do the stripes on the flag stand for?

You got the flag one, didn't you? But what about the other three? These are just a few of the questions people may be asked to answer if they are taking the test to become citizens of the United States. That's a good thing. A working knowledge of the governing processes and the history of our country can be reasonably expected of those who want to share in the benefits and responsibilities of being American.

2

The problem is that most native-born citizens probably can't pass the test. Americans are remarkably causal about their citizenship, not voting in sufficient numbers, not following the critical potential issues. Those of us to the Star-Spangled Banner born aren't tested in the same way converts are. In fact, the united States seems to have a bad case of what you might call natalism, privilege conferred by accident of birth, high or low. (Although there is still no privilege like the privilege of wealth. Who knew that National Guard service was so flexible that you could duck out nearly a year early because, as President Bush said in his ill-advised interview with Tim Russert, "I was going to Harvard Business School and worked it out with the military."   3

The latest citizens to be required to perform, as gadfly feminist politico Charlotte Whitton once said of women, twice as well to be thought half as good are gay men and lesbians. All these people want is what we hetero types take for granted: the opportunity to drop to one knee in a white-tablecloth restaurant and pledge eternal fealty in the eyes of the waiters and the world. But if gay people persist in this wild-eyed determination to marry, it's clear they will be held to that higher standard that outsiders have learned to expect.   4

In a recent sermon, Cardinal Edward Egan of New York, who somehow managed for a long time to contain his public outrage at pedophiles in the priestly ranks, decried the notion of same-sex marriage and referred to "the desecration of something sacred." The marriages we're talking about are civil marriages, which are so short of being sanctified in the eyes of the church that it will scarcely recognize their existence if you are Roman Catholic. And in a secular nation, why should church leaders be required to acknowledge civil marriage—or, for that matter, be attended to when they pass judgment on what they will not acknowledge? Let them police the rites they have right to regulate.   5

One of the chief arguments opponents have against same-sex marriage is that marriage is designed first and foremost to produce and shelter children. Naturally, we straight people don't have to conform to that standard. Infertile people, people who don't want to have kids, women who are past childbearing age: all of us get married as a matter of course, no questions asked. Unfortunately for those who rely on that argument, the barrenness of gay unions isn't accurate. In a soon-to-be-published book, "Gay Marriage: Why It Is Good for Gays, Good for Straights,   6 and Good for America," Jonathan Rauch reports that the most recent census found 28 percent of gay couples had kids. And that's probably an undercount. Opponents might also argue that the children of gay couples are not the sort of biological fruit of marriage to which we are accustomed. They might try telling that to straight people who have used IVF or a sperm bank, who are stepparents or adoptive parents.

Comedians have made jokes about the gay-marriage controversy along predictable lines: why shouldn't they have the same right to be miserable that the rest of us have? Rauch's book turns that off-handed ridicule of the institution on its head. In few books about matrimony will you read descriptions that so powerfully evoke the married state as a blessing for human beings. It is the yearning of the exile, the hunger of the disenfranchised. Even the dedication packs a wallop: "For Michael. Marry me, when we can." To characterize this sort of devotion as desecration is reprehensible. Anyone who defines marriage largely in terms of what happens in bed has never been married. Which may explain the Catholic Church's official reaction.   7

Like the naturalized citizens who are expected to know more about America than those of us born here, gay couples are being held to a standard the denizens of Vegas chapels and divorce courts have never had to meet: to justify the simple human urge, so taken for granted by the rest of us, to fully and legally come together. Just as it's common to see an immigrant take the oath and then kiss the ground, the result of all this enforced soul-searching may well be a fervor that will honor an embattled institution. Gay people are being asked to form a more perfect union. In the process, perhaps they can teach us something that we casual citizens and spouses badly need to learn.   8

Societal Suicide: Legalizing Gay Marriage Will Lead to More Family Breakdown and Crime

CHARLES COLSON

Charles Colson was the chief counsel for President Richard Nixon from 1969 to 1973 and was one of the Watergate Seven, jailed for Watergate-related changes. He is the founder of Prison Fellowship, a nonprofit organization devoted to Christian prison ministries and the chairman of the Wilberforce Forum, a conservative Christian political and social think tank and action group.

Is America witnessing the end of marriage? The Supreme   1
Judicial Court of Massachusetts has ordered that the state issue
marriage licenses to same-sex couples. (By late march, the Massachusetts legislature voted to recognize same-sex civil unions instead.) And unprecedented period of municipal lawlessness has
followed, with officials in California, New York, Oregon, and New
Mexico gleefully mocking their state constitutions and laws. The
result: Thousands of gays rushed to these municipalities to "marry,"
while much of the news media egged them on.

In the midst of the chaos, President Bush announced his   2
support for a Federal Marriage Amendment, which assures that
this contentious issue will be debated in every quarter of American life. It should be, because the consequences of having "gay
marriage" forced on us by judicial (or mayoral) fiat will fall on all
Americans—not just those who embrace it.

As a supporter of the amendment, I'm well aware of the   3
critical arguments. As the president noted, "After more than two
centuries of American jurisprudence, and millennia of human experience, a few judges and local authorities are presuming to
change the most fundamental institution of civilization. Their action
has created confusion on an issue that requires clarity."

He's right. Here's the clarity: marriage is the traditional   4
building block of human society, intended both to unite couples
and bring children into the world.

Tragically, the sexual revolution led to the decoupling of   5
marriage and procreation; same-sex "marriage" would pull them
completely apart, leading to an explosive increase in family col-
lapse, out-of-wedlock births and crime. How do we know this?

In nearly 30 years of prison ministry, I've witnessed the   6
disastrous consequences of family breakdown—in the lives of
thousands of delinquents. Dozens of studies now confirm the evidence I've seen with my own eyes. Boys who grow up without father are at least twice at likely as other boys to end up in prison.
Sixty percent of rapists and 72 percent of adolescent murderers
never knew or lived with their fathers.

Even in the toughest inner-city neighborhoods, just   7
10 percent of kids from intact families get into trouble, but 90
percent of those from broken families do.

Girls raised without a father in the home are five times   8
more likely to become mothers while still adolescents; children
from broken homes have more academic and behavioral

problems at school and are nearly twice as likely to drop out of high school.

Critics agree with this but claim gay "marriage" will not   9
weaken heterosexual marriage. The evidence says they're wrong.

Stanley Kurtz of the Hoover Institution writes: "It follows   10
that once marriage is redefined to accommodate same sex couples, that change cannot help but lock in and reinforce the very cultural separation between marriage and parenthood that makes gay marriage conceivable to begin with."

He cites Norway, where courts imposed same-sex   11
"marriage" in 1993—a time when Norwegians enjoyed a low out-of-wedlock birth rate. After the imposition of same-sex "marriage," Norway's out-of-wedlock birth rate shot up as the link between marriage and childbearing was broken and cohabitation became the norm.

Gay "marriage" supporters argue that most family tragedies   12
occur because of broken heterosexual marriages—including those of many Christians. They are right. We ought to accept our share of the blame, repent, and clean up our own house. But the fact that we have badly served the institution of marriage is not a reflection on the institution itself; it is a reflection on us.

As we debate the wisdom of legalizing gay "marriage," we   13
must remember that, like it or not, there is a natural moral order for the family. History and tradition—and the teachings of Jews, Muslims, and Christians—support the overwhelming empirical evidence: The family, led by a married mother and father, is the best available structure for both child-rearing and cultural health.

This is why, although some people will always pair off in   14
unorthodox ways, society as a whole must never legitimize any form of marriage other than that of one man and one woman, united with intention of permanency and the nurturing of children.

Marriage is not a private institution designed solely for   15
the individual gratification of its participants. If we fail to enact a Federal Marriage Amendment, we can expect, not just more family breakdown, but also more criminals behind bars and more chaos in our streets.

APPENDIX

Writing the Research Paper

Writing a research paper may at first seem like an overwhelming task to you, but it really is not. Although research papers do take more time than shorter, less complicated essays, they certainly should not cause the worry and anxiety that so many students seem to feel when they think about research assignments. After all, a research paper is just an extended essay supported with material that you have found in outside sources. And if you have written one of the essay assignments in Chapters 7 or 8, you have already practiced paraphrasing, quoting, and documenting source material.

GETTING STARTED

CHOOSING AN APPROPRIATE TOPIC

- As you choose your topic, make sure you understand the assignment. How long is the paper supposed to be? How many sources are required? When is it due? Does the assignment require argument, such as taking a position on the legalization of gambling in your state? Or does it ask for explanation and discussion, such as an examination of the effects of gambling on different personality types?

- Don't choose a topic that is too broad. If you have never written a research paper before, you might think you need an extra-large topic, but you don't. Trying to tackle a broad topic like the problems that gambling has caused different cultures throughout history will result in a paper that covers many different points in a very superficial way. The length of a good research paper comes from fewer points discussed in depth, with many supporting ideas and facts drawn from research.

DEVELOPING A PRELIMINARY THESIS

- As you know, the thesis states the central idea of your paper. Usually it is written as the last sentence of the introduction. If you are writing an argument, it is the statement your entire paper must prove: *The drawbacks of legalized gambling in California far outweigh any benefits.* If you are writing a factual report, it states the central point of the report: *One of the basic causes of homelessness is mental illness—either clinical depression or schizophrenia*

- If you know what position you want to argue or what point you want to make, write a preliminary thesis statement and move on to your research. However, if you do not know where you stand on an issue, write a question that you want your research to answer: *Should gambling be legalized in California? What are the primary causes of homelessness?* Once you have completed your research, replace your question with a statement of the conclusion you have drawn. That statement will now serve as your thesis.

DOING THE RESEARCH

First, a warning about research: A research paper is not a paraphrase of an encyclopedia article, nor is it a patchwork of quotations from your sources. It is a presentation of *your ideas,* supported by research. In other words, *you* and *your ideas* are a major part of the paper, even if your ideas were not clearly formed before you began your research. That said, let's look at some of the best sources for your research.

REFERENCE BOOKS

Sometimes the best way to start your research is to read general articles on your topic in encyclopedias or specialized reference works. You'll find these books in the reference section of the library. Use **general encyclopedias,** such as *The New Encyclopedia Britannica* or *Encyclopedia Americana.* Both will give you articles written by experts on the subject and will provide lists of other works you should read. **Specialized encyclopedias,** such as *Encyclopedia of Psychology* or *Encyclopedia of Biological Sciences,* can also be very helpful. Ask your librarian what other specialized reference works might provide you with information about your topic.

BOOKS

Books are an important source for many research papers. You can locate books on your topic by using the library catalog, which most libraries now make available through **online computer terminals.** Simply type in keywords related to your subject matter, as you would if you were searching for material on the Internet. The keywords you choose, of course, will be critical to a successful search. Don't give up if the words you use do not produce results at first. If you need to, ask one of the librarians which keywords might be appropriate for your topic. Before you leave your terminal to find the book on the library's shelves (called **stacks**), record its entire **call number** (a series of letters and numbers, usually toward the top or bottom of each entry on the computer) as well as the title and the author's name.

PERIODICALS

Periodicals consist of magazines, newspapers, and scholarly journals. These sources will have the most current research on your topic. To find periodicals, consult one of the **indexes** your library subscribes to. You will find some of them in printed, bound volumes in the reference section, but many popular indexes are available through the same online terminals as books. (Many school libraries now provide students with passwords to access these databases from home.) Even better, these **computerized indexes** often contain the entire article, which you can print or email to your home computer, saving you the trouble of having to find the physical magazine or newspaper in your library. Common computerized indexes are *InfoTrac, EBSCOhost,* and *Lexis Nex is.* Ask your librarian for help if using these important sources is confusing for you.

SOURCES FOR FACTS AND STATISTICS

To find facts and statistics, consult the library's volumes of *The Statistical Abstract of the United States, Information Please Almanac,* and *Facts on File.* You will find these and other volumes of statistics in the reference section. In addition, if your library subscribes to the *Opposing Viewpoints* computerized database, type in a keyword for your subject. When a list of sources appears, click on the "Statistics" tab at the top of the page to find articles that offer statistical information on your subject.

THE INTERNET

The Internet is a powerful source of information. Often a simple search using one keyword will produce thousands, even hundreds of thousands of **hits** (sites containing the keyword you entered). Typing the keyword *immigration* into a Google search, for example, will result in over 420 *million* hits. As you can see, using the Internet requires that you **focus** your search as well as carefully **evaluate** the information you find there. Here are some popular search engines and their world wide web addresses:

GOOGLE   http://google.com

YAHOO   http://www.yahoo.com

ALTAVISTA   http://www.altavista.com

HOTBOT   http://www.hotbot.com

LYCOS   http://www.lycos.com

To Focus Your Internet Search, Take the Following Steps:

- Use a more precise term. Using *illegal immigration* instead of *immigration*, for example, reduces the number of hits to 52 million (still an impossible number to work with).
- Put quotation marks around terms containing more than one word. Now the search engine will look only for documents that contain the two words in that specific order. *"Illegal immigration"* results in 18 million hits.
- Add another keyword or phrase, connecting it with AND. *"Illegal immigration" AND "border patrol"* results in 2 million hits.
- Limit your search to sites that are not commercially oriented. The last part of a web address, or URL (Uniform Resource Locater), identifies the nature of the website:

.com   commercial (sites designed to sell something or make a profit)

.net   commercial or personal

.org   a non-profit organization (aims to promote a cause)

.gov   government

.edu   college or educational institution

Consider limiting your search to .gov, .edu, and .org sites, which are generally the most reliable. For example, you can limit your search results to government sites by adding *site:gov* (no space between *site:* and *gov*) at the end of your keywords. *"Illegal immigration" AND "border patrol" site:gov* now produces 34,000 hits—still a very large number, but far fewer that 420 million!

Remember, *any* material drawn directly from the world wide web needs to be evaluated carefully.

To Evaluate Your Internet Sources, Consider the Following Questions:

- Is the source current? When was it created?
- Is the source reliable? (Restricting your search to .org, .gov, or .edu sites will help you avoid many unreliable sources.)
- Is the author qualified to write about your research topic? (Some .edu sites are written by students, not by experts on your topic.)
- Does the information seem fair and objective? (Even non-profit.org sites are often promoting a specific cause. Does the presentation seem fair?)

TAKING NOTES

- Before you take notes from any source, write down, print, or save all the information that you will need later for your Works Cited page:

FOR A BOOK	author, title, edition (if not the first), place of publication, publisher, and date of publication
FOR AN ARTICLE FROM A PERIODICAL	author, title of article, title of publication, date, page numbers, volume and issue numbers
FOR MATERIAL FROM A LIBRARY DATABASE OR THE INTERNET	same material as above, but also the name of the database, date of electronic publication, date you visited the site, and Internet address

- Make a copy of the article or portion of the book you intend to use. (Be sure to write all of the above publication information on the copy.) Now you can mark up this copy all you want.
- Read the source, underlining and highlighting major ideas and any places that seem to express significant points. Don't take notes yet. Just read and underline.
- Now take notes from what you have underlined. Use a separate sheet of paper (or note cards, if you prefer). As much as possible, use your own words in your notes. Next to each notation, identify the source and page number. If you write down *anything* word for word, place quotation marks around it and identify the source and page number.

  A warning: Some students skip taking notes and try to write their paper directly from the material they highlighted. Don't do it. The result is almost always a paper that reads like a string of loosely related quotations and summaries.

- When you have taken all of your notes, read them again. Mark those that seem particularly important. As best you can, identify notes that discuss similar ideas even though they come from different sources.

WRITING THE PAPER

ORGANIZING YOUR THOUGHTS AND WRITING THE FIRST DRAFT

- Once you have completed your research, set it aside for a moment and spend some time writing out your own thoughts. After all, your paper should present your views, as informed by the research you have done. What seem to be the most important issues in what you have read? Have your own ideas changed at all? Check the thesis that you started with. Does it still express the central idea that your research will support? If you need to revise it, do so now.

- The best way to organize your material is to think through your paper from first paragraph to last, *writing a rough outline as you do.* **Don't skip this step.** The temptation now will be to start writing the essay itself. However, you will find it *much easier* to write if you first think the paper through, writing down in brief phrases and sentences the basic ideas that you will include in each section. Write down your responses to questions like these:

    INTRODUCTION   What material should I include here? Should I open with background information? Do I have a striking anecdote or case study from my research that might make an effective opening?

    FIRST SECTION   What point should the first section of the body of my paper discuss? What material from my research should I include in this section? (Look through your notations from research to find material that should be included in your first section.) How many paragraphs will this section include?

    SECOND AND   Ask the same questions for each section, and write
    LATER SECTIONS   brief notes in the form of a rough outline.

- If you have prepared a thorough rough outline, you will now find it much easier to write the first full draft of the paper. Don't worry about the perfect writing style. Just follow your rough outline and present your ideas as clearly as you can.

INTEGRATING SOURCES INTO YOUR PAPER

- As you write your paper, you will present your ideas from research three ways: as *direct quotations, paraphrases,* and *summaries:*

    DIRECT QUOTATIONS   Direct quotations are word-for-word repetitions of the original source. Always place quotation marks around them. (**Exception:** Long quotations set off from the text do not use quotation marks.) Use direct quotations sparingly to avoid the appearance of a paper that is merely a string of quotations. No more than 10 to 15 percent of your paper should be direct quotations.

PARAPHRASES
Paraphrases are ideas from the original source written in your own words and writing style. Usually paraphrases are about the same length as the ideas were in their original form.

SUMMARIES
Summaries are ideas from the original source written in your own words and writing style. They differ from paraphrases in that summaries usually condense several paragraphs or more from the original source into a few sentences.

• Each direct quotation, paraphrase, or summary should be *integrated* into your paper with a transition. Do not simply "dump" one into your paragraph. Compare the following examples:

"DUMPED" QUOTATION
Many people believe that the residents of homeless shelters are just lazy and unmotivated, but such a view is much too simplistic. "Most people who end up in homeless shelters are suffering from schizophrenia, clinical depression, or post-traumatic stress syndrome."

QUOTATION WITH TRANSITION
Many people believe that the residents of homeless shelters are just lazy and unmotivated, but such a view is much too simplistic. **According to a recent study by Daniel Moriarty, a Stanford psychologist,** "Most people who end up in homeless shelters are suffering from schizophrenia, clinical depression, or post-traumatic stress syndrome."

DUMPED PARAPHRASE
Many people believe that the residents of homeless shelters are just lazy and unmotivated, but such a view is much too simplistic. Many of them are suffering from serious mental and emotional disorders.

PARAPHRASE WITH TRANSITION
Many people believe that the residents of homeless shelters are just lazy and unmotivated, but such a view is much too simplistic. **According to a recent study by Daniel Moriarty, a Stanford psychologist,** many of them are suffering from serious mental and emotional disorders.

 For a further discussion of integrating paraphrases and quotations into your paper, see pages 158–160.

AVOIDING PLAGIARISM

- Plagiarism occurs when you present someone else's words or ideas as if they were your own. When you directly quote from another work, you *must* use quotation marks as well as identify the source of the quotation. When you paraphrase or summarize from another work, you also *must* identify the source. Not doing so is plagiarism.

- A more subtle type of plagiarism occurs when you change only a few words in a passage, keeping most of the style of the original, and then present the passage as a paraphrase. When you paraphrase or summarize, use your own writing style. Try not to copy the style of the original.

DOCUMENTING YOUR SOURCES

If you use someone else's ideas, facts, examples, or statistics, you must *document* your source in two places:

- In *parenthetical references* within the body of the paper
- On the *Works Cited* page at the end of your paper

You must document sources even if you do not quote them directly and even if you only paraphrase or summarize the ideas of someone else. You do not need to document facts that are common knowledge, such as *Neil Armstrong was the first person to walk on the moon.*

PARENTHETICAL REFERENCES WITHIN THE BODY OF THE PAPER

Today's writers no longer use an elaborate footnote system together with Latin expressions at the bottom of the page. Instead, they use the method of the MLA (Modern Language Association) or the APA (American Psychological Association). Both methods use *parenthetical references,* although in slightly different ways. The following information is based on the MLA, the method used in English classes and the humanities.

Parenthetical references are placed within the paper directly after *all direct quotations, summaries,* or *paraphrases.* In them, you give readers just enough information so that they can find the full source on the Works Cited page at the end of your paper. The three most common parenthetical references are:

1. **Page number only.**   This is the most common parenthetical reference. Use only a page number if you have already identified the author within the transition:

   According to Royster, "Both groups could see the defeat of the Confederacy coming" (187).

Since you have given the last name of the author within the sentence, the reader can easily find the full source on your Works Cited page. The page number is all that you need in parentheses.

2. **Last name of author and page number.**   Include the last name of the
   author in the parentheses if you have not yet identified the author:

   Toward the spring of that year, the leaders of both armies knew that
   the days of the Confederacy were numbered (Royster 187).

3. **Title and page number.**   Use the title within the parentheses if your
   source does not have an author listed and if you haven't already mentioned the title in your text. You do not need to use the entire title. Include just enough of it to lead the reader to the right place on your
   Works Cited page.

   The bitterness has become "rancid in the veins of Southerners" ("Sherman's" 77).

The entire title is "Sherman's March and Southern Attitudes," but one word
is all that is needed to lead the reader to the article on the Works Cited page.

Special Situations in Parenthetical References

- **Citing a statement by one author that is quoted in the work of
  another author.** If your source quotes some *other* source and you also
  want to quote that other source, use "qtd. in" (quoted in):

  According to Anigami, "The circumstances of one's life are often a
  mirror of one's inner dynamics" (qtd. in Rangel 142).

  In this example, you have an article by *Rangel,* not by *Anigami.* Rangel
  has quoted what Anigami said or wrote, and you want to use the same
  quotation.

- **Citing a work by two or three authors.** In such a situation, include
  all of the last names in the citation:

  A recent article in *USA Today* reports that Bush's attempts to change the
  nation's immigration laws have divided his political base (Jackson and
  Kiely A4).

- **Citing material from the Internet or computerized indexes.** As
  with other sources, use the author's last name and page number if
  available. If no author is given, use the first major word of the title. Material downloaded from the Internet or from the library's periodical indexes *often does not show page numbers.* In that case, include in the
  parentheses only the author's last name or a portion of the title if no
  author is given:

  According to a May, 2006, article in the *National Review,* "The latest
  Gallup poll, from early April, has 47% of the public thinking that immigration should be decreased, 35% who want it left as is and only
  15% who want it increased" ("No Left Turn").

  This entry is downloaded from a computerized database that did not
  provide page numbers, so none is given here. In addition, no author
  was identified with the source, so part of the title is used instead.

Punctuation with Parenthetical References

Place the period that ends your sentence at the end of and outside the parentheses. Look at the examples above. Note that the period is placed after the parentheses, not before them.

(**Exception:** Quotations longer than four lines are set off by indenting them ten spaces from the left margin. No quotation marks are used, and the period is placed at the end of the last word, before the parentheses.)

THE WORKS CITED PAGE

The Works Cited page is the last page of a research paper. It is an alphabetical list of all the sources you have quoted, paraphrased, or summarized in your paper. There are precise conventions to be followed carefully when putting together this page:

- Begin the list on a new page after the last page of your text.
- Center the heading *Works Cited* at the top.
- Include only the sources that you have used in your paper.
- List the works alphabetically according to the last name of the author or, lacking that, using the first main word in the title.
- Begin typing the first line of each entry at the left-hand margin. Indent the second and subsequent lines five spaces (or one-half inch).
- Double-space all entries, and double-space between each entry.
- The main parts of each entry are the author, the title, and the publishing information. Separate each main part with periods.
- Underline the titles of books and magazines, and place quotation marks around the titles of articles.

Examples of Entries

In the following examples, if no author is given for your source, begin your entry with the title of the source instead.

- **Book**

  Author. <u>Title</u>. City: Publisher, Date.

  Royster, Charles. <u>The Destructive War</u>. New York: Random House, 1991.

- **Article in a Magazine Published Every Week or Two Weeks**

  Author. "Title of Article." <u>Title of Magazine</u> Full Date: Page number(s) of entire article. (Write a plus sign after the page number if the article is not printed on consecutive pages.)

  Quindlen, Anna. "Undocumented, Indispensable." <u>Newsweek</u> May 15, 2006: 78.

- **Article in a Magazine Published Every Month or Two Months**

  Author. "Title of Article." <u>Title of Magazine</u> Month and Year: Page number(s) of entire article. (Write a plus sign after the page number if the article is not printed on consecutive pages.)

  Slessarev-Jamir, Helene. "Looking for Welcome." <u>Sojourners Magazine</u> April 2006: 26-30.

- **Article in a Newspaper**

  Author. "Title of Article." <u>Title of Newspaper</u> Date, Section: Page number(s) of entire article. (Write a plus sign after the page number if the article is not printed on consecutive pages.)

  Rutenberg, Jim. "President Calls for Compromise on Immigration." <u>New York Times</u> 16 May 2006: A1+

- **Article in a Journal**

  Author. "Title of Article." <u>Title of Journal</u>. Volume Number. Issue Number (Year): Page number(s) of entire article.

  Tolson, David. "Sherman's Dastardly Deed." <u>Annals of the Confederacy</u>. 55.1 (1994): 367-80.

- **Article in an Anthology**

  Author. "Title of Article." <u>Title of Anthology</u>. Editor. City: Publisher, Date. Page number(s) of entire story or article.

  Blackmur, R. P. "The Method of Marianne Moore." <u>Selected Essays of R. P. Blackmur</u>. Ed. Denis Donoghue. New York: Ecco, 1986. 119-44.

- **Article from a Library's Computerized Database**

  Author. "Title of Article." [Title and dates of original sources as listed above for magazines and newspapers.] <u>Name of database</u>. Name of provider, if available. Name and location of library. Date of access and URL.

  Brush, Silla. "One Tough Border Collie." <u>U.S. News and World Report</u> April 17, 2006: 32. <u>Academic Search Premier</u>. EBSCOhost. Palomar College Lib., San Marcos, CA. 23 May 2006 <http://web11.epnet.com>

- **Material from an Internet Website**

  Author. "Title of Piece." <u>Title of Website</u>. Date published or last update (if available). Date of access and ULR.

  Bush, George W. "President Bush Addresses the Nation on Immigration Reform." <u>The White House</u>. 15 May 2006. 25 May 2006 <http://www.whitehouse.gov/news/releases/2006/05/20060515-8.html>.

- **Article in an Online Magazine or Newspaper**

  Author. "Title of Article." <u>Title of Online Magazine or Newspaper</u> Publication Date. Date of access and URL.

  Newman, Josie. "Canada Cracks Down on Rising Violence." <u>The Christian Science Monitor</u> 26 May 2006. 28 May 2006 <http://www.csmonitor.com/2006/0526/p07s02-woam.html>.

- **Article in an Online Reference Book or Encyclopedia**

  Author (if available). "Title of Article." <u>Title of Reference Book or Encyclopedia</u>. Date of article (if available). Date of access and URL.

"Focus on Film: *The Da Vinci Code*." <u>Encyclopedia Britannica Online</u>. Apr. 2006. 25 May 2006 <http://corporate.britannica.com/davinci/index.html>

- **No Author Given**

  Use the first main word of the title. Alphabetize according to that word.

  "The South's Anger." <u>The Knoxville Sentinel</u>. 25 Jan. 1945: E2-3.

- **More Than One Author**

  Use the last name for first author only. List subsequent authors by first and last names.

  Erianger, Steven and Alison Mitchell. "U.S. Officials Rethink Need to Deploy Troops." <u>The San Diego Union-Tribune</u>. 16 Nov. 1996: A1+

- **More Than One Work by the Same Author**

  For entries after the first one, use three hyphens and a period in place of the author's name. Alphabetize the works by the titles.

  Kooser, Ted. <u>Delights & Shadows</u>. Port Townsend, WA: Copper Canyon Press, 2004.

  ---. <u>Sure Signs</u>. Pittsburgh: University of Pittsburgh Press, 1980.

- **Radio or Television Program**

  <u>Name of Program</u>. Network. Local station. Broadcasting City. Date.

  <u>A Prairie Home Companion.</u> NPR. KPBS, St. Paul, Minnesota. 17 Nov. 2005.

- **Video or Audio Recording**

  Author or director. <u>Title</u>. Format. Producer, Release date. Running time.

  Hirsch, Henry. <u>The Civil War and the Twentieth Century</u>. CD. Warner Thompson, 1991. 120 min. (approx.).

- **Interview**

  Name of person. Personal, phone, or email. Date.

  Sanchez, Maria. Personal Interview. May 25, 2006.

Exploring ONLINE

Go to www.thomsonedu.com/devenglish/mcdonald for more help writing a research paper. Under "Chapter Resources" for the Appendix, click on "Exploring Online."

SAMPLE STUDENT RESEARCH PAPER

Roleson 1

Ryan Roleson

Professor McDonald

English 100

5 May 2005

A Story Still Being Written

The debate over legalization of euthanasia is a timeless battleground that has been fought upon for generations. Many years before our generations began arguing it, the ancient Greeks and Romans conflicted over the value of human life. Many thought that if life is unbearable, one has the right to commit suicide and viewed the use of euthanasia as a simple fact of life. However, others opposed euthanasia because they thought it was a violation of the commands of the gods, who valued human life regardless of its quality (Porter, Johnson, and Warren 90). Today, it is known as physician-assisted suicide, though it is also common to refer to it directly as euthanasia. Legalization of physician-assisted suicide is a complex and bitter debate that involves sharp and often bitter disagreement.

One reason for disagreement regards the ability of palliative care to stop or slow the physical pain of a hospitalized individual. Proponents of assisted death argue that in many cases, patients are not receiving appropriate pain relief, justifying euthanasia as a way to prevent further suffering: "In the United States alone, tens of millions of

Writer's name

Instructor

Course

Date

Title Centered

Double-spacing is used throughout.

Parenthetical reference is used for a paraphrase.

Thesis

Roleson 2

people—patients with cancer...and others—receive inadequate pain relief, causing unnecessary suffering and giving impetus to the euthanasia movement" (Porter, Johnson, and Warren 91). It is obvious that many people would prefer a quick, painless death to months of suffering in a cold, sterile hospital room. Paul Schotsmans, a professor of medical ethics in a major university in Belgium, writes about the painful death of his brother, a healthy, active man who was suddenly diagnosed with cancer: "The pain, the lack of air...regularly I had him in my arms during these days, as he was begging for air, begging for a nurse, reproaching me that I was not quick enough" (335). Though his brother finally dies in the hospital, Professor Schotsmans, who was once stalwart in his opposition to physician-assisted suicide, still experiences a dilemma. He opposes putting an end to another person's life, yet he asks, "Is it sometimes not better and more human to do this than let someone go through this process of suffering?" (335).

However, euthanasia can also be opposed for equally compelling reasons. According to Ersek, critics of euthanasia contend that suffering is no reason for killing. They say that helping someone die violates the sanctity of life, an idea that is basic to many religious beliefs (51). Furthermore, the American Nurses Association (ANA) has opposed euthanasia by the defining principle of nonmaleficence. Its position is that "nursing profession's covenant with society is to assist people in living the fullest lives possible, not to help them end their lives" (Ersek 51). Not only has

Roleson 3

the possibility of legalizing euthanasia been
challenged as outright murder, but it could also
lead to a higher likelihood of patients feeling
compelled to request aid in dying for less
justifiable reasons than physical pain. Critics of
euthanasia contend that if it were made legal,
palliative care would slide down the slippery slope
to preferring euthanasia over other medical
treatment. They fear that patients might be coerced
into assisted suicide because pain-killing drugs are
so expensive and caring for them takes so much time
and effort (Ersek 51). To put it bluntly, should we
have our grandparents killed simply because an
intensive-care retirement home costs too much?

Proponents of euthanasia respond by pointing out
the benefits of legalization. According to them,
some nurses and physicians already practice assisted
suicide, so legalization will provide accountability
and oversight (Ersek 52). For example, in Oregon,
the Department of Health and Human Services has
supervised assisted suicide since its implementation
in 1997. Each year, it publishes a report with
details of who prescribes medication, alternatives
discussed, and whether patients are impaired by
psychological disorders (Ersek 51). It is obvious
that euthanasia is a dangerous tool, but, to
proponents, its potential to relieve the suffering
of terminal hospital patients far outweighs the
possibility of its abuse.

Proponents also claim that "sanctity of life,"
which critics try to position against euthanasia,
should not be defined by mere existence. They point

Paraphrase is identified by author and page number.

Roleson 4

out, for example, that patients with paralyzing
disabilities should not be kept suffering in hospital
beds. The British House of Lords' decision in
Airedale NHS Trust v. Bland concerned a seventeen-
year-old comatose survivor kept alive for
approximately three years. The young man's parents
went to court to get permission to remove his life
support. The court eventually ruled that "existence
in a persistent vegetative state" does not benefit
the patient (Godlovitch, Mitchell, and Doig). A
Canadian court in Alberta also adopted this position
for a Canadian case and further defined it to include
the "sanctity of life." The court said that "...life
is sacred, not in the sense of bare existence, but in
a personal sense: how that patient construes a
meaningful life—their life as they see it and how
they wish to live" (Godlovitch, Mitchell, and Doig).

Opponents of legalization dispute the point by
further arguing that euthanasia, once legalized, is
bound to be abused. They hold that life is
inherently sacred, regardless of a person's
disabilities. For opponents of euthanasia, "life is
of such intrinsic value and the "slippery slope"
dangers are so evident that euthanasia cannot be
tolerated..." (Huxtable and Campbell). As an example
of such abuse, critics point out how far down the
"slippery slope" palliative care has gone in countries
such as the Netherlands, where euthanasia is legal:

> Nearly a third of all Dutch doctors
> hold physician-assisted suicide to be
> legitimate in very old people who are

Page numbers are not given when the printout from a computerized database does not provide them.

Ellipses are used to indicate omitted words.

Roleson 5

> tired of living. Congruent with this
> view, when the new Dutch law was de-
> bated and enacted in Parliament, the
> (now former) Health Minister stated that
> suicide pills should be distributed
> among the elderly. (Materstvedt).

Opponents contend that this kind of ethical abuse begins with its legalization. Simply because euthanasia is legal and being supervised by a government agency, that does not mean that it will not be abused.

Proponents respond that the right to life includes the right to death as well. Though the two may sound contradictory, it seems comical to suggest that the government has control over who enters the pearly gates of heaven. Proponents argue that a right to traditional types of palliative care includes the right to euthanasia: "People should have the right to make decisions about ending their own life in the same way they can choose or refuse other types of medical therapies" (Ersek 49-50). Proponents believe that not only does the necessity of autonomy include taking one's own life, but it also relieves unwanted feelings of separation on the part of a patient. As mentioned previously, Professor Schotsmans faced a similar situation while his brother was in the hospital. He comments on how lonely and isolated his brother was:"...medical and paramedical staff and family members have the chance to go away, to 'breathe' in normal life, but the dying patient remains left finally at his own" (336). Patients

Quotations longer than four lines are set off from the left margin by 10 spaces (one inch). No quotation marks are used.

are left alone to waste away in a hospital bed, while their friends and family continue to live their lives. To respect a patient's autonomy is to recognize that it is not enough to simply wait for a suffering person to die.

A final response from opponents of euthanasia consists of a different meaning of autonomy. Critics believe that "euthanasia...will damage autonomy in the most fundamental sense by eradicating the very possibility of future autonomous acting as such" (Materstvedt). Living all of life's opportunities, they say, is what gives a person autonomy. Furthermore, assisting in death is no simple favor: "Opponents of assisted suicide argue that the right to choose [euthanasia] doesn't extend to the right to die by asking health care officials to assist in hastening death" (Ersek 51).

The debate regarding the legalization of euthanasia is an emotionally charged battle that must be settled. Though some states or countries have implemented euthanasia, the conflict is far from over. Liberal proponents of euthanasia are just as sure as their conservative opponents of their opinions, and no end to this argument is in sight. Euthanasia has a long, hard road ahead of it before it reaches its destination. But let the growth of this debate bear sweet fruits by its end so that the most people can be helped in the least amount of time.

Roleson 7

Works Cited

Ersek, Mary. "Assisted Suicide: Unraveling a Complex
    Issue." Nursing 2005 35.4 (2005):48-52.

Godlovitch, Glenys, Ian Mitchell, and Christopher
    James Doig. "Discontinuing Life Support in
    Comatose Patients: An Example from Canadian
    Case Law." Canadian Medical Association Journal
    179.2 (2005): 1172-3. Academic Search Premier.
    EBSCOhost. Palomar College Lib. San Marcos, CA.
    11 May 2005 <http://web11.epnet.com>.

Huxtable, Richard and Alastair V. Campbell.
    "Palliative Care and the Euthanasia Debate:
    Recent Developments." Palliative Medicine 17
    (2003): 94-96. Academic Search Premier.
    EBSCOhost. Palomar College Lib. San Marcos, CA.
    11 May 2005 <http://web11.epnet.com>.

Materstvedt, Lars Johan. "Palliative Care on the
    'Slippery Slope' towards Euthanasia?"
    Palliative Medicine 17 (2003): 387-392.
    Academic Search Premier. EBSCOhost. Palomar
    College Lib. San Marcos, CA. 11 May 2005
    <http://web11.epnet.com>.

Porter, Theresa, Punporn Johnson, and Nancy A.
    Warren. "Bioethical Issues Concerning Death:
    Death, Dying, and End-of-Life Rights." Critical
    Care Nursing Quarterly 28.1 (2005): 85-92.

Schotsmans, Paul T. "The Ethical Claim of a Dying
    Brother." Christian Bioethics 9 (2003): 331-336.

New page is used for Works Cited page.

Double-spacing is used throughout.

Sources are listed alphabetically by last name.

Second and subsequent lines are indented 5 spaces.

Article from computerized database includes database information.

Credits

Chapter 1

p. 2: © Zits Partnership. King Features Syndicate; **p. 8**: Erma Bombeck, "Live Each Moment for What It's Worth," June 23, 1991. Copyright © 1991 by Erma Bombeck. All rights reserved. Reproduced by permission of Aaron M. Priest Literary Agency; **p. 9**: From *Will: The Autobiography of G. Gordon Liddy*, by G. Gordon Liddy, Copyright © 1980 by the author and reprinted by permission of St. Martin's Press, LLC; **p. 11**: Joseph T. O'Connor, "A View from Mount Ritter." From *Newsweek*, 5/25/98 © 1998 Newsweek, Inc. All rights reserved. Reprinted by permission.

Chapter 2

p. 38: © King Features Syndicate; **p. 43**: Russell, Bertrand. Excerpt from *The Autobiography of Bertrand Russell*, Vol. 1, pp. 3–4. Georg Allen & Unwin, 1967. Copyright © 1967 by the Bertrand Russell Peace Foundation Ltd. All rights reserved. Reproduced by permission of the Taylor & Francis Group; **p. 44**: "The Urge to Merge," from *Passages* by Gail Sheehy, copyright © 1974, 1976 by Gail Sheehy. Used by permission of Dutton, a division of Penguin Putnam Inc.; **p. 45**: "How to Stay Alive" by Art Hoppe; **p. 49**: © 1977, The Washington Post Writers Group, Reprinted with Permission; **p. 52**: From *Soul of a Citizen* by Paul Rogat Loeb, Copyright © 1999 by the author and reprinted by permission of St. Martin's Press, LLC; **p. 54**: © 1995, The Washington Post Writers Group, Reprinted with Permission; **p. 59**: Patricia O'Hara, "Charity Means You Don't Pick and Choose." From *Newsweek*, 12/23/02 © 2002 Newsweek, Inc. All rights reserved. Reprinted by permission.

Chapter 3

p. 76: *Cathy* © 1991 Cathy Guisewhite. Reprinted with permission of Universal Press Syndicate. All rights reserved; **p. 80**: © 1989, The Washington Post Writers Group, Reprinted with Permission; **p. 83**: Rudy Abramson, "A Matter of Honor," in *LA Times*, April 3, 1994, p. E1. Copyright © Rudy Abramson. All rights reserved. Reproduced by permission; **p. 89**: Chana Schoenberger, "Getting to Know about You and Me." From *Newsweek*, 9/20/93 © 1993 Newsweek, Inc. All rights reserved. Reprinted by permission; **p. 90**: From *Dave Barry Talks Back* by Dave Barry, copyright © 1991 by Dave Barry. Illustrations copyright © 1991 by Jeff MacNelly. Use by permission of Crown Publishers, a division of Random House, Inc; **p. 93**: Bob Chase, "Fear of Heights: Teachers, Parents, and Students Are Wary of Achievement" in *NEA Today*, April 26, 1998. Copyright © 1998 National Education Association. Reprinted by permission; **p. 98**: Sharon Zukin, "Attention Shoppers: Your Dreams In Aisle 3," in the *Chronicle Review*, December 19, 2003. Web Address http://chronicle.com/weekly/v50/i17/17b00501.htm All rights reserved. Reproduced by permission.

Chapter 4

p. 114: *Peanuts*: © United Feature Syndicate, Inc; **p. 126**: Barbara Ehrenreich, "Oh, Those Family Values" in *Time* magazine, July 18, 1994. Copyright © 1994 by Time Inc. All rights reserved. Reproduced by permission; **p. 129**: © 1993, The Washington Post Writers Group, Reprinted with Permission; **p. 131**: Alex Kotlowitz, "Colorblind" in *New York Times Magazine*, January 11, 1998, p. 22. Copyright ©1998 by the New York Times Co. All rights reserved. Reproduced by permission; **p. 136**: Copyright © 2003, the *Chronicle of Higher Education*. Reprinted with permission; **p. 146**: From *The Second Book of the Strange* by Lawrence D. Gadd, pp. 78-79 (1981). (Amherst, NY: Prometheus Books). Reprinted with permission.

Chapter 5

p. 152: *Calvin and Hobbes* © Watterson. Reprinted with permission of Universal Press Syndicate. All rights reserved; p. 155: Norman Cousins, "The Decline of Neatness" in *Time* magazine, April 2, 1990. Copyright © 1990 by Time Inc. All rights reserved. Reproduced by permission; **p. 165**: Mimi Avins, "The Bachelor: Silly, Sexist, and, to Many, Irresistible" in the *Los Angeles Times*, April 27, 2002. Copyright © 2002 by the Los Angeles Times. All rights reserved. Reproduced by permission; **p. 169**: John Hamerlinck, "Killing Women: a Pop-Music Tradition" in the *Humanist*, July-August 1995. All rights reserved. Reproduced by permission of the author; **p. 172**: Otto Friedrich, "The Changing Face of America" in *Time* magazine, July 8, 1985. Copyright © 1985 by Time Inc. All rights reserved. Reproduced by permission; **p. 176**: Dave Eggers, "Serve or Fail" in *New York Times Magazine*, June 13, 2004. Copyright © 2004 by the New York Times Co. All rights reserved. Reproduced by permission.

Chapter 6

p. 194: *Doonesbury* © 1986 G.B. Trudeau. Reprinted with permission of Universal Press Syndicate. All rights reserved; **p. 203**: Mark Mathabane, "Appearances Are Destructive" in the *New York Times*, August 26, 1993. All rights reserved. Reproduced by permission of the author; **p. 205**: Alfie Kohn, "Why Competition?" The *Humanist*, January/February 1980. All rights reserved. Reproduced by permission; **p. 210**: Elaine Minamide, "History 101: Pass the Popcorn, Please" in *San Diego Union-Tribune*. Copyright © 1998. All rights reserved. Reproduced by permission of the author; **p. 213**: Caspar Melville, "Hell Is Other iPods" in *New Humanist*, March/April 2005. All rights reserved. Reproduced by permission.

Chapter 7

p. 228: © King Features Syndicate; **p. 237**: Sidney Hook, "In Defense of Voluntary Euthanasia" in the *New York Times*, March 1, 1987. Copyright © 1987 by the New York Times Co. All rights reserved. Reproduced by permission; **p. 240**: Teresa R. Wagner, "Promoting a Culture of Abandonment" in the *San Diego Union Tribune*, June 25, 1998. Copyright © 1998 by Teresa R. Wagner, Family Research council. All rights reserved. Reproduced by permission of the author; **p. 242**: Kenneth Swift, "The Right to Choose Death" in latimes.com, June 25, 2005. All rights reserved. Reproduced by permission of the author; **p. 244**: Lawrence Rudden and Gerard V. Bradley, "Death and the Law: Why the Government Has an Interest in Preserving Life" in *World & I*, May 2003. Copyright © 2003 World & I. All rights reserved. Reproduced by permission; **p. 247**: Ruth C. Engs and Charles A. Hurley, "Should the Legal Drinking Age Be Lowered to 18 or 19?" in *CQ Researcher*, March 20, 1998, vol. 8, no. 11, p. 257. Copyright © 1998 by Congressional Quarterly Inc. All rights reserved. Reproduced by permission; **p. 249**: Elizabeth M. Whelan, "Perils of Prohibition." From *Newsweek*, 5/29/95 © 1995 Newsweek, Inc. All rights reserved. Reproduced by permission; **p. 252**: "The Minimum Legal Drinking Age," website http://www.ama-assn.org/ama/pub/category/13246.html. Adapted from Toomey, T. L., C. Rosenfeld, and A. C. Wagenaar, "The Minimum Legal Drinking Age: History, Effectiveness and Ongoing Debate," *Alcohol, Health and Research World*, vol. 20, no. 4, 1996, p. 214. Copyright © American Medical Association. All rights reserved. Reproduced by permission of the American Medical Association; **p. 254**: © 2001 by National Review Inc., 215 Lexington Avenue, New York, NY 10016. Reprinted by permission.

Chapter 8

p. 266: *Calvin and Hobbes* © Watterson. Dist. by Universal Press Syndicate. Reprinted with permission. All rights reserved; **p. 275**: Gary E. Johnson, "The Case for Drug Legalization" in *The World and I*, Feb. 2000, vol. 15, no. 2, p. 34. Copyright © 2000 by The World and I. All rights reserved. Reproduced by permission; **p. 279**: Rangel, Charles B., "Why Drug Legalization Should be Opposed" (as appeared in *Criminal Justice Ethics*, Volume 17, Number 2, [Summer/Fall 1998] pp. 2). Reprinted by permission of The Institute for Criminal Justice Ethics, 555 West 57th Street, Suite 601, New York, NY, 10019-1029; **p. 281**: Hodding Carter III, "We're Losing the Drug War Because Prohibition Never Works" in the *Wall Street Journal*, July 13, 1989, p.A15. Copyright © Dow Jones & Company, Inc. All rights reserved. Reproduced by permission; **p. 283**: Reprinted with permission from the March 1990 *Reader's Digest*. Copyright © 1990 by The Reader's Digest Assn., Inc; **p. 289**: Amitai Etzioni, "The Fast-Food Factories: McJobs Are Bad for Kids" in the *Washington Post*, August 24, 1986. All rights reserved. Reproduced by permission; **p. 294**: Michele Manges, "The Dead-End Kids" in the *Wall Street Journal*, February 9, 1990. Copyright © Dow Jones & Company, Inc. All rights reserved. Reproduced by permission; **p. 296**: Dennis McLellan, "Part-Time Work Ethic: Should Teens Go For It?" in the *Lost Angeles Times*, Nov. 7, 1986. All rights reserved. Reproduced by permission; **p. 301**: Maureen Brown, "Balancing Act: High School Students Making The Grade At Part-Time Jobs" in the *Los Angeles Times*, February 6, 1992. All rights reserved. Reproduced by permission.

Part Four

p. 402: McClain, Leanita. "The Middle-Class Black's Burden" from *A Foot in Each World: Articles and Essays*. Edited with an Introduction by Clarence Page Evanston: Northwestern University Press, 1986, pp. 12–15. Copyright © 1986 by Northwestern University Press. All rights reserved. Reproduced by permission; **p. 407**: Suzanne Pharr, "A Match Made in Heaven: Liberal Leftie Chats with a Promise Keeper" in *The Progressive*, August 1996, vol. 60, no. 8, p. 28. All rights reserved. Reproduced by permission of the author; **p. 414**: Michael Ryan, "Are You Living Mindlessly" in *Parade*, March 1, 1998. Copyright © Michael Ryan. All rights reserved. Reproduced by permission of Scovil, Chichak & Galen Literary Agency on behalf of the author; **p. 423**: David Daniels, "College Lectures: Is Anybody Listening?"; **p. 427**: William Henry III, " The Meaning of TV" in *Life* magazine. Copyright © 1969 by Life Magazine. All rights reserved. Reproduced by permission; **p. 430**: Paul Robinson, "TV Can't Educate" in the *New Republic*, August 12, 1978. All rights reserved. Reproduced by permission; **p. 436**: Madeline Drexler, "Don't Touch That Dial" in the *Boston Globe*, July 28, 1991. Copyright © Madeline Drexler. All rights reserved. Reproduced by permisson of the author; **p. 439**: Paul Greenberg, "The American Flag: A Symbol We Should Protect." Copyright © 1995, Los Angeles Times Syndicate. Reprinted by permission of the author; **p. 442**: Charles Levendosky, "Flag Burning and The First Amendment". Reprinted by permission of the author; **p. 444**: Robert Dole, "May Americans Do Battle to Save Our Flag" in *San Diego Union-Tribune*, December 17, 1995. Copyright © 1995. All rights reserved. Reproduced by permission of the author; **p. 446**: Jeffrey Kaplan, "Flag-Burning Ban: Protecting What It Symbolizes or the Symbol?" in *San Diego Union-Tribune*, December 14, 1995. Copyright © 1995. All rights reserved. Reproduced by permission; **p. 405**: "The Future/El Futuro" by Richard Rodriguez. Copyright © 1990 by Richard Rodriguez. Reprinted by permission of Georges Borchardt, Inc., on behalf of the author; **p. 412**: Copyright © 1995 *U.S. News & World Report*, L.P. Reprinted with permission; **p. 417**: © 1989, *Newsweek*. Reprinted with permission; **p. 420**: Paul Goodman, "A Proposal to Abolish Grading" from *Compulsory Mis-Education*. Horizon Press, 1964. Copyright © Paul Goodman. All rights reserved. Reproduced by permission of the author; **p. 434**: From *Mediaspeak* by Donna Woolfolk Cross, copyright © 1983 Donna Woolfolk Cross. Used by permission of Coward-McCann, Inc., a division of Penguin Group (USA) Inc; **p. 449**: Cleveland Amory, "The Trials of Animals." Originally published as "Needless Cruelty to Animals" in the *New York Times*, September 17, 1989. All rights reserved. Reproduced by permission; **p. 451**: Ronald Kline, "A Scientist: I Am the Enemy" in *Newsweek*, April 18, 1989. All rights reserved. Reproduced by permission of the author; **p. 453**: Anna Quindlen, "Desecration? Dedication!" in *Newsweek*, Feb. 23, 2004. Copyright © Anna Quindlen. All rights reserved. Reproduced by permission; **p. 455**: Charles Colson, "Societal Suicide, Legalizing Gay Marriage Will Lead to More Family Breakdown and Crime" in *Christianity Today*, June 2004, p. 72. Copyright © 2004 Christianity Today. All rights reserved. Reproduced by permission.

Appendix

p. 471: "A Story Still Being Written" by Ryan Roleson. Reproduced by permission.

Indexes

Subject Index

Boldface entries denote specific words discussed in the text.

Author/Title Index